MW01383076

GRAPHICS AND SOUND PROGRAMMING TECHNIQUES FOR THE MAC

Dan Parks Sydow

M&T BOOKS

M&T Books
A Division of MIS:Press, Inc.
A Subsidiary of Henry Holt and Company, Inc.
115 West 18th Street
New York, New York 10011

Limits of Liability and Disclaimer of Warranty

The Author and Publisher of this book have used their best efforts in preparing the book and the programs contained in it. These efforts include the development, research, and testing of the theories and programs to determine their effectiveness.

The Author and Publisher make no warranty of any kind, expressed or implied, with regard to these programs or the documentation contained in this book. The Author and Publisher shall not be liable in any event for incidental or consequential damages in connection with, or arising out of, the furnishing, performance, or use of these programs.

All products, names and services are trademarks or registered trademarks of their respective companies.

Wayzata sound files and QuickTime movie distributed with permission of Wayzata Technology. Screen snapshots of the Robot movie used with permission of Wayzata Technology.

Library of Congress Cataloging-in-Publication Data

    Graphics and sound programming for the Mac / by Dan Parks Sydow.
      p.   cm.
    Includes index.
    ISBN 1-55851-442-2
    1. Macintosh (Computer)—Programming.   2. Computer graphics.
  3. Computer sound processing.   I. Title.
    IN PROCESS
    006.6'765—dc20   95-40387
                                                CIP

10 9 8 7 6 5 4 3 2

Associate Publisher: *Paul Farrell*

Managing Editor: *Cary Sullivan*	**Production Editor:** *Anne Incao*
Development Editor: *Michael Sprague*	**Technical Editor:** *Pete Ferrante*
Copy Edit Manager: *Shari Chappell*	**Copy Editor:** *Winifred Davis*

Dedication

To Nadine and Taylor Ann

—Dan

Acknowledgments

Michael Sprague, Development Editor, M&T Books, for keeping things rolling and on schedule.

Anne Incao, Senior Production Editor, M&T Books, for another fine page layout effort.

Winifred Davis, Copy Editor, for making it appear that I really do know how to write!

Peter Ferrante, Apple Computer, for another helpful technical review.

Carole McClendon, Waterside Productions, for making this book happen.

Jeffery Garland, M.D., St. Joseph's Hospital, Milwaukee, Wisconsin, for choosing medicine as your profession, and for bypassing convention!

Karen Heine, RN, St. Joseph's Hospital, Milwaukee, Wisconsin, for providing help as both a professional and a person—Taylor's parents will always remember you!

CONTENTS

Why This Book Is for You

From the beginning, graphics and sound are what the Macintosh has been all about. For the Macintosh user, applications that include pictures, animation, movies, and sound have made working with computers fun. For the programmer, however, things haven't always been so fun. Such topics as pixel maps, asynchronous sound, and offscreen animation are all new experiences for any anyone coming from a programming background that doesn't include graphical user interface programming. Even those who have programmed the Mac for quite some time find these topics bewildering. Documentation is often sketchy and example source code hard to come by. Now, that's all changed.

This book provides detailed discussions, plenty of figures, slow walk-throughs of source code listings, and short, straight-to-the-point examples that will get all the fun and exciting multimedia features such as sound, speech, and animation out of the books and into your own programs.

If you are:

- A programmer who has been hesitant to try to add graphics and sound features to a program
- A programmer who has tried to understand such topics as off-screen animation, and given up

- Someone who wants a single reference for all of the most popular multimedia programming techniques
- A programmer looking for documentation on the newest Apple software, such as QuickDraw GX and QuickTime Musical Instruments
- A person who would like to know some of the basic game programming techniques such as asynchronous sound, flicker-free animation, and QuickTime movie-playing

...then this book is for you.

What You Need

To get the most out of this book, you'll need an understanding of either the C or C++ language. While you don't need to know advanced Macintosh programming techniques, you should be familiar with the Macintosh Toolbox and have programmed on the Macintosh.

Standalone, executable versions of each of the more than thirty example programs can be found on this book's CD. You can test drive them even if you don't own a compiler. To make changes to the code and recompile it, you'll need an integrated development environment (IDE). That's the fancy term for what used to be called a *compiler*. If you look on this book's CD you'll find that M&T Books has supplied a few versions of *each* example. Whether you have the THINK C, Symantec C++, or Metrowerks CodeWarrior C/C++ compiler, there are project files, source code files, and resource files that will work for you. There are also separate sets of project files for owners of PowerPC Macs and owners of Macs with a 680x0 CPU.

Because much of the code in the examples depends on Toolbox routines not found in System 6, you should try compiling the examples on a Mac that's running any version of System 7 or, soon, the Copland operating system.

Because the book comes bundled with a CD, you'll of course need a CD-ROM drive to access all the neat stuff on the CD. Or, you'll need to find a friend or coworker with a CD-ROM drive. He or she can copy the most important files from the CD to a few floppy disks for you.

What's on the CD

Source code, source code, source code. When learning programming techniques, you can never get too much source code to study. As mentioned, the CD holds several versions of each of the more than 30 example programs from the book—a different version for each of the most popular compilers.

You'll find that the CD has a folder that holds sound files—a couple dozen digitized sounds you can use in your own programs. There's also a few QuickTime movies you can play or edit—including the talking robot QuickTime movie pictured in Chapter 1.

Finally, there are numerous shareware and freeware programs on the CD—all related to graphics and sound, of course. You'll find such goodies as animation libraries, sound files converters, and a utility that turns pictures into pixel patterns (PixPats) that you can use as a desktop pattern or window background in your own programs.

CHAPTER 1

Introduction to Macintosh Graphics and Sound

Graphics and sound programming means multimedia. What exactly can you expect to *do* with multimedia programming? If you skim through this chapter before digging in, you'll get an overview of the many topics covered in this book. Getting a hint of what's in store will start you thinking—thinking about that game, instructional software, or movie, graphics, or sound-editing utility that's just waiting to be developed!

Graphics, Sound, and This Book

The nine chapters that make up this book offer a wealth of exciting programming topics and techniques—the next several pages summarize what you'll find in the 400-plus pages that follow.

Sound Playing

For a programmer, adding sound-playing features to applications that run on a computer known for its multimedia capabilities should be easy—and it is. A single Toolbox function will play a sound resource that's tucked in your application's resource fork. But if you want to play a sound while other action takes place—your programming efforts need to increase. Chapter 2 shows you how to do the easy stuff, such as playing a digitized sound—and the more difficult, such as playing a digitized sound while animation takes place. Figure 1.1 shows the window from one of the example programs in Chapter 2. Here the cartoon bear slides across ice as classical music plays.

FIGURE 1.1 Asynchronous sound—a Chapter 2 program
that plays music while animation takes place.

Sound Recording

If your application plays sounds, you might consider letting the user record the sounds to play. You can let the user do so right from within your own application. Figure 1.2 shows the standard Record dialog box that you can add to your programs—Chapter 3 examples show you how.

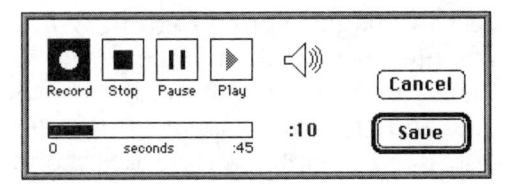

FIGURE 1.2 The standard Record dialog box
that you can add to any of your programs.

Speech

If you want your program to speak, you can digitize voices, store them
in your application's resource fork, and then use the sound-playing
techniques described in Chapter 3 to play these sounds. That, however,
takes careful planning of the exact text that is to be spoken and requires
a lot of disk space. Instead, you'll want to store as text the words that
your program will speak, then rely on the Speech Manager to speak
that text. Text is easy to type into a program or resource, is easy to edit,
can be entered by the user, and takes up very little disk space. Figure 1.3
shows a practical use for speech. Here, the user is allowed to type in
different phrases for a character in a game.

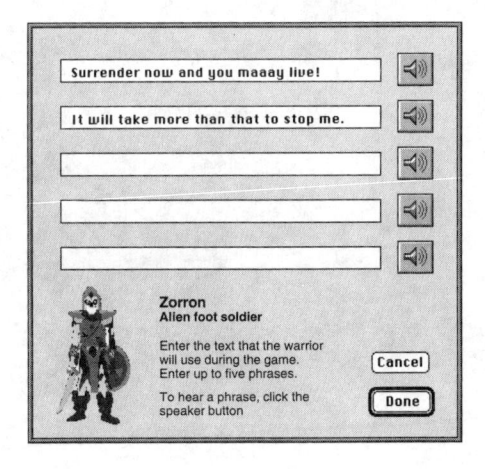

FIGURE 1.3 An example of a dialog box that takes advantage of the Speech Manager.

Using the Speech Manager, your program will not only have the ability to choose what to say, it will have the power to choose who will say it. That's because your Mac hosts a number of voice synthesizers—components that let your program speak in the voice of a child, an adult—even a robot. Read Chapter 4 for a description of how to add text-to-speech capabilities to your programs, and how to select from the numerous available voices.

Animation

Smooth, flicker-free color animation. What Macintosh game would be considered first-rate without it? If you've only experimented with moving an object on the screen, you've probably encountered the dreaded problem of flicker. In Chapter 5, you'll see how to use offscreen bitmaps to add smooth animation to any of your programs. Figure 1.4 shows how one of the example programs from this chapter looks. Here, the balloon smoothly glides across the background without flicker and without obscuring the background. In fact, as the balloon moves you'll even be able to see the background through the three clear, round panels in the balloon.

FIGURE 1.4 A Chapter 5 example program that displays flicker-free color animation.

QuickDraw GX

QuickDraw has been the source of all Macintosh graphics for a decade. Now there's a new QuickDraw—QuickDraw GX. This powerful, object-oriented version of QuickDraw works in conjunction with the old, original (but still useful) version—as shown in Figure 1.5. In Chapter 6, you'll see how your program can get ready for, and take advantage of, QuickDraw GX.

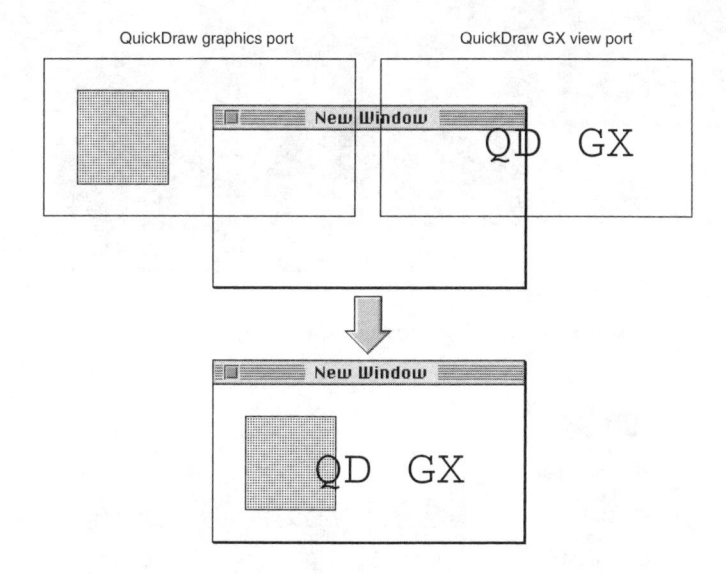

FIGURE 1.5 QuickDraw GX adds a new type of port—the view port—
to the Mac's graphics programming environment.

QuickTime Movies

Chapter 5 shows you how to create your own animated sequences and play them in an application. There is, of course, another way to achieve animation. Chapter 7 tells you all about QuickTime movies—how they're stored, how to open them, how to play them.

You're used to seeing QuickTime movies played in a window with a movie controller attached to it—like the ones shown in Figure 1.6. But a movie can also be played within a dialog box, with or without a controller. Figure 1.7 shows an example of a program that displays movies in an inset area of such a dialog box. Chapter 7 explains just how this can be done.

FIGURE 1.6 QuickTime movies that use movie controllers.

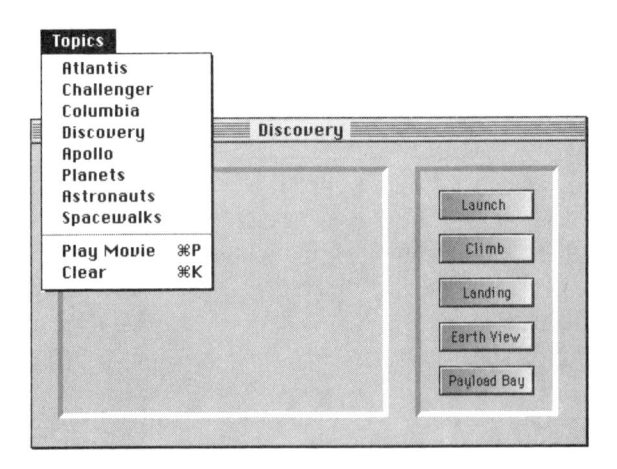

FIGURE 1.7 A dialog box with an area devoted to movie display.

QuickTime Musical Instruments

For the musically inclined, creating tracks of cool-sounding music is no problem. For the rest of us, a software package that includes more than 100 instruments and an interface that allows sounds from these instruments to be easily added to a program would be a blessing. Consider yourself saved—the QuickTime Musical Instruments extension is such a package. Chapter 8 shows you how to use this new extension to select instruments and then play music from them—within any of your applications. In that chapter, you'll also see how to display the Instrument Picker dialog box shown in Figure 1.8. This dialog box provides an interface that allows users of your program to choose the instruments they want to hear.

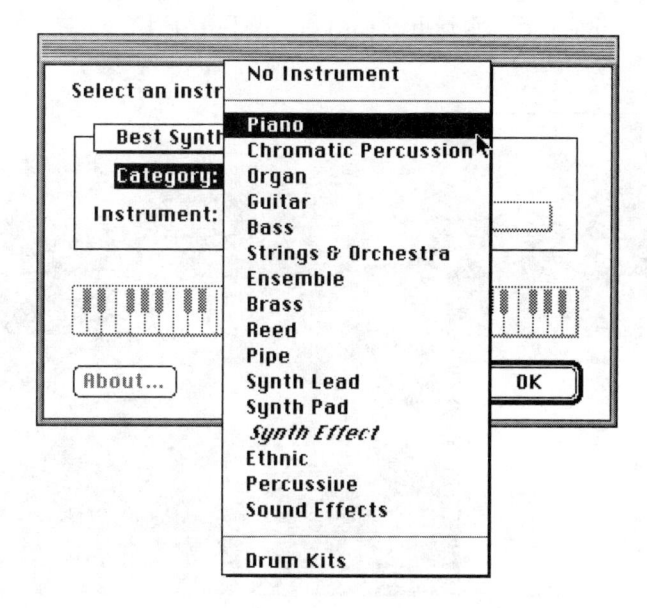

FIGURE **1.8** The Instrument Picker dialog box
can be easily added to any of your programs.

A Complete Example Program

The first eight chapters contain a total of more than 30 example programs—you'll find the listings in this book, the source files and projects on the CD. These example programs are short, simple, and to the point. That makes it easy for you to pull out the code you need for your own programs. If you're the type of programmer who also learns by seeing the source code for a more complete program—such as one with multiple window-handling capabilities, file editing, and menu items for opening and saving files—then Chapter 9 is for you. This chapter provides a complete walk-through of the source code for a QuickTime movie editing program. The FilmEdit program allows the user to open multiple movie files, play them one at a time or simultaneously, copy frames from one movie to another, and save any changes that are made. Figure 1.9 shows two different-size movies being played by FilmEdit.

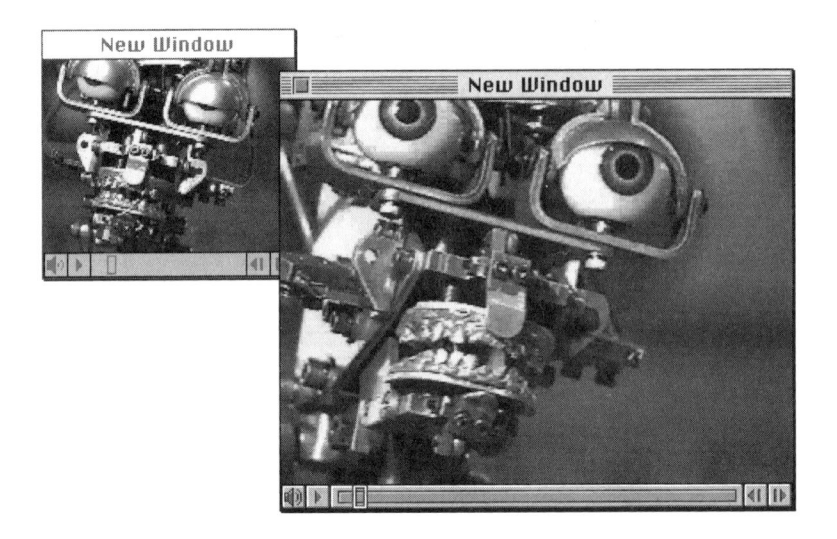

FIGURE 1.9 The Chapter 9 FilmEdit program allows multiple, different-size movies to be open at the same time.

Now...

Now you know what's in store for you in the next several hundred pages. You can jump to the chapter of interest right now, or read and learn from cover to cover. Either way, now is the time to begin.

CHAPTER 2

Sound Playing

The Mac has always been known for its graphics abilities—but its sound-playing powers are equally as impressive. In this chapter, you'll see how to take advantage of the latest release of the Sound Manager to add sound to any of your Mac applications.

Sounds can conveniently be stored as resources in the resource fork of a Macintosh application. Here you'll see how to load and play such a resource. You'll also learn how to allocate a sound channel in which to play a sound. The topic of sound channels will be especially important when you learn about *asynchronous sound playing*—the playing of a sound while other action takes place. Because asynchronous sound playing is such an important part of interesting and exciting applications such as games and multimedia educational software, this topic is covered in great detail. Here you'll see several examples of how to play a sound while animation takes place. Finally, you'll discover how to alter features of a sound, such as its volume and rate, as the sound plays.

The Sound Manager

The Sound Manager is a set of system software routines that provide programmers with the means of playing and altering existing sounds and recording new sounds.

The Sound Manager Version 3.0

The original Macintosh system software didn't include a Sound Manager—though there were a few sound-related Toolbox routines. The Sound Manager didn't exist until version 6.0 of the system software was released. With version 6.0.7 of the system software came an improved Sound Manager (version 2.0), and version 7.5 included the most powerful Sound Manager yet—version 3.0.

NOTE

Mac owners that haven't upgraded to System 7.5 can still use Sound Manager 3.0. Instead of having it as an integral part of the system software, however, a Mac owner running pre-System 7.5 software will need to obtain the Sound Manager 3.0 extension and add it to the Extensions folder on his or her computer.

Some of the Sound Manager routines covered in this chapter are available only to Mac owners who have version 3.0 (or, eventually, a higher version) of the Sound Manager. You can determine the version of the Sound Manager that is on the host machine by calling the Sound Manager routine `SndSoundManagerVersion()`. Calling this function once near the start of a program will provide the information necessary to determine if your application can run on the user's Macintosh. You'll find the code shown in the following snippet in each of the example programs listed in this chapter.

```
NumVersion   theSndMgrVers;

theSndMgrVers = SndSoundManagerVersion();

if ( theSndMgrVers.majorRev < 3 )
   ExitToShell();
```

Rather than simply calling ExitToShell() when encountering an error, call an application-defined error-handling routine.

SndSoundManagerVersion() returns a NumVersion—a data structure with four fields of Sound Manager version information. Check the majorRev field to see if it has a value of at least 3. If it does, the user has version 3.0 (or greater) of the Sound Manager.

Synchronous and Asynchronous Sound Play

The Sound Manager provides routines that allow your program to play sounds either synchronously or asynchronously. Synchronous sound play means that no other code will execute during the playing of the sound. While this mode of sound play is the easiest to program, it has the drawback of preventing on-screen action from taking place. If your program requires nonsound-related action to take place as a sound plays, you'll need to play sounds in an asynchronous mode. This chapter describes both types of sound playing, starting with the easier synchronous sound play.

Sound Resources

A digitized sound can conveniently be stored in the resource fork of an application, where it is always available for playing by the application.

About Sound Resources

A sound resource has a resource type of snd. Because all resource types must consist of four characters, the sound resource type ends with a blank space. Figures 2.1 and 2.2 show a sound resource in ResEdit and Resorcerer, respectively.

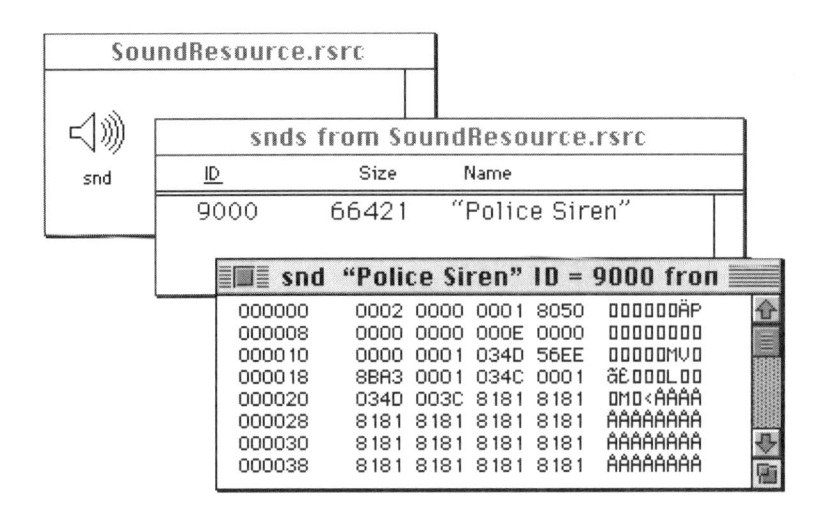

FIGURE **2.1** A snd sound resource, as viewed in ResEdit.

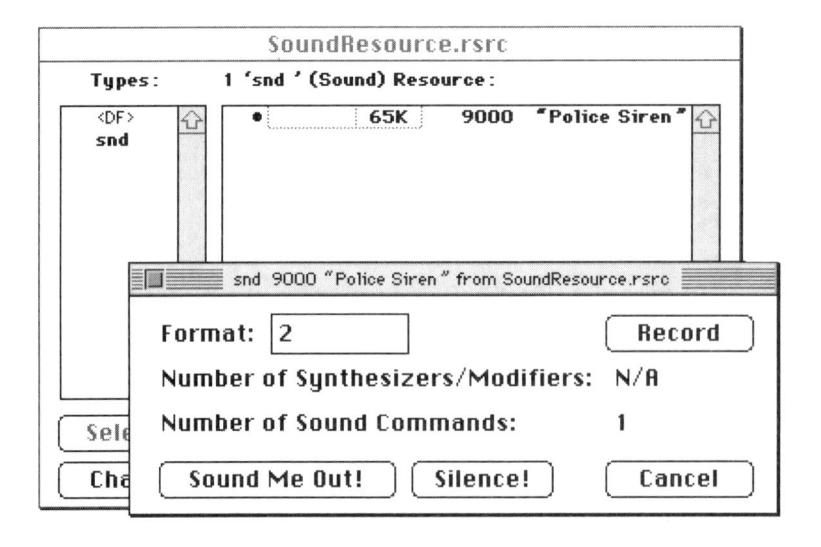

FIGURE **2.2** A snd sound resource, as viewed in Resorcerer.

You'll find that all of the `snd` resources shown in this book have a resource ID greater than 8191. Apple reserves IDs in the range of 0 to 8191 for its own system sound resources.

N O T E

From the two previous figures you can see that there's not much you can do to edit a sound resource—even with the aid of a graphical resource editor. This isn't much of a drawback, though—digitized sounds of just about any animal, person, or sound effect are available from a variety of sources. If a sound doesn't quite meet your needs, it is possible to edit it using a sound-editing application such as Macromedia's SoundEdit.

One source of sound resources is the software libraries of online services such as CompuServe, America Online, and eWorld. You can also buy a CD that contains a thousand or more sounds. Another option is to create sounds yourself by plugging a sound digitizer into one of the ports of your Mac. Finally, you can create them by using the Macintosh built-in microphone.

You can use the Sound control panel to record a sound using the Macintosh microphone. If you'd like to give users of your program the power to record and save sounds, you can do that too—the next chapter shows you how.

N O T E

Playing a Sound Resource

Every Mac has a number of sound resources in its System file—each system alert sound is a `snd` resource. If you include a call to the Toolbox routine `SysBeep()` in your source code, your program will play whichever system alert sound is currently selected in the user's Sound control panel.

```
SysBeep( 1 );
```

The value of the parameter to `SysBeep()` is unimportant. Any `short` value used here will produce the same result—the system alert sound will play a single time.

The parameter to `SysBeep()` used to determine the duration of the system beep. That was back when the Mac only had a single system alert sound—a simple beep. This now-useless parameter still exists for *backwards compatibility*—older programs that made use of the duration parameter will still work with newer system software.

Now, *Really* Playing a Sound Resource

While playing the system alert a single time does qualify as playing a sound resource, it's not what one generally thinks of when the time comes to add sound-playing capabilities to a program. Instead, you'll want your program to be able to play a sound resource that you've selected and, typically, included as part of your project's resource file (and, consequently, as a part of your program's resource fork). To do that you'll rely on the Toolbox function `SndPlay()`. Here's a snippet that includes a call to `SndPlay()`:

```
Handle   theHandle;
OSErr    theError;

theHandle = GetResource( 'snd ', 9000 );
theError = SndPlay( nil, (SndListHandle)theHandle, false );
```

The first parameter to `SndPlay()` is a pointer to a *sound channel*. Sound channels, described in more detail later in this chapter, are used by the Sound Manager to store information about sounds. Passing a `nil` pointer as the first parameter tells the Sound Manager to handle the details of allocating a sound channel.

If a sound is to be played in an altered form, such as at a different pitch then the one at which it was recorded, you'll need to allocate your own sound channel. If a sound is to be played asynchronously, you'll again need to allocate your own sound channel. Both of these topics are covered later in this chapter.

The second parameter to `SndPlay()` is a handle to the `snd` resource to play. You can load a `snd` resource into memory and receive a generic handle to this memory be calling the Toolbox function `GetResource()`—

as shown in the above snippet. This generic handle (type `Handle`) must be typecast to a `SndListHandle` in the call to `SndPlay()`.

The third parameter to `SndPlay()` indicates whether the sound should be played asynchronously or synchronously. A value of `true` tells the Sound Manager to play the sound asynchronously, while a value of `false` means the sound should be played synchronously.

N O T E   Ah, but if only life were so simple. Just passing a value of `true` as the final parameter to `SndPlay()` isn't enough to play the sound asynchronously. You also need to perform a few other steps, such as writing a callback routine. These details are, of course, described later in the chapter.

Figure 2.3 shows that `GetResource()` loads `snd` resource data in memory and `SndPlay()` sends that data to the Mac's speaker or speakers.

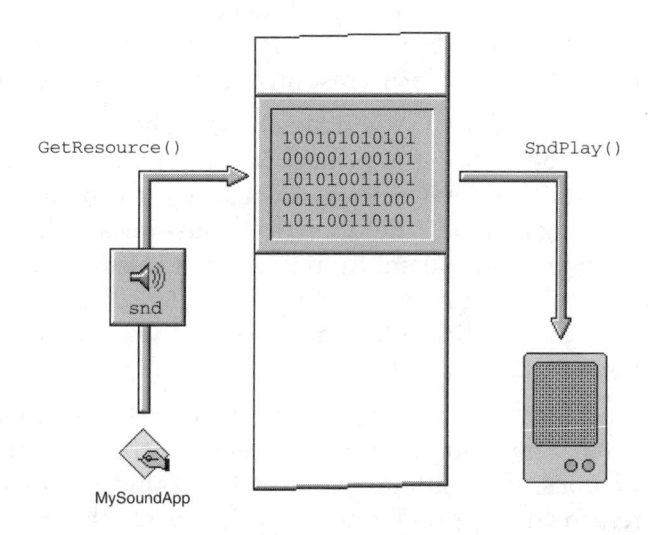

FIGURE 2.3 A call to `GetResource()` loads sound resource data into memory, while a call to `SndPlay()` plays that data.

Because the `SndPlay()` routine may move memory, lock the handle that leads to the sound data before calling `SndPlay()`. After the call to `SndPlay()` has completed, unlock the handle. The following snippet is an improvement over the previous one:

```
Handle  theHandle;
OSErr   theError;

theHandle = GetResource( 'snd ', 9000 );

HLock( theHandle );
   theError = SndPlay( nil, (SndListHandle)theHandle, false );
HUnlock( theHandle );
```

Using `SndPlay()` to play a `snd` resource is easy work. Simple enough, in fact, that you probably understand how sound playback works without the help of Figure 2.3. The `SndPlay()` function's ease of use is exactly why the figure has been included, though—to contrast the effort necessary to play a sound synchronously with that needed to play a sound asynchronously.

If your application will be playing more than one sound resource you'll find it useful to define a sound-playing function. The application-defined routine `PlaySoundResourceSynch()`, which is shown below, accepts a `SndChannelPtr` and the ID of a `snd` resource as its two parameters.

You've seen that to play a sound synchronously you need only pass a `nil` pointer to `SndPlay()`—the Sound Manager then handles sound channel allocation. The `PlaySoundResourceSynch()` function gives you the option of passing a value other than `nil`—just in case the sound is to be played in a way that is different from the way it was recorded. For now, simply pass `nil` as the first parameter to `PlaySoundResourceSynch()`. Later in this chapter you'll use the same routine with a sound channel pointer value other than `nil`.

The `PlaySoundResourceSynch()` routine loads the sound resource with that ID, plays the sound, and then releases the memory that the sound data occupies. If the attempt to load the sound resource fails, the routine will return the Apple-defined constant `resProblem` as the operating system error. If the resource loads successfully, but the call to `SndPlay()` fails, `PlaySoundResourceSynch()` will return the error reported by `SndPlay()`.

```
OSErr  PlaySoundResourceSynch( SndChannelPtr theChannel,
                               short         theResID )
{
   Handle  theHandle;
```

```
OSErr    theError;

theHandle = GetResource( 'snd ', theResID );

if ( theHandle == nil )
{
   return ( resProblem );
}
else
{
   HLock( theHandle );
      theError = SndPlay( theChannel, (SndListHandle)theHandle,
                         false );
   HUnlock( theHandle );

   ReleaseResource( theHandle );

   return ( theError );
}
}
```

To play a sound resource, pass `PlaySoundResourceSynch()` a `nil` pointer and the ID of a `snd` resource. As an example, consider the following snippet. It plays `snd` resource `11500`.

```
OSErr   theError;

theError = PlaySoundResourceSynch( nil, 11500 );
if ( theError != noErr )
   ExitToShell();
```

Chapter Example: SoundResource

The SoundResource program plays one sound resource, then quits. Because the program doesn't display menus or a window, it requires only a single resource—the police siren `snd` resource shown in Figure 2.4.

N O T E

The siren sound used here was, incidently, copied from a CD of over 1000 royalty-free sounds. CDs such as this are available from the various Mac software mail-order vendors.

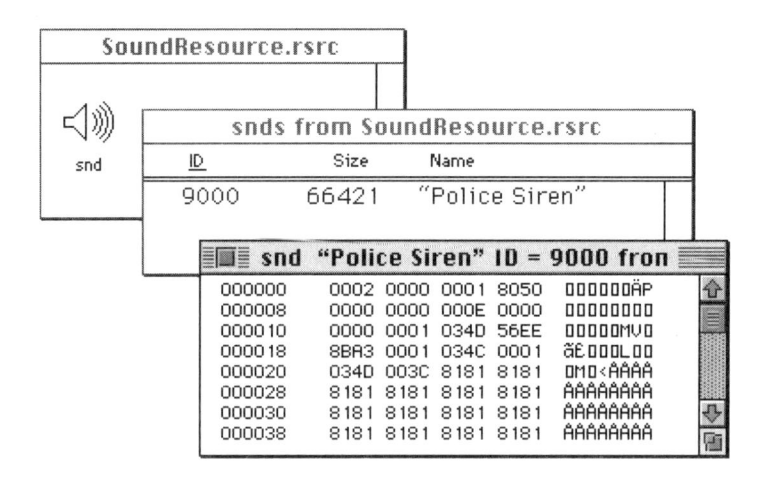

FIGURE 2.4 The SoundResource project requires only one resource—a snd resource.

If you'd like to play other sounds, replace the siren sound resource in the **SoundResource.rsrc** file with any other snd resource, then recompile the project. To play several sounds, add the desired snd resources to the project's resource file. Number the sound resources consecutively. Then alter main() by wrapping the call to PlaySoundResourceSynch() in a loop. The following code is an example that plays three sound resources (with IDs 9000, 9001, and 9002) in a row. Listed first is the original code from main(), followed by the code that should replace the original version.

```
// Original version
theResID = kPoliceSirenResID;
theError = PlaySoundResourceSynch( nil, theResID );
if ( theError != noErr )
   ExitToShell();

// Looping version
theResID = kPoliceSirenResID;
for ( i = 0; i < 3; i++ )
{
   theError = PlaySoundResourceSynch( nil, theResID );
   if ( theError != noErr )
      ExitToShell();
   ++theResID;
}
```

The source code listing for the SoundResource program follows.

```
//_____

#include <Sound.h>

//_____

void    InitializeToolbox( void );
OSErr   PlaySoundResourceSynch( SndChannelPtr, short );

//_____

#define    rPoliceSiren        9000

//_____

void  main( void )
{
    NumVersion   theSndMgrVers;
    short        theResID;
    OSErr        theError;

    InitializeToolbox();

    theSndMgrVers = SndSoundManagerVersion();
    if ( theSndMgrVers.majorRev < 3 )
       ExitToShell();

    theResID = rPoliceSiren;
    theError = PlaySoundResourceSynch( nil, theResID );
    if ( theError != noErr )
       ExitToShell();

}

//_____

OSErr  PlaySoundResourceSynch( SndChannelPtr theChannel,
                               short         theResID )
{
    Handle  theHandle;
    OSErr   theError;

    theHandle = GetResource( 'snd ', theResID );

    if ( theHandle == nil )
```

```
{
   return ( resProblem );
}
else
{
   HLock( theHandle );
      theError = SndPlay( theChannel, (SndListHandle)theHandle,
                           false );
   HUnlock( theHandle );

   ReleaseResource( theHandle );

   return ( theError );
}
}
```

Sound Channels

Any sound data in memory has a corresponding *sound channel* that holds a queue of sound-playing commands. When you call `SndPlay()` and pass a `nil` pointer as the first parameter, the Sound Manager takes care of the allocation of a sound channel. When your program is simply to play a sound synchronously, letting the Sound Manager take care of this task makes sense. If your program is to play a sound asynchronously, or if it is going to alter the way in which the a sound is played, your program needs access to the sound channel. In such cases, your program must allocate the sound channel so that it can use that channel at a later time.

Allocating and Disposing of a Sound Channel

To allocate a sound channel, use the Toolbox function `SndNewChannel()`. This routine allocates memory for a new *sound channel record* (of the type `SndChannel`) and returns a `SndChannelPtr`—a pointer that points to a sound channel record. A sound channel record is the data structure used to represent a sound channel. Your program can allocate memory for the sound channel record or, simply let the Sound Manager allocate this memory as in the following snippet:

```
SndChannelPtr    theChannel;
OSErr            theError;

theChannel = nil;
theError = SndNewChannel( &theChannel, 0, 0, nil );
```

The first parameter to `SndNewChannel()` is a pointer to a `SndChannelPtr`. If you pass a `nil` pointer as the first parameter (as shown above), `SndNewChannel()` will allocate the memory for a new sound channel record and return a pointer to that record. As described later, you'll then be able to use this pointer in subsequent sound-playing functions, such as `SndPlay()`.

The second parameter to `SndNewChannel()` is a constant that tells the Sound Manager what type of sound data is to be played on the new channel. Apple defines three constants that can be used here (`squareWaveSynth`, `waveTableSynth`, and `sampledSynth`), but you're just as well off if you pass a value of 0 so that the channel can be used for any type of sound.

The third parameter to `SndNewChannel()` supplies channel initialization information based on the type of sound that will be played (for instance, whether or not the sound is compressed). As was the case for the second parameter, pass a value of 0 here if you are uncertain of the exact type of sound that will be played from this channel.

The fourth parameter to `SndNewChannel()` is a pointer to a *callback routine*. A callback routine is an application-defined function that the Sound Manager executes (as opposed to being invoked by your own code) when a sound has finished playing on this channel. The callback routine is useful only for the playing of asynchronous sounds. For synchronous sound play, pass a `nil` pointer.

When `SndPlay()` is passed a `nil` pointer as its first parameter, the Sound Manager takes care of allocating a sound channel and disposing of that channel. When a sound channel is instead created by a call to `SndNewChannel()`, your program is responsible for its disposal. A call to the Toolbox function `SndDisposeChannel()` does that.

```
OSErr  theError;

theError = SndDisposeChannel( theChannel, true );
```

The first parameter to `SndDisposeChannel()` is a pointer to the sound channel to release from memory. The second channel is a `Boolean` value that tells whether a currently playing sound should be stopped (`true`) or whether `SndDisposeChannel()` should wait until the sound completes (`false`).

When a sound channel is created via a call to `SndNewChannel()`, a sound channel record is allocated in memory, as is a pointer to that record. The `SndNewChannel()` function disposes of the sound channel record, but has no effect on the pointer to it. After calling `SndDisposeChannel()`, also call the Toolbox function `DisposePtr()` to release the memory occupied by the sound channel pointer. `DisposePtr()` accepts a generic pointer as its one parameter, so you'll need to typecast the `SndChannelPtr` to the `Ptr` type. Figure 2.5 clarifies the allocation and deallocation of a sound channel.

```
OSErr   theError;

theError = SndDisposeChannel( theChannel, true );
DisposePtr( (Ptr)theChannel );
```

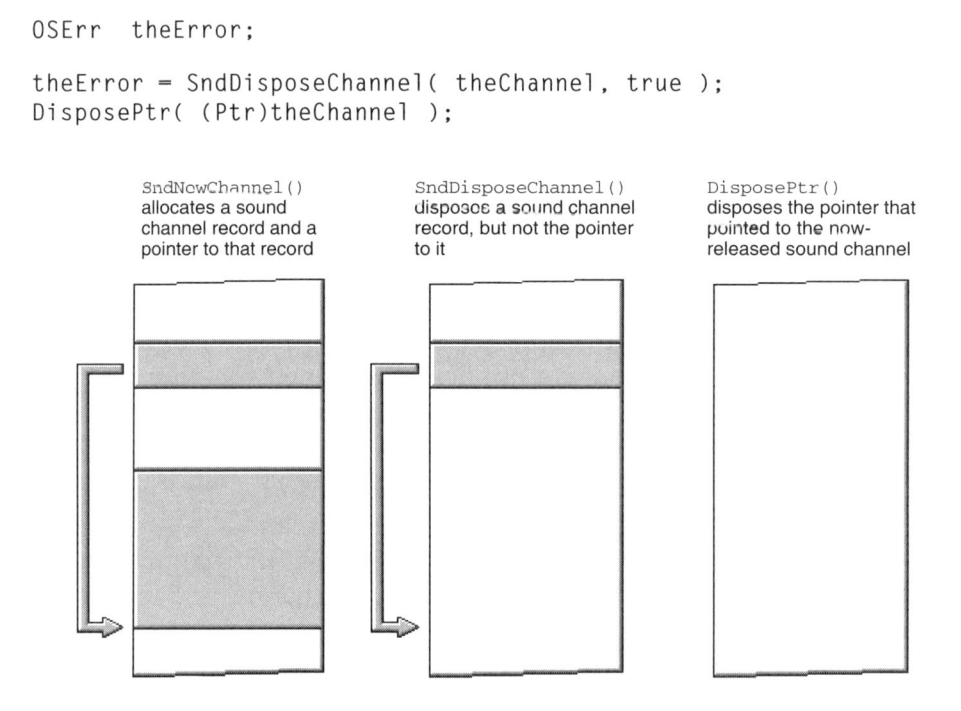

FIGURE 2.5 After using a sound channel, you must deallocate both the sound channel and the pointer that points to it.

NOTE A couple of quick reminders. Macintosh memory is shown with smaller addresses at the bottom of a figure. An object in memory starts at a lower address and ends at a higher address. Together, these two facts mean that a pointer to an object (which points to the *start* of an object), will appear to point to the *bottom* of the object.

You can combine the two memory disposal steps into one by writing a function such as DisposeOneSoundChannel():

```
OSErr  DisposeOneSoundChannel( SndChannelPtr theChannel )
{
   OSErr  theError;

   theError = SndDisposeChannel( theChannel, true );
   DisposePtr( (Ptr)theChannel );

   return ( theError );
}
```

Now that you're aware of the fact that both a sound channel and its pointer should be disposed of, the OpenOneSynchSoundChannel() function should make sense. This application-defined routine calls SndNewChannel() to allocate memory for a new sound channel, then returns a pointer to that channel, as follows:

```
SndChannelPtr  OpenOneSynchSoundChannel( void )
{
   SndChannelPtr  theChannel;
   OSErr          theError;

   theChannel = nil;
   theError = SndNewChannel( &theChannel, 0, 0, nil );

   if ( theError != noErr )
   {
      DisposePtr( (Ptr)theChannel );
      theChannel = nil;
   }

   return ( theChannel );
}
```

If the sound channel memory allocation succeeds, the pointer to the sound channel will be returned to the calling routine. If the allocation fails, `OpenOneSynchSoundChannel()` disposes of the memory occupied by the sound channel pointer and sets the pointer to `nil`. If the calling routine receives a `nil` pointer rather than a valid sound channel pointer, it can assume an error occurred. A typical call to `OpenOneSynchSoundChannel()` looks like this:

```
SndChannelPtr   theChannel;

theChannel = OpenOneSynchSoundChannel();
if ( theChannel == nil )
   ExitToShell();
```

NOTE

The name of the `OpenOneSynchSoundChannel()` function provides you with a hint that at least one change will need to be made to the function's code in order for it to allocate a sound channel that can be used for asynchronous sound play.

Using a Sound Channel

Once you've allocated a sound channel, you can use a pointer to it in any routine that requires a `SndChannelPtr`. For instance, rather than pass `nil` as the first parameter to `SndPlay()`, you can pass the newly allocated sound channel pointer, as follows:

```
SndChannelPtr   theChannel;
Handle          theHandle;
OSErr           theError;

theChannel = nil;
theError = SndNewChannel( &theChannel, 0, 0, nil );

// get handle to sound, lock it, then:
theError = SndPlay( theChannel, (SndListHandle)theHandle, false );
```

If you're using the application-defined function `PlaySoundResourceSynch()` to load and play a snd resource, then the above code becomes:

```
theChannel = nil;
theError = SndNewChannel( &theChannel, 0, 0, nil );
```

```
theError = PlaySoundResourceSynch( theChannel, theResID );
```

How does passing `SndPlay()` your own sound channel pointer differ from passing `SndPlay()` a `nil` pointer and letting the Sound Manager allocate a channel? In the above examples, there is no difference at all. But then, the above snippets are for demonstrative purposes only. The difference comes into effect when you send sound commands to a sound channel, then play the sound. The sound commands get stored in a queue in the sound channel record and are applied to sounds that are later played on that channel. Sound commands are covered in the next section.

Chapter Example: SoundChannelIntro

The SoundChannelIntro program does just what the previous example, SoundResource, did. It loads a `snd` resource into memory and uses a call to `SndPlay()` to play the sound data. The difference is that where SoundResource let the Sound Manager allocate and dispose of a sound channel (by passing `nil` to `SndPlay()`), SoundChannelIntro takes care of the memory allocation and disposal. While this serves no real benefit in this simple program, it does demonstrate a technique that you'll be using in each of the several remaining examples in this chapter.

The `OpenOneSynchSoundChannel()` and `DisposeOneSoundChannel()` functions found in Sound-ChannelIntro are identical to the versions developed in this section. The `PlaySoundResourceSynch()` function is an exact copy of the version used in this chapter's SoundResource program.

```
//_____

#include <Sound.h>

//_____

void            InitializeToolbox( void );
SndChannelPtr   OpenOneSynchSoundChannel( void );
OSErr           DisposeOneSoundChannel( SndChannelPtr );
OSErr           PlaySoundResourceSynch( SndChannelPtr, short );

//_____

#define    rPoliceSiren    9000
```

```
//_____

void  main( void )
{
   NumVersion      theSndMgrVers;
   short           theResID;
   OSErr           theError;
   SndChannelPtr   theChannel;

   InitializeToolbox();

   theSndMgrVers = SndSoundManagerVersion();
   if ( theSndMgrVers.majorRev < 3 )
      ExitToShell();

   theChannel = OpenOneSynchSoundChannel();
   if ( theChannel == nil )
      ExitToShell();

   theResID = rPoliceSiren
   theError = PlaySoundResourceSynch( theChannel, theResID );
   if ( theError != noErr )
      ExitToShell();

   theError = DisposeOneSoundChannel( theChannel );
   if ( theError != noErr )
      ExitToShell();
}

//_____

SndChannelPtr  OpenOneSynchSoundChannel( void )
{
   SndChannelPtr  theChannel;
   OSErr          theError;

   theChannel = nil;
   theError = SndNewChannel( &theChannel, 0, 0, nil );

   if ( theError != noErr )
   {
      DisposePtr( (Ptr)theChannel );
      theChannel = nil;
   }

   return ( theChannel );
}
```

```
//_____

OSErr  DisposeOneSoundChannel( SndChannelPtr theChannel )
{
   OSErr  theError;

   theError = SndDisposeChannel( theChannel, true );
   DisposePtr( (Ptr)theChannel );

   return ( theError );
}

//_____

OSErr  PlaySoundResourceSynch( SndChannelPtr theChannel,
                               short         theResID )
{
   Handle  theHandle;
   OSErr   theError;

   theHandle = GetResource( 'snd ', theResID );

   if ( theHandle == nil )
   {
      return ( resProblem );
   }
   else
   {
      HLock( theHandle );
         theError = SndPlay( theChannel, (SndListHandle)theHandle,
                             false );
      HUnlock( theHandle );

      ReleaseResource( theHandle );

      return ( theError );
   }
}
```

Sound Commands

When you call a Toolbox routine such as SysBeep() or SndPlay(), the Sound Manager issues *sound commands*, or instructions, to play the desired sound. Because SysBeep() and SndPlay() are high-level routines designed to shield the programmer from the complexity of sound play programming, the issuing of these sound commands takes place behind the scenes, without the programmer's intervention.

When you participate in the allocation of your program's own sound channel (rather than allowing the Sound Manager to do all the work), you gain the power to send sound commands of your choice to a sound channel. After you do that, any sounds played on that channel will be affected.

About Sound Commands

The `SndChannel` data type is used to keep track of information about a sound channel. Of the several `SndChannel` fields, the most important is the `queue` field. This data structure member holds the sound commands that affect the playing of a sound played on a particular sound channel. Figure 2.6 shows a sound channel pointer and a sound channel in memory, with emphasis on the `queue` field of the sound channel.

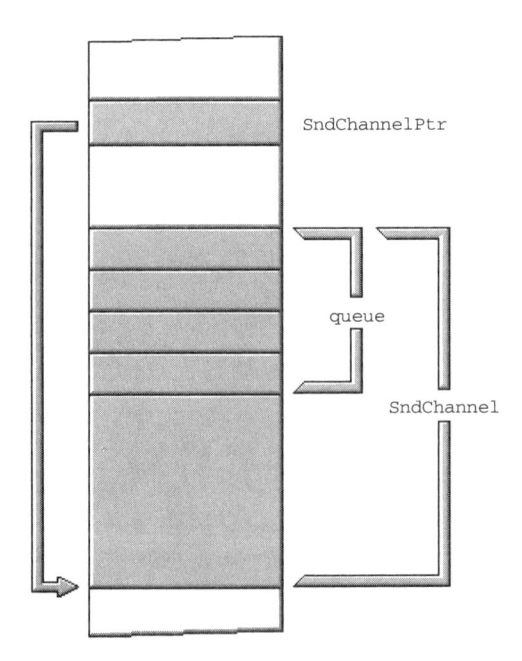

FIGURE 2.6 A channel's sound commands are kept in the queue field of a `SndChannel` data structure.

Sound commands affect the way in which a sound is played. Apple defines over two dozen constants, each representing one type of command. For instance, the freqCmd sound command changes the frequency of vibration of the sound waves that make up a sound—in short, the pitch of the sound changes.

To issue a sound command to a sound channel you'll first define the command, then call the Toolbox routine SndDoCommand(). Each sound command is represented by a SndCommand data structure that looks like this:

```
struct   SndCommand
{
   unsigned short   cmd;
   short            param1;
   long             param2;
};
```

The first field of the SndCommand holds the command number. The next two fields hold command options. The purpose of the option fields vary with the type of the command. For example, the frequency command (freqCmd) ignores the value in the first options parameter and uses the second options parameter to hold the sound's frequency. As a second example, consider the amplitude command, or ampCmd. For this command, the first options parameter holds the amplitude, or volume, of a sound. This volume is expressed by a short in the range of 0 to 255. The second options parameter is ignored. Coding to define a sound command that sets a channel to play a sound at approximately one-quarter volume (65 being approximately one-fourth of the maximum amplitude of 255) follows.

```
SndCommand   theCommand;

theCommand.cmd = ampCmd;
theCommand.param1 = 65;
theCommand.param2 = 0;
```

Once a command is set up, it needs to be added to the queue of a sound channel. To do this, call SndDoCommand().

```
SndChannelPtr   theChannel;
SndCommand      theCommand;
```

```
OSErr            theError;

theError = SndDoCommand( theChannel, &theCommand, false );
```

Figure 2.7 shows a sound channel in memory, with emphasis on the three fields that make up a single command in the sound channel's sound command queue.

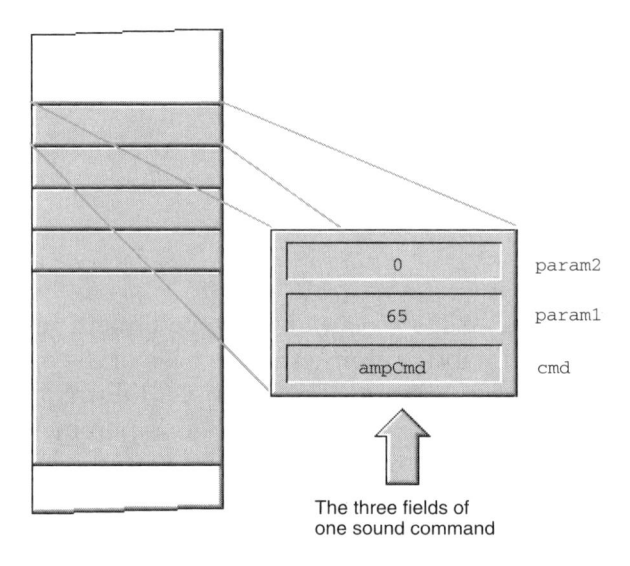

FIGURE 2.7 Each sound command is made up of three fields.

After setting up a command, issue it to a sound channel by calling the Toolbox function SndDoCommand().

```
SndCommand   theCommand;
OSErr        theError;

theError = SndDoCommand( theChannel, &theCommand, false );
```

The first parameter to SndDoCommand() is the sound channel to which the sound command should be queued. Before calling SndDoCommand() you'll allocate a sound channel by making a call to SndNewChannel(), as described earlier. The second parameter to SndDoCommand() is a pointer to the command itself. Fill the three fields of the command, then pass it to SndDoCommand().

When a new sound channel is created, it has a queue capable of holding 128 sound commands. If you are concerned about the unlikely event that your program may fill this queue, you can pass a value of `false` as the last parameter to `SndDoCommand()`. This tells the Sound Manager to wait for a free position if the queue is full. Passing a value of `true` tells the Sound Manager instead to return an error-result code (`queueFull`).

If your program will be issuing the same command to more than one channel, consider writing a function such as the application-defined routine `SetSoundAmplitude()`. When passed a sound channel and an amplitude, this function fills the fields of a sound command, issues the command to the channel (places it in the channel's queue), and returns a result code indicating whether the operation was successful or not.

```
OSErr  SetSoundAmplitude( SndChannelPtr theChannel, short theAmp )
{
    SndCommand   theCommand;
    OSErr        theError;

    theCommand.cmd = ampCmd;
    theCommand.param1 = theAmp;
    theCommand.param2 = 0;

    theError = SndDoCommand( theChannel, &theCommand, false );

    return ( theError );
}
```

It's important to keep in mind that in the above code, `SndDoCommand()` doesn't actually play a sound at the new amplitude. The call to `SndDoCommand()` only places the command in a channel's queue. You still need to load a sound resource into memory and call `SndPlay()` in order to play a sound. When you do that, the sound will be played at the new volume—provided you pass `SndPlay()` the affected sound channel. The following snippet shows how to play a sound at half volume (keeping in mind that the `ampCmd` accepts a value in the range of 0 (off) to 255 (full volume). The SoundCommands example program that follows demonstrates exactly how to use a sound channel.

```
SndChannelPtr  theChannel;
OSErr          theError;
```

```
// allocate a new sound channel here

theError = SetSoundAmplitude( theChannel, 127 );

// load a sound resource here

// pass SndPlay() theChannel to play the sound here
```

Chapter Example: SoundCommands

SoundCommands is very similar to the previous example program, SoundChannelIntro. Both use the same application-defined routines to allocate a new sound channel, play a sound resource, and deallocate the channel when done. The only difference between the two programs is that before SoundCommands plays the sound, it calls the application-defined function `SetSoundAmplitude()` to set the amplitude of the new sound channel.

The SoundCommands program plays a sound very quietly—the siren sound will play at about one-fifth of the volume set in the Sound control panel. To change the volume, try experimenting with the value of the `short` variable `theAmplitude`. Keep in mind that the range of `theAmplitude` should be from 0 to 255.

```
short   theAmplitude;

theAmplitude = 50;
theError = SetSoundAmplitude( theChannel, theAmplitude );
```

The following listing omits the `OpenOneSynchSoundChannel()`, `DisposeOne-SoundChannel()`, and `PlaySoundResourceSynch()` functions. If you'd like to see the listing for any of these functions, page back to the listing for the SoundChannelIntro example program.

```
//_____

#include <Sound.h>

//_____

void            InitializeToolbox( void );
```

```
SndChannelPtr   OpenOneSynchSoundChannel( void );
OSErr           DisposeOneSoundChannel( SndChannelPtr );
OSErr           PlaySoundResourceSynch( SndChannelPtr, short );
OSErr           SetSoundAmplitude( SndChannelPtr, short );

//_____

#define    rPoliceSiren        9000

//_____

void  main( void )

{
    NumVersion      theSndMgrVers;
    short           theResID;
    OSErr           theError;
    SndChannelPtr   theChannel;
    short           theAmplitude;

    InitializeToolbox();

    theSndMgrVers = SndSoundManagerVersion();
    if ( theSndMgrVers.majorRev < 3 )
       ExitToShell();

    theChannel = OpenOneSynchSoundChannel();
    if ( theChannel == nil )
       ExitToShell();


    theAmplitude = 50;
    theError = SetSoundAmplitude( theChannel, theAmplitude );
    if ( theError != noErr )
       ExitToShell();

    theResID = rPoliceSiren;
    theError = PlaySoundResourceSynch( theChannel, theResID );
    if ( theError != noErr )
       ExitToShell();

    theError = DisposeOneSoundChannel( theChannel );
    if ( theError != noErr )
       ExitToShell();
}
```

```
//_____

OSErr  SetSoundAmplitude( SndChannelPtr theChannel, short theAmp )
{
   SndCommand   theCommand;
   OSErr        theError;

   theCommand.cmd = ampCmd;
   theCommand.param1 = theAmp;
   theCommand.param2 = 0;

   theError = SndDoCommand( theChannel, &theCommand, false );

   return ( theError );
}
```

Asynchronous Sound Play

Asynchronous sound play allows both sound and animation to take place at the same time. An understanding of how asynchronous sound play works is paramount in creating exciting games and multimedia programs.

An Approach to Playing a Sound Asynchronously

Before jumping into the complete code necessary for playing a sound asynchronously, let's have a general introduction to asynchronous sound play.

To play a sound resource asynchronously, you'll first allocate a new sound channel using `SndNewChannel()`. You'll then load the sound resource to play and call `SndPlay()` play it. While these two routines are the same as the ones used to play a sound synchronously, the parameters that you'll pass to them will not be the same.

Once a sound is playing, your program will enter a loop. In each pass through the loop, a check will be made to see if the sound has finished playing. If it hasn't finished, an action will be performed. Typically, this action will be one step in an animation. For example, a digitized jet-engine sound could be loaded and a call to SndPlay() could be made to start playing the sound. In the body of the loop, a picture of an airplane could be shifted one pixel to the left at each pass through the loop—as long as the sound was still playing. The result would be an airplane flying across the screen from right to left, accompanied by the roar of its engine. When the sound stopped playing, the animation would also stop.

The following snippet shows, in general terms, how an animated sequence that is accompanied by sound could be played from within the main() routine of a program. Later in this chapter you'll see how the global variable gSoundPlaying gets set. You'll also see the development of CleanUpSoundIfFinished()—the function that deallocates an open sound channel when a sound is finished.

```
Boolean  gSoundPlaying;

void  main( void )
{
   EventRecord  theEvent;

  // initializations, open window

  while ( gDone == false )
  {
     WaitNextEvent( everyEvent, &theEvent, 15L, nil );

     CleanUpSoundIfFinished();

     if ( gSoundPlaying == true )
        MovePictureOnePixel();

     switch ( theEvent.what )
     {
        // handle mouseDown, keyDown, etc.
     }
  }
}
```

Figure 2.8 shows an overview of the steps necessary to play a sound asynchronously. On the next several pages this general description will be replaced with a more detailed look at these steps.

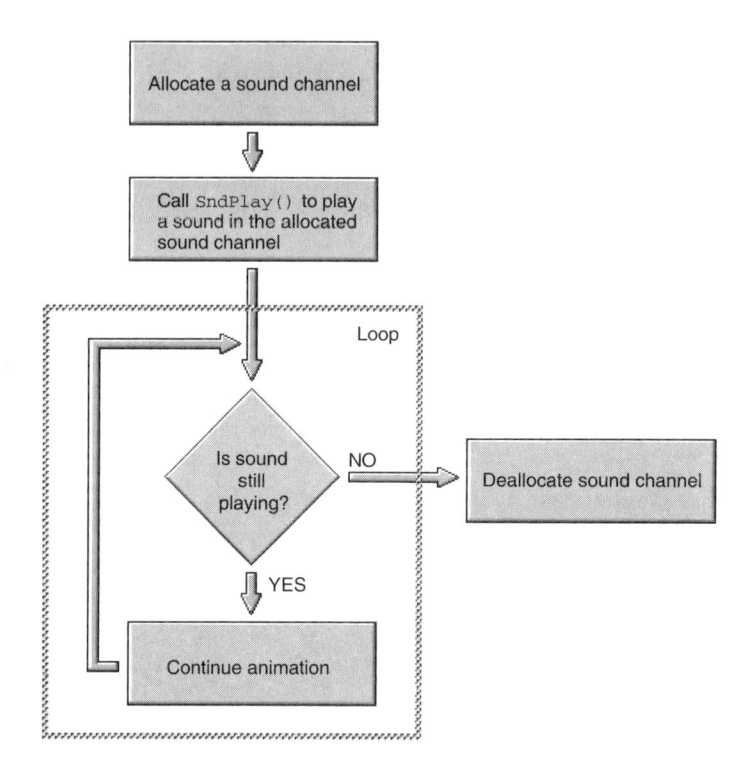

FIGURE **2.8** An overview of how sound and animation are carried out in unison.

The Callback Command and Callback Routine

The third parameter to the Toolbox function `SndPlay()` specifies whether the sound data referenced by the variable `theHandle` should be played asynchronously (`true`) or not (`false`). Earlier you saw that to play a sound *synchronously*, you pass `false` for the third parameter—as in this call:

```
theError = SndPlay( theChannel, (SndListHandle)theHandle, false );
```

Specifying that a sound be played synchronously (as has been the case up to this point) means that `SndPlay()` will let the Sound Manager take control of the Mac and play the sound from start to finish. No other action can take place until `SndPlay()` competes its execution. If, instead, you pass a value of `true` as the third parameter to `SndPlay()`, the routine will be executed in an altogether different manner. Instead of seizing control, the Sound Manager will share processor time with the rest of your program. That makes it possible to have `SndPlay()` play a sound and, at the same time, have your program cycle through the loop described on the previous pages.

Earlier, you learned that the loop body will perform a check to see if a sound channel currently has a sound playing. The way to determine if a sound is playing is to examine a flag variable that gets set by a *callback routine*. Simply put, a callback routine is called when, and only when, a sound has finished playing. The callback routine's purpose is to set a global flag variable that indicates to the rest of the program that the sound has indeed finished playing. It is the value of this global callback flag variable that the loop repeatedly checks.

Figure 2.9 illustrates how a callback routine works. In this figure, it's assumed that a cartoon police car moves from right to left as a siren sound plays. When `SndPlay()` is called to start the playing of the siren sound resource, the program sets a flag variable to indicate that a sound has started. In Figure 2.9, this flag is a global `Boolean` variable named `gSoundPlaying`. As the sound plays, the program frequently checks the value of `gSoundPlaying`. If the flag is still set to `true`, then the picture boundaries are moved a little to the left and the picture is redrawn. In the figure, this is done three times—in a real application, the check would be performed many more times so that animation would appear smooth.

When `SndPlay()` has finished, the Sound Manager will invoke the callback routine. The callback routine will change the value of `gSound-Playing` from `true` to `false`. Then, when the loop again tests the value of `gSoundPlaying`, it will find that this flag is now `false`. That tells the loop to stop performing the animation. The effect? When the sound stops, the animation stops, too.

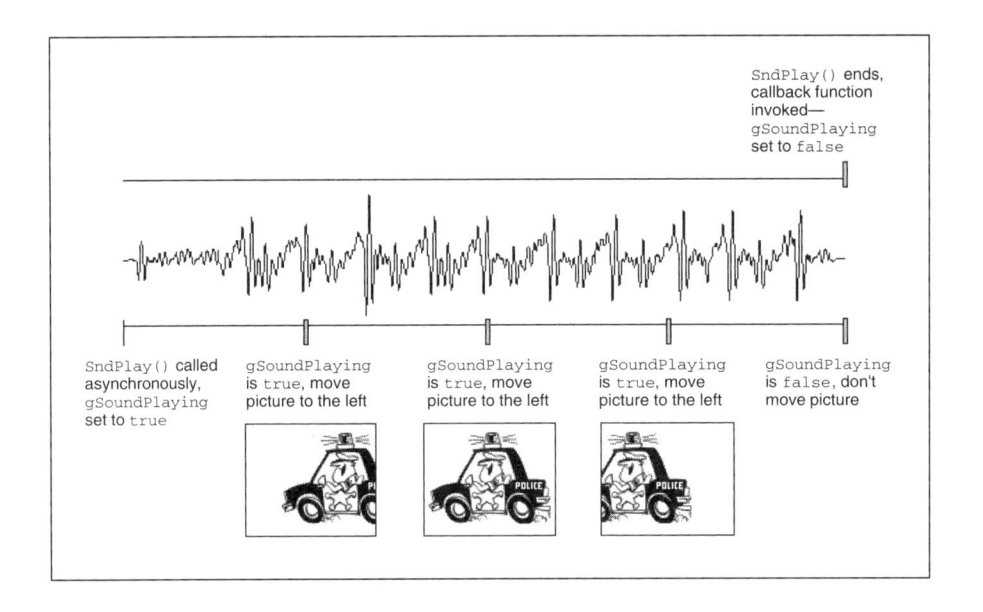

FIGURE 2.9 Animation continues as long as a
sound's callback routine hasn't set a flag to false.

It's important to note that while the callback routine is an application-defined function, it isn't called directly by your code. Instead, the Sound Manager will invoke it. Figure 2.9 implies that this code is different by placing it at the top of the figure, while the code called directly by the application (SndPlay() and the animation code) appears at the bottom of the figure.

How is it that the Sound Manager—and not your own code—invokes the callback routine? The answer lies within the sound channel record. A sound channel is represented in memory by a SndChannel data structure. You're familiar with the queue field of this structure—it holds the sound commands for a given channel. The callBack field is another member of the SndChannel structure. It holds a pointer to the channel's callback routine. Figure 2.10 labels a couple of the `SndChannel` data structure fields and shows that the `callBack` field holds a pointer to an application-defined callback routine in memory.

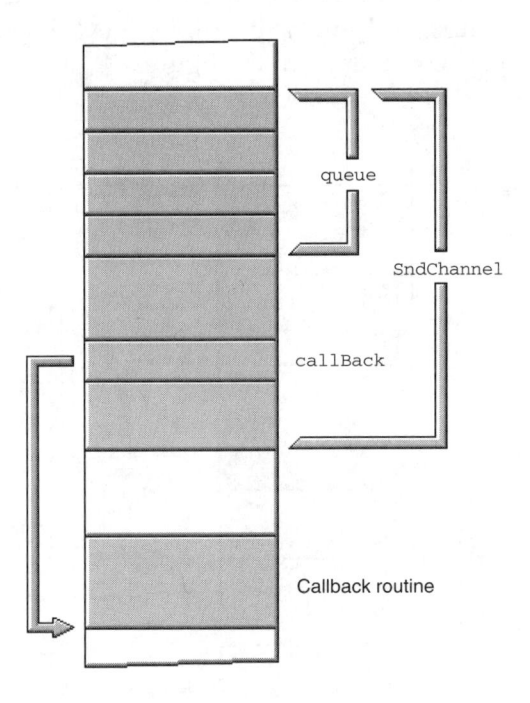

queue

SndChannel

callBack

Callback routine

FIGURE 2.10 A sound channel used for asynchronous sound play has a callback routine associated with it.

N O T E

The sound channel's queue holds 128 sound commands. For simplicity, the queue field in this and other figures shows a queue with room for only four commands. As an aside, this isn't entirely inaccurate—a programmer does in fact have control over the size of the queue.

When your application passes SndPlay() a SndChannelPtr, the Sound Manager takes various sound-playing commands found in the snd resource and places them in the sound channel's queue. Figure 2.11 shows two such sound commands added to the queue. Because the exact type of command is unimportant in this example, they're shown simply by the generic name "play command" in the figure.

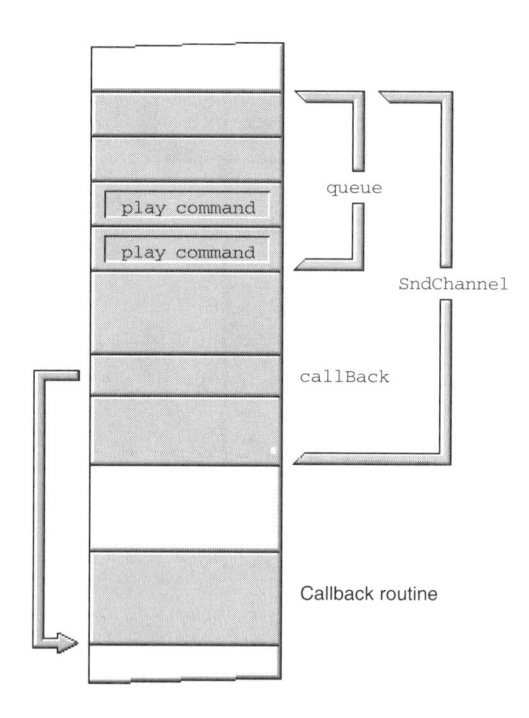

FIGURE 2.11 A sound channel about to play the sound data from a snd resource

After your program calls SndPlay() it should add a callBackCmd sound command to the sound channel's queue. Because SndPlay() has started the sound playing, this callBackCmd command will be the last sound command in the queue. Figure 2.12 shows a callBackCmd in the queue. Note that the callback command is the last entry in the queue—though the queue isn't full. Also notice that the start of the queue is shown at the lower end of the figure, corresponding to lower addresses.

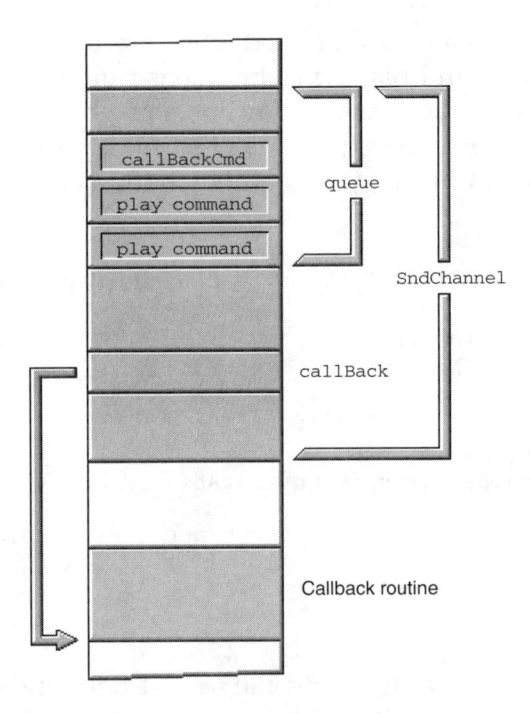

FIGURE 2.12 A callback command should be the last
sound command in a sound channel's queue.

Installing the Callback Command in the Command Queue

Recall that each sound command has three fields: the cmd field that holds a command number indicating the type of command and two option fields—param1 and param2—that hold information that varies depending on the type of command.

For a callback sound command, the command type is callBackCmd. With the callBackCmd command, the param1 and param2 fields are available for any purpose a particular application requires. For this chapter's example, the param1 field won't be needed and will simply be set to 0.

The param2 command will be used when a program using this chapter's asynchronous sound-playing technique is running on a 68K-based Mac. Below is an application-defined function named InstallCallbackCommand() that is called after SndPlay() starts. It's used to add, or install, a callback sound command in the queue of the sound channel currently playing the sound.

```
OSErr  InstallCallbackCommand( SndChannelPtr theChannel )
{
   OSErr        theError;
   SndCommand   theCommand;

   theCommand.cmd    = callBackCmd;
   theCommand.param1 = 0;
   theCommand.param2 = SetCurrentA5();

   theError = SndDoCommand( theChannel, &theCommand, true );

   return ( theError );
}
```

The setting of the cmd field and the param1 field of the sound command is simple enough to follow. The assignment of the param2 option field may not seem as straightforward.

The call to the Toolbox function SetCurrentA5() sets the param2 field to the value in the A5 register. This value is a pointer to the section of the application partition that holds the application's global variables. By storing this pointer value in the sound-channel command queue, the callback routine will have a backup value of this pointer should the A5 register contents be changed later on. Figure 2.13 illustrates that both the A5 register in the CPU and the param2 field of the callback sound command hold the same address.

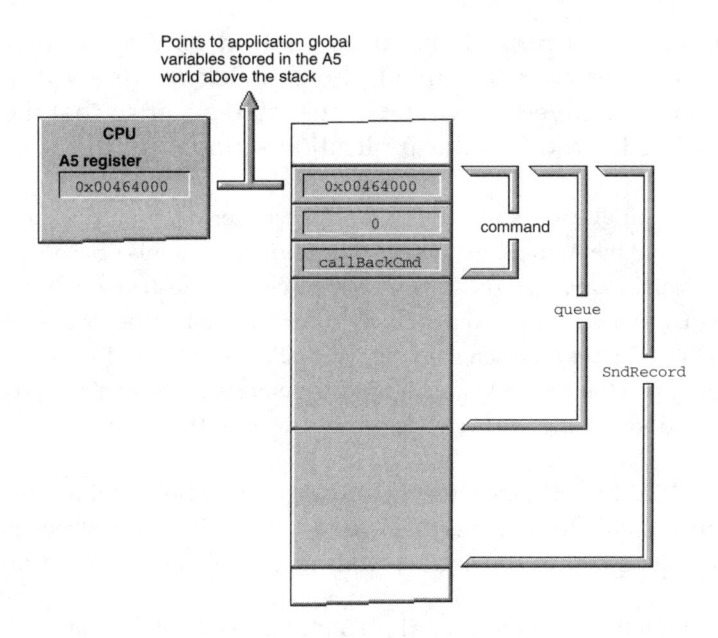

FIGURE 2.13 The param2 field of the callback command
holds the A5 register pointer value.

The reason this pointer value is stored in the sound channel's queue has to do with the nature of a callback routine. A callback routine isn't invoked by a call from your code. Instead, it's called by the system. When it is called, other code may be executing. If this other code happens to be a Toolbox function, the value in the A5 register might not be a pointer to the application's global variables. That's because a Toolbox function has the power to save the A5 register value, use and alter the register's contents, and then restore the register to its initial condition. Should a callback routine start executing *while* a Toolbox routine is executing (which is possible because a sound playing asynchronously plays while other code executes), the callback routine will insert the `param2` value (the saved A5 value) in the A5 register so that the callback routine knows how to find the application's global variables.

If you already know about the A5 register, read on. If you don't know about the A5 register, but feel the information in this very brief overview is satisfactory, read on. If, however, you aren't satisfied with this discussion, take a side trip to Appendix B—it provides all of the details about the A5 register and its importance when working with callback routines. Because the topics of the A5 register and the A5 world are Macintosh memory topics, and not directly related to graphics and sound, they've been relegated to an appendix.

The `InstallCallbackCommand()` function should be invoked just after an asynchronous call to `SndPlay()` is made. That has the effect of placing the `callBackCmd` last in the sound channel's sound command queue.

```
theError = SndPlay( theChannel, (SndListHandle)theHandle, true );

theError = InstallCallbackCommand( theChannel );
```

At first glance it may seem that the above snippet plays the sound and then, when the sound is finished, installs the callback routine. This isn't the case. You're thinking back to synchronous sound play, where `SndPlay()` started a sound, then took control until the sound was finished. No other code executed until `SndPlay()` completed. Remember, `SndPlay()` is now playing a sound asynchronously. That means `SndPlay()` starts the sound, and then the program carries on. In the above code, that means that the `InstallCallbackCommand()` routine is invoked immediately after `SndPlay()` is called—just after the sound starts playing, but before the sound finishes.

The Sound Callback Routine

When a sound channel is to be used to play a sound *synchronously*, the channel is allocated with the last parameter to `SndNewChannel()` set to `nil`:

```
SndChannelPtr   theChannel;
OSErr           theError;
```

```
theChannel = nil;
theError = SndNewChannel( &theChannel, 0, 0, nil );
```

When a sound channel is to be used for asynchronous sound play, this last parameter should instead be a universal procedure pointer (UPP) that points to an application-defined callback routine. When `SndNewChannel()` is called in this manner, a callback routine becomes associated with the sound channel named as the first parameter. That tells the Sound Manager what routine to use as a sound's callback function. The following code shows how a call to `SndNewChannel()` looks when allocating a sound channel for asynchronous play:

```
SndChannelPtr    theChannel;
OSErr            theError;
SndCallBackUPP   theCallBackUPP;

theCallBackUPP = NewSndCallBackProc( SoundChannelCallback );

theChannel = nil;
theError = SndNewChannel( &theChannel, 0, 0, theCallBackUPP );
```

The `SndCallBackUPP` is an Apple-defined data type that turns out to be nothing more than a `UniversalProcPtr`—a *universal procedure pointer*, or UPP. The `NewSndCallBackProc()` function is a Toolbox routine that, when passed the name of an application-defined routine, creates a UPP for that function. In the above snippet, the application-defined routine is named `SoundChannelCallback()`. This UPP is then passed to `SndNewChannel()`. These steps are necessary so that the Sound Manager can have a pointer to the callback function that you've written.

 Universal procedure pointer? `UniversalProcPtr`? UPP? These terms aren't familiar to you? They should be. They're an important part of programming the PowerPC. They all mean the same thing: a pointer that

NOTE points to a function. The UPP replaces the `ProcPtr` type that was used in the past. The Apple universal header files use UPPs so that the same source code can properly compile for both older 68K-based Macs and the newer PowerPC-based Macs.

Finally, you'll need to write the application-defined callback routine. The format of this function is as follows: the `pascal` keyword, a return type of `void`, the function name, and a `SndChannelPtr` parameter and a `SndCommand` parameter. An example follows.

```
pascal void  SoundChannelCallback( SndChannelPtr theChannel,
                                   SndCommand    theCommand )
```

Generally, the only purpose of a callback routine is to let the rest of your application know that an asynchronous sound has finished playing. You can do that by defining a couple of global flag variables and setting them to the appropriate value in the callback routine. This chapter's example defines a `Boolean` named `gCallbackExecuted` to let the program know whether the callback routine has executed and a `Boolean` named `gSoundPlaying` to let the program know if a sound is currently playing. A simple version of a callback routine follows.

```
pascal void  SoundChannelCallback( SndChannelPtr theChannel,
                                   SndCommand    theCommand )
{
   gCallbackExecuted = true;
   gSoundPlaying = false;
}
```

The above version of `SoundChannelCallback()` is included here to demonstrate just how little there is to a callback routine. But to make this function usable, you need to surround the two assignment statements with some utility code. As mentioned earlier, at the time the system invokes a callback routine, there's no way to know what other code will be executing. If a Toolbox function is being carried out, the callback routine should save the value in the A5 register (the Toolbox may be using this register for its own purposes) and then set the A5 register to a value that points to the application global variables. Only then can the callback routine make use of any application global variables. Finally, as the callback routine ends it should restore the A5 register to the condition it found it in. That is, it should replace the contents of the A5 register with whatever value was in the register at the time the callback routine was invoked. That allows the Toolbox function to finish executing after the callback routine has finished.

To save the current value of the A5 register and to change the value in the register, call the Toolbox routine `SetA5()`:

```
long  theA5;

theA5 = SetA5( theCommand.param2 );
```

Now you see why the callBackCmd that was placed in the sound channel
sound command queue set param2 to the application's A5 value. By
saving the application's A5 value early on, it's been preserved for use by
the callback routine. SetA5() saves the current A5 value (the one used
by the Toolbox routine that SoundChannelCallback() may be interrupting) in a variable named theA5. Then SetA5() sets the A5 register to the
param2 value.

  With the A5 register pointing to the application's global variable
section in memory, the callback routine can access global variables:

```
gCallbackExecuted = true;
gSoundPlaying = false;
```

Before exiting, the callback routine should restore the A5 register to the
condition it was in when the callback routine started. Another call to
SetA5() does this. This time the parameter is the local variable theA5.
This variable holds the value A5 had when the routine started. The
value returned by SetA5() is placed in variable theA5. Since the routine
is ending, this value is ignored.

```
theA5 = SetA5( theA5 );
```

The following is a version of the callback routine that takes the A5 register
into consideration:

```
pascal void  SoundChannelCallback( SndChannelPtr theChannel,
                                   SndCommand      theCommand )
{
    long  theA5;

    theA5 = SetA5( theCommand.param2 );

    gCallbackExecuted = true;
    gSoundPlaying = false;

    theA5 = SetA5( theA5 );
}
```

Keeping track of the A5 register can be a little tricky. Figure 2.14 may clear things up a bit. The light-background snippets represent code in an application, while the darker-background snippets represent the code for a Toolbox routine. In the top snippet you can see that the application's A5 value is stored in the `param2` field of a sound command. If you follow the arrow down you can see where this saved value will be used—in the callback routine. Follow the arrows for each of the three saved A5 values to see where each is later used.

Figure 2.14 emphasizes that the callback routine is capable of interrupting an executing Toolbox routine—that's the reason the A5 register value has to be stored and restored. In the figure, the hypothetical Toolbox routine `ToolboxFunc()` is in the middle of executing when the Sound Manager invokes the `SoundChannelCallback()` routine. When `SoundChannelCallback()` completes, control returns to the Toolbox routine—which then finishes up.

NOTE

Figure 2.14 was lifted directly from Appendix B. Remember, if this A5 topic is giving you grief, take a diversion to that appendix now.

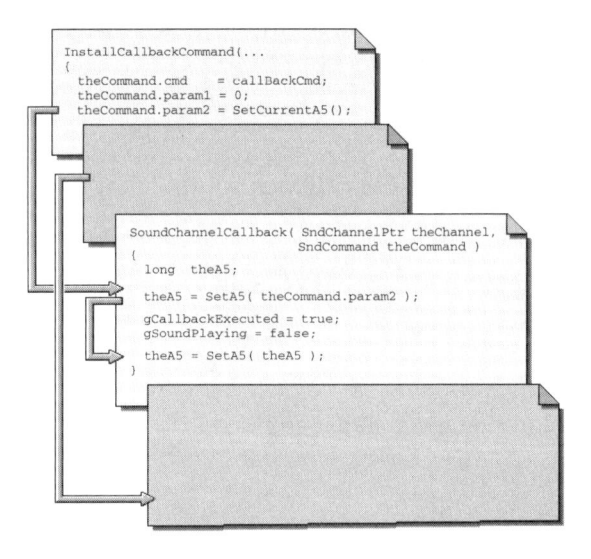

FIGURE 2.14 The A5 value is initially saved so that it can be used
by the callback routine at a later time.

Before you can say that the callback routine is complete, you have to account for the fact that this code might be compiled on either a 68K compiler of a PowerPC compiler. To do that, add a couple of #ifndef compiler directives to the routine. An #ifndef directive tells the compiler "if not defined, do the following…" Use the powerc identifier after the #ifndef directive. If a 68K compiler is being used, powerc will not be defined, and the code that follows will be compiled. If a PowerPC compiler is being used, powerc will be defined and the code under the #ifndef will not be compiled.

```
#ifndef powerc
    theA5 = SetA5( theCommand.param2 );
#endif
```

NOTE

Writing your code such that it compiles using either a 68K compiler or a PowerPC compiler is a fact of life you should be dealing with. For a more thorough reference to PowerPC programming, look at the M&T book *Programming the PowerPC* or the *PowerPC System Software* version of *Inside Macintosh*.

Because a native PowerPC application doesn't keep global variables in an A5 world, this is exactly the effect you want—the calls to SetA5() will be skipped. The final version of the callback routine—complete with A5 code and #ifndef directives—used in this chapter's example program, follows.

```
pascal void  SoundChannelCallback( SndChannelPtr theChannel,
                                   SndCommand    theCommand )
{
    long  theA5;

    #ifndef powerc
        theA5 = SetA5( theCommand.param2 );
    #endif

    gCallbackExecuted = true;
    gSoundPlaying = false;

    #ifndef powerc
        theA5 = SetA5( theA5 );
```

```
#endif
}
```

Now that the #ifndef directive and PowerPC code have been mentioned, it's time to point out that the InstallCallbackCommand() routine discussed a little earlier should also include an #ifndef powerc directive. Rather than always setting param2 to the current A5 value, check to see if the code is being compiled on a 68K compiler or a PowerPC compiler. If a 68K compiler is being used, make the call to SetCurrentA5(). If a PowerPC compiler is being used, then the param2 field of the callback command won't be used, and you can simply set param2 to 0. The new, final version of InstallCallbackCommand() follows:

```
OSErr  InstallCallbackCommand( SndChannelPtr theChannel )
{
   OSErr       theError;
   SndCommand  theCommand;

   theCommand.cmd    = callBackCmd;
   theCommand.param1 = 0;
#ifndef powerc
      theCommand.param2 = SetCurrentA5();
#else
      theCommand.param2 = 0;
#endif

   theError = SndDoCommand( theChannel, &theCommand, true );

   return ( theError );
}
```

Starting the Sound and Animation

Playing a sound asynchronously requires several main steps and a few lesser ones. The six main steps used in this book's approach are as follows:

1. Allocate a new sound channel, specifying a callback routine for that channel.
2. Load a sound resource into memory.
3. Set a global flag that states that a sound is playing.

4. Call `SndPlay()` to begin asynchronous sound play.

5. Install a `callBackCmd` sound command in the queue of the sound channel that is playing the sound.

6. Within a loop, perform animation as the sound plays.

These six main steps can all be taken care of within a single application-defined routine. The `PlaySoundResourceAsynch()` function, which is used in this chapter's asynchronous sound example program, needs only a `snd` resource ID passed to it in order to start sound play.

NOTE The `PlaySoundResourceAsynch()` routine, and the application-defined functions that it calls, can be used unchanged in many programs. The only exception is the `AnimateWhileSoundPlays()` routine. This function will be application-specific. That is, the animated action it performs while sound plays will vary depending on your program's animation requirements.

```
short         gSoundPlaying = false;
SndChannelPtr gSoundChannel = nil;
Handle        gSoundHandle  = nil;

void  PlaySoundResourceAsynch( short theResID )
{
   OSErr  theError;

   gSoundChannel = OpenOneAsynchSoundChannel();
   if ( gSoundChannel == nil )
      ExitToShell();

   gSoundHandle = GetResource( 'snd ', theResID );
   if ( gSoundHandle == nil )
      ExitToShell();

   DetachResource( gSoundHandle );
   HLock( gSoundHandle );

   gSoundPlaying = true;

   theError = SndPlay( gSoundChannel, (SndListHandle)gSoundHandle,
                       true );

   if ( theError == noErr )
      theError = InstallCallbackCommand( gSoundChannel );
```

```
    else
       ExitToShell();

    AnimateWhileSoundPlays();
}
```

The first of the five steps handled by PlaySoundResourceAsynch(), the allocation of a new sound channel, is taken care of in a call to the application-defined function OpenOneAsynchSoundChannel(). This function is very similar to the OpenOneSynchSoundChannel() routine described earlier in this chapter. The chief differences are that the new routine creates a universal procedure pointer for a callback function, then passes that UPP to the Toolbox routine SndNewChannel(). A brief description of creating a UPP appears earlier in this chapter.

```
SndChannelPtr  OpenOneAsynchSoundChannel( void )
{
    SndChannelPtr    theChannel;
    OSErr            theError;
    SndCallBackUPP   theCallBackUPP;

    theCallBackUPP = NewSndCallBackProc( SoundChannelCallback );

    theChannel = nil;
    theError = SndNewChannel( &theChannel, 0, 0, theCallBackUPP );

    if ( theError != noErr )
    {
       DisposePtr( (Ptr)theChannel );
       theChannel = nil;
    }

    return ( theChannel );
}
```

After the sound channel has been allocated, a call to GetResource() handles the second step—the loading of a sound resource into memory. After loading the resource data, a call to DetachResource() is made. This Toolbox routine detaches the sound resource from its resource file. When a sound is played synchronously, this step isn't important—no other action can take place. When a sound is played asynchronously, almost anything can happen as the sound plays—including the closing of a resource file. You'll want the sound resource detached from its file in case this happens. By detaching the resource from the file in which it hails from, you remove any dependency on the resource file.

NOTE The closing of a resource file isn't a random event—your code would have to deliberately do that. In a small application, you'll know whether or not this happens. A large application that keeps resources in separate resource files, however, may have several calls to a routine that closes a resource file.

After the resource is detached from its file, a call to `HLock()` locks the resource data in memory. This is in preparation for the call to `SndPlay()`. Unlike the synchronous sound-playing function developed earlier, there is no call to `HUnlock()` in the asynchronous sound-playing function. When a sound is playing asynchronously, it can be interrupted by the user before `SndPlay()` finishes. That means that the call to `HUnlock()` shouldn't follow the call to `SndPlay()`. Instead, it should appear in a function that is called repeatedly from within a loop—the same loop that will be performing any actions that take place while the sound plays. That loop will be discussed a little later.

Just before the sound is played, a global flag should be set to show the rest of the program that a sound is playing. This is the third of the six steps listed above.

```
gSoundPlaying = true;
```

The next step is the actual playing of the sound—finally! A call to `SndPlay()`, with the last parameter set to `true`, starts a sound playing asynchronously. The first parameter to `SndPlay()` is the `SndChannelPtr` that was returned by the call to `OpenOneAsynchSoundChannel()` function that was made earlier in `PlaySoundResourceAsynch()`.

```
theError = SndPlay( gSoundChannel, (SndListHandle)gSoundHandle,
                    true );
```

Just after `SndPlay()` is invoked, the fifth of the six steps—the adding of the callback sound command to the sound command queue of the sound channel that is playing the sound—is performed. The application-defined routine `InstallCallbackCommand()`, described earlier, takes care of this.

```
theError = InstallCallbackCommand( gSoundChannel );
```

Figure 2.15 adds a few concise comments to the `PlaySoundResourceAsynch()` routine to sum up the tasks that this important function handles.

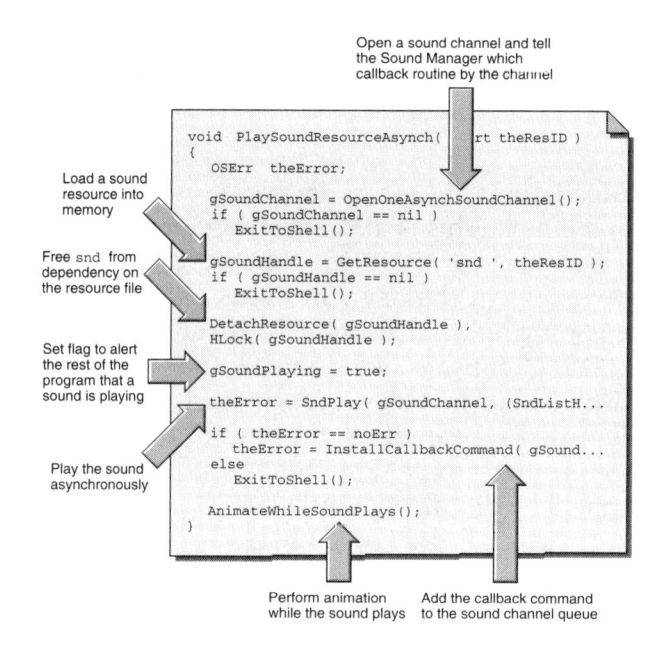

FIGURE 2.15 The `PlaySoundResourceAsynch()` routine performs the steps necessary to run an animation as a sound plays.

The last step is to enter a loop that performs some on-screen action while the sound plays. The application-defined routine `AnimateWhileSoundPlays()` holds that loop.

Performing Animation While a Sound Plays

After `PlaySoundResourceAsynch()` makes a call to `SndPlay()` to start a sound playing, `AnimateWhileSoundPlays()` is called to perform the animation that will accompany the sound. It's important to keep in mind that when `SndPlay()` is called asynchronously, the Sound Manager does not take control of the program. Instead, the code that follows the call to SndPlay() executes as the sound plays. That means that just after the sound starts, AnimateWhileSoundPlays() will be called. A typical version of this routine follows.

```
void  AnimateWhileSoundPlays( void )
{
   Boolean  loopDone = false;

   while ( loopDone == false )
   {
      CleanUpSoundIfFinished();

      if ( gSoundPlaying == true )
         MovePictureOnePixel();
      else
         loopDone = true;
   }
}
```

At each pass through the while loop in AnimateWhileSoundPlays(), a call is made to an application-defined routine named CleanUpSoundIf-Finished(). The purpose of this routine is to dispose of the sound channel when the sound is finished. Because an application can't predict when a playing sound will end, it needs to call this function frequently. When the sound does finish, the Sound Manager will invoke the sound channel's callback routine. The callback function will set the global Boolean flag variable gCallbackExecuted to true. When CleanUpSoundIfFinished() notices this, the function unlocks the sound handle (which had been locked just before SndPlay() started to play the sound), releases the sound resource data from memory, and disposes of the sound channel. The function also sets the gCallbackExecuted to false so that if CleanUpSoundIf-Finished() gets called again, the function won't try to dispose of the now nonexistent sound channel.

```
void  CleanUpSoundIfFinished( void )
{
   OSErr  theError;

   if ( gCallbackExecuted == true )
```

```
{
    HUnlock( gSoundHandle );
    ReleaseResource( gSoundHandle );
    gSoundHandle = nil;

    theError = DisposeOneSoundChannel( gSoundChannel );
    if ( theError != noErr )
        ExitToShell();

    gSoundChannel = nil;
    gCallbackExecuted = false;
    }
}
```

The job of AnimateWhileSoundPlays() is to perform the action that accompanies the sound. To determine if the sound is playing, the routine checks the value of the global flag gSoundPlaying. Recall that this Boolean variable is set to true when SndPlay() is called, and set to false in the callback routine. When the sound finishes playing, the Sound Manager will interrupt AnimateWhileSoundPlays() to execute the callback routine. When the callback function finishes, AnimateWhile-SoundPlays() will resume. At that time gSoundPlaying will be false, and the loop—and the animation—will end.

As long as gSoundPlaying is true, the animation will continue. In this example, that animation consists of a picture being moved one pixel to the left—the application-defined function MovePictureOnePixel() does that. The asynchronous sound example that appears later in this chapter describes this routine. Once the callback routine is invoked and gSoundPlaying is toggled to false, the local variable loopDone gets set to true and the loop, animation, and the AnimateWhileSoundPlays() function, end.

Figure 2.8, located back near the start of the asynchronous-sound section of this chapter, gave a broad overview of how a sound is played asynchronously. Figure 2.16 updates Figure 2.8 by filling in the names of the functions that handle the basic sound-playing tasks.

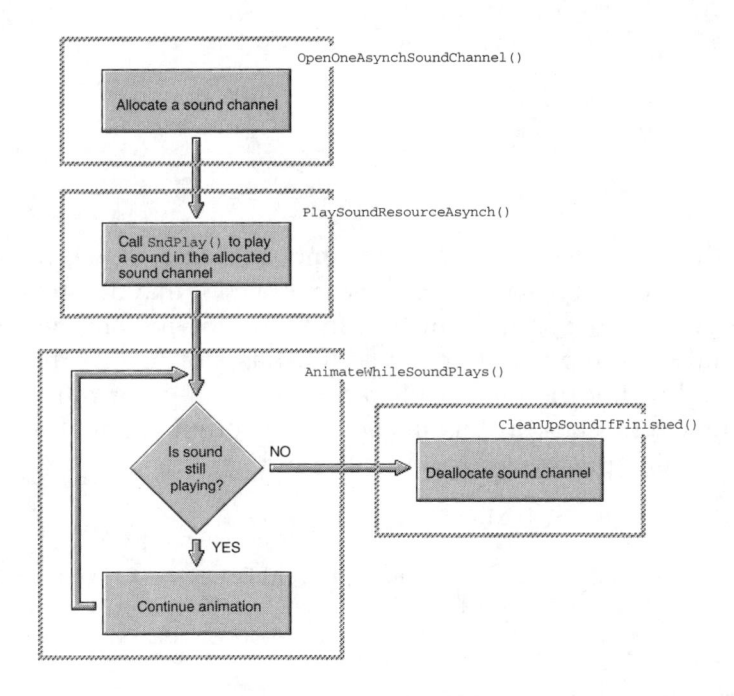

FIGURE 2.16 The application-defined functions that make asynchronous sound play possible.

Before finishing off with an example program, let's look at the answer to a question you may have regarding the disposing of the sound channel. To determine when to dispose of the channel, CleanUpSoundIfFinished() is called from within the while loop found in AnimateWhileSoundPlays(). Rather than calling this routine at every pass through the loop, perhaps it could be called just a single time—when the global gSoundPlaying flag becomes false:

```
while ( loopDone == false )
{
    if ( gSoundPlaying == true )
        MovePictureOnePixel();
```

```
   else
   {
      CleanUpSoundIfFinished();
      loopDone = true;
   }
}
```

While this approach will work in some instances, it will fail in others. Consider a version of AnimateWhileSoundPlays() that doesn't stop animation as soon as the sound finishes. In the following snippet, animation might take place even after the sound has stopped. If the sound has finished, but the picture hasn't reached the edge of the window, the animation continues. In this instance, the sound channel will inadvertently remain open even though the sound has finished.

```
while ( loopDone == false )
{
   if ( (gSoundPlaying == true) || (gAtEdge == false) )
      MovePictureOnePixel();
   else
   {
      CleanUpSoundIfFinished();
      loopDone = true;
   }
}
```

Instead of calling CleanUpSoundIfFinished once, as is done above, call it each pass through the loop—as shown earlier.

Chapter Example: AsynchSndPlay

The AsynchSndPlay example program is a simple demonstration of asynchronous sound play. When you start the program you'll see an empty window. Pressing any key starts a cartoon bear sliding on a block of ice across the window from right to left. Figure 2.17 shows the bear in the window. As the bear moves, you'll hear classical music playing. When the animation stops a short time later, the music will stop as well. You can replay the sound by again pressing any key. When you do, the bear will start moving from the point at which he stopped. And, of course, the music will again play as the bear moves. To quit the program, wait until the animation and sound stop, then click the mouse button.

FIGURE 2.17 The AsynchSndPlay program displays
a picture that moves while a sound plays.

NOTE Why is a cartoon polar bear sliding along to the music of the 18th-century composer George Frideric Handel? Who cares! What's important here is that while a sound is playing, other action is taking place on the screen. That's the definition of asynchronous sound—a technique you'll need to master if you're going to write multimedia programs or games.

The AsynchSndPlay project requires three resources: a `PICT`, a `snd `, and a `WIND`. Figure 2.18 shows the resource IDs of each. You can replace the picture or the sound with resources of your own—just make sure to give the `PICT` an ID of `128` and the `snd ` an ID of `9000`, in order to match the numbers used in the source code.

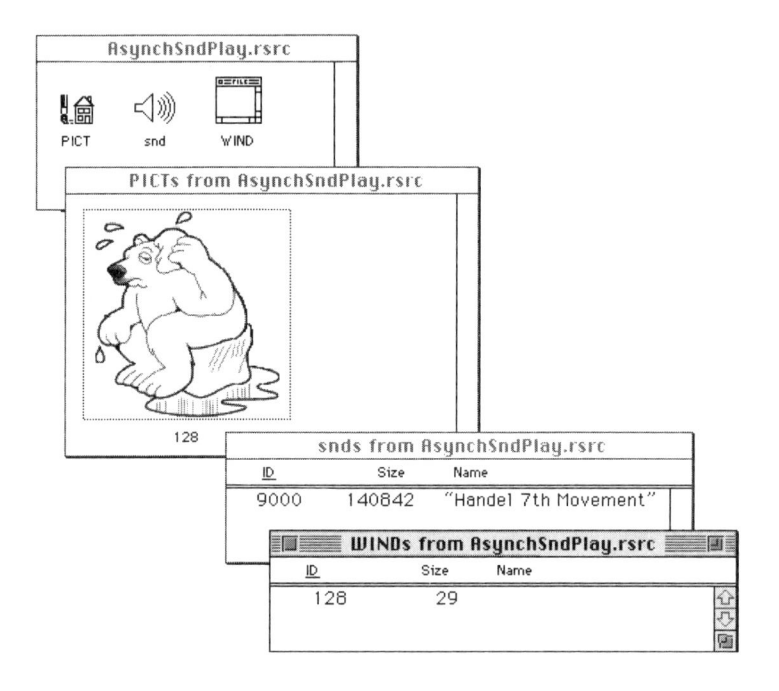

FIGURE 2.18 The three resources used in the
AsynchSndPlay program, as viewed in ResEdit.

Most of the routines that make up the AsynchSndPlay program have
been described in this chapter. Before presenting the source code listing,
a quick look is in order for the few routines that haven't yet been covered.
The main() function is shown below, with an explanation following.

```
void  main( void )
{
   NumVersion    theSndMgrVers;
   EventRecord   theEvent;

   InitializeToolbox();

   theSndMgrVers = SndSoundManagerVersion();
   if ( theSndMgrVers.majorRev < 3 )
      ExitToShell();

   OpenDisplayWindow();
   LoadAndSetupPicture();
```

Chapter 2 - Sound Playing

```
while ( gDone == false )
{
    WaitNextEvent( everyEvent, &theEvent, 15L, nil );

    switch ( theEvent.what )
    {
        case mouseDown:
            gDone = true;
            break;

        case keyDown:
            PlaySoundResourceAsynch( rMusicSound );
            break;
    }
}
}
```

After initializing the Toolbox and verifying that the user has Sound Manager version 3.0 or later, main() calls the application-defined routines OpenDisplayWindow() and LoadAndSetupPicture() to open a window and load the PICT resource into memory. A handle to the picture is stored in the global variable gThePicture, and the starting boundaries of the picture are stored in the global rectangle variable gTheRect.

```
void  OpenDisplayWindow( void )
{
    WindowPtr  theWindow;

    theWindow = GetNewWindow( rDisplayWindow, nil, (WindowPtr)-1L );
    ShowWindow( theWindow );
    SetPort( theWindow );
}
```

```
//_____
```

```
void  LoadAndSetupPicture( void )
{
    short  theWidth;
    short  theHeight;
    short  left = 475;
    short  top = 10;

    gThePicture = GetPicture( rBearPicture );
    gTheRect = (**gThePicture).picFrame;
    theWidth = gTheRect.right - gTheRect.left;
```

```
    theHeight = gTheRect.bottom - gTheRect.top;
    SetRect( &gTheRect, left, top, left + theWidth, top +
    theHeight );
}
```

The picture handle and boundary rectangle are stored in global variables so that their values will be retained as the program runs. When it comes time to move the picture one pixel to the left, MovePictureOnePixel() simply offsets the variable gTheRect one pixel, then calls DrawPicture():

```
void  MovePictureOnePixel( void )
{
    OffsetRect( &gTheRect, -1, 0 );
    DrawPicture( gThePicture, &gTheRect );
}
```

For smoother animation you'll use graphic worlds rather than moving a picture. That topic is described in Chapter 5.

NOTE

To play a sound and run the animation, a user of AsynchSndPlay presses any key. A keystroke causes a keyDown event to occur, which is picked up by WaitNextEvent(). In response to the keyDown event, main() calls PlaySoundResourceAsynch() to start the sound and animation.

Now, the complete source code listing for AsynchSndPlay follows below. As you look over the listing, keep in mind that many of the routines can be used "as is" in your own programs that will take advantage of asynchronous sound. In particular, in their present form SoundChannel-Callback(), InstallCallbackCommand(), CleanUpSoundIfFinished(), and PlaySoundResourceAsynch() may all meet your needs.

```
//_____

#include <Sound.h>

//_____

pascal void    SoundChannelCallback( SndChannelPtr, SndCommand );
OSErr          InstallCallbackCommand( SndChannelPtr );
void           CleanUpSoundIfFinished( void );
```

```
void            PlaySoundResourceAsynch( short );
void            AnimateWhileSoundPlays( void );
void            InitializeToolbox( void );
void            OpenDisplayWindow( void );
void            LoadAndSetupPicture( void );
void            MovePictureOnePixel( void );
SndChannelPtr   OpenOneAsynchSoundChannel( void );
OSErr           DisposeOneSoundChannel( SndChannelPtr );

//_____

#define    rMusicSound          9000
#define    rDisplayWindow        128
#define    rBearPicture          128

//_____

short           gSoundPlaying     = false;
Boolean         gCallbackExecuted = false;
SndChannelPtr   gSoundChannel     = nil;
Handle          gSoundHandle      = nil;
Boolean         gDone             = false;
PicHandle       gThePicture;
Rect            gTheRect;

//_____


void  main( void )
{
   NumVersion    theSndMgrVers;
   EventRecord   theEvent;

   InitializeToolbox();

   theSndMgrVers = SndSoundManagerVersion();
   if ( theSndMgrVers.majorRev < 3 )
      ExitToShell();

   OpenDisplayWindow();
   LoadAndSetupPicture();

   while ( gDone == false )
   {
      WaitNextEvent( everyEvent, &theEvent, 15L, nil );

      switch ( theEvent.what )
```

```
        {
           case mouseDown:
             gDone = true;
             break;

           case keyDown:
             PlaySoundResourceAsynch( rMusicSound );
             break;
        }
     }
}

//_____

void  PlaySoundResourceAsynch( short theResID )
{
   OSErr  theError;


   gSoundChannel = OpenOneAsynchSoundChannel();
   if ( gSoundChannel == nil )
      ExitToShell();

   gSoundHandle = GetResource( 'snd ', theResID );
   if ( gSoundHandle == nil )
      ExitToShell();

   DetachResource( gSoundHandle );
   HLock( gSoundHandle );

   gSoundPlaying = true;
   theError = SndPlay( gSoundChannel, (SndListHandle)gSoundHandle,
                    true );

   if ( theError == noErr )
      theError = InstallCallbackCommand( gSoundChannel );
   else
      ExitToShell();

   AnimateWhileSoundPlays();
}

//_____

void  AnimateWhileSoundPlays( void )
{
```

```
   Boolean  loopDone = false;

   while ( loopDone == false )
   {
      CleanUpSoundIfFinished();

      if ( gSoundPlaying == true )
         MovePictureOnePixel();
      else
         loopDone = true;
   }
}

//_____

void  CleanUpSoundIfFinished( void )
{
   OSErr  theError;

   if ( gCallbackExecuted == true )
   {
      HUnlock( gSoundHandle );
      ReleaseResource( gSoundHandle );
      gSoundHandle = nil;

      theError = DisposeOneSoundChannel( gSoundChannel );
      if ( theError != noErr )
         ExitToShell();

      gSoundChannel = nil;
      gCallbackExecuted = false;
   }
}

//_____

OSErr  InstallCallbackCommand( SndChannelPtr theChannel )
{
   OSErr       theError;
   SndCommand  theCommand;

   theCommand.cmd    = callBackCmd;
   theCommand.param1 = 0;
   #ifndef powerc
      theCommand.param2 = SetCurrentA5();
   #else
```

```
      theCommand.param2 = 0;
   #endif

   theError = SndDoCommand( theChannel, &theCommand, true );

   return ( theError );
}

//_____

pascal void  SoundChannelCallback( SndChannelPtr theChannel,
                                    SndCommand     theCommand )
{
   long  theA5;

   #ifndef powerc
      theA5 = SetA5( theCommand.param2 );
   #endif

   gCallbackExecuted = true;
   gSoundPlaying = false;

   #ifndef powerc
      theA5 = SetA5( theA5 );
   #endif
}

//_____

SndChannelPtr  OpenOneAsynchSoundChannel( void )
{
   SndChannelPtr    theChannel;
   OSErr            theError;
   SndCallBackUPP   theCallBackUPP;

   theCallBackUPP = NewSndCallBackProc( SoundChannelCallback );

   theChannel = nil;
   theError = SndNewChannel( &theChannel, 0, 0, theCallBackUPP );

   if ( theError != noErr )
   {
      DisposePtr( (Ptr)theChannel );
      theChannel = nil;
   }

   return ( theChannel );
```

```
}

//_____

OSErr  DisposeOneSoundChannel( SndChannelPtr theChannel )
{
   OSErr  theError;

   theError = SndDisposeChannel( theChannel, true );
   DisposePtr( (Ptr)theChannel );

   return ( theError );
}

//_____

void  OpenDisplayWindow( void )
{
   WindowPtr  theWindow;

   theWindow = GetNewWindow( rDisplayWindow, nil, (WindowPtr)-1L );
   ShowWindow( theWindow );
   SetPort( theWindow );
}

//_____

void  LoadAndSetupPicture( void )
{
   short  theWidth;
   short  theHeight;
   short  left = 475;
   short  top = 10;

   gThePicture = GetPicture( rBearPicture );
   gTheRect = (**gThePicture).picFrame;
   theWidth = gTheRect.right - gTheRect.left;
   theHeight = gTheRect.bottom - gTheRect.top;
   SetRect( &gTheRect, left, top, left + theWidth, top +
    theHeight );
}

//_____

void  MovePictureOnePixel( void )
{
   OffsetRect( &gTheRect, -1, 0 );
```

```
   DrawPicture( gThePicture, &gTheRect );
}
```

More Asynchronous Sound

Not only can a sound be played while animation takes place, but that sound can have its characteristics altered while the animation continues.

Allowing User Input While a Sound Plays

In the AnimateWhileSoundPlays() function of last section's Asynch-SndPlay program, a loop was used to move a picture across a window as a sound played. While looping is a powerful programming device, it can have one serious drawback: for the entire time that a loop executes, it takes control of a program and locks out the user. This may be an acceptable practice for programs that run on certain machines, but it runs counter to the notion of how an event-driven program should operate.

While a loop generally does take control of a program, it doesn't have to. You already know that fact from working with the event loop of any Mac program. The call that is at the heart of an event loop—WaitNextEvent()—makes it possible for the user to constantly interact with the program. By looking for,—and processing—keyboard and mouse events, WaitNextEvent() allows the user to set the course of action for a program.

Typically, a Macintosh programmer will include just a single call to WaitNextEvent() in a program—the call that appears in the event loop. This is done because one call is usually adequate—not because there is a restriction on the number of times WaitNextEvent() can appear in a program. When it makes sense to use an additional call to WaitNext-Event(), a program should do so. As you may have guessed, this makes perfect sense for last section's AsynchSndPlay program.

Adding a call to WaitNextEvent() in the AnimateWhileSoundPlays() function allows the function to watch for user-input. One likely scenario is that the user may want to stop the asynchronous sound from playing before it's finished. The following new version of AnimateWhileSound-

Plays() responds to a keyDown event by calling a new application-defined routine named StopSoundPlaying() and then setting the loop-ending local Boolean variable loopDone to true.

```
void   AnimateWhileSoundPlays( void )
{
    EventRecord   theEvt;
    Boolean       loopDone = false;

    while ( loopDone == false )
    {
        CleanUpSoundIfFinished();

        if ( gSoundPlaying == true )
            MovePictureOnePixel();
        else
            loopDone = true;

        WaitNextEvent( everyEvent, &theEvt, 15L, nil );

        switch ( theEvt.what )
        {
            case keyDown:
                StopSoundPlaying();
                loopDone = true;
                break;
        }
    }
}
```

StopSoundPlaying() sets the global flags gCallbackExecuted to true and gSoundPlaying to false. Then the CleanUpSoundIfFinished() function is called to dispose of the sound channel.

```
void   StopSoundPlaying( void )
{
    if ( gSoundChannel != nil )
    {
        gCallbackExecuted = true;
        gSoundPlaying = false;
    }
    CleanUpSoundIfFinished();
}
```

The `StopSoundPlaying()` is called by the application—not by the Sound Manager (as the callback routine is). Because the application is terminating the sound early, the Sound Manager doesn't get the chance to issue the callback command. That's why the `StopSoundPlaying()` routine has to "artificially" set `gCallbackExecuted` to `true`. When `CleanUpSound-IfFinished()` begins to exccute, it will note that this flag is `true` and will dispose of the sound channel.

Because the `keyDown`-handing code in `AnimateWhileSoundPlays()` sets the `loopDone` flag to `true`, the loop will end regardless of the value of `gSoundPlaying`. However, `StopSoundPlaying()` makes no assumptions about the routine that calls it. It sets `gSoundPlaying` to `false` in case the calling function relies on this flag to end the loop.

 Having a keystroke as the event that triggers some action makes for a clear, easy-to-follow example. Your program can apply the same event-handling principle in a more complex way. For example, your animation routine could respond to `mouseDown` events in the menu bar rather than `keyDown` events. Then, rather than pressing a key, the user could stop a sound by making a **Stop Sound** menu selection from a Sound menu.

Chapter Example: AsynchSndEvt

The AsynchSndEvt program that you'll find on the CD in this chapter's folder of examples is almost identical to the AsynchSndPlay example. Once again a polar bear slides to the classical music of Handel. The difference is that AsynchSndEvt uses the new version of `AnimateWhile-SoundPlays()` and the `StopSoundPlaying()` routine. That allows the user to stop a sound that is playing by pressing any key. Another keystroke will restart the sound from the beginning.

As you look over the AsynchSndEvt source code, take note of the fact that there are two calls to `WaitNextEvent()`. As always, one call appears in the event loop. When ever a sound *isn't* playing, this is the call to `WaitNextEvent()` that processes events. When a sound isn't playing the program responds to `keyDown` and `mouseDown` events in `main()`. Once a sound is playing, the program will be in the `while` loop of `Animate-WhileSoundPlays()`. That means that when a sound *is* playing, it is the call to `WaitNextEvent()` in `AnimateWhileSoundPlays()` that processes events. When a sound is playing, only `keyDown` events will be processed.

```
// main() handles events when a sound isn't playing.
// A click of the mouse quits the program, a press of a
// key plays a sound asynchronously.

void  main( void )
{
    ...
    ...
    while ( gDone == false )
    {
        WaitNextEvent( everyEvent, &theEvent, 15L, nil );

        switch ( theEvent.what )
        {
            case mouseDown:
                gDone = true;
                break;

            case keyDown:
                PlaySoundResourceAsynch( ksnd resourceID );
                break;
        }
    }
}

// AnimateWhileSoundPlays() handles events during sound play.
// Mouse clicks are ignored, a press of a key stops the sound.

void  AnimateWhileSoundPlays( void )
{
    EventRecord  theEvt;
    Boolean      loopDone = false;

    while ( loopDone == false )
    {
        ...
        ...
        WaitNextEvent( everyEvent, &theEvt, 15L, nil );

        switch ( theEvt.what )
        {
            case keyDown:
                StopSoundPlaying();
```

```
                loopDone = true;
                break;
          }
      }
}
```

There's one final addition to the AsynchSndEvt source code that is worthy of note. The `PlaySoundResourceAsynch()` routine now starts with a check to verify that `gSoundChannel` isn't `nil`:

```
void  PlaySoundResourceAsynch( short theResID )
{
   OSErr  theError;

   if ( gSoundChannel != nil )
      StopSoundPlaying();

   // rest of routine is the same as the previous version
}
```

The AsynchSndEvt program won't ever make use of this addition, but it is a useful one nonetheless. If you ever make a change to the program such that it stops and restarts a sound in response to pressing a key, `StopSoundPlaying()` will be called from within `PlaySoundResource-Asynch()`.Consider the following version of `AnimateWhileSoundPlays()`. It has two lines of `keyDown`-handling code commented out, and one new line in their place.

```
void  AnimateWhileSoundPlays( void )
{
   EventRecord   theEvt;
   Boolean       loopDone = false;

   while ( loopDone == false )
   {
      CleanUpSoundIfFinished();

      if ( gSoundPlaying == true )
         MovePictureOnePixel();
      else
         loopDone = true;

      WaitNextEvent( everyEvent, &theEvt, 15L, nil );
```

```
        switch ( theEvt.what )
        {
            case keyDown:
//              StopSoundPlaying();
//              loopDone = true;
                PlaySoundResourceAsynch( ksnd resourceID );  // NEW
                break;
        }
    }
}
```

In the above version of `AnimateWhileSoundPlays()`, a keystroke will call
`PlaySoundResourceAsynch()`. Because a sound is already playing, a
sound channel is already allocated, and a pointer to it is held in the
global `SndChannelPtr` variable `gSoundChannel`. When `AnimateWhile-`
`SoundPlays()` calls `PlaySoundResourceAsynch()`, the test of the value of
`gSoundChannel` will reveal that this variable is not a `nil` pointer, and the
current sound should thus be stopped:

```
void  PlaySoundResourceAsynch( short theResID )
{
    OSErr  theError;

    if ( gSoundChannel != nil )
        StopSoundPlaying();
    ...
    ...
```

What would happen if the above test of `gSoundChannel` wasn't made?
`PlaySoundResourceAsynch()` would go on to allocate a new sound channel
and place a pointer to it in `gSoundChannel`. Because the original sound
would be playing in a channel pointed to by `gSoundChannel`, this would
result in the very troubling situation.

   As a test, alter the AsynchSndEvt source code to match this new
example: comment out the `StopSoundPlaying()` call and the `loopDone`
assignment under the `keyDown` case section in `AnimateWhileSound-`
`Plays()`. If you do that, then recompile and run the project, you'll find
that when a sound is playing, the sound stops, then restarts, each time a
key is pressed.

Sound Commands and Asynchronous Sound Play

The Toolbox function `SndDoCommand()` adds a sound command to the sound command queue of a sound channel. You've used this routine to add a callback command to the sound channel that is playing a sound asynchronously. As Figure 2.19 shows, a call to `SndPlay()` starts issuing the commands in a queue to the speaker—starting with the first command in the queue (shown lower in memory). The figure also shows that a call to `SndDoCommand()` adds a sound command to the end of a queue.

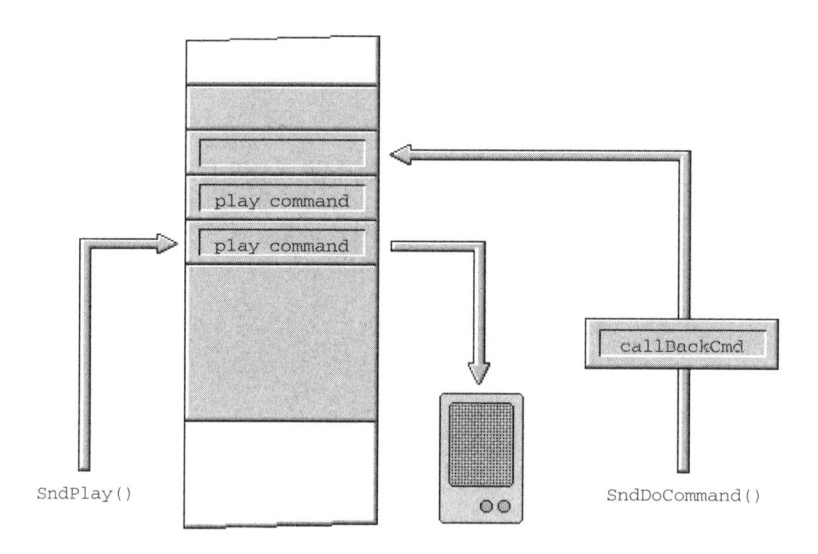

FIGURE 2.19 A call to `SndDoCommand()` adds a command to a sound channel queue.

The Toolbox includes a second routine that works with sound commands—`SndDoImmediate()`. Like `SndDoCommand()`, `SndDoImmediate()` accepts a sound channel pointer and a sound command as parameters. Unlike `SndDoCommand()`, `SndDoImmediate()` issues a sound command directly to the sound hardware of a Mac. The sound channel sound command queue is bypassed entirely. Figure 2.20 shows `SndDoImmediate()` sending a command to change the amplitude, or volume, of a sound that is currently playing.

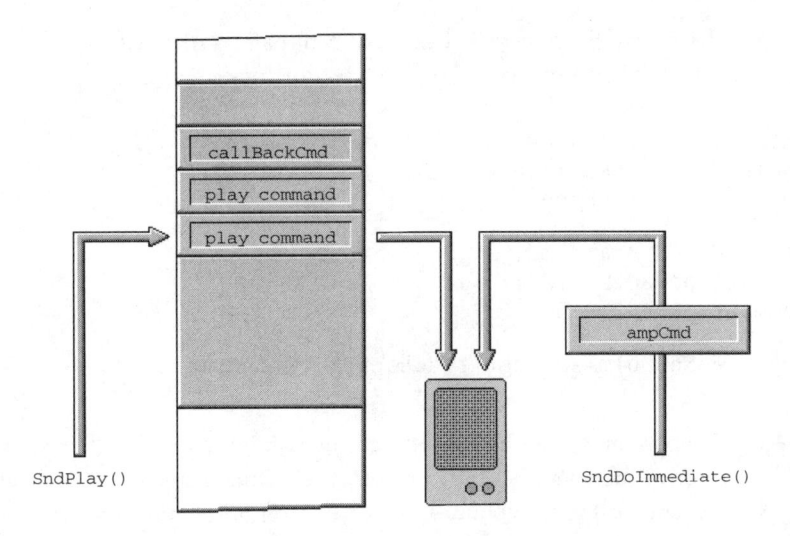

FIGURE 2.20 A call to SndDoImmediate() immediately processes a sound channel.

When combined with asynchronous sound, a routine that immediately affects a sound channel is a powerful programming tool. When a program starts a sound, a call to SndDoImmediate() lets the user change a characteristic of the sound as it plays.

SndDoImmediate() and Sound Volume

SndDoImmediate() works with a variety of sound commands, one of which is the ampCmd sound command introduced earlier in this chapter. In this chapter's SoundCommands example program, you saw the ampCmd used in a call to SndDoCommand(). Recall that the ampCmd varies the amplitude, or volume, of a sound. For the amplitude command the cmd field is ampCmd, the param1 field is the desired amplitude, and the param2 field is unused. The param1 field has a range of 0 to 255, with 0 turning the sound off and 255 setting the sound to 100 percent of the sound level currently set by the user in the user's Sound control panel. The following snippet will change the volume of a playing sound to one-half its current volume. As soon as the call to SndDoImmediate() is made, the sound playing on theChannel will drop in volume by 50 percent (because a `param1` value of 127 is approximately one half of the maximum `param1` value of 255).

```
SndChannelPtr   theChannel;
SndCommand      theCommand;
OSErr           theError;

theCommand.cmd = ampCmd;
theCommand.param1 = 127;
theCommand.param2 = 0;

theError = SndDoImmediate( theChannel, &theCommand );
```

N O T E   Keep in mind that the amplitude is in relation to the sound level set by the user in the user's **Sound** control panel. Thus a single `param1` value will generate different volumes, depending on how loud the user has set the volume of the Mac's speaker. For instance, don't assume that a half volume setting of 127 will always play a sound at half the maximum level that a Mac can deliver. If the user has his or her **Sound** control-panel sound level set to 1, the sound will play at a volume midway between 0 and 1 on the **Sound** control-panel scale—and that's a *very* quiet sound.

This chapter's next example program uses a routine named `SetSound-Amplitude()` to change the volume of a sound. Pass `SetSoundAmplitude()` a sound channel pointer and the new amplitude, and the function will immediately change the volume of whatever sound is currently playing on the sound channel pointed to by the `SndChannelPtr` parameter.

```
OSErr  SetSoundAmplitude( SndChannelPtr theChannel, short theAmp )
{
   SndCommand   theCommand;
   OSErr        theError;

   theCommand.cmd = ampCmd;
   theCommand.param1 = theAmp;
   theCommand.param2 = 0;

   theError = SndDoImmediate( theChannel, &theCommand );

   return ( theError );
}
```

This same routine, with one change, appears much earlier in this chapter—in the SoundCommands example program. There, a call to SndDoCommand() was used in place of SndDoImmediate().

Earlier you saw how to add event handling to the loop that performs the animation accompanying a sound that is playing asynchronously. The following snippet shows how that technique could be expanded upon. In the following example, a keyDown event is handled by first determining which particular key was pressed by the user. If the key was the minus key on the numeric keypad of the keyboard, SetSoundAmplitude() is called to turn the sound volume down to half volume. If any other key is pressed, the sound and animation are stopped—just as they were in the previous example program, AsynchSndEvt.

```
void  AnimateWhileSoundPlays( void )
{
    ...
    ...

    while ( loopDone == false )
    {
        ...
        ...

        WaitNextEvent( everyEvent, &theEvt, 15L, nil );

        switch ( theEvt.what )
        {
            case keyDown:
                theChar = theEvt.message & charCodeMask;
                switch ( theChar )
                {
                    case '-':
                        theError = SetSoundAmplitude( gSoundChannel, 127 );
                        if ( theError != noErr )
                            ExitToShell();
                        break;
                    default:
                        StopSoundPlaying();
                        loopDone = true;
                        break;
```

```
            }
            break;
         }
      }
   }
}
```

The MoreSndCommands example program that appears a little later provides a complete version of the above AnimateWhileSoundPlays() snippet.

N O T E

SndDoImmediate() and Sound Pitch

Your application can use SndDoImmediate() to change the rate of play of a sound. The rateCmd sound command allows the frequency of a playing sound to be lowered or raised. A lower frequency corresponds to a lower pitch, and produces a lower sound—like a bass drum. A higher frequency corresponds to a higher pitch, and generates a higher sound—as in a violin. The rateCmd also alters the duration of a sound. A lower rate not only lowers the sound's frequency, it also slows the sound down. A higher rate increases the sound's frequency and speeds up the sound.

The rate command requires a cmd field of rateCmd, a param1 field that is unused, and a param2 field that is a hexadecimal long value. A param2 value of 0x00010000 plays a sound at 22 kHz—the rate at which most sampled sounds are recorded. Other rates all use this 22 kHz value as a base. That is, to play a sound at twice its normal rate, or 44 kHz, use 0x00020000 for the param2 value. A value of 0x00030000 plays a sound at 66 kHz. To slow a sound to 11 kHz, set param2 to 0x00008000.

If your hexadecimal skills are a little rusty, here's why 0x00008000 is one-half of 0x00010000.

0x00010000 in decimal is (1) x (16x16 x16 x16), or 65,536.
0x00008000 in decimal is (8) x (16x16 x16), or 32,768.

N O T E

The following snippet will change the rate of a playing sound to 66 kHz.

```
SndChannelPtr   theChannel;
SndCommand      theCommand;
OSErr           theError;

theCommand.cmd = rateCmd;
theCommand.param1 = 0;
theCommand.param2 = 0x00030000;

theError = SndDoImmediate( theChannel, &theCommand );
```

The MoreSndCommands example program found on this book's CD includes a routine named SetSoundRate(). Pass SetSoundRate() a sound-channel pointer and a long variable (in hexadecimal), and the function will immediately change the rate of the playing sound.

```
OSErr  SetSoundRate( SndChannelPtr theChannel, long theRate )
{
   SndCommand   theCommand;
   OSErr        theError;

   theCommand.cmd = rateCmd;
   theCommand.param1 = 0;
   theCommand.param2 = theRate;

   theError = SndDoImmediate( theChannel, &theCommand );

   return ( theError );
}
```

As was done for the amplitude of a sound, the sound's rate can be controlled by the user from the event-handling section of the animation loop. In the following snippet, pressing the **f** key (for "fast") will set the sound that is playing to 66 kHz.

```
void  AnimateWhileSoundPlays( void )
{
   . . .
   . . .

   while ( loopDone == false )
   {
```

```
    ...
    ...

    WaitNextEvent( everyEvent, &theEvt, 15L, nil );

    switch ( theEvt.what )
    {
        case keyDown:
            theChar = theEvt.message & charCodeMask;
            switch ( theChar )
            {
                case 'f':
                    theError = SetSoundRate( gSoundChannel,
                                             0x00030000 );
                    if ( theError != noErr )
                        ExitToShell();
                    break;
                default:
                    StopSoundPlaying();
                    loopDone = true;
                    break;
            }
            break;
    }
    }
}
```

Chapter Example: MoreSndCommands

The MoreSndCommands example program represents the final return of the sliding bear and Handel's 7th Symphony. This version of the sliding-bear program gives the user the ability to vary both the amplitude and rate of the classical score that accompanies the bear's slide.

To change the amplitude of the sound, the SetSoundAmplitude() routine developed on the preceding pages is used. The changing of the sound's rate is handled by another function you've recently seen— SetSoundRate().

Once again, it's the call to WaitNextEvent() in the loop of Animate-WhileSoundPlays() that makes it possible for the user to gain control of the sound. If the event is a keyDown event, AnimateWhileSoundPlays() will begin by determining which key was pressed. If the key was the +

or - key on the numeric keypad, the sound's amplitude will change. Pressing the - key lowers the amplitude by 30 on the scale of 0 to 255. Repeatedly pressing the - key will continually lower the volume of the sound until the level approaches 0. Pressing the + key raises the amplitude 30. Before lowering or raising the volume, a check is made to ensure that the amplitude will not go out of the param1 range of 0 to 255. Here's the amplitude-related case sections used in AnimateWhileSoundPlays():

```
case '+':
   if ( theAmplitude <= 225 )
      theAmplitude += 30;
   theError = SetSoundAmplitude( gSoundChannel, theAmplitude );
   if ( theError != noErr )
      ExitToShell();
   break;

case '-':
   if ( theAmplitude >= 30 )
      theAmplitude -= 30;
   theError = SetSoundAmplitude( gSoundChannel, theAmplitude );
   if ( theError != noErr )
      ExitToShell();
   break;
```

The user can change the rate of play of the sound by pressing one of three keys. The **f** key (for "fast') sets the sound playing at 66 kHz. This increased rate will produce sound that is played very fast. The **s** key (for "slow") sets sound play to 11 kHz—resulting in a sound that plays at half its normal speed. Pressing the **p** key (for "play") plays the sound at its normal 22 kHz rate. Here's a snippet that shows the case sections for these three keystrokes:

```
#define     k11kHzFreqRate     0x00008000
#define     k22kHzFreqRate     0x00010000
#define     k44kHzFreqRate     0x00020000
#define     k66kHzFreqRate     0x00030000

case 'p':
   theError = SetSoundRate( gSoundChannel, k22kHzFreqRate );
   if ( theError != noErr )
      ExitToShell();
   break;
```

```
case 's':
   theError = SetSoundRate( gSoundChannel, k11kHzFreqRate );
   if ( theError != noErr )
      ExitToShell();
   break;

case 'f':
   theError = SetSoundRate( gSoundChannel, k66kHzFreqRate );
   if ( theError != noErr )
      ExitToShell();
   break;
```

AnimateWhileSoundPlays(), shown below, holds the code that differs from the AsynchSndEvt program. To see the full listing for the MoreSndCommands program, refer to the **MoreSndCommands.c** source-code file found on the included CD.

```
void  AnimateWhileSoundPlays( void )
{
   EventRecord   theEvt;
   Boolean       loopDone = false;
   char          theChar;
   OSErr         theError;
   short         theAmplitude = 255;

   while ( loopDone == false )
   {
      CleanUpSoundIfFinished();

      if ( gSoundPlaying == true )
         MovePictureOnePixel();
      else
         loopDone = true;

      WaitNextEvent( everyEvent, &theEvt, 15L, nil);

      switch ( theEvt.what )
      {
         case keyDown:
            theChar = theEvt.message & charCodeMask;
            switch ( theChar )
            {
               case '+':
```

```
                  if ( theAmplitude <= 225 )
                     theAmplitude += 30;
                  theError = SetSoundAmplitude( gSoundChannel,
                  theAmplitude );
                  if ( theError != noErr )
                     ExitToShell();
                  break;
               case '-':
                  if ( theAmplitude >= 30 )
                     theAmplitude -= 30;
                  theError = SetSoundAmplitude( gSoundChannel,
                     theAmplitude );
                  if ( theError != noErr )
                     ExitToShell();
                  break;
               case 'p':
                  theError = SetSoundRate( gSoundChannel,
                  k22kHzFreqRate );
                  if ( theError != noErr )
                     ExitToShell();
                  break;
               case 's':
                  theError = SetSoundRate( gSoundChannel,
                  k11kHzFreqRate );
                  if ( theError != noErr )
                     ExitToShell();
                  break;
               case 'f':
                  theError = SetSoundRate( gSoundChannel,
                  k66kHzFreqRate );
                  if ( theError != noErr )
                     ExitToShell();
                  break;
               default:
                  StopSoundPlaying();
                  loopDone = true;
                  break;
            }
            break;
      }
   }
}
```

Summary

Version 3.0 of the Sound Manager provides you, the programmer, with the routines necessary to play and alter sounds. Before adding sound-playing capabilities to your program, you'll want to call `SndSoundManagerVersion()` to verify that the user has this version of the Sound Manager as part of his or her system software.

Sounds can conveniently be stored as `snd` resources in the resource fork of a Macintosh application. To load a sound into memory, call `GetResource()`. To play the loaded sound, call `SndPlay()`. For simple synchronous sound play, you can let the Sound Manager take care of the allocation of a sound channel from which a sound is played. For the more complex asynchronous sound play (sound playing that allows other action, such as animation, to take place), your program will become involved.

Playing a sound asynchronously requires that a callback routine be associated with the sound channel from which the sound will be played. The callback routine gets invoked by the Sound Manager when the asynchronous sound finishes playing. The purpose of this function is to set a flag variable that indicates to the rest of the program that the sound has finished playing.

CHAPTER 3

Sound Recording

The Sound Manager, described in Chapter 2, is the set of Toolbox routines that provides your programs with the capabilities to play sounds through either the Mac's built-in speakers or a pair of external speakers. Sound Manager routines such as SndDoCommand() and SoundDoImmediate() allow your programs to alter the way in which a sound is played.

The Sound Input Manager—the topic of this chapter—is the set of Toolbox routines that gives your applications the power to record sounds. The most important of these routines is the one that displays and controls the standard Sound Recording dialog box. By including this dialog box in your program, you provide a standard interface that is recognizable to the user. Once the user records a sound using this dialog box, your program can play the sound back at any time or save it to a sound resource in a resource file. Each of these topics is covered in this chapter.

Sound Input Devices

From the very oldest Macintosh to the most current model, each has had a built-in speaker. That means that your program doesn't have to check for the presence of sound-playing hardware before it plays a sound. The same is not true for sound recording. While all current Macs come with built-in sound recording capabilities, many older models don't. So before your program attempts to record a sound, it should first make a check to verify that the host computer does indeed have a *sound input device*. For this task you can use a short application-defined routine such as the IsSoundInputAvailable() function described below. An example of a call to this function is shown here:

```
Boolean  soundInputPresent;

soundInputPresent = IsSoundInputAvailable();
if ( soundInputPresent == false )
   ExitToShell();
```

Here's a look at IsSoundInputAvailable(), followed by a description of how this function determines whether an input device is available.

```
Boolean  IsSoundInputAvailable( void )
{
   OSErr     theError;
   long      theResult;
   Boolean   inputAvail;

   theError = Gestalt( gestaltSoundAttr, &theResult );
   if ( theError != noErr )
      ExitToShell();

   inputAvail = theResult & ( 1 << gestaltHasSoundInputDevice );
   if ( inputAvail > 0 )
      return ( true );
   else
      return ( false );
}
```

IsSoundInputAvailable() calls the Toolbox routine Gestalt() to request system information. By passing the Apple-defined constant gestaltSoundAttr as the first parameter (the *selector code*), IsSoundInputAvailable() is requesting information about the host machine's sound capabilities. This information is returned by the system in the *response parameter*—the long variable theResult.

With gestaltSoundAttr as the selector code, Gestalt() returns several pieces of sound-related information. Each piece of information occupies just a single bit in the filled-in variable theResult. To get the one piece of information of importance here (whether a sound input device is available on the user's Mac), you'll need to perform some bit-shifting. That's what the shift-left operator (<<) is used for in IsSoundInputAvailable(). If the bit in question (gestaltHasSoundInputDevice) is turned on, then sound input is available, and a value of true should be returned to the calling function.

The `IsSoundInputAvailable()` routine checks to see only if there is a sound input device available—it makes no attempt to determine what type of microphone is present. Because the sound recording Toolbox routine you'll use to record sounds works with any microphone, the detail of what kind of microphone is connected to a Mac is unimportant to your application.

If a user has more than one sound input device on his or her Macintosh, only one will be current at any time. The user makes this choice using the Sound control panel. Figure 3.1 shows the Sound control panel for a Mac that has two sound input devices: a built-in microphone and a MacRecorder sound digitizer connected to one of the ports. Your application won't have to check to see which of these devices is in use—your program will simply verify that there is a device, then it will go ahead and allow sound recording.

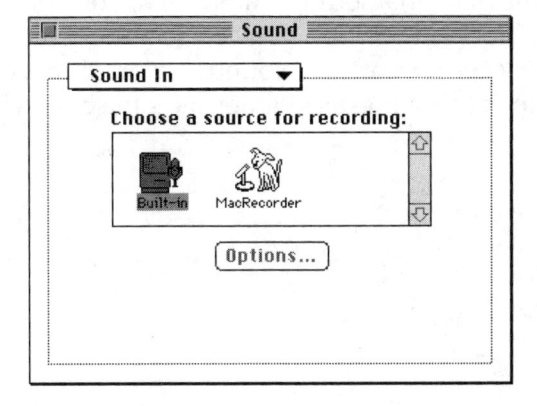

FIGURE 3.1 The Sound Input screen of the Sound control panel.

Recording a Sound to Memory

The Sound Input Manager makes it easy for you to add sound recording capabilities to any of your Mac applications. It only takes a call to the Toolbox routine `SndRecord()` to display the standard Sound Recording dialog box pictured in Figure 3.2. Once this dialog box is on the screen, the Toolbox and the Sound Input Manager will handle the user's actions—whether they involve recording, pausing, stopping, or playing back a sound.

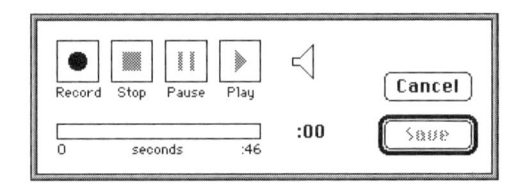

FIGURE 3.2 The standard Sound Recording dialog box.

Sound Data and Memory

When your program uses the `SndRecord()` routine to allow the user to record a sound, the sound data will be recorded to memory. Before calling `SndRecord()`, your program will allocate a block of heap memory in which to hold this data. In allocating this block, your program will obtain a handle to this block. Figure 3.3 shows a section of an application heap that holds a block of memory for sound data and a `SndListHandle` that references the block (via a master pointer, as is the case with all handles).

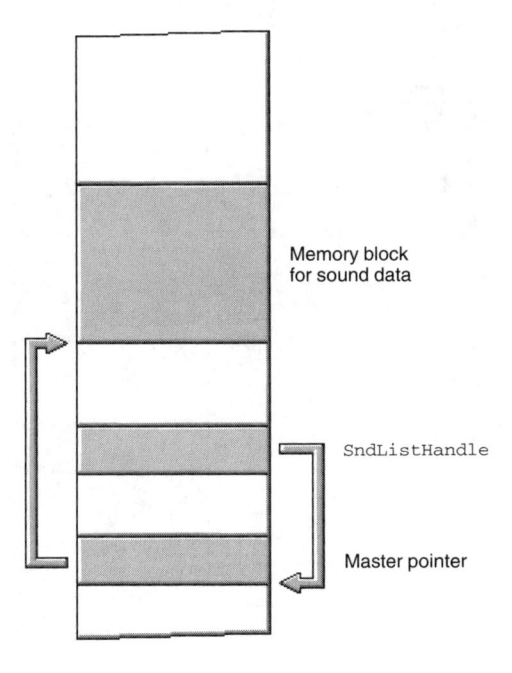

FIGURE 3.3 The data for a recorded sound is held
in a block of memory referenced by a handle.

When it comes time to allow the user to record a sound, your program
will call SndRecord() to display the standard Sound Recording dialog
box. When the user clicks the **Record** button in this dialog box, the Sound
Input Manager will route incoming sound from the sound input device
(such as the built-in microphone) to the block of memory that has been
allocated for the sound data. Figure 3.4 illustrates this.

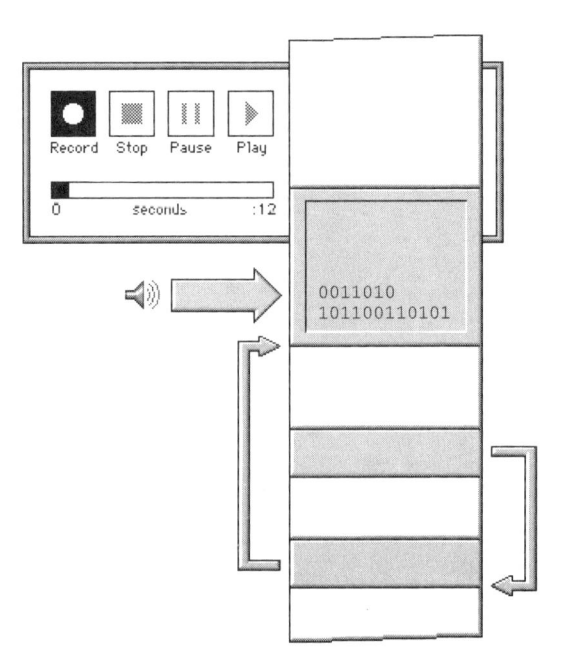

FIGURE 3.4 The standard Sound Recording dialog box sends
recorded sound data to a block of heap memory.

The Sound Recording dialog box records a sound directly to memory. The more memory you have available to record to, the more sound data you can record. More data translates to a longer sound. A small block will allow a sound of only a few seconds in length to be recorded; a large block can hold several minutes of recorded sound. The larger the memory block, the longer the sound that the user is allowed to record. The question that arises is this: How large a block should your program allocate for the sound data? The answer: As large a block as can be spared by your application. That answer, of course, begs another question: How can you tell how much memory your application has to spare? The answer to that question is provided by the Toolbox function `PurgeSpace()`.

Allocating a Memory Block for Sound Data

You know the total amount of heap space that will be given to your application—that figure is set up in your Symantec or Metrowerks compiler environment. Figure 3.5 shows the Project panel of the Metrowerks CodeWarrior Preferences dialog box. Here, a project has set the resulting application's heap size to 1 megabyte. From this 1024 KB of memory will come the block that will hold recorded sound data.

 If you're using a Symantec compiler, you'll use the **Set Project Type** menu item in the Project menu to set the application heap size.

NOTE

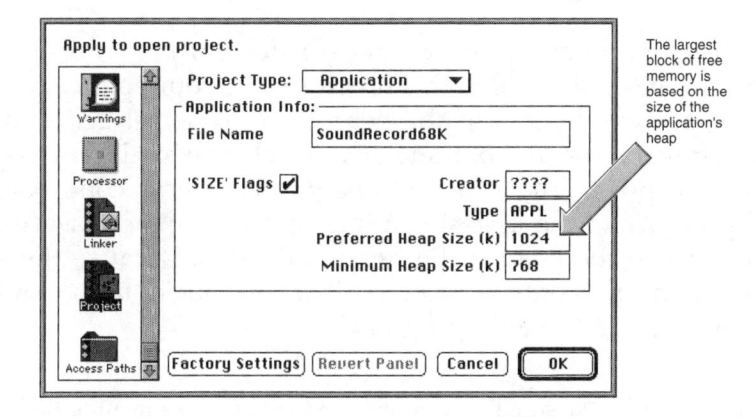

FIGURE 3.5 Metrowerks owners use the Preferences dialog box to set an application's heap size.

 Both the Symantec and Metrowerks compilers provide a default heap size of 384 KB. Now that you know sound data will be saved directly into this heap memory, you'll probably want to increase the heap size of any projects you're creating that include sound-recording capabilities.

NOTE

A sound data memory block must occupy contiguous heap memory, that is, the block must occupy adjacent free bytes. Because there will be other objects in the application heap besides the sound data block, and because these blocks may break up the available free memory into small blocks of unknown sizes, your program shouldn't make assumptions about the part of the heap that it can reserve for the sound data block. If you've set your application heap size to 1 MB, there's no guarantee that a block anywhere near that size will be free. Instead, just before allocating the block, your program should call the Toolbox function `PurgeSpace()` to check on the availability of free RAM:

```
long   theTotalHeap;
long   theContigMem;

PurgeSpace( &theTotalHeap, &theContigMem );
```

Contrary to its name, `PurgeSpace()` doesn't *purge,* or *deallocate,* any memory. Instead, a call to this function tells your application how much free space would exist if the heap were to be purged. After a call to `PurgeSpace()`, the first parameter will hold the total free space (in bytes) in the heap if the heap were to be purged. The second parameter will hold the size of the largest contiguous block of memory (in bytes) that will exist in the heap if the heap is purged. Because the sound data must reside in a contiguous block, it is the value of the second parameter that is of interest to your program.

To make sure that your application has access to all of the available application heap, call the Toolbox routine `MaxApplZone()` near the start of the program. The SoundRecord program listed later in this chapter provides an example.

N O T E

Figure 3.6 provides an example of the information returned by a call to `PurgeSpace()`. This figure shows part of the Metrowerks MW Debug window both before and after a call is made to `PurgeSpace()`. Before the call, the variable `theContigMem` has a random value that doesn't reflect the free memory space. After the call, the variable `theContigMem` has a value (1,035,972 bytes) close to the 1 MB partition size (1,048,576 bytes) this example application program is given.

If you're using a Symantec compiler, your debugger window will look different. This example is straightforward enough, however, that Figure 3.6 should suffice—you shouldn't have to follow along in your own compiler.

N O T E

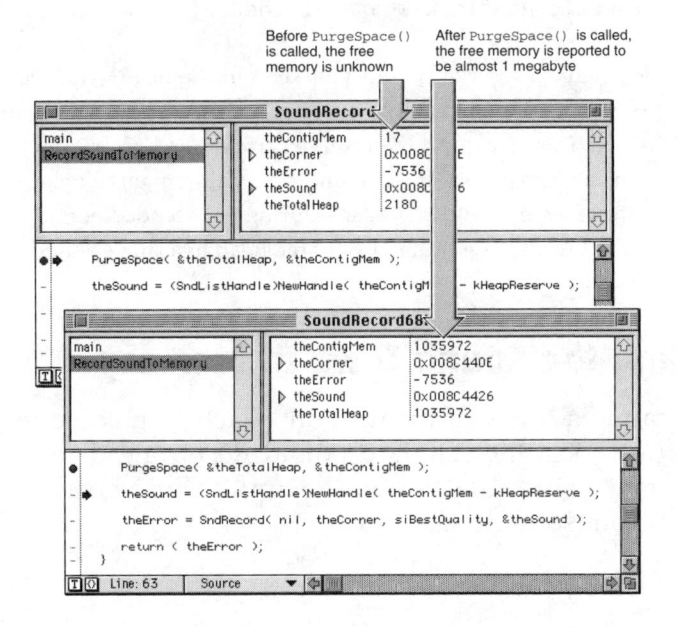

FIGURE 3.6 The Metrowerks debugger shows how `PurgeSpace()` returns the amount of available heap memory.

After calling `PurgeSpace()`, call the Toolbox function `NewHandle()` to allocate a block for the sound data. The size of the block should be the `theContigMem` value returned by `PurgeSpace()`, minus some number of bytes that you'd like to keep reserved for your program's use. If a contiguous block this size isn't available, `NewHandle()` will purge the heap to free up the necessary amount of memory. The following snippet determines the amount of free contiguous memory, then allocates a block that is 75 KB less than that amount. The handle that is returned by the call to `NewHandle()` is typecast to the `SndListHandle` data type before being assigned to the variable `theSound`.

```
#define    kHeapReserve    75 * 1024

SndListHandle    theSound;
long             theTotalHeap;
```

```
long            theContigMem;

PurgeSpace( &theTotalHeap, &theContigMem );

theSound = (SndListHandle)NewHandle( theContigMem - kHeapReserve );
```

NOTE How large a reserve should you keep in the heap? That depends. If your program will immediately save or play the recorded sound and then purge its data from memory, the reserve can be small—less than the 75 KB used in the above snippet. If the sound data will remain in memory for a longer period of time, the reserve should be larger—during an extended period of its execution, your program won't want to dedicate most of the heap to a single sound.

Recording the Sound Data to Memory

After allocating a block of memory in which to hold sound data, call `SndRecord()` to post the standard Sound Recording dialog box. Before doing so, make sure that the **SoundInput.h** universal header file is included in your source code:

```
#include <SoundInput.h>

SndListHandle   theSound;
OSErr           theError;
Point           theCorner = { 50, 20 };

theError = SndRecord( nil, theCorner, siBestQuality, &theSound );
```

The first parameter to `SndRecord()` is a pointer to an optional filter function. If used, this function specifies how the dialog box will handle user actions (such as keystrokes and mouse clicks). The `SndRecord()` routine handles sound recording, pausing, stopping, and playing, so your program most likely will not benefit from a filter function. If that is the case, pass a `nil` pointer here.

The second parameter to `SndRecord()` determines the screen placement of the standard Sound Recording dialog box. Because the dialog box is always the same size, you need only specify the left and top coordinates (as a `Point` variable) in order for the dialog box to be positioned properly. In the above snippet, the top of the dialog box will appear 50 pixels from the top of the screen and the left side will appear 20 pixels from the left of the screen.

The third parameter to `SndRecord()` is used to tell the Sound Input Manager at which quality level to record incoming data. Use one of the three Apple-defined constants—`siGoodQuality`, `siBetterQuality`, or `siBestQuality`—for this parameter. Your choice of quality value, along with the size of the sound data memory block, determines the duration of the sound that can be recorded. The lower the recording quality, the longer the sound that can be recorded. This is the result of compression of the sound data. A lower-quality sound has compression performed on it. Compression conserves memory but sacrifices sound quality.

For voice recording you'll generally use `siGoodQuality`. For sounds that have a critical need to be recorded at the highest quality, use `siBestQuality`. The `siBetterQuality` records sounds that are a quality and storage compromise between `siGoodQuality` and `siBestQuality`.

Near the end of this chapter you'll find a short study of how these three sound qualities affect both recording length and disk storage space.

N O T E

The final parameter to `SndRecord()` is the pointer to the block of memory that is to be devoted to holding the new sound data. The following snippet sets up the memory block, then displays the standard Sound Recording dialog box.

```
SndListHandle   theSound;
OSErr           theError;
Point           theCorner = { 50, 20 };
long            theTotalHeap;
long            theContigMem;

PurgeSpace( &theTotalHeap, &theContigMem );

theSound = (SndListHandle)NewHandle( theContigMem - kHeapReserve );

theError = SndRecord( nil, theCorner, siBestQuality, &theSound );
```

Chapter Example: SoundRecord

The SoundRecord program does nothing more than display the standard Sound Recording dialog box. Figure 3.7 shows this dialog box as it looks recording a sound.

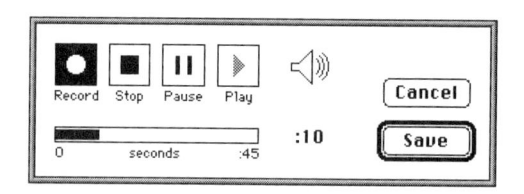

FIGURE 3.7 The standard Sound Recording dialog box
after the **Record** button has been clicked.

You can press the **Record** button and speak into the built-in microphone on your Mac to record a sound. Press the **Stop** button to end recording, then press the **Play** button to play the sound back. You can do this as often as you wish; the dialog box won't be dismissed until you press either the **Cancel** or **Save** button.

Once the standard Sound Recording dialog box is posted, all of its functionality is handled by the SndRecord() function. This routine will maintain control of the program until either the **Cancel** or **Save** button is clicked by the user. When that happens, the program ends. SoundRecord won't save a recorded sound. To do that, you'll need to add calls to a few Resource Manager functions. A description of how to save a recorded sound and an example program that does it appear later in this chapter.

The SoundRecord program carries out its few tasks from main(), the listing of which follows.

```
void  main( void )
{
   NumVersion    theSndMgrVers;
   OSErr         theError;
   Boolean       soundInputPresent;

   InitializeToolbox();
```

```
   MaxApplZone();

   theSndMgrVers = SndSoundManagerVersion();
   if ( theSndMgrVers.majorRev < 3 )
      ExitToShell();

   soundInputPresent = IsSoundInputAvailable();
   if ( soundInputPresent == false )
      ExitToShell();

   theError = RecordSoundToMemory();
   if ( theError == userCanceledErr )
      ExitToShell();
}
```

When your application is launched, its heap size isn't set to the size you specified when you built the application with your development environment. Instead, the heap starts out small and grows "on demand." As your program requests memory blocks, the heap expands to meet those demands. If you make a call to PurgeSpace() early in a program, you'll see that this function returns only a small value as the available heap memory—not the large amount of free heap RAM that you might expect it to return. To set your application's heap to its maximum size, call the Toolbox routine MaxApplZone() early in your program. After initializing the Toolbox, the main() function of the SoundRecord program calls MaxApplZone(). Later, when PurgeSpace() is called, the true largest free block size will be reported.

It's a good idea to call MaxApplZone() in all your Mac programs, not just ones that work with sound. Call the function once, just after initializing the Toolbox.

NOTE

After initializing the Toolbox and expanding the heap to its maximum size, main() verifies that Sound Manager 3.0 or later is present on the user's machine, as discussed in Chapter 2. Next, the application-defined routine IsSoundInputAvailable() is called to make sure that a sound input device is connected to the user's Macintosh. Finally, an application-defined function named RecordSoundToMemory() is called. A close examination of this function will reveal that it consists of the sound recording code discussed earlier in this chapter, including the call to SndRecord().

If the user clicks the **Cancel** button in the standard Sound Recording dialog box that `SndRecord()` posts, the `RecordSoundToMemory()` routine will return the Apple-defined result code of `userCanceledErr`. The RecordSound program chooses to exit if this happens; your program will handle the user's decision not to record a sound in a way that is appropriate to the purpose of your application. As mentioned, if the user clicks the **Save** button, the dialog is dismissed and no action is taken.

```
//_____

#include <Sound.h>
#include <SoundInput.h>

//_____

void      InitializeToolbox( void );
Boolean   IsSoundInputAvailable( void );
OSErr     RecordSoundToMemory( void );

//_____

#dcfine    kHeapReserve     75 * 1024

//_____

void  main( void )
{
   NumVersion   theSndMgrVers;
   OSErr        theError;
   Boolean      soundInputPresent;

   InitializeToolbox();

   MaxApplZone();

   theSndMgrVers = SndSoundManagerVersion();
   if ( theSndMgrVers.majorRev < 3 )
      ExitToShell();

   soundInputPresent = IsSoundInputAvailable();
   if ( soundInputPresent == false )
      ExitToShell();
```

```
   theError = RecordSoundToMemory();
   if ( theError == userCanceledErr )
      ExitToShell();
}

//_____

Boolean  IsSoundInputAvailable( void )
{
   OSErr    theError;
   long     theResult;
   Boolean  inputAvail;

   theError = Gestalt( gestaltSoundAttr, &theResult );
   if ( theError != noErr )
      ExitToShell();

   inputAvail = theResult & ( 1 << gestaltHasSoundInputDevice );
   if ( inputAvail > 0 )
      return ( true );
   else
      return ( false );
}

//_____

OSErr  RecordSoundToMemory( void )
{
   SndListHandle  theSound;
   OSErr          theError;
   Point          theCorner = { 50, 20 };
   long           theTotalHeap;
   long           theContigMem;

   PurgeSpace( &theTotalHeap, &theContigMem );

   theSound = (SndListHandle)NewHandle( theContigMem - kHeapReserve );

   theError = SndRecord( nil, theCorner, siBestQuality, &theSound );

   ReleaseResource( (Handle)theSound );

   return ( theError );
}
```

Playing Back a Recorded Sound

Once a sound has been recorded to memory, your program can play it back at any time. This section of the chapter is short for good reason; in Chapter 2, you learned how to play a sound that is stored in memory.

Using the Handle to the Recorded Sound

In the SoundRecord example just described, the application-defined function `RecordSoundToMemory()` declared a local `SndListHandle` variable named `theSound`. After a call to `SndRecord()`, this variable held a handle to whatever sound the user recorded. Because the handle to the sound data was a local variable, when the dialog box was dismissed any reference to the sound data in memory was lost. This wasn't a concern for the SoundRecord program—it only allowed the user to play back a recorded sound via the **Play** button of the standard Sound Recording dialog box. A more likely case is that your application will want to preserve the sound handle so that the user's sound can either be played back after the Sound Recording dialog box has been dismissed or saved to disk as a `snd` resource.

In this section's SoundHandle program, the sound handle will be declared outside of `RecordSoundToMemory()` and passed to this routine. When the routine ends, the sound handle value will be a valid reference to the recorded sound data in memory. At any point in the program the sound can be played by passing this handle to the Toolbox routine `SndPlay()`. Here's how a call to the new version of `RecordSoundToMemory()` would look:

```
OSErr          theError;
SndListHandle  theSound;

theError = RecordSoundToMemory( &theSound );
if ( theError == userCanceledErr )
   ExitToShell();
```

Note that the address of the variable `theSound` is passed so that changes to `theSound` made by `RecordSoundToMemory()` will be preserved after the function has completed. The new version of `RecordSoundTo-Memory()` follows the same steps as the old version: the largest contiguous block of free heap memory is determined, a block that size (less a reserve) is allocated, and a call to `SndRecord()` is made.

```
OSErr  RecordSoundToMemory( SndListHandle *theSound )
{
    OSErr  theError;
    Point  theCorner = { 50, 20 };
    long   theTotalHeap;
    long   theContigMem;

    PurgeSpace( &theTotalHeap, &theContigMem );

    *theSound = (SndListHandle)NewHandle( theContigMem -
    kHeapReserve );

    theError = SndRecord( nil, theCorner, siBestQuality, theSound );

    return ( theError );
}
```

N O T E

Take note of two subtle changes to `RecordSoundToMemory()`. Because the address of a `SndListHandle` is passed as a parameter, this line from the old version of the function:

```
    theSound = (SndListHandle)NewHandle( theContigMem - kHeapReserve );
```

becomes:

```
    *theSound = (SndListHandle)NewHandle( theContigMem - kHeapReserve );
```

The new version of the function must dereference `theSound` (which is now a pointer to a `SndListHandle` rather than a `SndListHandle`) before using it here. Conversely, in the call to `SndRecord()`, `theSound` is passed as the last parameter, rather than `&theSound`—as was the case in the previous version of `RecordSoundToMemory()`. The last parameter to `SndRecord()` must be a pointer to `SndListHandle`. In this new version of `RecordSoundToMemory()`, that's what `theSound` is.

The new version of `RecordSoundToMemory()` doesn't release the sound handle, as the old version did. Instead, the sound data is kept in memory for later use. Now that the sound data is in memory and the program has a handle to that memory, the sound data can be played at any time. You can pass the handle to an application-defined routine designed for that purpose. When your application is through playing the sound, it can free up the memory occupied by the sound data by calling `Release-Resource()`. The following snippet calls a routine that plays the sound referenced by the passed sound handle and then releases the memory that handle references.

```
theError = PlaySoundSynchFromHandle( theSound );
if ( theError != noErr )
   ExitToShell();

ReleaseResource( (Handle)theSound );
```

The `PlaySoundSynchFromHandle()` is similar to the Chapter 2 routine `PlaySoundResourceSynch()`. That routine had additional code that loaded a `snd ` resource into memory. Because the standard Sound Recording dialog box has provided a handle to a sound in memory, there's no need for this new routine to load a sound.

```
OSErr  PlaySoundSynchFromHandle( SndListHandle theHandle )
{
   OSErr   theError;

   if ( theHandle != nil )
   {
      HLock( (Handle)theHandle );
         theError = SndPlay( nil, theHandle, false );
      HUnlock( (Handle)theHandle );

      return ( theError );
   }
}
```

Your application could, of course, use the asynchronous sound playing techniques discussed in Chapter 2 to play the sound while other action takes place on screen, if there is a need to do so.

N O T E

Chapter Example: SoundHandle

When you run the SoundHandle example program, you'll see the same thing you witnessed when you ran SoundRecord: the standard Sound

Recording dialog box. Like that program, SoundHandle allows you to use this dialog box to record and play back your own sounds. Again, like SoundRecord, clicking the **Cancel** button terminates the program. The one difference between SoundHandle and SoundRecord comes when you click on the **Save** button. Doing that dismisses the dialog box, then plays the recorded sound one more time; this is something that SoundRecord couldn't do. In that program, once the Sound Recording dialog box was dismissed the recorded sound could not be accessed. Here, in SoundHandle, the handle to the sound data is preserved after the Sound Recording dialog box is dismissed, and consequently, the sound data can be accessed at any time.

NOTE You've probably noticed that the source code for InitializeToolbox()— a routine used in every program in this book—isn't provided in every source code listing. You should be familiar with that very basic routine by now. To save a little ink, the SoundHandle listing and the listing for the next example don't include the source for IsSoundInputAvailable(). You'll find that listing in the SoundRecord example earlier in this chapter.

```
//_____

#include <Sound.h>
#include <SoundInput.h>

//_____

void       InitializeToolbox( void );
Boolean    IsSoundInputAvailable( void );
OSErr      RecordSoundToMemory( SndListHandle * );
OSErr      PlaySoundSynchFromHandle( SndListHandle );

//_____

#define    kHeapReserve      75 * 1024

//_____

void  main( void )
{
    NumVersion      theSndMgrVers;
    OSErr           theError;
    SndListHandle   theSound;
```

```
    Boolean        soundInputPresent;

    InitializeToolbox();

    MaxApplZone();

    theSndMgrVers = SndSoundManagerVersion();
    if ( theSndMgrVers.majorRev < 3 )
       ExitToShell();

    soundInputPresent = IsSoundInputAvailable();
    if ( soundInputPresent == false )
       ExitToShell();

    theError = RecordSoundToMemory( &theSound );
    if ( theError == userCanceledErr )
       ExitToShell();

    theError = PlaySoundSynchFromHandle( theSound );
    if ( theError != noErr )
       ExitToShell();

    ReleaseResource( (Handle)theSound );
}

//_____

OSErr  RecordSoundToMemory( SndListHandle *theSound )
{
    OSErr  theError;
    Point  theCorner = { 50, 20 };
    long   theTotalHeap;
    long   theContigMem;

    PurgeSpace( &theTotalHeap, &theContigMem );

    *theSound = (SndListHandle)NewHandle( theContigMem -
    kHeapReserve );

    theError = SndRecord( nil, theCorner, siBestQuality, theSound );

    return ( theError );
}

//_____

OSErr  PlaySoundSynchFromHandle( SndListHandle theHandle )
```

```
{
   OSErr    theError;

   if ( theHandle != nil )
   {
      HLock( (Handle)theHandle );
         theError = SndPlay( nil, theHandle, false );
      HUnlock( (Handle)theHandle );

      return ( theError );
   }
}
```

Saving a Recorded Sound to a snd Resource

Your application may want to play a user-recorded sound, but not right away. Rather than keep the sound data (which may be quite memory-intensive) in the heap, your program can save the sound to a resource and then release the memory the sound data occupies. When it comes time to play the sound, the sound resource data can be loaded back into memory in preparation for a call to SndPlay().

Some programs may allow a user to record sounds and save them as sound resources in a separate resource file—possibly for use by other programs. Here again your application can make use of the fact that saving sound data from memory to disk is an easy task.

The Format of Sound Data in Memory

When the standard Sound Recording dialog box is used to record a sound, the sound's data ends up in a block of memory. Conveniently, the sound data is stored in the format that matches a snd resource. As you've seen, that makes it possible (and very easy) to play back the sound data using a call to SndPlay(). Likewise, having the sound data already in the format of a snd resource makes it possible (and, again, easy) to save the sound data as a snd resource in a resource file. Figure 3.8 emphasizes the fact that sound data in memory matches the layout of snd resource data.

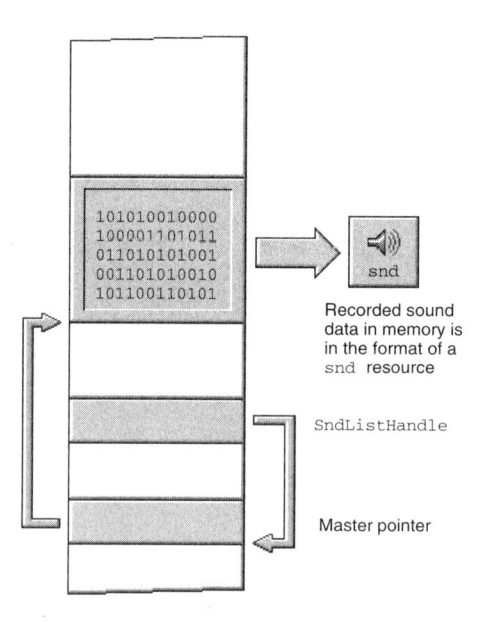

FIGURE **3.8** When sound data is saved to memory,
it is done so in the format of a snd resource.

Saving Sound Data to a snd Resource

Saving sound data to a snd resource involves three steps, each of which corresponds to a Resource Manager Toolbox call:

1. Call CurResFile() to get the file reference number of the current resource file.
2. Call AddResource() to add the sound data to the resource map in memory.
3. Call UpdateResFile() to add the sound data to a resource in a resource file.

Here's a snippet that uses the above three routines:

```
SndListHandle  the Sound;
OSErr          theError;
```

```
short            theResourceFileRef;

theResourceFileRef = CurResFile();

AddResource( (Handle)theSound, 'snd ', 9000, "\pNew Sound" );

UpdateResFile( theResourceFileRef );
```

The Toolbox routine `CurResFile()` returns a `short` value that is a file reference number to the current resource file. If your program hasn't explicitly opened any resource files, then the resource fork of your application will be considered the current resource file. This reference number will be used in a subsequent call to `UpdateResFile()`.

To add a resource to the resource map—the map in memory that serves as a guide to resources on disk—call the Toolbox function `AddResource()`:

```
AddResource( (Handle)theSound, 'snd ', 9000, "\pNew Sound" );
```

The first parameter to `AddResource()` is a handle to the data in memory that is to be saved as a resource. The second parameter is the four-character resource type that the data is to be saved to. The third parameter is the resource ID that should be given to the saved resource. The final parameter is the name that should be given to the resource. Note that this isn't the name of a file; it is the name that will be given to the individual resource in the file it is saved to.

The call to `AddResource()` adds the new resource to the resource map in memory; it doesn't add the new resource to the resource file on disk. To do that, call the Toolbox routine `UpdateResFile()`. Pass this routine the reference number that was obtained in the earlier call to `CurResFile()`.

```
UpdateResFile( theResourceFileRef );
```

The above steps are the minimum steps necessary to save sound data in memory to a snd resource in a resource file. The application-defined function `SaveSoundFromMemoryToResource()` uses those steps and a few others to ensure a proper saving of the resource to file.

```
#define   kSndResIDMaxReserved      8191

long  SaveSoundFromMemoryToResource( SndListHandle theSound )
```

```
{
   long    theResID;
   OSErr   theError;
   short   theResourceFileRef;

   theResourceFileRef = CurResFile();

   do
   {
      theResID = UniqueID( 'snd ' );
   } while ( theResID <= kSndResIDMaxReserved );

   AddResource( (Handle)theSound, 'snd ', theResID, "\pNew Sound" );
   theError = ResError();
   if ( theError != noErr )
      ExitToShell();

   UpdateResFile( theResourceFileRef );
   theError = ResError();
   if ( theError != noErr )
      ExitToShell();

   return ( theResID );
}
```

After obtaining a reference number to the current resource file, SaveSound-FromMemoryToResource() calls the Toolbox routine UniqueID() to select an ID that will be given to the resource that is about to be created. While your program could select the ID itself, doing so would provide no guarantee that a resource of the type being saved, with that same ID, doesn't already exist. The UniqueID() function searches open resource files (including the current one) for resources of the type specified in the parameter passed to it. It takes note of the IDs of all such resources and returns an ID that is not used.

Calling UniqueID() a single time would be adequate for coming up with an ID that is unique for the snd resource to be created. However, it wouldn't ensure that the ID was out of the range that Apple reserves for its own system sound resources—0 through 8191. That's why SaveSoundFromMemoryToResource() calls UniqueID() from within a loop. When UniqueID() returns a value outside this range, a valid ID is considered to be found and the loop ends.

After an ID is selected, AddResource() and UpdateResFile() are called in the manner described before the SaveSoundFromMemoryToResource() listing. Following each call, the Toolbox function ResError() is called to verify that no error occurred. If an error did occur, the SaveSound-FromMemoryToResource() function handles the error by simply exiting the program.

When SaveSoundFromMemoryToResource() has completed, the ID of the new sound resource is returned to the calling function. That allows the rest of the program to use this new sound resource. Any time the program wants to use the new sound resource, it should pass this ID to GetResource() to load the snd data to memory.

Chapter Example: SaveSound

Like the previous two programs in this chapter, SaveSound displays the standard Sound Recording dialog box to allow the user to record a new sound. Unlike the other two programs, SaveSound provides the dialog box with a functional **Save** button. When the user clicks **Save**, the dialog box will be dismissed and the new recording will be saved to the resource fork of the SaveSound application.

Before the program exits, the newly recorded sound will be played. This is done simply to prove that the sound data was in fact saved to a snd resource. Consider this snippet, taken from main():

```
theNewSoundID = SaveSoundFromMemoryToResource( theSound );

ReleaseResource( (Handle)theSound );
theSound = nil;

theError = PlaySoundResourceSynch( theNewSoundID );
```

The above code saves sound data to a resource. SaveSoundFromMemory-ToResource() returns the new resource's ID to the variable theNewSoundID. Then main() releases the sound data, and, just to make sure that the program can't access that data in memory, sets theSound to nil. Next, the application-defined routine PlaySoundResourceSynch() is called. This function was lifted directly from Chapter 2. When passed the ID of a sound resource, `PlaySoundResourceSynch()` calls `GetResource()` to load the resource to memory and then calls `SndPlay()` to play the sound data. Purging the sound data from memory and then loading the `snd` resource and playing the user-recorded sound provides proof that the user-recorded sound data was properly saved as a `snd` resource in the application's resource fork.

You can verify that SoundSave always gives a new `snd` resource a unique ID when it writes sound data to its resource fork. To do this, use your compiler to build a stand-alone version of SoundSave. Then, from the Finder, double-click on the **SoundSave** icon to run the program. Record and save a sound. After clicking the **Save** button, the program will quit. Next, from the Finder again, run SoundSave. Record a sound and save it. Now run your resource editor (ResEdit or Resorcerer). Use it to open the SoundSave application (don't open the **SoundSave.rsrc** file, open the SoundSave application). If you look at the `snd` resources in the application you'll find the two resources created from running the program twice—one resource per execution of SoundSave. Notice that the `snd` resources have different IDs and that both have IDs greater than 8191. Figure 3.9 shows a look at SoundSave using ResEdit.

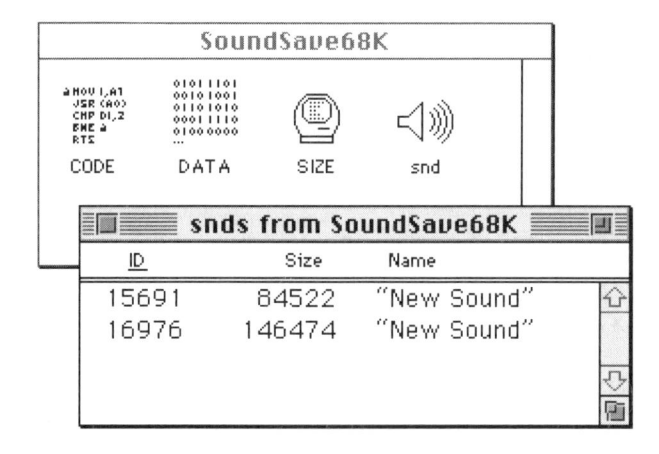

FIGURE 3.9 The SoundSave program will save a new sound to its own resource fork each time the program runs.

NOTE

You don't have to have your application save the sound resource to the application's resource fork, of course. You can save it to any open resource file. The SaveSound example saves the sound resource to its own fork to keep the source code listing focused on the process of creating a snd resource rather than on resource file management techniques. If your program will be used over a network, it *shouldn't* write data to its own resource fork. It should instead save the sound resource to a new or existing resource file. For information on working with multiple resource files, refer to the M&T book *More Mac Programming Techniques* or the *More Macintosh Toolbox* volume of *Inside Macintosh*. These books show you how to create a new resource file, open it, write to it, save the changes, close it, and, at a later time, reopen the file and read it. After reading about these techniques, combine them with this book's technique for saving a sound resource.

```
//_____

#include <Sound.h>
#include <SoundInput.h>

//_____

void       InitializeToolbox( void );
Boolean    IsSoundInputAvailable( void );
OSErr      RecordSoundToMemory( SndListHandle * );
long       SaveSoundFromMemoryToResource( SndListHandle );
OSErr      PlaySoundResourceSynch( short );

//_____

#define    kHeapReserve              75 * 1024
#define    kSndResIDMaxReserved         8191

//_____

void  main( void )
{
    NumVersion      theSndMgrVers;
    OSErr           theError;
    SndListHandle   theSound;
    long            theNewSoundID;
    Boolean         soundInputPresent;

    InitializeToolbox();

    MaxApplZone();
```

```
      theSndMgrVers = SndSoundManagerVersion();
      if ( theSndMgrVers.majorRev < 3 )
         ExitToShell();

      soundInputPresent = IsSoundInputAvailable();
      if ( soundInputPresent == false )
         ExitToShell();

      theError = RecordSoundToMemory( &theSound );
      if ( theError == userCanceledErr )
         ExitToShell();

      theNewSoundID = SaveSoundFromMemoryToResource( theSound );

      ReleaseResource( (Handle)theSound );
      theSound = nil;

      theError = PlaySoundResourceSynch( theNewSoundID );
      if ( theError != noErr )
         ExitToShell();
}

//_____

OSErr   RecordSoundToMemory( SndListHandle *theSound )
{
   OSErr   theError;
   Point   theCorner = { 50, 20 };
   long    theTotalHeap;
   long    theContigMem;

   PurgeSpace( &theTotalHeap, &theContigMem );

   *theSound = (SndListHandle)NewHandle( theContigMem -
   kHeapReserve );

   theError = SndRecord( nil, theCorner, siBestQuality, theSound );

   return ( theError );
}

//_____

long  SaveSoundFromMemoryToResource( SndListHandle theSound )
{
   long    theResID;
   OSErr   theError;
```

```
    short   theResourceFileRef;

    theResourceFileRef = CurResFile();

    do
    {
        theResID = UniqueID( 'snd ' );
    } while ( theResID <= kSndResIDMaxReserved );

    AddResource( (Handle)theSound, 'snd ', theResID, "\pNew Sound" );
    theError = ResError();
    if ( theError != noErr )
        ExitToShell();

    UpdateResFile( theResourceFileRef );
    theError = ResError();
    if ( theError != noErr )
        ExitToShell();

    return ( theResID );
}

//_____

OSErr  PlaySoundResourceSynch( short theResID )
{
    Handle   theHandle;
    OSErr    theError;

    theHandle = GetResource( 'snd ', theResID );

    if ( theHandle == nil )
    {
        return ( resProblem );
    }
    else
    {
        HLock( theHandle );
            theError = SndPlay( nil, (SndListHandle)theHandle, false );
        HUnlock( theHandle );

        ReleaseResource( theHandle );

        return ( theError );
    }
}
```

Sound Quality and Disk Storage Space

When your application calls SndRecord() to display the standard Sound Recording dialog box, the dialog box will display the amount of time that the user can use to record a single sound. Figure 3.10 illustrates this.

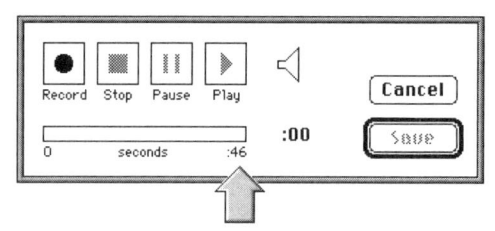

Maximum length of a single recording

FIGURE 3.10 The standard Sound Recording dialog box specifies
the amount of time available for a single sound recording.

The time displayed in this dialog box is dependent on two factors. The first is the size of the memory block to which the sound data will be saved. Recall that this memory block is set up with a call to NewHandle(), and the handle returned by this function is passed as the fourth parameter to SndRecord():

```
OSErr   theError;
Point   theCorner = { 50, 20 };
long    theTotalHeap;
long    theContigMem;

PurgeSpace( &theTotalHeap, &theContigMem );

*theSound = (SndListHandle)NewHandle( theContigMem - kHeapReserve );

theError = SndRecord( nil, theCorner, siBestQuality, theSound );
```

The second factor used to determine the maximum duration of the sound that can be recorded is the quality at which the sound is recorded. The third parameter to SndRecord() can be one of three Apple-defined constants, each of which represents a different sound-quality recording level:

```
theError = SndRecord( nil, theCorner, siBestQuality, theSound );
theError = SndRecord( nil, theCorner, siBetterQuality, theSound );
theError = SndRecord( nil, theCorner, siGoodQuality, theSound );
```

The higher the quality, the less time that is allotted for the recording. The primary reason for this is compression. A lower-quality sound uses compression during sound recording. This has the advantage of allowing a longer sound to fit in the same amount of memory and the disadvantage of decreasing the quality of the sound.

To provide a rough idea of the differences in sound time and quality that the three recording quality constants provide, you can run a simple test using the source code for the SoundSave example program. First, build a version of SoundSave using the following call to SndRecord():

```
theError = SndRecord( nil, theCorner, siBestQuality, theSound );
```

Next, run the newly created SoundSave program. Take note of the amount of time that can be used to record a sound; this time appears in the standard Sound Recording dialog box. In the top section of Figure 3.11 you can see that in one test this time was 46 seconds. Now record a 10-second sound; a 10-second clip of music will work fine. Click the **Save** button to save the sound and exit the SoundSave application. Open the SoundSave program using your resource editor. Examine the snd resource that was added to the application's resource fork. In the top section of Figure 3.11 you can see that in one test the 10-second sound takes up approximately 200 KB of disk space.

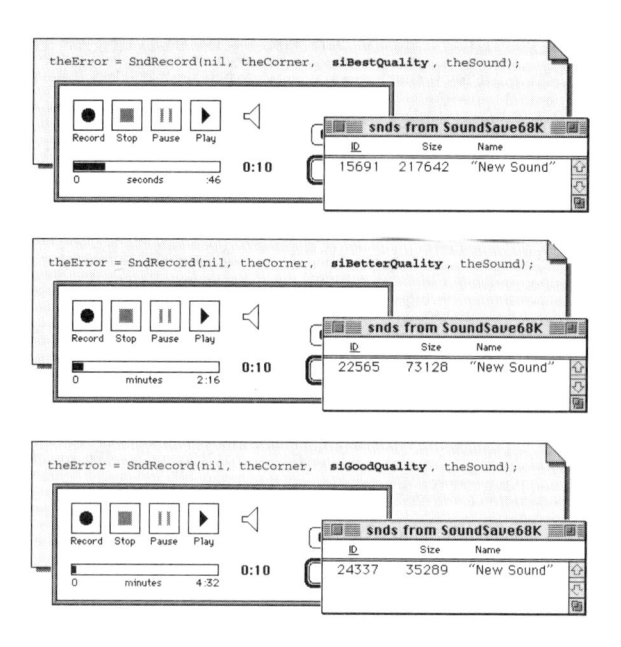

FIGURE 3.11 Changing the sound recording quality affects both the amount of time available for sound recording and the size of a recorded sound.

Now repeat the previous test—this time using the siBetterQuality sound quality in place of siBestQuality:

```
theError = SndRecord( nil, theCorner, siBetterQuality, theSound );
```

Leave the application heap size at whatever value it was set at for the first test (the SoundSave project comes with the heap size set to 1024 KB, or 1 MB). After changing the one line of code, build a new version of SoundSave. Run the stand-alone application and again note the time that is allotted to sound recording. In Figure 3.11 you can see that with siBetterQuality, the time increased from 46 seconds to 2 minutes and 16 seconds. Note that the size of the memory block used to hold the sound remained approximately the same between the running of the two versions of SoundSave.

After recording another 10-second sound (using the same 10-second music clip), Figure 3.11 shows that the size of the saved snd resource dropped from about 200 KB to about 70 KB.

The same test was repeated one last time with a sound quality of siGoodQuality. The result was a recording time of 4 minutes and 32 seconds. The snd resource size turned out to be about 35 KB.

What observation can you make from this test? This isn't a scientific test designed for accuracy. Instead, it provides a general feel for how the recording quality affects recording times. A more important observation, however, might be that this real-world test resulted in time values that closely match the compression used for the three sound qualities. The siBestQuality quality, which uses no compression, allowed a 46-second recording. The siBetterQuality quality, which uses 3:1 compression, allowed a 136-second recording—very close to three times the 46-second siBestQuality time. The siGoodQuality, which uses 6:1 compression, allowed a 272-second recording—very close to six times the 46-second siBestQuality time.

Summary

The Sound Manager gives your program the ability to play sounds. The Sound Input Manager gives your application the ability to record sounds. Before your program attempts to record a sound it should verify that the user's Mac has a sound input device. Generally, this device will be the built-in microphone.

The Sound Input Manager Toolbox routine that you'll become most familiar with is SndRecord(). This function posts the standard Sound Recording dialog box. For the duration that this dialog box is on the screen, SndRecord() controls your program. This powerful Toolbox routine takes care of user mouse clicks in the dialog box. These actions include recording, pausing, stopping, and playing sounds.

You can use Resource Manager functions to save a recorded sound that is in memory to a resource file that resides on the user's hard disk.

CHAPTER 4

Speech

In Chapter 2, you saw how the Sound Manager allows sounds to be played, while in Chapter 3 you read how the Sound Input Manager allows sounds to be recorded. Together, these two managers can be used to record and play back digitized speech. But there is a far easier way to add speech capabilities to your Mac applications. The Speech Manager includes functions that allow your program to turn text into spoken words. Whether the text comes from a string that is hard-coded into your source code, one that is read in from a string resource, or one that is entered in a dialog's Edit box by the user, the Speech Manager knows how to turn those characters into speech that emits from the user's audio hardware.

Besides being an easier way to add new speech phrases to a program, using text and the Speech Manager to generate speech offers additional advantages to using digitized sound resources. One advantage is the savings in disk "real estate." Whereas a single digitized sentence may often require over 100 MB of disk storage, the same sentence stored as text will need only a couple of dozen bytes of disk space—one byte per character in the sentence. A second advantage to using the Speech Manager rather than digitized speech is the voice option. While the digitized speech comes in one voice only—the voice in which it was originally recorded—speech generated from text can be spoken in any number of different-sounding voices.

In this chapter, you'll see exactly how to easily turn text into speech by using the Speech Manager and sound synthesizers. You'll also learn about the topics covered in the preceding paragraphs: speaking text from strings that you include in your source code or in resources, or that are supplied by the user. You'll also see how to generate speech in a variety of voices—including speech that sounds like that spoken by a robot.

The Speech Manager

In Chapter 3, you saw that the Sound Input Manager uses the Sound Manager to access the audio hardware connected to a user's Macintosh. In this chapter, you'll see that the Speech Manager does the same.

The Sound Manager can be used to play sounds—either from sound resources or sound files—through the Macintosh speakers. With the assistance of the Speech Manager, the Sound Manager can also speak words that originate as text. The use of the Sound Manager by the Speech Manager is transparent to the user and to the programmer. For that reason, there's no need to worry if you've skipped Chapter 2 of this book—you won't need information from that chapter in order to understand the topics covered in this chapter.

The Speech Manager and Speech Synthesizers

The Speech Manager is used to allow a program to generate *synthesized speech*—speech that results from the conversion of text to spoken sound. The Speech Manager itself doesn't perform the conversion, however. Instead, this manager passes text to a *speech synthesizer* and relies on this synthesizer's built-in dictionaries and sets of pronunciation rules in order to pronounce the text properly. The Speech Manager is capable of using different synthesizers to speak text. Figure 4.1 shows several extensions found in the Extensions folder of the System Folder—including the Speech Manager extension and the MacinTalk Pro speech synthesizer extension.

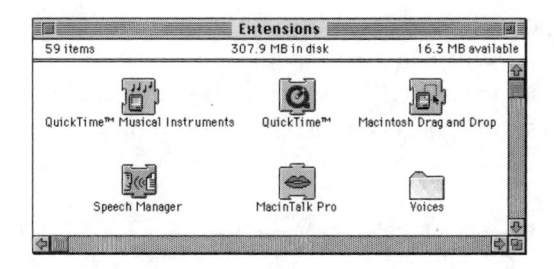

FIGURE 4.1 The Speech Manager and the MacinTalk Pro speech synthesizer are both system software extensions.

After the speech synthesizer applies its pronunciation rules to the text that the Speech Manager passes it, the synthesizer passes the converted data to the Sound Manager for output to the Mac's audio hardware. Figure 4.2 shows the path that text takes to become speech. In the figure, the data is passed to the MacinTalk Pro speech synthesizer for processing—but a different synthesizer could be used instead.

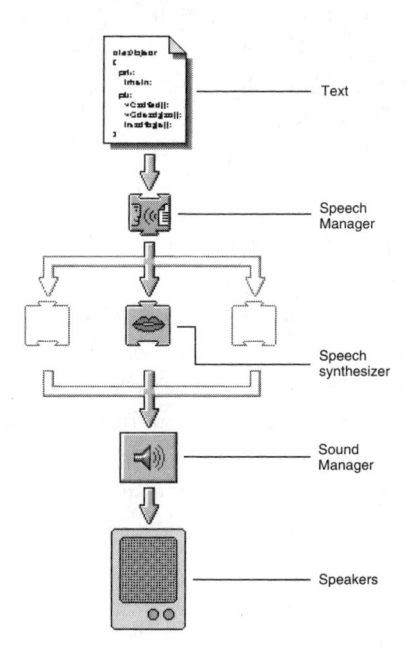

FIGURE 4.2 The Speech Manager uses a speech synthesizer and the Sound Manager to generate speech from text.

Figure 4.2 shows the text that is to be spoken as words in a text file. The text doesn't have to appear in a document, though. As you'll see in this chapter, it can also be entered into an Edit box in a dialog box by the user, it can be a string resource, or it can be hard-coded into an application.

Voices and Speech Synthesizers

If you look back at Figure 4.1, you'll see that the figure provides a hint that there's more software involved in speech generation than what is shown in Figure 4.2. The Macintosh allows text to be spoken in different voices. A *voice* is information held in a data structure. This information specifies different qualities of speech that result in the speech having characteristics such as that of a old man, a young woman, a small boy, or even a robot. If your application doesn't specify a particular voice, text will be spoken using the *system-default voice*.

Voices are designed for specific speech synthesizers. Figure 4.3 shows several voice files found in the Voices folder in the Extensions folder of the System Folder. The three voice files at the bottom of Figure 4.3 are used by the MacinTalk synthesizer. The three voice files at the top of the figure are used by the speech synthesizer that comes built into the Speech Manager extension.

N O T E Earlier, it was stated that the Speech Manager doesn't actually speak. Instead, it routes text to a speech synthesizer. A *synthesizer* is a code component in a resource file or the resource fork of a file. A speech synthesizer can appear anywhere in the System Folder—including within the Speech Manager itself. The resource fork of the Speech Manager extension includes a speech synthesizer—used with some voices—that guarantees that a Mac with the Speech Manager will always have at least one speech synthesizer as well. If you removed the synthesizer code from the Speech Manager, you'd still have a functional Speech Manager.

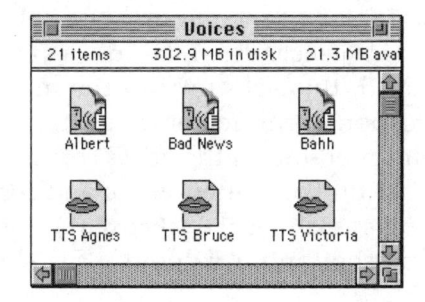

FIGURE 4.3 Voice files can be found in a folder the System Folder—
usually in the Extensions folder.

 The Extensions folder of your Mac should already have the Speech Manager, MacinTalk Pro, and the Voices folder in it—they're all added as part of your System install. If they're not there, look on your system disks or CD. For System 7.5, search for the Install Speech icon. Launch the installer, click the **Continue** button, then select **Custom Install** from the pop-up menu. Check the **Text-to-Speech Software** checkbox and click the **Install** button.

Checking for the Availability of the Speech Manager

Macintosh computers don't have built-in speech capabilities—they need the Speech Manager software. Before your program attempts to speak text, it should first call `Gestalt()` to verify that the host computer has this system software extension. As was done for sound recording in Chapter 3, you can use a short application-defined routine to make this check. The following snippet makes a call to a function named `IsSpeechAvailable()`.

```
Boolean  speechPresent;

speechPresent = IsSpeechAvailable();
if ( speechPresent == false )
   ExitToShell();
```

The IsSpeechAvailable() function makes a call to Gestalt() with a selector code of gestaltSpeechAttr. Like the gestaltSoundAttr selector code used in Chapter 3, this selector returns more than one piece of information in the response parameter. To extract the information you need, use the left shift operator on the gestaltSpeechMgrPresent bit and perform a logical AND on the shifted value and response parameter. If the bit in question (gestaltSpeechMgrPresent) is turned on, then the Speech Manager is present and a value of true should be returned to the calling routine.

```
Boolean  IsSpeechAvailable( void )
{
   OSErr    theError;
   long     theResult;
   Boolean  speechAvail;

   theError = Gestalt( gestaltSpeechAttr, &theResult );
   if ( theError != noErr )
      ExitToShell();

   speechAvail = theResult & ( 1 << gestaltSpeechMgrPresent );
   if ( speechAvail > 0 )
      return ( true );
   else
      return ( false );
}
```

Speaking a String

If your application requires only simple speech generation—such as the speaking of a string using the system, or default, voice, then the SpeakString() Toolbox function may be all your program needs.

The SpeakString() Toolbox Function

The Speech Manager provides a very simple means of generating speech—the SpeakString() function. To use SpeakString(), pass in a Pascal string—as shown in the following snippet. SpeakString() will have the Speech Manager generate the speech for the string and broadcast the speech through the Mac's speakers. Note that the snippet includes the **Speech.h** universal header file—as should any code that makes use of speech functions.

```
#include <Speech.h>

OSErr   theError;

theError = SpeakString( "\pYes, it's really this easy!" );
```

The string that gets passed to `SpeakString()` can also be a variable. The following snippet gives the same results as the above code:

```
OSErr   theError;
OSErr   theString = "\pYes, it's really this easy!";

theError = SpeakString( theString );
```

After calling `SpeakString()`, you can compare the returned `OSErr` value to the Apple-defined constant `noErr` to verify that the call was successful:

```
theError = SpeakString( theString );
if ( theError != noErr )
   ExitToShell();
```

Chapter Example: QuickSpeech

QuickSpeech is the simplest example of generating speech. The program begins by initializing the Toolbox and then calling the application-defined `IsSpeechAvailable()` to determine if the user's Macintosh has the Speech Manager extension. This function is identical to the version developed earlier in this chapter.

When it is known that the Speech Manager is present, QuickSpeech calls `SpeakString()` to speak a single string.

```
//_____

#include <Gestalt.h>
#include <Speech.h>
```

```
//_____

void    InitializeToolbox( void );
Boolean IsSpeechAvailable( void );

//_____

void  main( void )
{
   OSErr    theError;
   Boolean  speechPresent;

   InitializeToolbox();

   speechPresent = IsSpeechAvailable();
   if ( speechPresent == false )
      ExitToShell();

   theError = SpeakString( "\pTesting 1 2 3 Testing 123);
   if ( theError != noErr )
      ExitToShell();
}

//_____

Boolean  IsSpeechAvailable( void )
{
   OSErr    theError;
   long     theResult;
   Boolean  speechAvail;

   theError = Gestalt( gestaltSpeechAttr, &theResult );
   if ( theError != noErr )
      ExitToShell();

   speechAvail = theResult & ( 1 << gestaltSpeechMgrPresent );
   if ( speechAvail > 0 )
      return ( true );
   else
      return ( false );

}
//_____

void  InitializeToolbox( void )
{
   InitGraf( &qd.thePort );
```

```
    InitFonts();
    InitWindows();
    InitMenus();
    TEInit();
    InitDialogs( 0L );
    FlushEvents( everyEvent, 0 );
    InitCursor();
}
```

Speaking More Than One String

In Chapter 2, you saw that by the use of the `SndPlay()` Toolbox function, the Sound Manager can produce sound asynchronously. The Speech Manager can also produce asynchronous sound. In fact, asynchronously generated speech is the norm for the Speech Manager.

Asynchronous speech means that before the call to `SpeakString()` completes, control will be returned to your program—and the code following the call to `SpeakString()` will execute. This asynchronous speech generation must be taken into account if your program is to speak more than one string. Consider the following *incorrect* example:

```
theError = SpeakString( "\pThis is string #1." );

theError = SpeakString( "\pThis is the second string." );
```

Rather than speak two strings one after the other, the Speech Manager will generate speech for both strings at almost the same time—an undesirable result. To force the Speech Manager to generate synchronous speech—one string spoken *after* the other, use the `SpeechBusy()` Toolbox function.

After the first call to `SpeakString()`, use `SpeechBusy()` in a "do nothing" `while` loop. Because `SpeakString()` generates speech asynchronously, the while loop will be executed almost immediately after the call to `SpeakString()`. `SpeechBusy()` will return a value of `true` if speech is taking place, `false` if it isn't. That means that as long as the first call to `SpeakString()` is still executing, `SpeechBusy()` will keep returning a value of `true`. The result will be that the program will remain at the `while` loop until the first `SpeakString()` completes. Only then will `SpeechBusy()` return a value of `false`, sending the program on to the second call to `SpeakString()`. Here's the snippet that corrects the preceding wrong example:

```
theError = SpeakString( "\pThis is string #1." );

while ( SpeechBusy() == true )
   ;

theError = SpeakString( "\pThis is the second string." );
```

N O T E   Saying that `SpeechBusy()` returns a value of `true` or `false` is a simplification. `SpeechBusy()` doesn't actually return a `Boolean` value. It returns the number of active *speech channels*. While the details of speech channels aren't discussed until later in this chapter, this brief discussion will introduce them. The `SpeakString()` function automatically opens a speech channel to use in speaking a string, and then closes the channel when finished speaking. If `SpeechBusy()` is called while `SpeakString()` is speaking text, `SpeechBusy()` will return a value of 1 (or more than 1 if other speech channels are also active). This nonzero value correlates to `true`—and means the `while` statement will continue to cycle through the "do nothing" loop.

This next snippet does the same task as the preceding one—it just adds a little error-checking.

```
theError = SpeakString( "\pThis is string #1." );
if ( theError != noErr )
   ExitToShell();

while ( SpeechBusy() == true )
   ;

theError = SpeakString( "\pThis is the second string." );
if ( theError != noErr )
   ExitToShell();
```

Chapter Example: WaitSpeech

WaitSpeech demonstrates how to include a call to SpeechBusy() so that two strings can be called one after the other. When WaitSpeech runs, it will say the phrase "This is string number 1. This is the second string."

```
void  main( void )
{
    Str255    theString = "\pThis is the second string.";
    OSErr     theError;
    Boolean   speechPresent;

    InitializeToolbox();

    speechPresent = IsSpeechAvailable();
    if ( speechPresent == false )
        ExitToShell();

    theError = SpeakString( "\pThis is string #1." );
    if ( theError != noErr )
        ExitToShell();

    while ( SpeechBusy() == true )
        ;

    theError = SpeakString( theString );
    if ( theError != noErr )
        ExitToShell();
}
```

User Input and Speech

SpeakString() will speak the text of a string no matter where the string comes from. If your program needs to generate speech based on text provided by the user, SpeakString() may again be your solution.

Your applications can obtain user-entered strings just as they always have—by displaying a dialog box that contains one or more edit boxes. After the user enters text and dismisses the dialog box, call the Toolbox function `GetDialogItem()` to get a handle to an edit box. Then pass that handle to the Toolbox function `GetDialogItemText()` to retrieve the text from that edit box. Finally, save the string so that it can be spoken later, or immediately use the retrieved text as the parameter in a call to `SpeakString()`. The following snippet performs these tasks in order to speak the text found in an Edit box with a dialog item number of 3.

```
#define       kPhraseEdit      3

DialogPtr  theDialog;
short      theType;
Handle     theHandle;
Rect       theRect;
Str255     theString;
OSErr      theError;

GetDialogItem( theDialog, kPhraseEdit, &theType, &theHandle,
    &theRect );
GetDialogItemText( theHandle, theString );
theError = SpeakString( theString );
```

Chapter Example: InputSpeech

The InputSpeech program allows the user to enter text into the Edit box item of a dialog box. When the user clicks on the **Speak** button, the program retrieves the text and speaks it. By repeatedly clicking the **Speak** button, the user can have the computer speak the phrase as many times as desired. Figure 4.4 shows the InputSpeech dialog box.

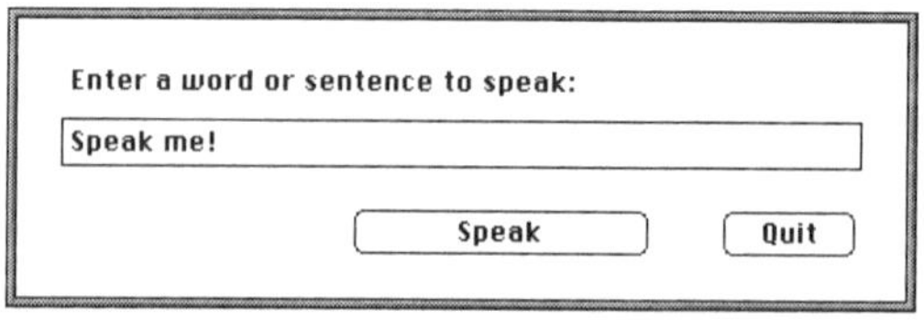

FIGURE 4.4 The dialog box displayed by the InputSpeech program.

The InputSpeech project requires just two resources: a DLOG and a DITL. The DITL, with the item number of each item shown, appears in Figure 4.5.

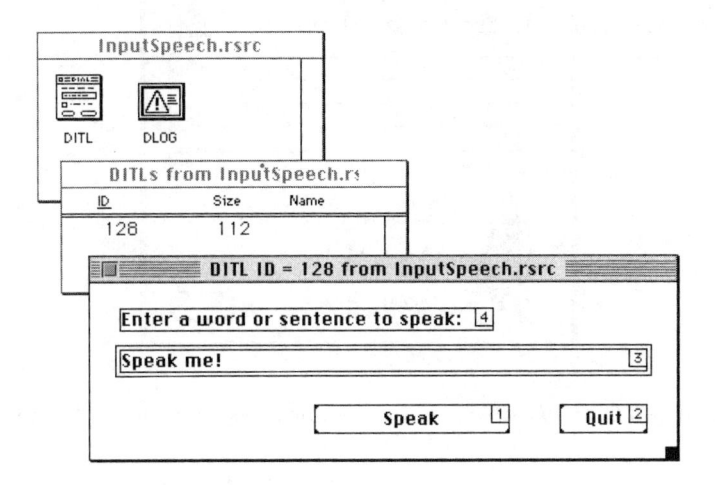

FIGURE 4.5 The DITL resource used by the InputSpeech program.

InputSpeech checks for the availability of the Speech Manager, then opens a dialog box. When the user clicks on DITL item number 1, the text from item number 3 (kPhraseEdit) is obtained and sent to the speaker via a call to SpeakString():

```
GetDialogItem( theDialog, kPhraseEdit,
               &theType, &theHandle, &theRect );
GetDialogItemText( theHandle, theString );
theError = SpeakString( theString );
if ( theError != noErr )
   ExitToShell();
break;
```

The technique used in the InputSpeech program can easily be expanded to provide user-input for a program with a more sophisticated interface. Figure 4.6 shows one possible example. Here, the user-entered phrases can be played back immediately—as in InputSpeech—and can be saved. Clicking the **Done** button would save each phrase as a string in a global array of strings. That would allow the program to play back the strings at any time.

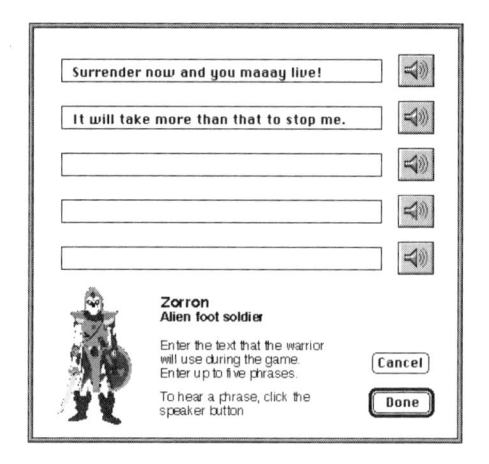

FIGURE 4.6 An example of implementing speech into an application.

```
//_____

#define        rSpeechDialog        120
#define        kSpeakButton          1
#define        kQuitButton           2
#define        kPhraseEdit           3

//_____

void   main( void )
{
   Boolean   speechPresent;

   InitializeToolbox();

   speechPresent = IsSpeechAvailable();
   if ( speechPresent == false )
      ExitToShell();

   OpenSpeechDialog();
}

//_____

void  OpenSpeechDialog( void )
{
```

```
DialogPtr    theDialog;
short        theItem;
Boolean      allDone = false;
short        theType;
Handle       theHandle;
Rect         theRect;
Str255       theString;
OSErr        theError;

theDialog = GetNewDialog( rSpeechDialog, nil, (WindowPtr)-1L );
ShowWindow( theDialog );
SetPort( theDialog );

while ( allDone == false )
{
   ModalDialog( nil, &theItem );

   switch ( theItem )
   {
      case kSpeakButton:
         GetDialogItem( theDialog, kPhraseEdit,
                        &theType, &theHandle, &theRect );
         GetDialogItemText( theHandle, theString );
         theError = SpeakString( theString );
         if ( theError != noErr )
            ExitToShell();
         break;
      case kQuitButton:
         allDone = true;
         break;

   }
}
DisposeDialog( theDialog );
}
```

Resource Strings and Speech

Up to this point you've seen that SpeakString() uses strings that were hard-coded into a program and strings that were obtained from a dialog box Edit box item. You can also use SpeakString() with strings that are saved as resources in a string list resource—a STR# resource.

Figure 4.7 shows a few of the many strings held in the resource file of a program that is used to keep inventory of a computer store's computer wares. When an employee checks to see if a particular computer model is in stock, the inventory will load two of the strings from the STR# resource and then call SpeakString() twice to speak a phrase such as "Power Mac 6100 slash 66 is back ordered."

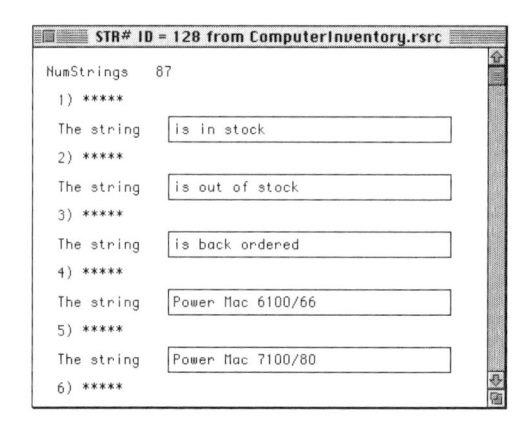

FIGURE 4.7 An example of a STR# resource.

The source code listing could include a #define directive for each string in the STR# resource:

```
#define        rStringList                  128
#define        kInStockStrIndex              1
#define        kOutStockStrIndex             2
#define        kBackOrderStockStrIndex       3
#define        kPowerMac6100_66StrIndex      4
#define        kPowerMac7100_80StrIndex      5
...
...
```

When it comes time to speak the on-hand status of a computer, call the Toolbox routine GetIndString() to load the string from the string resource to memory. Then call SpeakString()—as shown in the following snippet.

```
short   theStringIndex;

theStringIndex = kPowerMac7100_80StrIndex;
```

```
GetIndString( theString, rStringList, theStringIndex );
theError = SpeakString( theString );
```

Since the preceding example relies on calling SpeakString() twice to generate one sentence from two strings, it's important to keep in mind the asynchronous nature of the Speech Manager. In the following snippet the SpeechBusy() function is called so that the two phrases will be spoken one after the other.

```
theStringIndex = kPowerMac7100_80StrIndex;

GetIndString( theString, rStringList, theStringIndex );
theError = SpeakString( theString );

while ( SpeechBusy() == true )
    ;

theStringIndex = kBackOrderStockStrIndex;

GetIndString( theString, rStringList, theStringIndex );
theError = SpeakString( theString );
```

Chapter Example: ResourceSpeech

The ResourceSpeech example displays a dialog box with three buttons in it—as shown in Figure 4.8. Clicking on the **Speak Short String** button causes the phrase "Correct" to be spoken. Clicking on the **Speak Long String** button results in the phrase "Congratulations, that's correct" to be spoken.

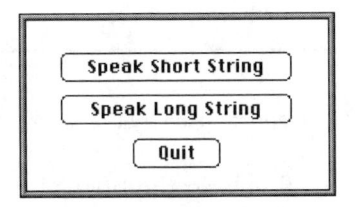

Figure 4.8 The dialog box displayed by the ResourceSpeech program.

Figure 4.9 shows the resource file for the ResourceSpeech project, with emphasis on the dialog item numbers of the file's one DITL resource.

Figure 4.10 shows the resource file's one STR# resource and the two strings it holds.

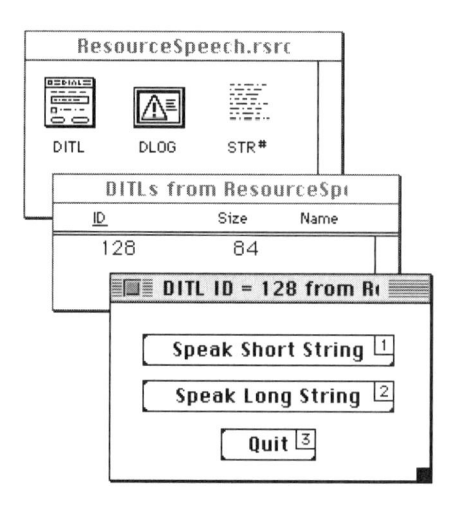

FIGURE 4.9 The DITL resource used by the ResourceSpeech program.

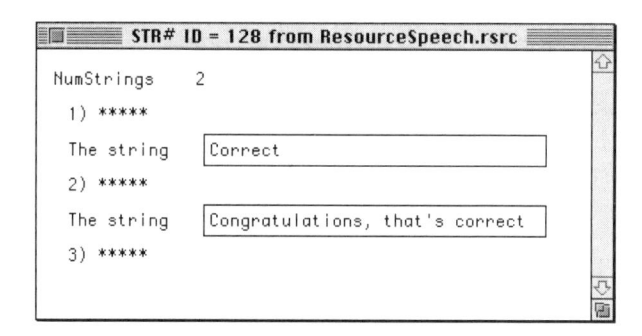

FIGURE 4.10 The STR# resource used by the ResourceSpeech program.

ResourceSpeech begins by checking the host Mac for speech capabilities, then opens the program's dialog box. A click on either **Speak** button results in a call to GetIndString() with the appropriate STR# index, and then a call to SpeakString(). The following code executes when the **Speak Short String** button (DITL item number 1, or kSpeakShortButton) gets clicked:

```
GetIndString( theString, rStringList, kShortStrIndex );
theError = SpeakString( theString );
if ( theError != noErr )
    ExitToShell();
```

The following is the source code listing for the ResourceSpeech example.

```
//_____

#define        rSpeechDialog          128
#define        kSpeakShortButton        1
#define        kSpeakLongButton         2
#define        kQuitButton              3
#define        rStringList            128
#define        kShortStrIndex           1
#define        kLongStrIndex            2

//_____

void   main( void )
{
    Boolean   speechPresent;

    InitializeToolbox();

    speechPresent = IsSpeechAvailable();
    if ( speechPresent == false )
        ExitToShell();
    OpenSpeechDialog();
}

//_____

void   OpenSpeechDialog( void )
{
    DialogPtr   theDialog;
    short       theItem;
    Boolean     allDone = false;
    Str255      theString;
    OSErr       theError;

    theDialog = GetNewDialog( rSpeechDialog, nil, (WindowPtr)-1L );
    ShowWindow( theDialog );
    SetPort( theDialog );

    while ( allDone == false )
```

```
   {
      ModalDialog( nil, &theItem );

      switch ( theItem )
      {
         case kSpeakShortButton:
            GetIndString( theString, rStringList, kShortStrIndex );
            theError = SpeakString( theString );
            if ( theError != noErr )
               ExitToShell();
            break;

         case kSpeakLongButton:
            GetIndString( theString, rStringList, kLongStrIndex );
            theError = SpeakString( theString );
            if ( theError != noErr )
               ExitToShell();
            break;

         case kQuitButton:
            allDone = true;
            break;
      }
   }
   DisposeDialog( theDialog );
}
```

Speech Channels

In Chapter 2, you saw that whenever sound data is processed by the Sound Manager, a sound channel is involved. Processing speech is similar—whenever text is spoken from the Macintosh speakers, a speech channel is involved. When you call SpeakString(), the Speech Manager takes care of allocating a speech channel. The Speech Manager is also responsible for using that same channel to produce the speech and disposing of the speech channel when speech has finished. When you call SpeakString(), you'll notice that the speech is always spoken in the same voice—the system default voice. If your application needs to use a different voice, it should allocate its own speech channel and use that channel when generating speech. Since SpeakString() doesn't have a provision for using an application-specified speech channel, you'll use the SpeakText() Toolbox function when using your own channel.

Allocating and Disposing of a Speech Channel

To allocate a speech channel, use the Toolbox routine NewSpeechChannel(). This function allocates memory for a new speech channel record—a structure of type SpeechChannelRecord. NewSpeechChannel() then returns a SpeechChannel—a pointer to the new speech channel record. The following snippet allocates a new speech channel.

```
SpeechChannel   theChannel;
OSErr           theError;

theError = NewSpeechChannel( nil, &theChannel );
```

The first parameter to NewSpeechChannel() is a pointer to a voice specification data structure. As you'll see later in this chapter, this data structure corresponds to the voice that is to be used for speech generated through this one speech channel. Using a nil pointer as this first parameter—as done here—tells the Speech Manager to use the system default voice.

The second parameter to NewSpeechChannel() is a pointer to a speech channel. When NewSpeechChannel() finishes executing, this parameter will hold a newly allocated speech channel. You'll use this speech channel in subsequent calls to SpeakText().

NOTE

A variable of type SpeechChannel is generally referred to as a speech channel—even though it is a pointer to a SpeechChannelRecord. That's because your application won't ever directly use a SpeechChannelRecord— it's used internally by the Speech Manager. If you look at the definition of the SpeechChannelRecord data type, you'll see that it consists of nothing more than a single 4-byte field that serves as a pointer to other data:

```
struct SpeechChannelRecord
{
    long  data[1];
};
```

After using a speech channel to speak text, you'll need to deallocate the memory it occupies. To do that, call the Toolbox function `Dispose-SpeechChannel()`. The only parameter required by `DisposeSpeechChannel()` is the identification of speech channel to dispose.

```
OSErr  theError;

theError = DisposeSpeechChannel( theChannel );
```

NOTE You might recall from Chapter 2 that when a sound channel is disposed of, both the sound channel data structure and the sound channel pointer were disposed of:
```
theError = SndDisposeChannel( theChannel, true );
DisposePtr( (Ptr)theChannel );
```

For a speech channel, you need only call `DisposeSpeechChannel()`. That call will deallocate both the `SpeechChannel` and the `SpeechChannelRecord`.

NOTE

If you write a routine to open a new speech channel, include a call to `DisposeSpeechChannel()` in the event that the call to `NewSpeechChannel()` returns an error. The application-defined function `OpenOneSpeechChannel()` will be used in the remaining examples in this chapter:

```
SpeechChannel  OpenOneSpeechChannel( void )
{
    SpeechChannel  theChannel;
    OSErr          theError;

    theError = NewSpeechChannel( nil, &theChannel );

    if ( theError != noErr )
    {
        theError = DisposeSpeechChannel( theChannel );
        theChannel = nil;
    }
    return ( theChannel );
}
```

If the speech channel memory allocation goes smoothly, the sound channel will be returned to the calling routine. If the allocation fails,

`OpenOneSpeechChannel()` disposes of the memory occupied by the speech channel and sets the pointer to `nil`. If the calling routine receives a `nil` pointer instead of a valid speech channel, the calling function will assume an error occurred. Here's a call to `OpenOneSpeechChannel()`:

```
SpeechChannel  theChannel;

theChannel = OpenOneSpeechChannel();
if ( theChannel == nil )
   ExitToShell();
```

Using a Speech Channel

After allocating a speech channel, use the channel in a call to `SpeakText()`. Rather than speak a single string, `SpeakText()` speaks text from a buffer. The second parameter to `SpeakText()` is a pointer to the first byte in the buffer, while the third parameter is the number of bytes to be spoken from that buffer. The first parameter is the speech channel to use. The following is an example that allocates a new speech channel, calls `SpeakText()` to speak a sentence, then deallocates the speech channel.

```
OSErr          theError;
SpeechChannel  theChannel;
Str255         theString =  "\pUsing my own speech channel";

theChannel = OpenOneSpeechChannel();

theError = SpeakText( theChannel, (Ptr)(theString + 1),
                      theString[0] );

while ( SpeechBusy() == true )
   ;

theError = DisposeSpeechChannel( theChannel );
```

N O T E Like `SpeakString()`, `SpeakText()` generates asynchronous speech. So it's important that you call `SpeechBusy()` in a loop before disposing of the speech channel that `SpeakText()` uses. Remember, the code that follows the call to `SpeakText()` will execute before `SpeakText()` completes talking.

In the above snippet, the variable `theString` is considered the text buffer. The first byte to speak from that buffer is the second byte of the string, not the first—the first byte of a Pascal-formatted string holds the length of the string. In C, an array name serves as a pointer to the array. Adding to the array name adds to the address of the start of the array. With that in mind, theString holds the address of the start of the string, while theString + 1 holds the address of the next byte in the string—the first character in the string. Finally, because SpeakText() requires a generic pointer to a buffer, the string variable needs to be typecast to type Ptr.

The last parameter to SpeakText() is the number of bytes that should be used from the buffer. As mentioned, the first byte of a Pascal-formatted string holds the length of the string. For this reason, it is the value of the first byte of theString that should be used here.

The above example speaks one string of text—just as earlier examples that used SpeakString() did. The only difference is that this new example required the extra work of allocating a new sound channel and then disposing of that channel. At first glance, that doesn't seem much of an improvement over the SpeakString() way of generating speech. The advantage to this new method doesn't show up in the above snippet—or in the SpeechChannelIntro program presented next. Instead, the small amount of extra work pays off in the following section when a speech channel and SpeakText() are used together to speak a string using a voice other than the system default voice.

Chapter Example: SpeechChannelIntro

The SpeechChannelIntro program ties together the snippets from this section an presents them in a simple program that opens a new speech channel, speaks a sentence using that channel, and then disposes of the channel.

```
//_____

void            InitializeToolbox( void );
Boolean         IsSpeechAvailable( void );
SpeechChannel   OpenOneSpeechChannel( void );

//_____

void  main( void )
```

```c
{
    OSErr          theError;
    Boolean        speechPresent;
    SpeechChannel  theChannel;
    Str255         theString = "\pUsing my own speech channel";

    InitializeToolbox();

    speechPresent = IsSpeechAvailable();
    if ( speechPresent == false )
        ExitToShell();

    theChannel = OpenOneSpeechChannel();
    if ( theChannel == nil )
        ExitToShell();

    theError = SpeakText( theChannel, (Ptr)(theString + 1),
                          theString[0] );
    if ( theError != noErr )
        ExitToShell();

    while ( SpeechBusy() == true )
        ;

    theError = DisposeSpeechChannel( theChannel );
    if ( theError != noErr )
        ExitToShell();
}

//_____

SpeechChannel  OpenOneSpeechChannel( void )
{
    SpeechChannel  theChannel;
    OSErr          theError;
    theError = NewSpeechChannel( nil, &theChannel );

    if ( theError != noErr )
    {
        theError = DisposeSpeechChannel( theChannel );
        theChannel = nil;
    }

    return ( theChannel );
}
```

Voices

One of the primary reasons for creating a speech channel is so that you can associate a particular voice with the text that is to be spoken. Without an application-defined speech channel, your application must settle for the system-default voice used by the SpeakString() function.

Specifying a Voice

Voices are stored as files in the System Folder of a user's Macintosh—as are speech synthesizers used with the voices. While you might know which voices and which synthesizers are present on your Mac, you have no way of knowing what users of your application might have on their computers. That means that rather than specifying one particular voice, your program should specify one or more characteristics the desired voice should have. After that, your program should cycle through the voices that are available on the user's machine. When a voice that has characteristics matching the desired ones is found, that voice should be associated with the channel that is to be used to speak a buffer of text.

Each voice has a VoiceDescription data structure that holds information about that voice. The following snippet shows that structure:

```
struct    VoiceDescription
{
    long        length;
    VoiceSpec   voice;
    long        version;
    Str63       name;
    Str255      comment;
    short       gender;
    short       age;
    short       script;
    short       language;
    short       region;
    long        reserved[4];
};
```

Of most interest in selecting a voice will be the gender and age fields of the VoiceDescription structure. The gender field will always have a value matching one of three Apple-defined constants:

```
enum
{
    kNeuter  = 0,
    kMale    = 1,
    kFemale  = 2
};
```

The kMale and kFemale gender values are self-explanatory. The other, kNeuter, is used to describe a voice that is robotic-sounding. If your program wants to see if a voice generates speech in a male voice, it should include a snippet similar to the following:

```
VoiceDescription  theVoiceDesc;

// get a voice description for a voice

// now check to see if the voice has characteristics matching
// the desired ones:
if ( theVoiceDesc.gender == kMale )
    // voice matches, use it to generate speech
```

The above snippet uses a comment in place of one important step: obtaining a voice description structure for a voice. That topic will be covered in the next section.

The age field of the VoiceDescription structure yields the approximate age that a speaker of this voice would have. If you'd like to generate speech using a voice that sounds as if it were that of a teenager, you might have a test such as the following:

```
if ( ( theVoiceDesc.age > 12 ) && ( theVoiceDesc.age < 20 ) )
    // voice matches, use it to generate speech
```

If you'd like the voice to be that of a teenage male, combine the above two tests:

```
if ( theVoiceDesc.gender == kMale )
   if ( ( theVoiceDesc.age > 12 ) && ( theVoiceDesc.age < 20 ) )
      // voice matches, use it to generate speech
```

Obtaining a Voice Description for a Voice

To begin a search for a voice that matches your program's specifications, call the Toolbox function `CountVoices()`:

```
OSErr  theError;
short  theNumVoices;

theError = CountVoices( &theNumVoices );
```

As its name implies, `CountVoices()` searches the user's system to find all available voices, counts them, and returns the total in the parameter. This returned value should then be used as the index in a `for` loop. The purpose of the loop is to examine each voice in turn, searching for one that has characteristics matching the program's needs—such as a voice of a middle-aged man.

```
for ( theIndex = 1; theIndex <= theNumVoices; theIndex++ )
{
   // examine each voice until a middle-aged man match is found
}
```

Within the loop body, getting a `VoiceDescription` for a voice is a two-step process. First, a `VoiceSpec` is needed. The `VoiceSpec` is used to provide a unique reference to each voice. The `VoiceSpec` data structure consists of two fields: an identification number of the speech synthesizer for which the voice was created and an identification number of the voice itself. Any number of voices can share the same speech synthesizer ID, but each voice of these voices with the same synthesizer ID will have a voice ID that is unique. To get a `VoiceSpec` for a voice, call the Toolbox function `GetIndVoice()`:

```
OSErr      theError;
short      theIndex;
VoiceSpec  theVoiceSpec;

theError = GetIndVoice( theIndex, &theVoiceSpec );
```

The first parameter to GetIndVoice() is an index that tells which voice is of interest. This parameter must have a value no less than 1, for the first voice, and no greater than the total number of voices currently present in the user's system—as reflected in the value returned by CountVoices(). The following shows how the voice-searching loop is shaping up:

```
OSErr       theError;
short       theNumVoices;
short       theIndex;
VoiceSpec   theVoiceSpec;

theError = CountVoices( &theNumVoices );

for ( theIndex = 1; theIndex <= theNumVoices; theIndex++ )
{
    theError = GetIndVoice( theIndex, theVoiceSpec );
    // examine the voice specified by theVoiceSpec
}
```

A voice description can be obtained by making a call to the Toolbox function GetVoiceDescription():

```
theError = GetVoiceDescription( theVoiceSpec, &theVoiceDesc,
                            sizeof( theVoiceDesc ) );
```

The first parameter to GetVoiceDescription() is the VoiceSpec for the voice of interest. The VoiceSpe is the one returned by the preceding call to GetIndVoice(). The second parameter is a pointer to a variable of type VoiceDescription. After the call to GetVoiceDescription() is complete, this data structure will be filled with information about the voice specified by the VoiceSpec. The final parameter to GetVoiceDescription() is the number of bytes in a VoiceDescription data structure. Use the sizeof() function to get this value.

At this point, enough is known about a voice to make a decision as to whether it is one that matches the program's needs. An updated version of the voice-checking loop follows.

```
OSErr           theError;
short           theNumVoices;
short           theIndex;
```

```
VoiceSpec          theVoiceSpec;
VoiceDescription   theVoiceDesc;

theError = CountVoices( &theNumVoices );

for ( theIndex = 1; theIndex <= theNumVoices; theIndex++ )
{
   theError = GetIndVoice( theIndex, theVoiceSpec );

   theError = GetVoiceDescription( theVoiceSpec, &theVoiceDesc,
                                   sizeof( theVoiceDesc ) );

   // compare fields of the VoiceDescription with the desired
   // voice characteristics to see if this voice is a match

   // if voice matches, exit loop
   // else loop again and check the next indexed voice
}
```

This loop can be included in a function that is used to return the VoiceSpec for a voice that fits a certain requirement. Consider as an example the GetVoiceSpecBasedOnGender() routine listed below. When passed a pointer to a VoiceSpec and a gender value, the function loops until it finds a voice of the specified gender. When it does, the loop is exited and the function returns the VoiceSpec of the voice. Notice that because the VoiceSpec is passed in as a pointer, the parameters to GetIndVoice() change from:

```
theError = GetIndVoice( theIndex, &theVoiceSpec );
```

to the following:

```
theError = GetIndVoice( theIndex, theVoiceSpec );
```

The same applies to the first parameter to GetVoiceDescription(). If the function cycles through all of the voices that are available on the user's Mac, and a match is never found, the function returns a value of kNoMatchingVoiceErr. This is an application-defined constant that tells the caller that no matching voice was found. It is then up to the caller to determine how to proceed.

```
#define       kNoMatchingVoiceErr       -999

OSErr  GetVoiceSpecBasedOnGender( VoiceSpec *theVoiceSpec,
                                  short       theGender )
{
    OSErr              theError;
    short              theNumVoices;
    short              theIndex;
    VoiceDescription   theVoiceDesc;

    theError = CountVoices( &theNumVoices );
    if ( theError != noErr )
        return ( theError );

    for ( theIndex = 1; theIndex <= theNumVoices; theIndex++ )
    {
        theError = GetIndVoice( theIndex, theVoiceSpec );
        if ( theError != noErr )
            return ( theError );

        theError = GetVoiceDescription( theVoiceSpec, &theVoiceDesc,
                                        sizeof( theVoiceDesc ) );
        if ( theError != noErr )
            return ( theError );

        if ( theVoiceDesc.gender == theGender )
            return ( noErr );
    }
    return ( kNoMatchingVoiceErr );
}
```

The following indicates how an application would call `GetVoiceSpec-BasedOnGender()` to obtain a `VoiceSpec` for a robotic voice:

```
OSErr      theError;
short      theGender;
VoiceSpec  theVoiceSpec;

theGender = kNeuter;
theError = GetVoiceSpecBasedOnGender( &theVoiceSpec, theGender );
```

Once a `VoiceSpec` is obtained, it can be used in a call to `NewSpeechChannel()` to open a speech channel:

```
theError = NewSpeechChannel( &theVoiceSpec, &theChannel );
```

After the channel is open, text generated from it will use the robotic voice. Calls to SpeakText(), SpeechBusy(), and DisposeSpeechChannel() follow the opening of the new speech channel:

```
theError = SpeakText( theChannel, (Ptr)(theString + 1),
                      theString[0] );
while ( SpeechBusy() == true )
   ;
theError = DisposeSpeechChannel( theChannel );
```

If your application will use voices, you'll want to replace the application-defined function OpenOneSpeechChannel() with a routine that includes a VoiceSpec as a parameter. Then, rather than opening the speech channel with a first parameter of nil, use the passed VoiceSpec:

```
SpeechChannel  OpenOneSpeechChannelVoice( VoiceSpec theVoiceSpec )
{
   SpeechChannel  theChannel;
   OSErr          theError;
   theError = NewSpeechChannel( &theVoiceSpec, &theChannel );
   if ( theError != noErr )
   {
      theError = DisposeSpeechChannel( theChannel );
      theChannel = nil;
   }
   return ( theChannel );
}
```

Chapter Example: ChangeVoice

The ChangeVoice program opens a dialog box like the one shown in Figure 4.11. This dialog box allows the user to set the voice to that of a young boy, a woman, a robot, or the system-default voice. After setting the voice, a click on the **Play Speech** button results in a spoken sentence using the selected voice. ChangeVoice speaks the same sentence regardless of the voice selected.

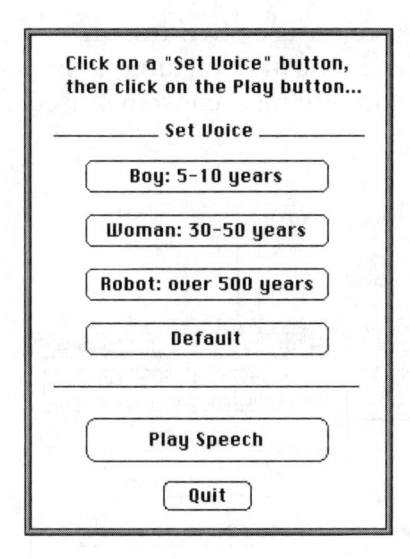

FIGURE **4.11** The dialog box displayed by the ChangeVoice program.

ChangeVoice relies on an application-defined function named `Get-VoiceSpecBasedOnAgeGender()`. This routine is very similar to the `GetVoiceSpecBasedOnAgeGender()` function developed a couple of pages back. The difference between the two functions is that the new routine looks for a voice that meets two requirements rather than one—the new function loops until a voice of the specified gender and specified age range is found. The following snippet executes in response to a click on the **Boy: 5–10 years** button.

```
OSErr       theError;
short       theAgeLo;
short       theAgeHi;
short       theGender;
VoiceSpec   theVoiceSpec;
theGender = kMale;
theAgeLo  =  5;
theAgeHi  = 10;
theError = GetVoiceSpecBasedOnAgeGender( &theVoiceSpec, theAgeLo,
                                 theAgeHi, theGender );
```

The ChangeVoice project uses two resources: a DLOG and a DITL. The dialog items are shown in the DITL pictured in Figure 4.12. Following the figure are the application-defined constants used to represent the DITL and its items.

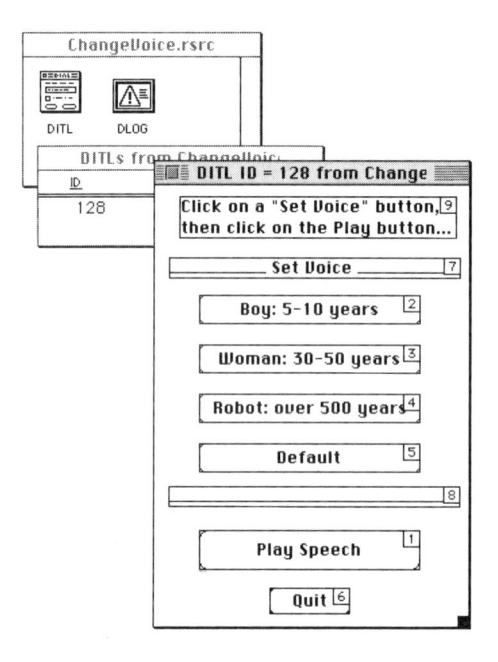

FIGURE 4.12 The DITL resource used by the ChangeVoice program.

```
#define        rSpeechDialog                    128
#define        kPlaySpeechButton                  1
#define        kSetSpeechYoungBoyButton           2
#define        kSetSpeechMiddleAgeWomanButton     3
#define        kSetSpeechRobotButton              4
#define        kSetSpeechDefaultButton            5
#define        kQuitButton                        6
```

One point of interest in the code is the manner in which the program gets a VoiceSpec for the system-default voice:

```
OSErr          theError;
VoiceSpec      theDefaultVoiceSpec;
```

```
VoiceDescription  theVoiceDesc;

theError = GetVoiceDescription( nil, &theVoiceDesc,
                                sizeof( theVoiceDesc ) );

theDefaultVoiceSpec = theVoiceDesc.voice;
```

The GetVoiceDescription() function is usually called with a VoiceSpec as the first parameter. If, instead, a value of nil is passed, a VoiceDescription for the system-default voice will be returned. So far, you've seen the gender and age fields of this structure. Among the many other fields in this structure is the voice field. This field is a VoiceSpec structure for the voice being described. By assigning the voice field to a VoiceSpec variable, the program can at any time speak text in the system-default voice by opening a new speech channel with theDefaultVoiceSpec as the first parameter to a call to OpenSpeechChannel().

```
//_____

void            InitializeToolbox( void );
Boolean         IsSpeechAvailable( void );
SpeechChannel   OpenOneSpeechChannelVoice( VoiceSpec );
void            OpenSpeechDialog( void );
OSErr           GetVoiceSpecBasedOnAgeGender( VoiceSpec *, short,
                                              short, short );

//_____

#define         rSpeechDialog                    128
#define         kPlaySpeechButton                  1
#define         kSetSpeechYoungBoyButton           2
#define         kSetSpeechMiddleAgeWomanButton     3
#define         kSetSpeechRobotButton              4
#define         kSetSpeechDefaultButton            5
#define         kQuitButton                        6
#define         kNoMatchingVoiceErr             -999

//_____

void  main( void )
{
    Boolean  speechPresent;
    InitializeToolbox();
    speechPresent = IsSpeechAvailable();
    if ( speechPresent == false )
```

```
      ExitToShell();
   OpenSpeechDialog();
}

//_____

void  OpenSpeechDialog( void )
{
   DialogPtr          theDialog;
   short              theItem;
   Boolean            allDone = false;
   OSErr              theError;
   SpeechChannel      theChannel;
   Str255             theString = "\pMilwaukee, that's in
   Minnesota right?";
   short              theAgeLo;
   short              theAgeHi;
   short              theGender;
   VoiceSpec          theDefaultVoiceSpec;
   VoiceSpec          theVoiceSpec;
   VoiceDescription   theVoiceDesc;

   theDialog = GetNewDialog( rSpeechDialog, nil, (WindowPtr)-1L );
   ShowWindow( theDialog );
   SetPort( theDialog );

   theError = GetVoiceDescription( nil, &theVoiceDesc,
                                   sizeof( theVoiceDesc ) );

   theDefaultVoiceSpec = theVoiceDesc.voice;
   theVoiceSpec = theDefaultVoiceSpec;
   while ( allDone == false )
   {
      ModalDialog( nil, &theItem );

      switch ( theItem )
      {
         case kSetSpeechYoungBoyButton:
            theGender = kMale;
            theAgeLo  =  5;
            theAgeHi  = 10;
            theError = GetVoiceSpecBasedOnAgeGender( &theVoiceSpec,
                                                     theAgeLo,
                                                     theAgeHi,
                                                     theGender );

            break;
```

```c
        case kSetSpeechMiddleAgeWomanButton:
            theGender = kFemale;
            theAgeLo  = 30;
            theAgeHi  = 50;
            theError = GetVoiceSpecBasedOnAgeGender( &theVoiceSpec,
                                                     theAgeLo,
                                                     theAgeHi,
                                                     theGender );
            break;

        case kSetSpeechRobotButton:
            theGender = kNeuter;
            theAgeLo  =   500;
            theAgeHi  = 10000;
            theError = GetVoiceSpecBasedOnAgeGender( &theVoiceSpec,
                                                     theAgeLo,
                                                     theAgeHi,
                                                     theGender );
            break;

        case kSetSpeechDefaultButton:
            theVoiceSpec = theDefaultVoiceSpec;
            break;

        case kPlaySpeechButton:
            theChannel = OpenOneSpeechChannelVoice( theVoiceSpec );
            if ( theChannel == nil )
                ExitToShell();
            theError = SpeakText( theChannel, (Ptr)(theString + 1),
                                  theString[0] );
            while ( SpeechBusy() == true )
                ;
            theError = DisposeSpeechChannel( theChannel );
            if ( theError != noErr )
                ExitToShell();
            break;

    case kQuitButton:
        allDone = true;
        break;
}
if ( theError == kNoMatchingVoiceErr )
{
    SysBeep( 0 );
    theVoiceSpec = theDefaultVoiceSpec;
}
```

```
      else if ( theError != noErr )
         ExitToShell();
   }
   DisposeDialog( theDialog );
}

//_____

OSErr  GetVoiceSpecBasedOnAgeGender( VoiceSpec *theVoiceSpec,
                                     short      theAgeLo,
                                     short      theAgeHi,
                                     short      theGender )
{
   OSErr               theError;
   short               theNumVoices;
   short               theIndex;
   VoiceDescription    theVoiceDesc;

   theError = CountVoices( &theNumVoices );
   if ( theError != noErr )
      return ( theError );

   for ( theIndex = 1; theIndex <= theNumVoices; theIndex++ )
   {
      theError = GetIndVoice( theIndex, theVoiceSpec );
      if ( theError != noErr )
         return ( theError );
      theError = GetVoiceDescription( theVoiceSpec, &theVoiceDesc,
                                      sizeof( theVoiceDesc ) );
      if ( theError != noErr )
         return ( theError );

      if ( (theVoiceDesc.age >= theAgeLo) &&
           (theVoiceDesc.age <= theAgeHi) )
         if ( theVoiceDesc.gender == theGender )
            return ( noErr );
   }
   return ( kNoMatchingVoiceErr );
}

//_____

SpeechChannel  OpenOneSpeechChannelVoice( VoiceSpec theVoiceSpec
   )
{
   SpeechChannel  theChannel;
```

```
OSErr           theError;
theError = NewSpeechChannel( &theVoiceSpec, &theChannel );
if ( theError != noErr )
{
   theError = DisposeSpeechChannel( theChannel );
   theChannel = nil;
}
return ( theChannel );
}
```

Summary

The Speech Manager is a system software extension that, with the aid of speech synthesizers and the Sound Manager, converts text into speech. Speech Manager functions, such as `SpeakString()` and `SpeakText()`, allow your program to generate speech from any string.

To generate speech using the system-default voice, just call `SpeakString()` with a string as the lone parameter. To generate speech using other voices—a man, a woman, a child, or a robot—call `SpeakText()` instead. `SpeakText()` requires that your application first create a sound channel from which the speech will be played.

CHAPTER 5

Animation

Everybody wants to do animation. It's the first thing a new programmer wants to do after figuring out how to write "Hello World" to a window, and it's what a number-crunching engineer wants to do for fun. Animation is easy—if you're content with the annoying flicker that accompanies the animated objects produced by repeatedly drawing a picture to a window. If you want slick, smooth, flicker-free animation, a little extra work is in order.

The extra work involved in generating professional-looking animated effects comes from gaining an understanding of a single Toolbox function—CopyBits(). In this chapter you'll see how to use this powerful function in conjunction with offscreen bitmaps and offscreen graphics worlds to create both black-and-white and color animation. You'll find out how CopyBits() is used to move an object across any background—without obscuring that background, and without the noticeable screen flicker seen in some programs.

If you're interested in programming games, this chapter and Chapter 2 will help you reach that goal. If you combine the color animation techniques found in this chapter with the sound-playing techniques provided in Chapter 2, you'll be well on your way to writing the next great Macintosh game.

Monochrome Animation and CopyBits()

Understanding the Toolbox function CopyBits() is a must for any programmer interested in producing smooth animation. As its name implies, CopyBits() copies a bit image—a collection of bits—from one location to another. In this section CopyBits() will be used on monochrome images. Later, this same function will be used to generate color animation.

Bit Images and BitMaps

A graphical image can be thought of as having two representations. The first, and most obvious, is the screen representation—the image as it appears visually. The second is its representation in memory. For monochrome images, each screen pixel that makes up an image on the screen has a corresponding bit in memory used to keep track of the state of the pixel. If an image pixel appears black, its corresponding bit in memory has a value of 1, or "on." If an image pixel appears white, its corresponding memory bit has a value of 0, or "off."

The above discussion implies that a pixel is not the same as a bit. That's true. In discussions that deal less specifically with graphical images, though, you may see the words interchanged.

NOTE

To form a graphical image, bits are grouped together in a data structure known as a BitMap—represented by the BitMap data structure:

```
struct  BitMap
{
   Ptr     baseAddr;
   short   rowBytes;
   Rect    bounds;
};
```

While graphical images vary in size, each `BitMap` data structure is always the same size. That's possible because the `BitMap` data type doesn't actually hold the `BitMap` bit information. Instead, this data resides elsewhere in memory. The first field of a `BitMap` (the `baseAddr` field) is a pointer to the first byte of this data.

The second field of a `BitMap` specifies how many bytes appear in a single row of the graphical image. For alignment purposes, all images are held in rows that have a byte length divisible by 2. Consider the bit image shown in Figure 5.1. The letter "T" that this image forms is seven bits across at its widest point. Yet the bit image is 16 bits, or two bytes, across. Whether this image had a width of 1 bit, 16 bits, or any value in between, it would occupy two bytes across. For the example shown in Figure 5.1, the `rowBytes` field of the `BitMap` data structure representing this image would have a value of 2, for two bytes across.

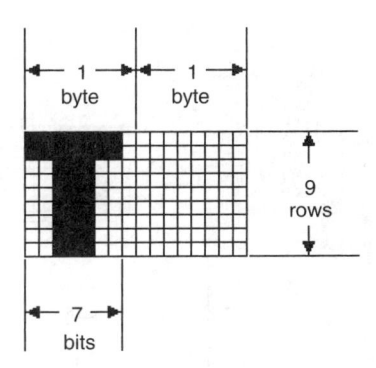

FIGURE **5.1** The `BitMap` data structure keeps track of
the number of bytes in a bit image.

The third field of the `BitMap` is a rectangle that specifies the boundaries of the image. This rectangle encompasses the image without taking into consideration any byte padding. Again referring to Figure 5.1, the image would have a bounding rectangle seven pixels across and nine pixels vertically. The values that make up the bounding rectangle may or may not be normalized (use the point (0, 0) as a reference point). Thus for the image in Figure 5.1, the bounding rectangle could have coordinates such as the following:

```
bounds.left      30
bounds.right     37
bounds.top       50
bounds.bottom    59
```

By keeping track of the number of bytes in a row and the coordinates of an image, the size in bytes of an image can be determined. Using the following equation makes the image in Figure 5.1 occupy 18 bytes.

```
image byte size = rowBytes * ( bounds.bottom - bounds.top )
```

In C, a `BitMap` is referenced using a pointer. In Figure 5.2, you can see that a pointer to a `BitMap` is used to access a `BitMap` data structure. The `BitMap` data structure in turn references the `BitMap` data in another part of memory. Figure 5.2 shows the bit values in the bit image memory, along with the image that those bit values would form.

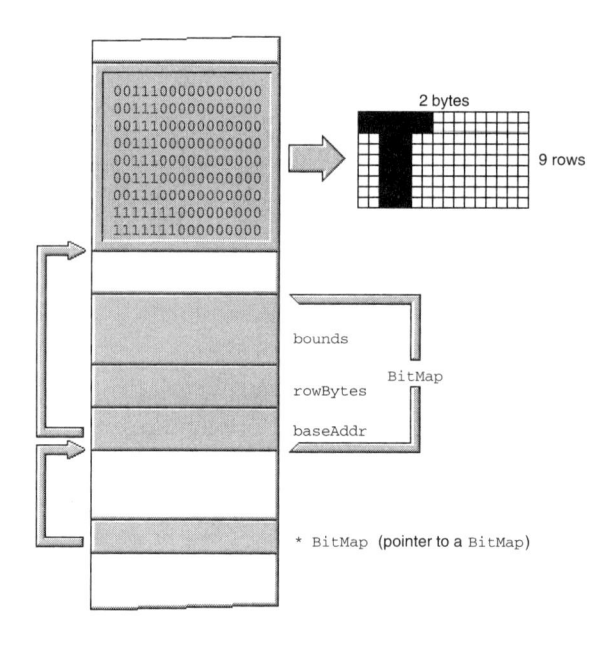

FIGURE 5.2 The `baseAddr` field of a `BitMap`
points to the actual bit image in memory.

The individual bits that make up the bit image appear to form an upside-down "T" in Figure 5.2. As you look at this figure (and all others in this book), keep the Macintosh memory-addressing convention in mind: smaller, or lower, addresses are shown at the bottom of a figure. That's why a figure shows a pointer pointing to what appears to be the bottom of an object in memory. This "bottom" is actually the start of the object.

Once again, it is important to remember the distinction between bits and pixels. An image that exists in a BitMap structure exists as bit values in memory—it doesn't appear in a window. A program can have several images stored in BitMaps, and each of these images will be invisible to the user. Not until an image is drawn to a window's port does it become visible.

You've just seen that a BitMap holds a graphic image. But how does this "invisible" BitMap image contribute to animation? The answer lies in the number of BitMaps used to create an animated effect. Offscreen animation works in the following way. Your program will allocate memory for three BitMaps. A window will be opened, which will add a fourth BitMap. As you'll see on the next pages, a window always has its own BitMap. To draw a single frame from an animated sequence, your program will make use of each of these four BitMaps. One BitMap will be used to hold a background picture, a second will be used to hold a foreground picture, and a third will be used as a mixture BitMap—it will hold a BitMap that is the combined image of the foreground BitMap overlaid upon the background BitMap. It is this mixture BitMap that will be copied to the final BitMap—the one that holds the contents of the open window. Figure 5.3 illustrates.

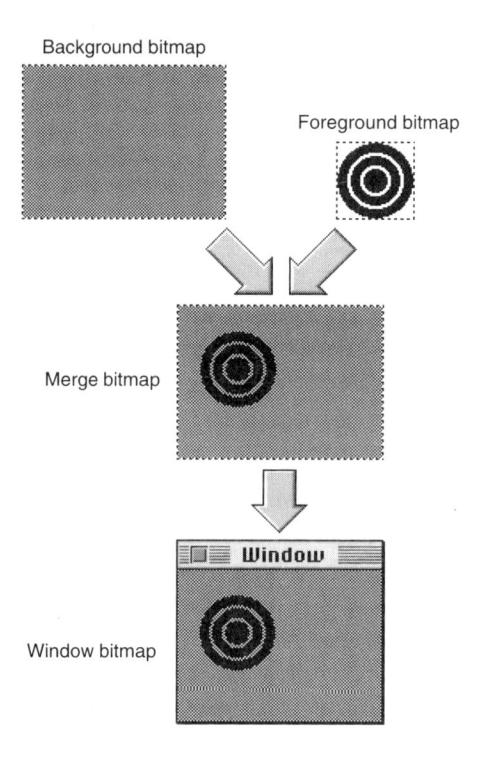

FIGURE 5.3 Smooth animation is produced by combining a foreground with a background offscreen.

Because `BitMap` images are simply bits in memory, the blending of the `BitMaps` is invisible to the user—it takes place "behind the scene." To create animation, the coordinates of the foreground `BitMap` are slightly moved, the foreground and background `BitMaps` are again combined to form the merge `BitMap`, and this new merge `BitMap` is again copied to the window. The result? The flicker that is apparent with other types of animation doesn't exist. That's because the mixing of the `BitMaps` takes place in memory—not in the window.

BitMaps, Graphics Ports, and Windows

When you create a new window, whether by a call to `GetNewWindow()` or `NewWindow()`, the Window Manager allocates memory for a `WindowRecord` data structure and returns a `WindowPtr` to your program. A `WindowPtr` is a pointer to the first field in that structure—the `port` field. A `WindowRecord` is a data structure consisting of several fields that hold descriptive information about a window. The first field, the `port` field, is of type `GrafPort`. Figure 5.4 shows a `WindowRecord` in memory.

 To emphasize the topic being discussed, only select fields of the `WindowRecord` data structure will be shown—and these fields will not be to scale with the entire `WindowRecord` structure. This applies to other data structures pictured

N O T E   in figures as well.

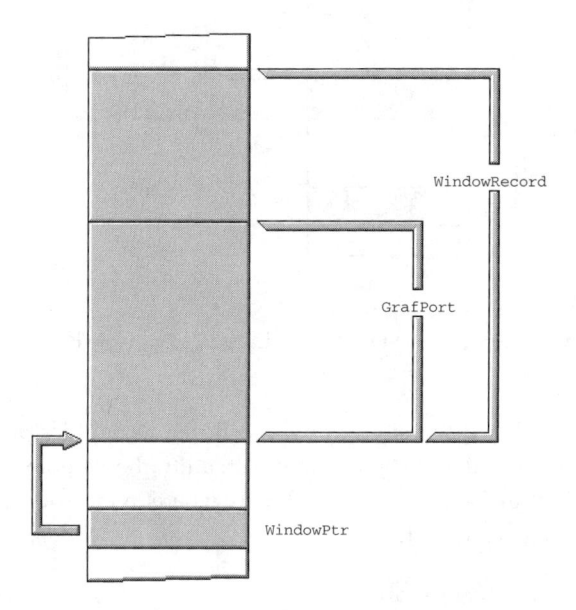

FIGURE 5.4 A `WindowPtr` points to the first field in a `WindowRecord`—a field of type `GrafPort`.

A `GrafPort` is a data structure that consists of several fields. The second field in a `GrafPort` is the `portBits` field, which is of type `BitMap`. The `GrafPort` of a `WindowRecord` holds information about the drawing environment of the window (such as the font that text will be displayed in), while the `BitMap` of a `WindowRecord` holds the bit image representing the contents of the window. Figure 5.5 shows the `BitMap` and `GrafPort` of a `WindowRecord`.

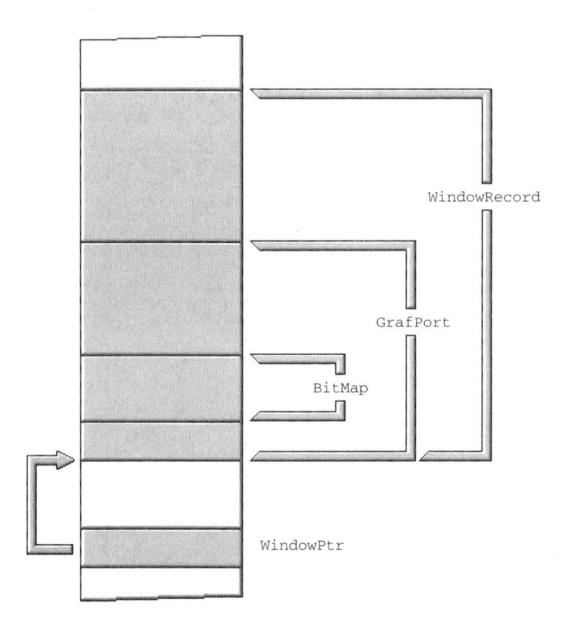

FIGURE 5.5 A `GrafPort` contains a field of type `BitMap`.

 From earlier discussions you'll recall that a graphics port's `BitMap` field doesn't hold the `BitMap` image itself, but rather, a pointer to the bit image that is elsewhere in memory. Exactly where in memory the bit image ends up is of no concern to you.

N O T E

BitMaps and Graphics Ports Without Windows

The preceding text and figures have shown that both a `BitMap` and a graphics port are a part of a window—they're fields of a `WindowRecord` data structure. But each can also exist on its own. That is, you can allocate memory for a BitMap or GrafPort without creating a new window. This is exactly what you'll do when performing offscreen animation. Figure 5.6 shows a section of memory after a GrafPtr variable has been declared and set to point at memory allocated for a GrafPort. As shown in the figure, this new graphics port will be used to hold an image that will serve as a background over which animation will take place.

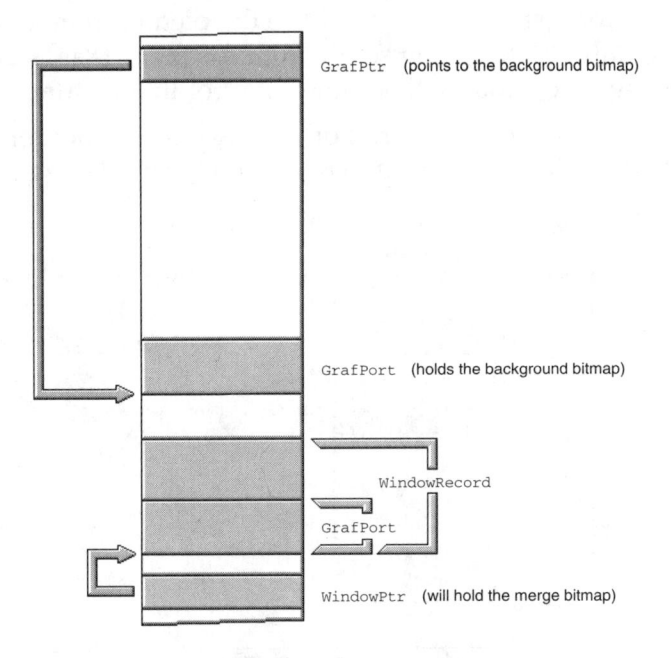

FIGURE 5.6 A GrafPtr variable is used to access a GrafPort drawing environment.

Figure 5.6 shows what memory might look like for a program that opens a window (pointed to by a WindowPtr variable) and also creates an additional graphics port (pointed to by a GrafPtr variable). In the figure, the graphics port that isn't a part of the WindowRecord is assumed to hold a BitMap that will be used to hold the background of the offscreen drawing. This graphics port is pointed to by a GrafPtr variable.

Both the `BitMap` data type and the `GrafPort` data type will be of interest to you when performing offscreen animation. As mentioned, you'll use four bitmaps (each represented by a `BitMap` data structure) when performing animation. Rather than just allocating `BitMap` data structures, you'll instead allocate `GrafPort` data structures. A `GrafPort` includes a `BitMap` as one of its fields—and it has the additional benefit of keeping track of the drawing environment for that `BitMap` structure. That means, for instance, you could use the picture from a `PICT` resource as a background `BitMap`, then set the font for the `BitMap`'s `GrafPort` and draw a string of text that will become a part of that picture.

Figure 5.7 shows this same area of memory after another `GrafPort` is allocated. This one will be used to hold a foreground image.

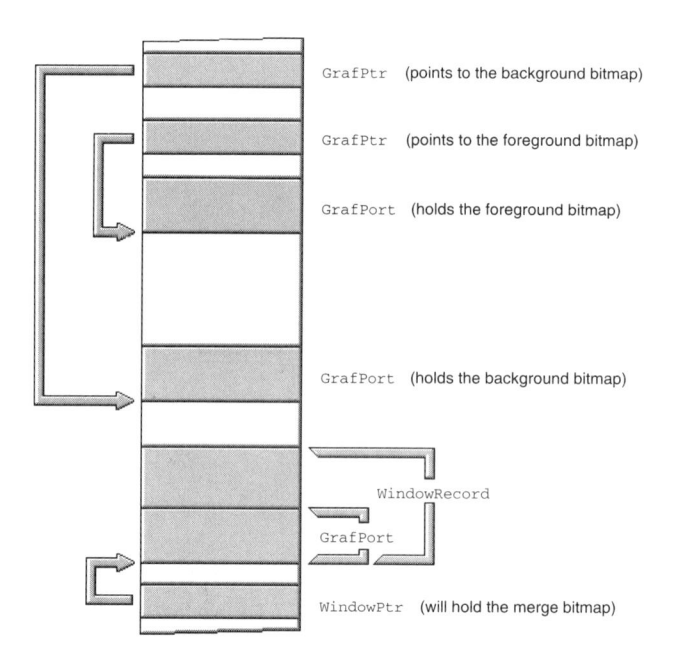

FIGURE 5.7 An application can create more than one `GrafPort`.

Figure 5.8 shows memory after another graphics port is allocated. The BitMap associated with this graphics port will be used to hold the result of combining two bitmaps.

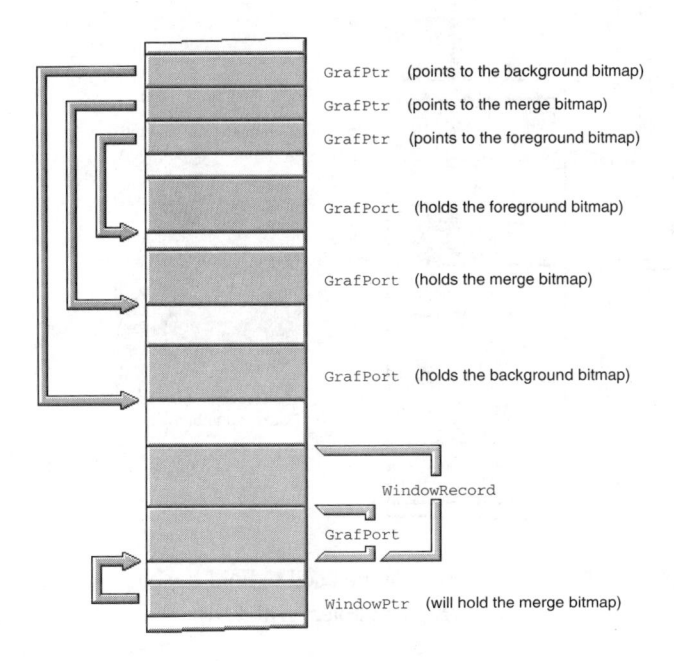

GrafPtr   (points to the background bitmap)

GrafPtr   (points to the merge bitmap)

GrafPtr   (points to the foreground bitmap)

GrafPort   (holds the foreground bitmap)

GrafPort   (holds the merge bitmap)

GrafPort   (holds the background bitmap)

WindowRecord

GrafPort

WindowPtr   (will hold the merge bitmap)

FIGURE 5.8 For animation, three GrafPorts—
and three GrafPtr pointers—will be used.

Allocating a GrafPort, and the BitMap that accompanies it, reserves memory for these data structures—but doesn't place any image in the area of memory reserved for the BitMap. To do that, you'll make the new GrafPort the active port and draw to it. In Figure 5.9, the graphics port used to hold a background has been drawn to. In this example assume that a picture of a gray rectangle was loaded from a PICT resource and drawn to the graphics port.

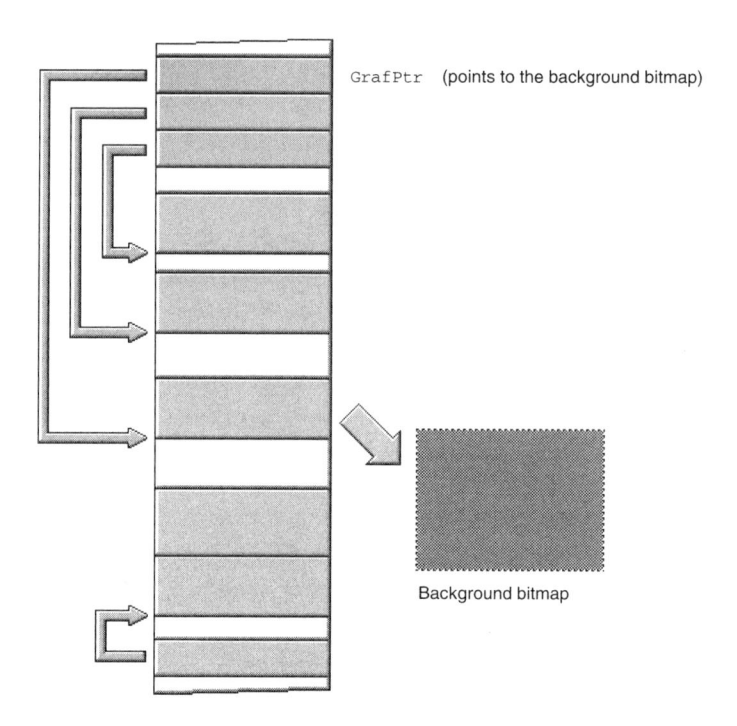

GrafPtr (points to the background bitmap)

Background bitmap

FIGURE 5.9 A GrafPort can be used to hold the background over which an object will move.

Next, the graphics port that will be used to hold the image resulting from the merging of a background image and a foreground image is sized to match the background BitMap. Nothing is drawn to this BitMap at this time. Then the graphics port that is used to hold a foreground image is drawn to. Figure 5.10 illustrates.

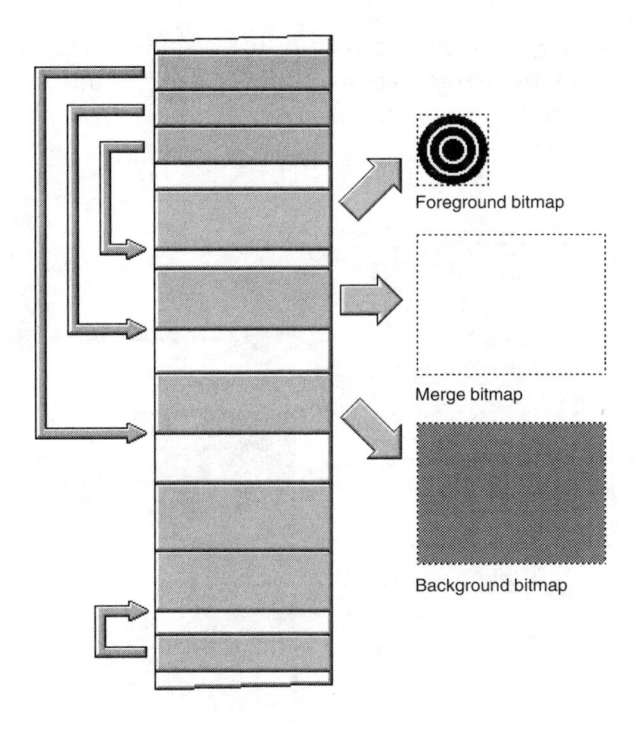

FIGURE 5.10 Three offscreen graphics ports are used to hold a foreground, background, and combined image.

Each `GrafPtr` in Figure 5.10 leads to a `GrafPort`. Each `GrafPort` has a field that is a `BitMap`. Each `BitMap` has a `baseAddr` field that points to an area in memory that holds the actual bit image.

N O T E

To create a single scene, or frame, for animation, the background BitMap is copied to the merge BitMap. Then the foreground BitMap is copied to that same merge BitMap—directly over the background. The result is shown in Figure 5.11.

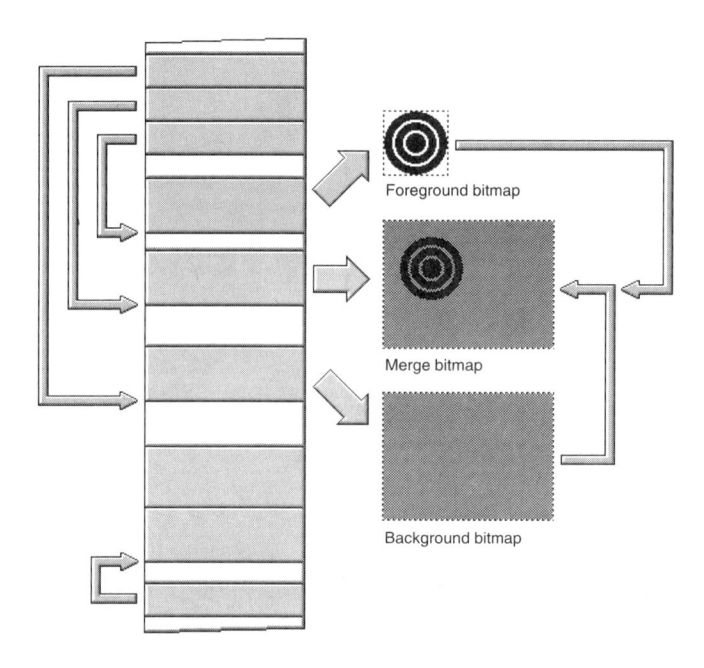

Foreground bitmap

Merge bitmap

Background bitmap

FIGURE 5.11 The merge BitMap is created by copying a background BitMap and a foreground BitMap to a single graphics port.

Now, with the combining of the background and foreground taken care of—and taken care of in memory rather than in a window—the completed scene is copied to the BitMap that holds the contents of the window. Figure 5.12 illustrates.

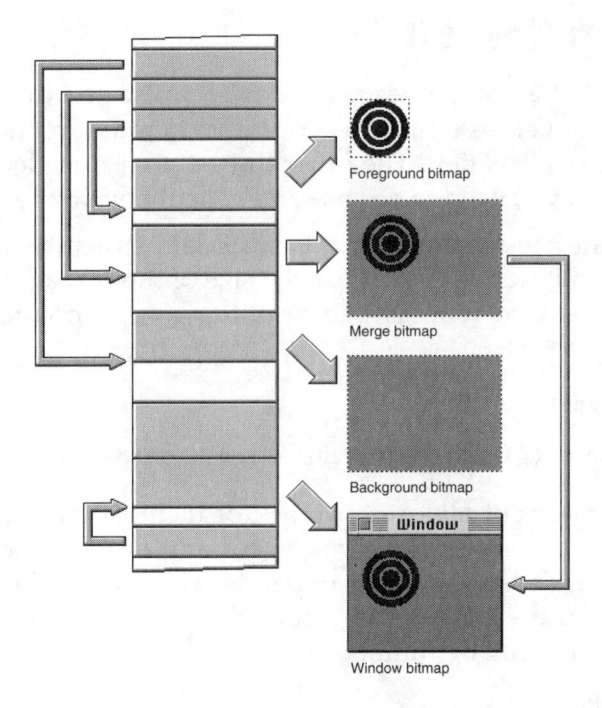

FIGURE 5.12 The combined BitMap is copied to a window.

The preceding steps show how a single frame appears in a window—but how does this lead to animation? The copying of the background and foreground to the merge BitMap, and then the copying of the merge BitMap to the window, take place within a loop. After the merge BitMap is copied to the window BitMap, the coordinates of the foreground BitMap get changed slightly. Then the merging of the BitMaps, and the blasting of this merged BitMap to the window, are repeated. The result is that the image appears to have moved slightly. And, best of all, no noticeable flicker has taken place.

Creating a New BitMap

The `BitMap` that accompanies a window gets created during the call to `NewWindow()` or `GetNewWindow()`—your program doesn't need to be concerned with its allocation. The other three `BitMaps` needed for offscreen drawing, however, need to be created explicitly by your application.

To allocate the memory for a `BitMap` data structure, make a call to the Toolbox routine `NewPtr()`. Pass the size of the `BitMap` structure as the only parameter, and typecast the resulting generic pointer to a pointer that points to a `BitMap`:

```
BitMap   *theBitMapPtr;

theBitMapPtr = (BitMap *)NewPtr( sizeof( BitMap ) );
```

The above statement allocates a block of memory the size of a `BitMap` structure, but doesn't provide values for any of the three fields of this data structure. Those values are dependent on the graphic image that is to be stored in the `BitMap`. As a refresher, here's another look at the `BitMap` data structure definition:

```
struct  BitMap
{
   Ptr     baseAddr;
   short   rowBytes;
   Rect    bounds;
};
```

Begin by getting the bounding rectangle of the image that is to be stored in the new `BitMap`. For instance, if the image is saved as a `PICT` resource, load the `PICT` and find its framing rectangle from the `picFrame` field of the `Picture` structure that defines the picture. You can call the Toolbox routine `OffsetRect()` to ensure that the rectangle has a left coordinate of 0 and a top coordinate of 0—as done in this snippet:

```
PicHandle   thePicture;
Rect        theRect;

thePicture = GetPicture( 128 );

theRect = (**thePicture).picFrame;
OffsetRect( &theRect, - theRect.left, - theRect.top );
```

The `bounds` field of a `BitMap` holds the bounding rectangle of the image. Use the `BitMap` pointer to access the `bounds` field, and set it to the bounding rectangle for the picture that is to be stored:

```
theBitMapPtr->bounds = theRect;
```

Determining the value that is to be stored in the `rowBytes` field requires a little work. You can get the number of bits in a row by simply looking at the width the picture's bounding rectangle:

```
theRect.right - theRect.left
```

Unfortunately, the `rowBytes` field is a byte value, not a bit value. And there is the byte padding to consider—`rowBytes` is always a multiple of two bytes. You can be assured that the image's `rowBytes` value includes the necessary padding, as follows. Begin by taking the bounding rectangle width and adding 7 to it, then divide by 8. This returns the number of bytes needed, without concern for padding. Adding 7 forces the division to return the correct byte value. For instance, if an image is 10 pixels wide, dividing by 8 would yield a byte value of 1 (the remainder gets *truncated*, or dropped). By adding 7, the 10 pixel width becomes 17, and division by 8 gives a 2-byte row value—as desired.

```
BitMap    *theBitMapPtr;
Rect        theRect;

theBitMapPtr->rowBytes = (theRect.right - theRect.left + 7) / 8;
```

Now it's time to consider the padding. To do this, divide the `rowBytes` value by 2 and examine the remainder (use the C modulus operator, %, to return the remainder of an integer division). If `rowBytes` isn't an even value, increment it by 1 so that it is even:

```
if ( ( theBitMapPtr->rowBytes % 2 ) != 0 )
   theBitMapPtr->rowBytes++;
```

The following snippet shows how `rowBytes` can be calculated:

```
BitMap    *theBitMapPtr;
Rect        theRect;
short       theTest;
```

```
theBitMapPtr->rowBytes = (theRect.right - theRect.left + 7) / 8;
theTest = theBitMapPtr->rowBytes / 2;
if ( ( 2 * theTest ) != theBitMapPtr->rowBytes )
   theBitMapPtr->rowBytes++;
```

The last `BitMap` field to fill is the `baseAddr` field—the address at which the bit image will be stored. When memory is allocated for a `BitMap` structure, the memory for the `BitMap` itself isn't allocated. To do that, you'll need the byte size of the image. The `rowBytes` field tells how many bytes across the image is. This value multiplied by the bit height of the image gives the image size in bytes. For an example, refer back to Figure 5.1. Use the following code to verify that the graphic image in that figure requires an 18-byte bitmap.

```
short   theImageHeight;
short   theImageByteSize;

theImageHeight = theRect.bottom - theRect.top;
theImageByteSize = theBitMapPtr->rowBytes * theImageHeight;
```

With the size of the image calculated, allocate memory for the bitmap.

```
theBitMapPtr->baseAddr = NewPtr( theImageByteSize );
```

Rather than using the `BitMap` directly, it will be accessed through a graphics port. This allows graphics environment information to be saved along with the `BitMap` if desired. It also makes writing to the `BitMap` easy—Toolbox calls like `SetPort()` work on graphics ports. The allocation of a graphics port follows:

```
GrafPtr   theGrafPtr;

theGrafPtr = (GrafPtr)NewPtr( sizeof( GrafPort ) );
```

To initialize the fields of the new graphics port, call the Toolbox function `OpenPort()`. This call has the additional benefit of making the new graphics port the current port—something that needs to be done before a `BitMap` can be paired with the new port:

```
BitMap   *theBitMapPtr;

OpenPort( theGrafPtr );
SetPortBits( theBitMapPtr );
```

One of the fields of a graphics port is a `BitMap`. Creating a new graphics port doesn't associate the new `BitMap` that you've just created with the new graphics port. The call to the Toolbox function `SetPortBits()` does that. It matches the `BitMap` that is passed to it to whichever port is current.

At this point, the new `BitMap` is ready to be drawn to. Because you'll want to perform the above steps three times—once for each of the three offscreen `BitMaps` used in the animation—you'll want to turn the above steps into a function. The `MakeNewBitMapAndSetPort()` function accepts a pointer to a rectangle that holds the boundaries of a graphic image. The function then creates a new `BitMap`, creates a new graphics port, ties the two together, makes the graphics port current, and then returns a pointer to the new port.

 The `MakeNewBitMapAndSetPort()` function uses the coordinates of the passed-in rectangle, but doesn't make any changes to them. So the function doesn't need a pointer to the rectangle. Yet that's what gets passed to it.

N O T E Macintosh C parameter-passing conventions state that a parameter that is greater than four bytes in size should be passed by reference—that is, as a pointer. A `Rect` variable is larger than four bytes, so it should be passed as a pointer.

```
GrafPtr MakeNewBitMapAndSetPort( Rect *theRectPtr )
{
   BitMap   *theBitMapPtr;
   short    theImageHeight;
   short    theImageByteSize;
   GrafPtr  theGrafPtr;

   theBitMapPtr = (BitMap *)NewPtr( sizeof( BitMap ) );
   if ( theBitMapPtr == nil )
      ExitToShell();

   theBitMapPtr->bounds = *theRect;

   theBitMapPtr->rowBytes = (theRect->right - theRect->left + 7) / 8;
   if ( ( theBitMapPtr->rowBytes % 2 ) != 0 )
      theBitMapPtr->rowBytes++;

   theImageHeight = theRect->bottom - theRect->top;
   theImageByteSize = theBitMapPtr->rowBytes * theImageHeight;
   theBitMapPtr->baseAddr = NewPtr( theImageByteSize );
   if ( theBitMapPtr->baseAddr == nil )
      ExitToShell();
```

```
   theGrafPtr = (GrafPtr)NewPtr( sizeof( GrafPort ) );
   if ( theGrafPtr == nil )
      ExitToShell();

   OpenPort( theGrafPtr );

   SetPortBits( theBitMapPtr );

   return( theGrafPtr );
}
```

Before calling `MakeNewBitMapAndSetPort()`, obtain the bounding rectangle of the image that is to be drawn to the new `BitMap`. Then call the function. `MakeNewBitMapAndSetPort()` will return a pointer to the new graphics port that holds the new `BitMap`. `MakeNewBitMapAndSetPort()` makes this graphics port the current one, so any drawing that takes place will end up in the new `BitMap`. If you're using a picture as the graphics image, the following snippet will draw that picture to the new `BitMap`. Remember, the drawing sets bit values in memory—it doesn't affect what the user sees in any open windows.

```
GrafPtr      theBackGrafPtr;
PicHandle    theBackPicture;
Rect         theRect;

theBackPicture = GetPicture( 128 );

theRect = (**theBackPicture).picFrame;
OffsetRect( &theRect, - theRect.left, - theRect.top );

theBackGrafPtr = MakeNewBitMapAndSetPort( &theRect );
DrawPicture( theBackPicture, &theRect );
```

Copying a BitMap

After using a function like `MakeNewBitMapAndSetPort` to create three `BitMaps`—one for the foreground image, one for the background image, and one to hold the combination of the other two—your program will need to copy images from one `BitMap` to another. As you've certainly surmised, `CopyBits()` is the Toolbox function that handles this chore.

As part of the offscreen animation process, the background `BitMap` must be copied to the merge `BitMap`. Here's the `CopyBits()` call that takes care of that task:

```
GrafPtr   theBackGrafPtr;
GrafPtr   theMergeGrafPtr;

CopyBits( &(theBackGrafPtr->portBits),
          &(theMergeGrafPtr->portBits),
          &(theBackGrafPtr->portBits.bounds),
          &(theMergeGrafPtr->portBits.bounds),
          srcCopy,
          nil );
```

At first glance, the six parameters to CopyBits() may make the function call seem a little imposing. This needn't be the case, though, as each parameter serves an easily understood purpose. Once you understand one call to CopyBits(), all others will quickly be understood. The above snippet places each parameter on a separate line so that you can quickly see where one ends and the next begins.

The first parameter is the BitMap that is to be copied—the source BitMap. The portBits field of a graphics port is a BitMap. In the above example, theBackGrafPtr is the GrafPtr returned by a call to the application-defined routine MakeNewBitMapAndSetPort(). When that function created a BitMap, it associated it with a graphics port. *Associated* means that the function set the graphics port's portBits field to this BitMap.

The second parameter to CopyBits() is the BitMap that is to be copied to—the destination BitMap. Again, the GrafPtr and BitMap used in the above snippet are the result of calling MakeNewBitMapAndSetPort().

The third parameter is the bounding rectangle of the source BitMap. Recall that the MakeNewBitMapAndSetPort() routine placed the graphic image's bounding rectangle in the bounds field of the newly created BitMap, then put that BitMap in the portBits field of the newly created graphics port. The fourth parameter is the bounding rectangle of the destination BitMap. Because the first four parameters are all greater than four bytes in size, each is passed using the & operator.

The fifth parameter to CopyBits() specifies a *copy mode*. The mode tells CopyBits() how the bits of the source image should be placed over the bits of the destination image. Using the Apple-defined constant srcCopy tells CopyBits() to stamp the source image over the destination image, obscuring anything under the source. Because the above snippet is copying the background BitMap to the destination BitMap, whatever currently lies at the destination should be covered by the background

BitMap. If `CopyBits()` is being used in an animation loop, then the merge `BitMap` will hold the most recent frame of an animation. The background `BitMap` is now used to "erase" this frame—as shown in Figure 5.13. The next step (shown in the next snippet) will be to copy the foreground `BitMap` to the merge `BitMap`.

The final parameter to `CopyBits()` is a `RgnHandle` that serves as a clipping mask. This mask will alter how the resulting image is clipped in the destination rectangle. Pass `nil` here to ignore this clipping mask.

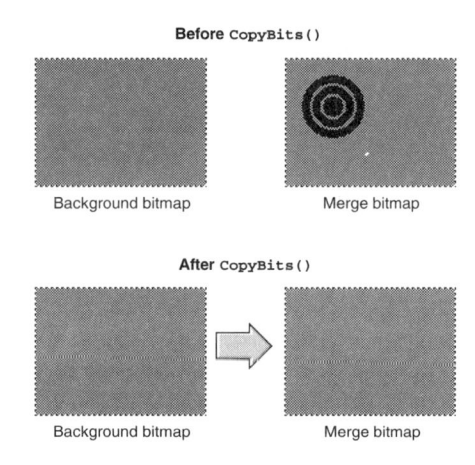

FIGURE 5.13 The background `BitMap` is being used to erase what is about to become the previous scene in an animation.

The previous snippet copied the background `BitMap` to the merge `BitMap`. The following snippet copies the foreground `BitMap` to the merge `BitMap`. Here, four of the six parameter values will change from the preceding call to `CopyBits()`.

```
GrafPtr   theForeGrafPtr;
GrafPtr   theMergeGrafPtr;
short     foreImageWidth;
short     foreImageHeight;
Rect      theRect;
```

```
SetRect( &theRect, 15, 15, 15 + foreImageWidth, 15 + foreImageHeight );

CopyBits( &(theForeGrafPtr->portBits),
          &(theMergeGrafPtr->portBits),
          &(theForeGrafPtr->portBits.bounds),
          &theRect,
          srcOr,
          nil );
```

In the above snippet, the source `BitMap` is now `theForeGrafPtr->portBits` rather than `theBackGrafPtr->portBits`. The source-bounding rectangle is now `theForeGrafPtr->portBits.bounds` rather than `theBackGrafPtr->port-Bits.bounds`. The destination rectangle is now one that defines where the foreground image should be drawn—Figure 5.14 shows two examples. In the top part of this figure, the left top corner of the foreground `BitMap` is set to appear at point (15, 15). In the bottom part of the figure, the left top corner is set to appear at point (65, 15).

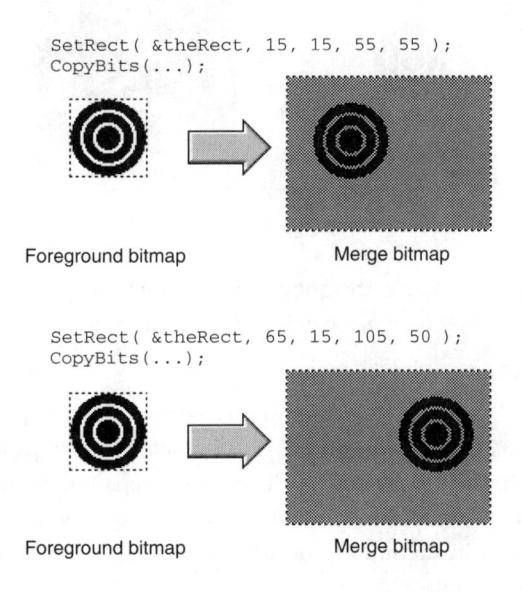

FIGURE **5.14** The destination rectangle defines where the foreground `BitMap` will be placed against the background `BitMap`.

Finally, the copy mode parameter to CopyBits() will now be srcOr rather than srcCopy. Using a mode of srcOr tells CopyBits() to copy only the black bits of the source BitMap to the destination BitMap. Where white bits appear in the source image, CopyBits() will allow destination bits to show through. Figure 5.15 illustrates.

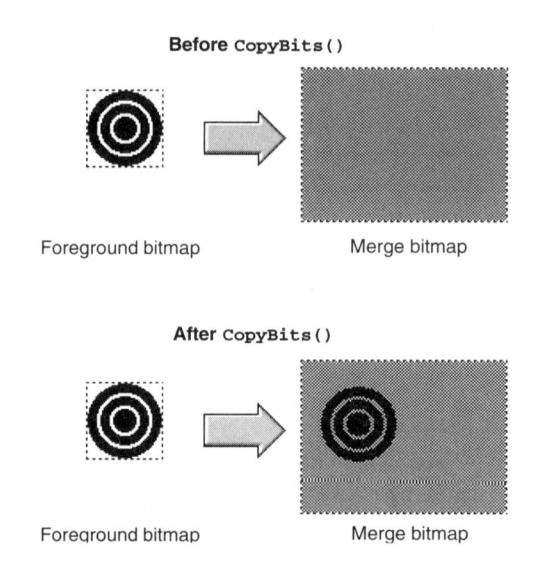

FIGURE 5.15 Using the srcOr copy mode tells CopyBits() to copy only black bits from the source BitMap.

NOTE Back in Figure 5.12 you saw the background BitMap being copied to the merge BitMap. In Figure 5.15, you see the foreground BitMap being copied to the merge BitMap. These two steps follow one another to create a single frame in an animation. Notice that if these steps took place in a window—rather than in memory—the user would see flicker as the background BitMap covered the previous frame.

After the foreground image has been added to the merge `BitMap`, the merge `BitMap` is ready for display in a window. Another call to `CopyBits()` takes care of this:

```
GrafPtr    theMergeGrafPtr;
WindowPtr  theWindow;

CopyBits( &(theMergeGrafPtr->portBits),
          &(theWindow->portBits),
          &(theMergeGrafPtr->portBits.bounds),
          &(theWindow->portRect),
          srcCopy,
          nil );
```

In this third call to `CopyBits()` the source `BitMap` is `theMergeGraf-Ptr->portBits` and the destination `BitMap` is the `BitMap` of the window that will display the animation—`theWindow->portBits`. Back in Figure 5.5, you saw that a `WindowPtr` points to the `GrafPort` field of a `WindowRecord`, and that the `GrafPort` field holds a `BitMap` field.

The source rectangle in this call to `CopyBits()` is the bounding rectangle of the merge `BitMap`: `theMergeGrafPtr->portBits.bounds`. The destination rectangle is the contents of the window—defined by the `portRect` field of the window's `GrafPort`.

The image that is in the window just before this call to `CopyBits()` is about to become the previous frame of the animation. That means that the merge `BitMap` that is now being copied to the window should obscure the contents of the window. Using the Apple-defined constant `srcCopy` does that.

Chapter Example: CopyBitsB&W

The CopyBitsB&W program demonstrates how the `CopyBits()` function can be used to create smooth, flicker-free black-and-white animation. When the program runs, the user sees a small toothbrush moving up and down over a large set of teeth. A click of the mouse button ends the program. Figure 5.16 shows how CopyBitsB&W looks when running.

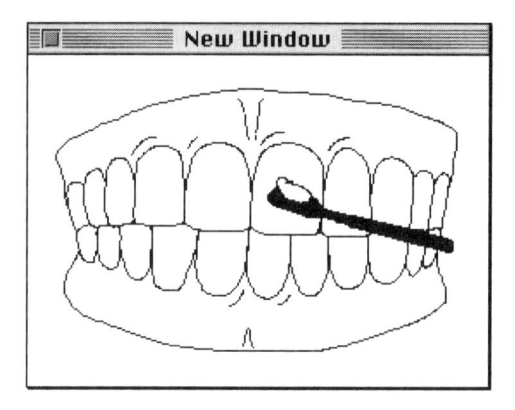

FIGURE 5.16 The CopyBitsB&W program in action.

NOTE

Dental students, dentists, and orthodontists—take note. The next edition of this book *might* use a `CopyBits()` example that also includes flossing.

Figure 5.17 shows the two `PICT` resources used in the CopyBitsB&W project. `PICT 128`, of course, serves as the background image and `PICT 129` becomes the foreground image.

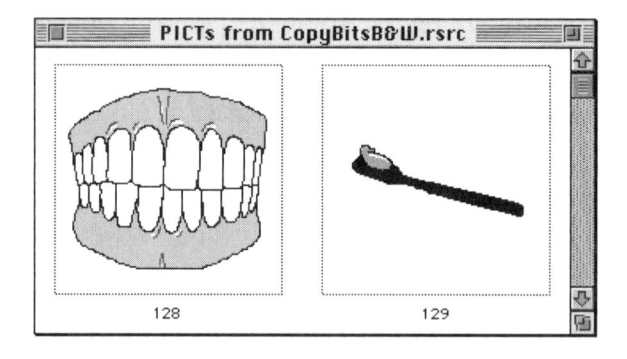

FIGURE 5.17 The two PICT resources used in the CopyBitsB&W project.

NOTE Notice that the two PICT resources are grayscale images. When you run the CopyBitsB&W program, however, the images will appear in monochrome—the gray pixels will appear white. Later in this chapter, you'll see how to use CopyBits() with images with a greater pixel depth.

CopyBitsB&W uses all of the techniques described earlier in this chapter. First, three BitMaps are created using the same application-defined MakeNewBitMapAndSetPort() routine that you saw several pages back. Each time this function is called, a new BitMap is created and a pointer to the GrafPort that holds that BitMap is returned.

Figure 5.18 shows the three BitMaps in memory. In the figure, you can see that the background and foreground BitMaps have been copied to the merge BitMap, and the merge BitMap is being copied to the window BitMap.

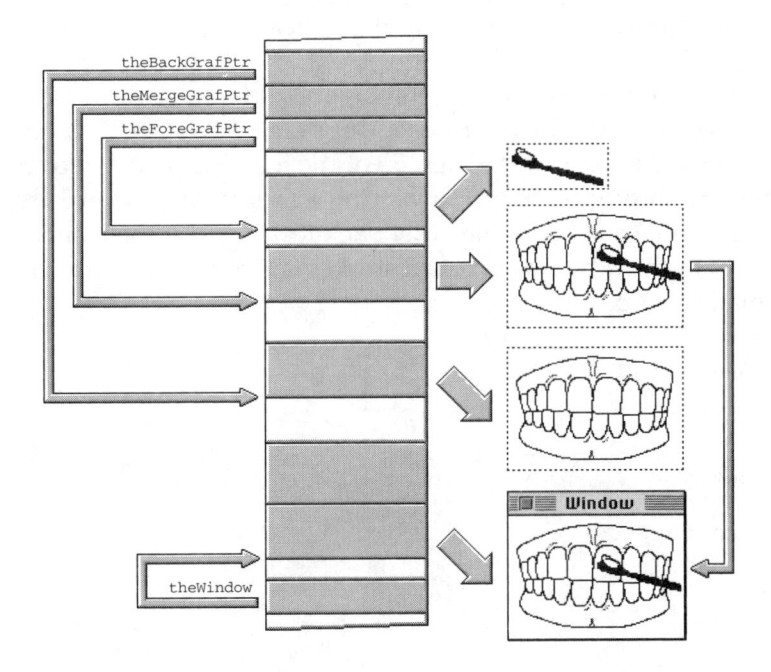

FIGURE 5.18 The CopyBitsB&W program uses three off screen BitMaps to produce flicker-free animation.

The initial placement of the toothbrush is determined just after the toothbrush PICT is loaded into memory. The bounding rectangle for the picture is found and stored in the Rect variable theRect. Those coordinates are then used to determine the picture's width and height. After that, the coordinates are changed to match the desired starting location for the brush. When the program runs, the top left corner of the brush will initially appear at point (135, 50) of the window. The code that sets up the foreground BitMap rectangle follows:

```
Rect        theRect;
short       theWidth;
short       theHeight;
short       left = 135;
short       top  = 50;

theWidth = theRect.right - theRect.left;
theHeight = theRect.bottom - theRect.top;
SetRect( &theRect, left, top, left + theWidth, top + theHeight );
```

Animation is carried out from within a while loop. A counter in the loop body ensures that the brush moves down 50 pixels, then up 50 pixels, over and over. At passes 1 through 50 of the loop, the brush moves down. At passes 51 through 100, the brush moves up. At pass 101, the cycle starts anew. The count variable is set back to 1 and the top is incremented for the start of the downward brush stroke. The following snippet outlines the animation loop.

```
short  count = 0;

while
{
   ++count;

   if ( count <= 50 )
      ++top;
   else if ( ( count > 50 ) && ( count <= 100 ) )
      —top;
   else
   {
      count = 1;
      ++top;
   }
```

```
    // copy background BitMap to merge BitMap

    SetRect( &theRect, left, top, left + theWidth, top + theHeight );

    // copy foreground BitMap to merge BitMap

    // copy merge BitMap to window BitMap
}
```

Now, the complete listing of CopyBitsB&W follows:

```
//_____

#define      rDisplayWindow          128
#define      rBackPicture            128
#define      rForePicture            129

//_____

void      InitializeToolbox( void );
GrafPtr   MakeNewBitMapAndSetPort( Rect * );

//_____

void   main( void )
{
    WindowPtr   theWindow;
    GrafPtr     theBackGrafPtr;
    GrafPtr     theForeGrafPtr;
    GrafPtr     theMergeGrafPtr;
    PicHandle   theBackPicture;
    PicHandle   theForePicture;
    Rect        theRect;
    short       theWidth;
    short       theHeight;
    short       left = 135;
    short       top  = 50;
    short       count = 0;

    InitializeToolbox();

    HideCursor();

    theBackPicture = GetPicture( rBackPicture );
    if ( theBackPicture == nil )
        ExitToShell();
```

```
theRect = (**theBackPicture).picFrame;
OffsetRect( &theRect, - theRect.left, - theRect.top );

theWidth = theRect.right - theRect.left;
theHeight = theRect.bottom - theRect.top;

theWindow = GetNewWindow( rDisplayWindow, nil, (WindowPtr)-1L );
SizeWindow( theWindow, theWidth, theHeight, true );
ShowWindow( theWindow );

theBackGrafPtr = MakeNewBitMapAndSetPort( &theRect );
DrawPicture( theBackPicture, &theRect );

theMergeGrafPtr = MakeNewBitMapAndSetPort( &theRect );

theForePicture = GetPicture( rForePicture );
if ( theBackPicture == nil )
   ExitToShell();

theRect = (**theForePicture).picFrame;

theWidth = theRect.right - theRect.left;
theHeight = theRect.bottom - theRect.top;
SetRect( &theRect, left, top, left + theWidth, top + theHeight );

theForeGrafPtr = MakeNewBitMapAndSetPort( &theRect );
DrawPicture( theForePicture, &theRect );

while ( !Button() )
{
   ++count;

   if ( count <= 50 )
      ++top;
   else if ( ( count > 50 ) && ( count <= 100 ) )
      -top;
   else
   {
      count = 1;
      ++top;
   }

   CopyBits( &(theBackGrafPtr->portBits),
             &(theMergeGrafPtr->portBits),
             &(theBackGrafPtr->portBits.bounds),
             &(theMergeGrafPtr->portBits.bounds),
             srcCopy,
```

```
                    nil );

        theRect = theForeGrafPtr->portBits.bounds;

      SetRect( &theRect, left, top, left + theWidth, top + theHeight );

        CopyBits( &(theForeGrafPtr->portBits),
                  &(theMergeGrafPtr->portBits),
                  &(theForeGrafPtr->portBits.bounds),
                  &theRect,
                  srcOr,
                  nil );

        CopyBits( &(theMergeGrafPtr->portBits),
                  &(theWindow->portBits),
                  &(theMergeGrafPtr->portBits.bounds),
                  &(theWindow->portRect),
                  srcCopy,
                  nil );
    }
}

//_____

GrafPtr MakeNewBitMapAndSetPort( Rect *theRectPtr )
{
    BitMap   *theBitMapPtr;
    short     theImageHeight;
    short     theImageByteSize;
    GrafPtr   theGrafPtr;

    theBitMapPtr = (BitMap *)NewPtr( sizeof( BitMap ) );
    if ( theBitMapPtr == nil )
        ExitToShell();

    theBitMapPtr->bounds = *theRectPtr;

    theBitMapPtr->rowBytes =
                (theRectPtr->right - theRectPtr->left + 7) / 8;
    if ( ( theBitMapPtr->rowBytes % 2 ) != 0 )
        theBitMapPtr->rowBytes++;

    theImageHeight = theRectPtr->bottom - theRectPtr->top;
    theImageByteSize = theBitMapPtr->rowBytes * theImageHeight;
    theBitMapPtr->baseAddr = NewPtr( theImageByteSize );
    if ( theBitMapPtr->baseAddr == nil )
        ExitToShell();
```

```
theGrafPtr = (GrafPtr)NewPtr( sizeof( GrafPort ) );
if ( theGrafPtr == nil )
   ExitToShell();

OpenPort( theGrafPtr );
SetPortBits( theBitMapPtr );

return( theGrafPtr );
}
```

Color Animation and GWorlds

Monochrome is boring. Color is cool. If you're like most programmers, you might have skipped the preceding section that dealt with black-and-white animation and jumped right to this section. If you did, please, go back and read it now. That section's in-depth discussion of offscreen animation, and its example program that uses CopyBits(), provides much of the background for the topics presented in the remainder of this chapter.

Color Images and PixMaps

Earlier you saw that the BitMap is used to keep track of a monochrome graphical image. A reminder of what the BitMap data structure looks like follows:

```
struct  BitMap
{
   Ptr     baseAddr;
   short   rowBytes;
   Rect    bounds;
};
```

For color images, a pixel map is used. The PixMap data structure is used to keep track of a color image. Color images require more data, and the PixMap data structure reflects that fact.

```
struct  PixMap
{
```

```
Ptr            baseAddr;
short          rowBytes;
Rect           bounds;
short          pmVersion;
short          packType;
long           packSize;
Fixed          hRes;
Fixed          vRes;
short          pixelType;
short          pixelSize;
short          cmpCount;
short          cmpSize;
long           planeBytes;
CTabHandle     pmTable;
long           pmReserved;
};
```

As you look at the PixMap definition, you'll notice that its first three fields are the same as the three fields that make up the BitMap data structure. Like the BitMap, the PixMap doesn't hold the data that makes up an image. Instead, it holds a pointer to that data, along with additional descriptive information.

Pixel Maps, Color Graphics Ports, and the GWorld

QuickDraw uses a GrafPort and a BitMap to display the black-and-white contents of window. Color QuickDraw uses a CGrafPort and a PixMap to display the color contents of a window. In your study of monochrome animation, you saw that BitMaps and GrafPorts can exist without windows—they can be created off screen. For monochrome animation, you created three offscreen GrafPorts (accessed through GrafPtr variables), each of which held a BitMap. You'll use a similar approach for color animation. Instead of creating GrafPorts, however, you'll create CGrafPorts (accessed through CGrafPtr variables), each of which will hold a pixel map.

Because color graphics ports are complex structures, Apple has defined a special environment that makes working with the CGrafPort and the PixMap easier. The *offscreen graphics world*, or GWorld, exists to simplify working with offscreen color images. The GWorld is based on the CGrafPort—the first field of a GWorld is a color graphics port. When you work with a GWorld, your program will use a `GWorldPtr`. This pointer points to the first field of the GWorld, the `CGrafPort` field.

After the color graphics port, remaining fields of the GWorld data structure are private—you won't find them listed in the universal header files. Because there is no GWorld data structure to point to, a `GWorldPtr` is defined to be a `CGrafPtr`:

```
typedef  CGrafPtr  GWorldPtr;
```

Keeping the contents of a GWorld private is all right with you, the programmer—a graphics world is supposed to provide you with a simple interface for working with offscreen color images. As such, there is no need for your program to manipulate individual GWorld fields. Toolbox routines will handle those tasks.

Checking for the Availability of GWorlds

Before using color graphics worlds, verify that the user's machine supports this feature of Color QuickDraw. As you've seen in previous chapters, calling a simple application-defined routine that returns a `Boolean` value works well. In this chapter, that function is `AreGWorlds-Available()`:

```
Boolean  graphicsWorldsPresent;

graphicsWorldsPresent = AreGWorldsAvailable();
if ( graphicsWorldsPresent == false )
   ExitToShell();
```

The `AreGWorldsAvailable()` function makes a call to `Gestalt()` with a selector code of `gestaltQuickdrawFeatures`. Like some other selector codes, the `gestaltQuickdrawFeatures` selector returns more than one piece of information in the response parameter. To extract the needed information, use the left shift operator on the `gestaltHasDeepGWorlds` bit and perform a logical AND on the shifted value and response parameter. If the bit in question—`gestaltHasDeepGWorlds` is turned on, then color graphics worlds are supported and a value of `true` should be returned to the calling routine.

```
Boolean  AreGWorldsAvailable( void )
{
   OSErr    theError;
   long     theResult;
   Boolean  worldAvail;

   theError = Gestalt( gestaltQuickdrawFeatures, &theResult );
   if ( theError != noErr )
      ExitToShell();

   worldAvail = theResult & ( 1 << gestaltHasDeepGWorlds );
   if ( worldAvail > 0 )
      return ( true );
   else
      return ( false );
}
```

Creating a GWorld and its PixMap

The Toolbox function NewGWorld() is used to create a color offscreen graphics world. Before calling NewGWorld() your program should establish the size of the pixel map that the graphics world will use to hold a pixel image. Typically, a graphics world will be the size of a picture that will be used as a moving object in an animation. The following snippet sets a global Rect variable to the size of a picture stored in a PICT resource. To ensure that the rectangle has its top left coordinate at point (0, 0), OffsetRect() is called.

```
#define        rForePicture           128

Rect        gGWorldPixMapRect;
PicHandle   theForePicture;

theForePicture = GetPicture( rForePicture );
gGWorldPixMapRect = (**theForePicture).picFrame;
OffsetRect( &gGWorldPixMapRect, - gGWorldPixMapRect.left,
            - gGWorldPixMapRect.top );
```

Next, NewGWorld() is called to create a new graphics world—as shown in this snippet:

```
GWorldPtr  gForeGWorldPtr;
```

```
theError = NewGWorld( &gForeGWorldPtr, 0, &gGWorldPixMapRect,
                      nil, nil, noNewDevice );
```

When NewGWorld() has completed execution, the first parameter will hold a pointer to a newly created graphics world. The remaining parameters supply NewGWorld() with information about some of the properties the new GWorld should be created with.

The second parameter to NewGWorld() is the pixel depth for the offscreen world. The pixel depth is the number of bits used to hold color information about a single pixel. Passing a value of 0 tells NewGWorld() to determine the pixel depth to use. If only one monitor is in use, NewGWorld() will then use the pixel depth of that monitor. If more than one monitor is in use, NewGWorld() will determine which monitor, or monitors, the rectangle used as the third parameter is found. The pixel depth of the screen with the greatest pixel depth will then be used.

The third parameter is the bounding rectangle to be used for the pixel map that is a part of the new graphics world. The fourth parameter to NewGWorld() is a handle to a color table. Passing a nil value here (and a value of 0 as the second parameter) tells NewGWorld() to use the color table of the monitor used to determine the pixel depth.

The fifth parameter specifies which graphics device should be used. Passing a value of nil here tells NewGWorld() to use the GDevice structure of the monitor used to determine the pixel depth.

The final parameter to NewGWorld() allows your program to supply optional information about the new graphics world. Passing the Appledefined constant noNewDevice tells NewGWorld() to *not* create a new GDevice structure.

When working with an offscreen graphics world, you'll often be accessing the graphics world's pixel map. Because the internals of the GWorld are private, the Toolbox provides a function that returns this pixel map to your program. That means your code won't have to worry about where in the GWorld structure the PixMap field is located. You can call the Toolbox function GetGWorldPixMap() to get a PixMapHandle to a graphics world PixMap:

```
PixMapHandle  gForePixMap;

gForePixMap = GetGWorldPixMap( gForeGWorldPtr );
```

Pass GetGWorldPixMap() a pointer to a graphics world and the function will return a handle to that graphics world's pixel map. Figure 5.19 shows what happens when GetGWorldPixMap() is called. In the figure, you can see that a GWorld contains a PixMapHandle as one of its fields. Like any handle, the PixMapHandle points to a master pointer, which in turn points to the desired structure. GetGWorldPixMap() takes care of determining where the GWorld PixMapHandle points to, and returns this value to your program. Your program can store this information in a local or global PixMapHandle variable. As your program executes, this variable should be used to access the GWorld's pixel map.

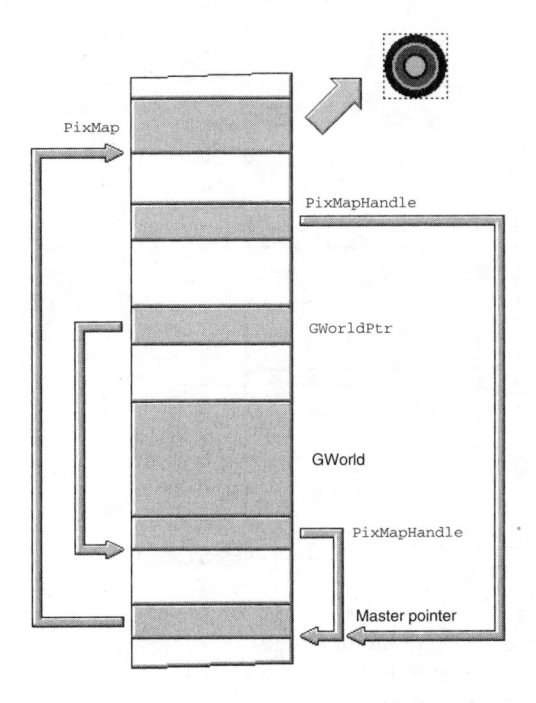

FIGURE 5.19 GetGWorldPixMap() returns a handle to a GWorld's pixel map.

N O T E

A PixMapHandle points to a master pointer. The master pointer points to a PixMap. The PixMap has a baseAddr field that points to an area in memory that holds the actual pixel image. Figure 5.19 doesn't show where the baseAddr field leads—it just shows the pixel map you'll find at whatever location baseAddr references.

Using GWorlds for Animation

The pixel map that is a part of a graphics world is used in color animation much as the `BitMap` is used in monochrome animation. Figure 5.20 shows that an animation uses four pixel maps: three of the pixel maps are from GWorlds, while the fourth holds the contents of a color window.

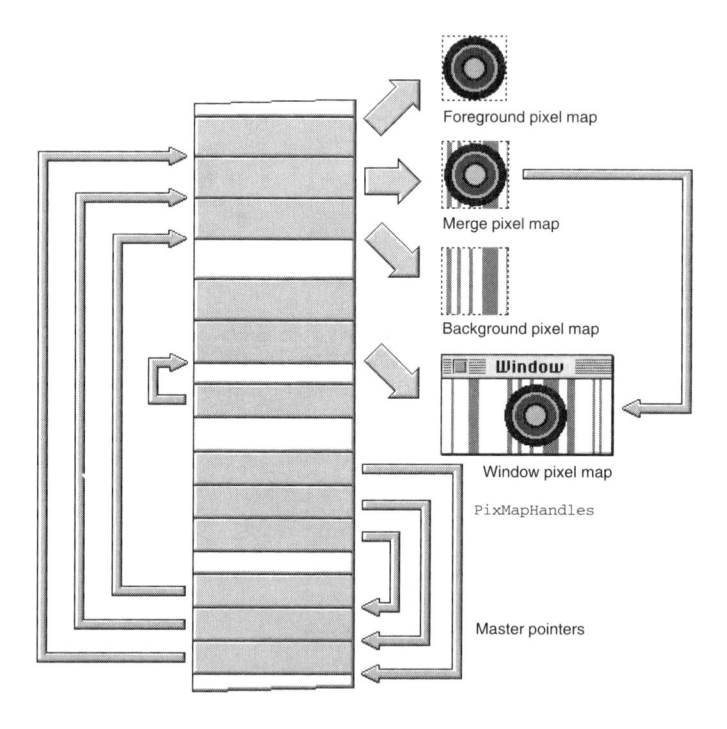

Foreground pixel map

Merge pixel map

Background pixel map

Window pixel map

PixMapHandles

Master pointers

FIGURE 5.20 Color animation uses three offscreen pixel maps.

Figure 5.20 hints that in this book color animation will employ a different strategy than was used for black-and-white animation. For monochrome animation, the background and merge offscreen `BitMaps` were the same size as the window that was to display the animation. For color animation, all three offscreen pixel maps will be the size of the offscreen foreground pixel map—that means that each of the offscreen pixel maps will be smaller—usually much smaller—than the window pixel map that displays the animation. Because there's much more data for the Mac to keep track of in the display of color than there is in the display of black and white, this approach will keep the animation moving quickly.

CopyBits() and Color Animation

You saw earlier that one way to perform monochrome animation was to save the entire background to a merge `BitMap`, then overlay the foreground `BitMap` onto the merge `BitMap`, and then copy this combined `BitMap` to the animation window `BitMap`. For color animation, a few extra steps are necessary.

Over the next several pages you'll see how the `CopyBits()` Toolbox function can be used to move an object a single pixel from left to right in a window. While this may not seem like a lofty goal, keep in mind that once you understand how the object moves smoothly across this short distance, you'll know everything you need to about animation—further movement of the object is done by simply looping through the code described here.

Figure 5.21 shows what the animation window looks like for the example that will be examined next. In this window, a very small framed rectangle (six pixels by five pixels) moves across a background that includes several vertical lines. The movement of this object will be illustrated in several figures—each of which includes enlarged views of the four pixel maps used in the animation. Figure 5.21 gives you an idea of how a pixel map will be shown in the figures.

Animation window

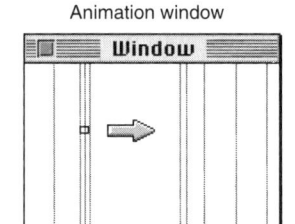

Enlarged view of a section of the above window

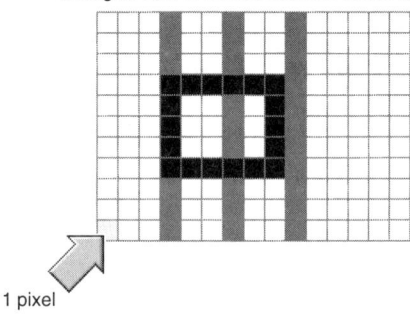

1 pixel

FIGURE 5.21 The figures used to clarify the following example
will include an enlarged view of an area of a window.

Before stepping through the copying of pixel maps, the GWorlds and
`PixMapHandles` have to be set up. The following global variables will be
used in the upcoming example:

```
GWorldPtr       gForeGWorldPtr;
GWorldPtr       gBackGWorldPtr;
GWorldPtr       gMergeGWorldPtr;
PixMapHandle    gForePixMap;
PixMapHandle    gBackPixMap;
PixMapHandle    gMergePixMap;
Rect            gGWorldPixMapRect;
Rect            gWindowPixMapRect;
WindowPtr       gDisplayWindow;
```

The three `GWorldPtr` variables will be used in calls to `NewGWorld()` to create
three new graphics worlds. After that, the `PixMapHandle` variables
(obtained from calls to `GetGWorldPixMap()`) will be used to access the off-

screen pixel maps. The `gGWorldPixMapRect` variable establishes the size of each of the three offscreen pixel maps. This rectangle will have a top left point of (0, 0), and its coordinates won't change as the program runs. The `gWindowPixMapRect` will be the same size as the pixel map rectangle—but it won't be *normalized* to (0, 0). And its coordinates will change. This rectangle will be used to hold the coordinates of a rectangle in the animation window. The rectangle will be the area involved in the animation at any given moment. See Figure 5.22 for clarification.

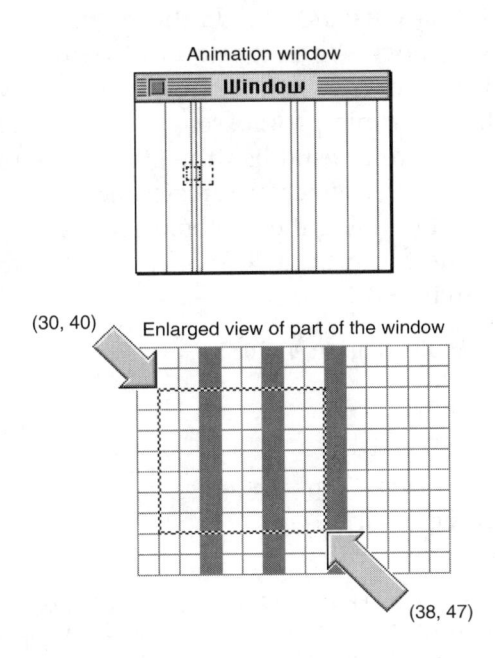

FIGURE 5.22 A global `Rect` variable will be used
to keep track of a rectangle in the animation window.

In Figure 5.22, the solid-framed rectangle that will be the moving object has not yet been drawn to the window. Instead, the window at the top of the figure shows two dashed rectangles. These rectangles won't appear in the animation—they're shown merely as a reference to where the animation will be taking place. The larger rectangle represents the area of the window that will be shown in an enlarged view in the following figures. The inner rectangle represents the area of the window that the program will be working with. This rectangle serves two purposes. First, the area in this rectangle will be copied to preserve the current background. Second, this is the area in which the merge pixel map will be drawn—notice that this rectangle is the same dimensions as the off-screen pixel maps. As the animation moves to the right, one pixel at a time, the coordinates of this rectangle will change, one pixel at a time.

Near the start of the program, the GWorlds and `PixMapHandles` are set up. The following application-defined function performs these tasks. `CreateGWorldsAndPixMaps()` loads the picture that will serve as the foreground into memory. When created in a paint or draw program, this picture should be created with a one-pixel-wide white border— you'll see why as the example progresses. `CreateGWorldsAndPixMaps()` uses the size of this picture to establish the size of the pixel maps used by the three graphics worlds—which are created next. Handles to the pixel maps are then obtained by calling the Toolbox function `GetGWorldPixMap()` three times. Finally, the foreground GWorld is made the current port and the picture is drawn to it.

```
void  CreateGWorldsAndPixMaps( void )
{
   PicHandle   theForePicture;
   QDErr       theError;

   theForePicture = GetPicture( rForePicture );
   if ( theForePicture == nil )
      ExitToShell();

   gGWorldPixMapRect = (**theForePicture).picFrame;
   OffsetRect( &gGWorldPixMapRect, - gGWorldPixMapRect.left,
               - gGWorldPixMapRect.top );

   theError = NewGWorld( &gForeGWorldPtr, 0, &gGWorldPixMapRect,
                         nil, nil, noNewDevice );
   theError = NewGWorld( &gBackGWorldPtr, 0, &gGWorldPixMapRect,
                         nil, nil, noNewDevice );
   theError = NewGWorld( &gMergeGWorldPtr, 0, &gGWorldPixMapRect,
                         nil, nil, noNewDevice );

   gForePixMap = GetGWorldPixMap( gForeGWorldPtr );
   gBackPixMap = GetGWorldPixMap( gBackGWorldPtr );
   gMergePixMap = GetGWorldPixMap( gMergeGWorldPtr );

   SetGWorld( gForeGWorldPtr, nil );
```

```
DrawPicture( theForePicture, &gGWorldPixMapRect );
}
```

Each of the next several figures will include four pixel maps—as shown in Figure 5.23. The three pixel maps on the left of the figure are the off-screen pixel maps that are each a part of an offscreen graphics world. For each of these pixel maps, the entire pixel map is shown—seven rows of eight pixels. The larger pixel map on the right of the figure represents a part of the window pixel map. Since the traveling rectangle will only be shown moving a single pixel from left to right, only a part of the window pixel map is needed to demonstrate what's going on.

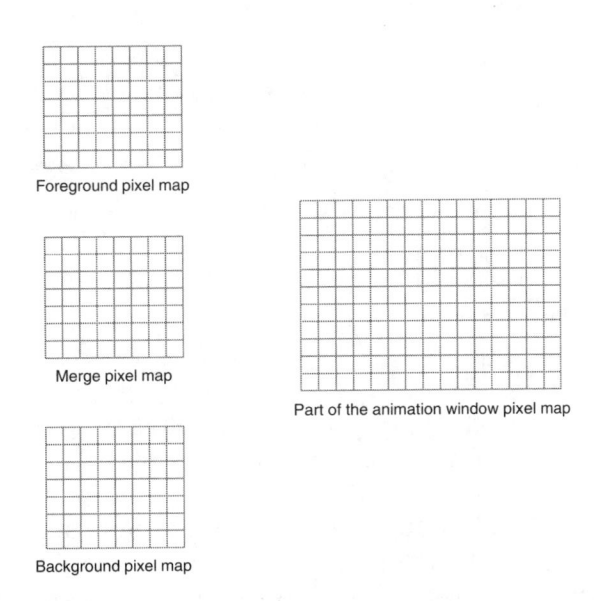

Foreground pixel map

Merge pixel map

Part of the animation window pixel map

Background pixel map

FIGURE 5.23 The next several figures will use this format
to display the contents of pixel maps.

The object that will be traveling across the window is first drawn to the offscreen foreground pixel map. Drawing that normally takes place in a window can be directed to an offscreen graphics world by first calling SetGWorld(). Because a pointer to a graphics world is also a pointer to a color graphics port, subsequent calls to QuickDraw routines like DrawPicture() will result in drawing taking place off screen—as shown in Figure 5.24. As mentioned, when the picture was copied from the paint program in which it was created, a border of white pixels was included. The foreground pixel map includes this border.

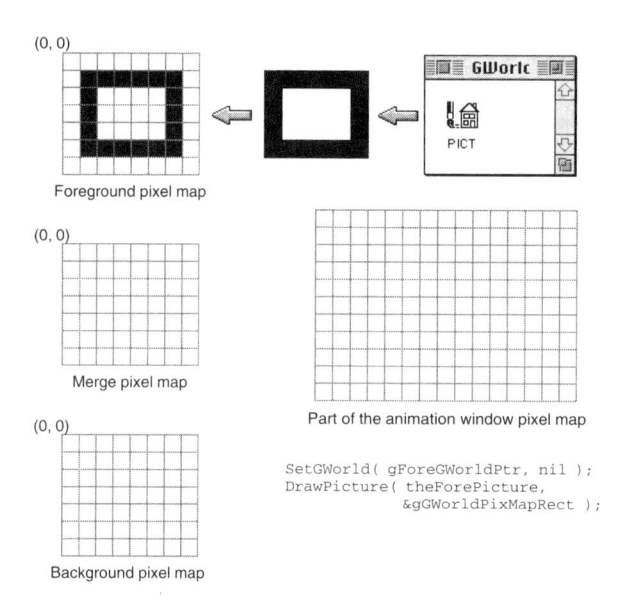

(0, 0)

Foreground pixel map

(0, 0)

Merge pixel map

(0, 0)

Background pixel map

Part of the animation window pixel map

```
SetGWorld( gForeGWorldPtr, nil );
DrawPicture( theForePicture,
             &gGWorldPixMapRect );
```

FIGURE 5.24 A picture can be drawn to an offscreen pixel map using a call to DrawPicture().

Animation will take place from within a loop. Before starting the loop— and before the object is first drawn to the window—the area of the window that is to hold the object is preserved. A simple application-defined routine named PrepareForAnimation() handles this chore.

```
void  PrepareForAnimation( void )
{
   gWindowPixMapRect = gGWorldPixMapRect;
   OffsetRect( &gWindowPixMapRect, 30, 40 );

   CopyBits( &(gDisplayWindow->portBits), (BitMap *)(*gBackPixMap),
             &gWindowPixMapRect, &gGWorldPixMapRect, srcCopy, nil );

   CopyBits( (BitMap *)(*gBackPixMap), (BitMap *)(*gMergePixMap),
```

```
                 &gGWorldPixMapRect, &gGWorldPixMapRect, srcCopy, nil );
}
```

`PrepareForAnimation()` begins by setting the coordinates of the window rectangle. First, `gWindowPixMapRect()` is set to the size of the pixel map rectangles—`gGWorldPixMapRect`. That gives the rectangle coordinates of (0, 0, 8, 7). A call to `OffsetRect()` moves this rectangle to the onscreen location where the animation is to start. This example starts the animation in a rectangle at coordinates (30, 40, 38, 47). Figure 5.25 shows how the examples pixel maps look at this point.

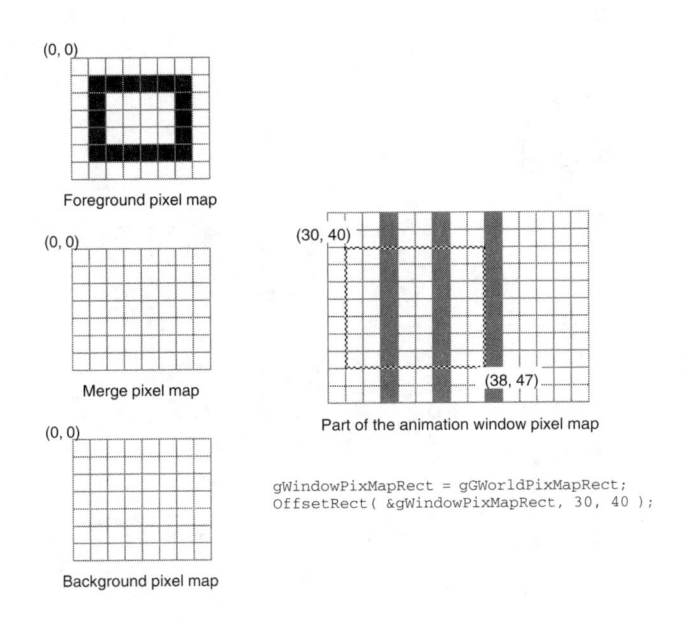

FIGURE 5.25 A rectangle is set up in the animation window.

`PrepareForAnimation()` makes two calls to `CopyBits()`. The first call saves the `gWindowPixMapRect` area to the offscreen background pixel map—as shown in Figure 5.26. From this chapter's introduction to `CopyBits()`, you'll recall that the first and second parameters to this function must each be a pointer to a `BitMap`. For color animation, though, you'll be working with the `PixMap` data type. That means that some typecasting will be in order. In this first call to CopyBits(), the source pixel map is the window's pixel map. Because gDisplayWindow has been declared to be a WindowPtr, no typecasting is needed here—the portBits field of the GrafPort that a WindowPtr points to is defined to be a BitMap. The destination pixel map gBackPixMap, though, needs to be typecast. Dereferencing this PixMapHandle once provides its pointer. Using (BitMap *) to typecast the result satisfies CopyBits().

```
CopyBits( &(gDisplayWindow->portBits), (BitMap *)(*gBackPixMap),
          &gWindowPixMapRect, &gGWorldPixMapRect, srcCopy, nil );
```

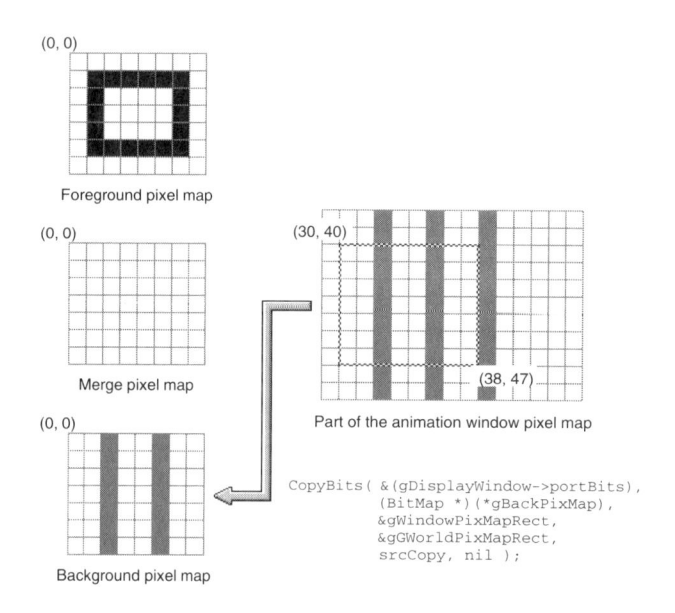

FIGURE 5.26 The contents of the animation window rectangle are copied to the offscreen background pixel map.

The second call to CopyBits() copies the offscreen background pixel map to the offscreen merge pixel map—as shown in Figure 5.27. Recall that the rectangle gGWorldPixMapRect has (and will have throughout the program) coordinates of (0, 0, 8, 7).

```
CopyBits( (BitMap *)(*gBackPixMap), (BitMap *)(*gMergePixMap),
         &gGWorldPixMapRect, &gGWorldPixMapRect, srcCopy, nil );
```

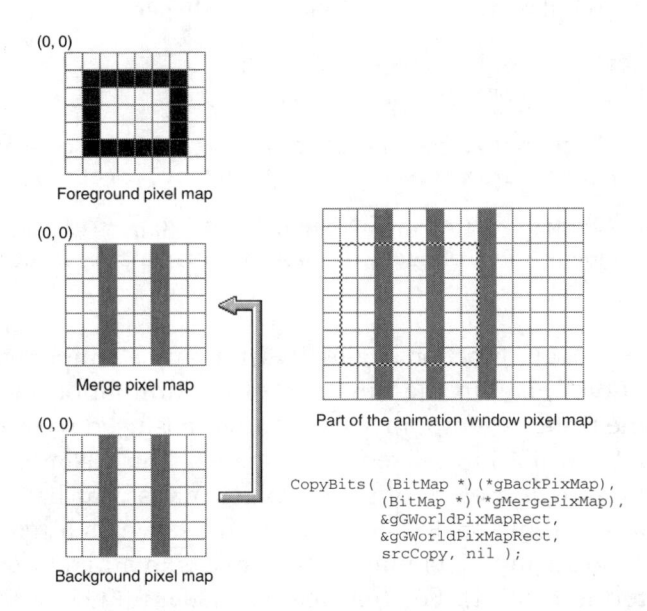

FIGURE 5.27 The contents of the offscreen background pixel map
are copied to the offscreen merge pixel map.

The remainder of the animation is handled from within a loop. Each pass through the loop executes a function that calls CopyBits() five times. A typical version of this application-defined function follows:

```
void  AnimateOneFrame( void )
{
    Rect   theTempRect;

    theTempRect = gGWorldPixMapRect;
    OffsetRect( &theTempRect, 1, 0 );

    CopyBits( (BitMap *)(*gForePixMap), (BitMap *)(*gMergePixMap),
             &gGWorldPixMapRect, &theTempRect, transparent, nil );

    CopyBits( (BitMap *)(*gMergePixMap), &(gDisplayWindow->portBits),
             &gGWorldPixMapRect, &gWindowPixMapRect, srcCopy, nil );
```

```
    OffsetRect( &gWindowPixMapRect, 1, 0 );

    CopyBits( &(gDisplayWindow->portBits), (BitMap *)(*gMergePixMap),
              &gWindowPixMapRect, &gGWorldPixMapRect, srcCopy, nil );

    theTempRect = gGWorldPixMapRect;
    OffsetRect( &theTempRect, -1, 0 );

    CopyBits( (BitMap *)(*gBackPixMap), (BitMap *)(*gMergePixMap),
              &gGWorldPixMapRect, &theTempRect, srcCopy, nil );

    CopyBits( (BitMap *)(*gMergePixMap), (BitMap *)(*gBackPixMap),
              &gGWorldPixMapRect, &gGWorldPixMapRect, srcCopy, nil );
}
```

The `AnimateOneFrame()` function begins by setting up a temporary rectangle that is shifted one pixel in the direction of the animation movement—one pixel to the right. A temporary `Rect` variable is used so that `gGWorld-PixMapRect` retains its normalized coordinates. The `gGWorldPixMapRect` rectangle was used to define offscreen pixel maps that have a top left coordinate of (0, 0). In `CopyBits()` calls it will serve as a reference that can be used to grab any pixel map (which exists in a pixel map that has (0, 0) as its top left point). For that reason, `gGWorldPixMapRect` should preserve its original coordinates.

```
Rect   theTempRect;

theTempRect = gGWorldPixMapRect;
OffsetRect( &theTempRect, 1, 0 );

CopyBits( (BitMap *)(*gForePixMap), (BitMap *)(*gMergePixMap),
          &gGWorldPixMapRect, &theTempRect, transparent, nil );
```

The `CopyBits()` call copies the offscreen foreground pixel map to the offscreen merge pixel map. `gGWorldPixMapRect` is used as the source rectangle, so the entire foreground pixel map is copied. The shifted temporary rectangle is used as the destination, so the foreground will appear in the merge pixel map shifted one pixel to the right—as shown in Figure 5.28. The rightmost column of foreground pixels will be cut off. That's all right, since the foreground picture was intentionally created with an "empty" one pixel border. The Apple-defined constant `transparent` is used as the copy mode. This mode tells `CopyBits()` to ignore any white pixels in the source pixel map.

NOTE For black-and-white `BitMap` copying, the `srcOr` copy mode was used to ignore white pixels. For color copying, use transparent instead. This mode actually tells `CopyBits()` to ignore all source pixels that don't match the destination background color. This background is usually—but not always—white. Color windows may have a nonwhite background.

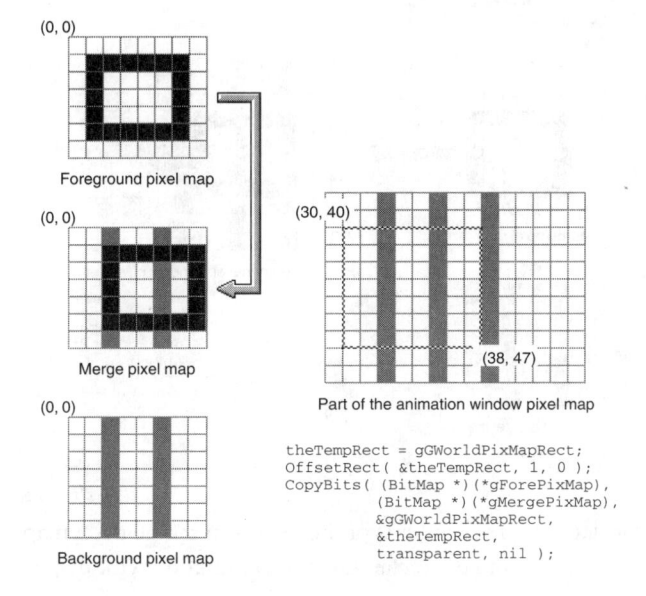

FIGURE 5.28 The contents of the offscreen foreground pixel map are shifted on pixel to the right, then copied to the offscreen merge pixel map.

The next call to `CopyBits()` blasts the offscreen pixel map to the window— as shown in Figure 5.29. Since this is the first rectangle object to be drawn to the window, no movement will be noticed. The next pass through the loop will provide proof that this call to `CopyBits()` shifts the object one pixel to the right.

```
CopyBits( (BitMap *)(*gMergePixMap), &(gDisplayWindow->portBits),
          &gGWorldPixMapRect, &gWindowPixMapRect, srcCopy, nil );
```

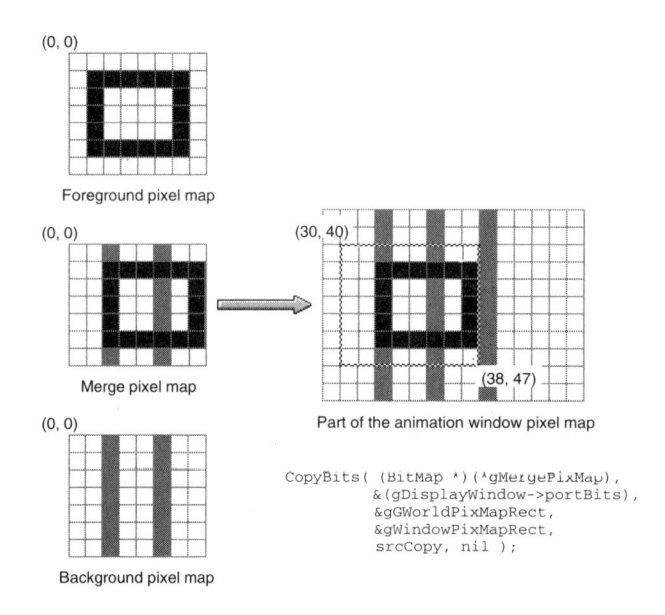

FIGURE 5.29 The contents of the offscreen merge pixel map are copied to the rectangle in the animation window.

There are three calls to `CopyBits()` remaining in the `AnimateOneFrame()` function. Preparation for the next frame of animation—one that will be drawn one pixel to the right of the one that was just copied to the window—begins with the first call. First, the global rectangle variable `gWindowPixMapRect`—the rectangle that keeps track of where in the window animation is taking place—is offset by a single pixel. Compare

Figure 5.30 to Figure 5.29 to see that the window rectangle does indeed enclose an area one pixel to the right of the previous area.

```
OffsetRect( &gWindowPixMapRect, 1, 0 );
```

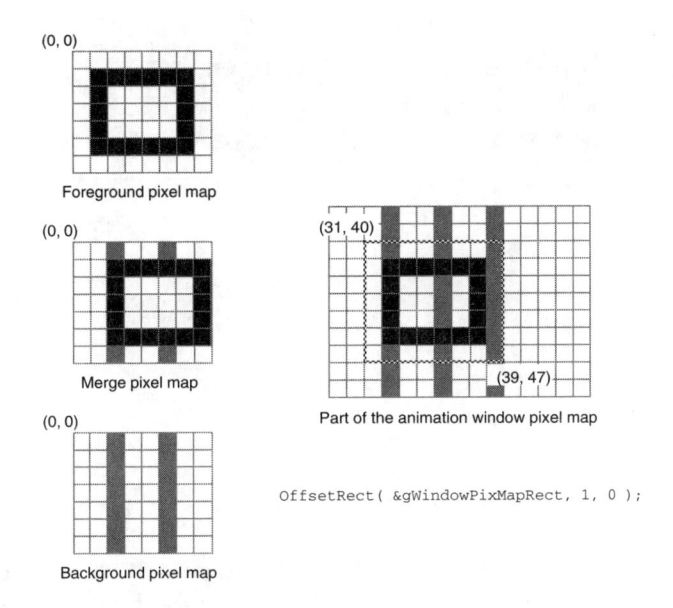

FIGURE **5.30** After the object is drawn to the window, the window rectangle is shifted one pixel to the right.

A call to CopyBits() copies the newly enclosed area of the window to the offscreen merge pixel map. Figure 5.31 illustrates. As you'll soon see, this step is necessary in order to preserve the new pixels that are now in the window rectangle—the rightmost column of pixels.

```
CopyBits( &(gDisplayWindow->portBits), (BitMap *)(*gMergePixMap),
        &gWindowPixMapRect, &gGWorldPixMapRect, srcCopy, nil );
```

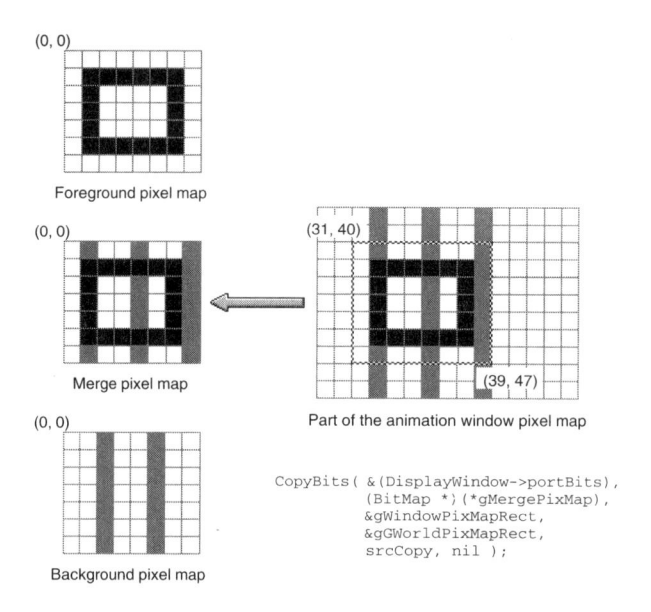

FIGURE 5.31 The contents of the animation window rectangle
are copied to the offscreen merge pixel map.

Once again, the temporary rectangle is set to match the coordinates of
the offscreen pixel map rectangle. This time, though, the temporary rectangle is then shifted one pixel to the left rather than one pixel to the right.
A call to `CopyBits()` then copies the offscreen background pixel map to the
offscreen merge pixel map. As Figure 5.32 shows, this has the effect of
stamping over almost the entire pixel map that was just copied from the
window to the merge pixel map. *Almost* is the key word in that last
sentence. Since the destination rectangle has been shifted one pixel to the
left, the rightmost column of pixels in the merge pixel map will be preserved. That's the only reason the pixel map was copied from the window
to the merge pixel map in the previous step—to save this one column.

What this latest `CopyBits()` does is to create a merge pixel map that holds the background that appears in the window rectangle. Note that he contents of the offscreen merge pixel map is the same as the window pixel map—minus the black rectangle.

```
theTempRect = gGWorldPixMapRect;
OffsetRect( &theTempRect, -1, 0 );

CopyBits( (BitMap *)(*gBackPixMap), (BitMap *)(*gMergePixMap),
          &gGWorldPixMapRect, &theTempRect, srcCopy, nil );
```

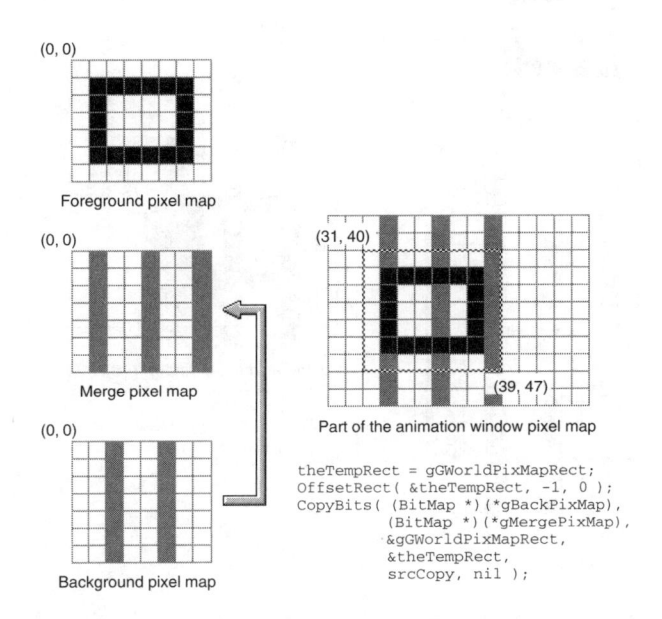

FIGURE 5.32 The contents of the offscreen background pixel map are shifted one pixel to the left and then copied to the offscreen merge pixel map.

Now, the rebuilt window background that is in the offscreen merge pixel map is copied to the offscreen background pixel map—as shown in Figure 5.33. There it will be saved for, and used in, the next pass through the animation loop.

```
CopyBits( (BitMap *)(*gMergePixMap), (BitMap *)(*gBackPixMap),
         &gGWorldPixMapRect, &gGWorldPixMapRect, srcCopy, nil );
```

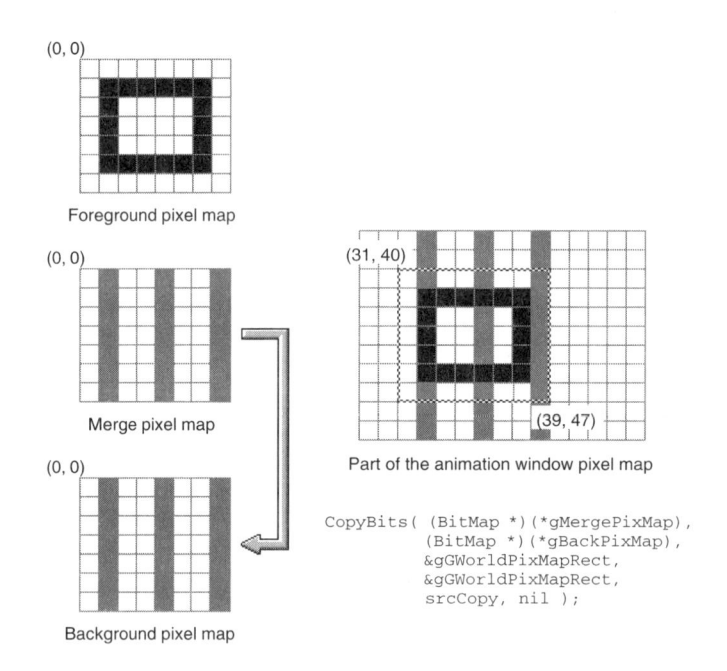

FIGURE 5.33 The offscreen merge pixel map is saved by storing it in the offscreen background pixel map.

That completes one pass through the animation loop. The next pass through the loop will begin with the offscreen foreground pixel map getting copied to the offscreen merge pixel map. Again, transparent mode will be used. The next step will be to send the contents of the offscreen merge pixel map to the window. In this example, the rectangle will then appear to move one pixel to the right. Figure 5.34 shows the first step of the next pass through the loop, while Figure 5.35 shows the second step.

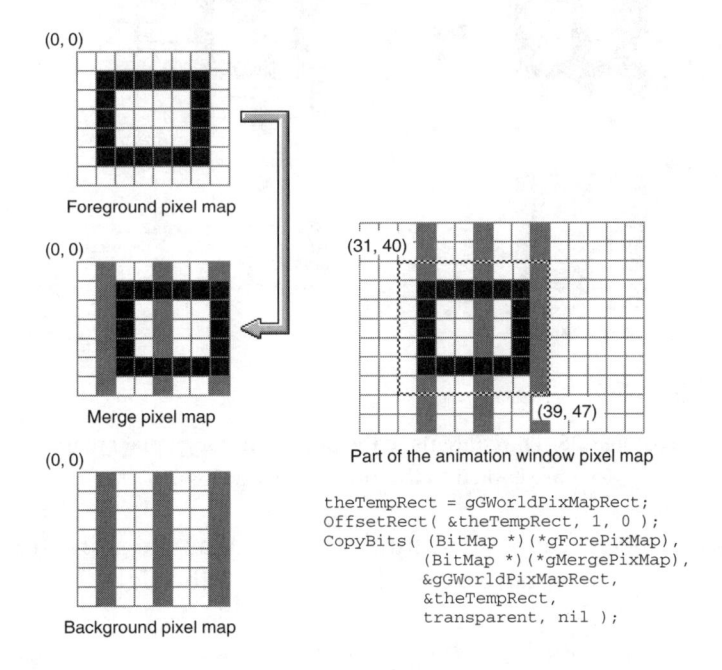

```
theTempRect = gGWorldPixMapRect;
OffsetRect( &theTempRect, 1, 0 );
CopyBits( (BitMap *)(*gForePixMap),
          (BitMap *)(*gMergePixMap),
          &gGWorldPixMapRect,
          &theTempRect,
          transparent, nil );
```

FIGURE 5.34 The contents of the offscreen foreground pixel map are shifted one pixel to the right and then copied to the offscreen merge pixel map.

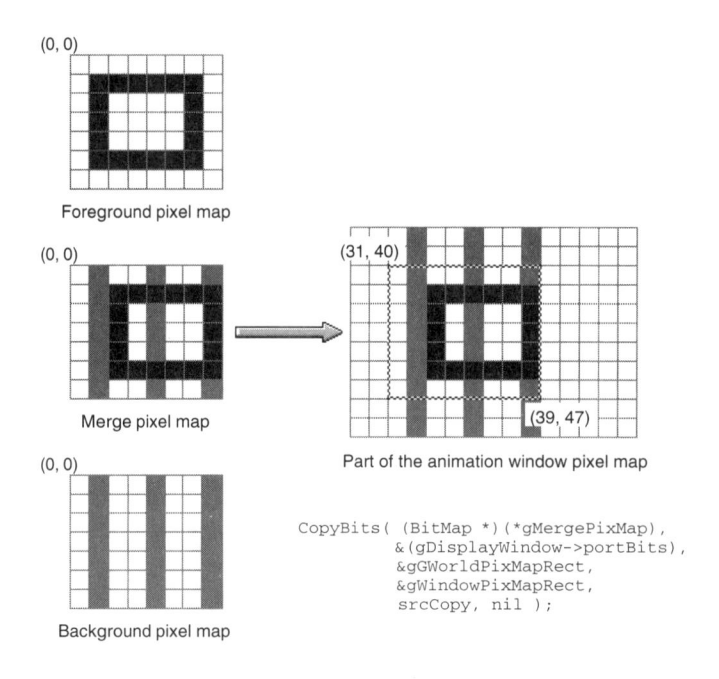

```
CopyBits( (BitMap *)(*gMergePixMap),
          &(gDisplayWindow->portBits),
          &gGWorldPixMapRect,
          &gWindowPixMapRect,
          srcCopy, nil );
```

FIGURE 5.35 The contents of the offscreen merge pixel map
are copied to the animation window.

Calls to `AnimateOneFrame()` continue for as long as the animation runs—each call moves the rectangle object one pixel to the right.

Chapter Example: GWorlds

The GWorlds example program opens a large, color window that holds the picture shown in Figure 5.36. As the program runs, a multicolored hot-air balloon moves horizontally across the window, from left to right. When the balloon reaches the right edge of the window, it starts back to the left. Because the GWorlds program uses offscreen graphics worlds, the animation is flicker-free. To quit the program, click the mouse button.

FIGURE **5.36** The result of running the GWorld program.

The GWorlds project requires a single WIND resource and two PICT resources—the PICTs are shown in Figure 5.37. The pixels that make up the three circles in the balloon picture were drawn in white to demonstrate that the background picture can be made to show through parts of a foreground picture. Not evident in the figure is the fact that the balloon picture has a one-pixel-wide white border surrounding it. Figure 5.38 shows the balloon picture pasted against a black background so that you can see the area that this picture occupies.

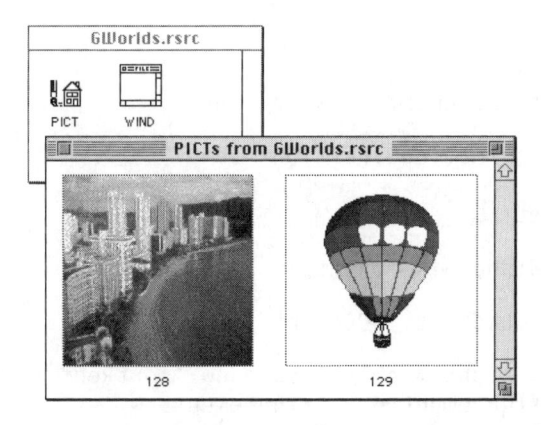

FIGURE **5.37** The two PICT resources used in the GWorlds project.

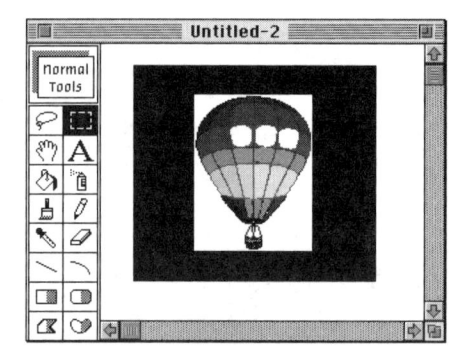

FIGURE 5.38 The foreground picture is framed by white pixels.

The GWorlds example program uses the routines developed in this chapter: `AreGWorldsAvailable()`, `CreateGWorldsAndPixMaps()`, `Prepare-ForAnimation()`, and `AnimateOneFrame()`. In all cases, these routines are identical to—or very similar to—the versions you're familiar with.

The earlier discussions of animation used an object that moved in just one direction. In the GWorlds example program, the balloon moves both to the right and to the left. To determine in which direction the balloon should move, the program adds a short routine named `Determine-AnimationDirection()`.

```
#define       kXincrement       1

short   gCurrentXIncrement = kXincrement;

void   DetermineAnimationDirection( void )
{
   Rect   theRect;

   theRect = gWindowPixMapRect;

   OffsetRect( &theRect, gCurrentXIncrement, 0 );

   if ( theRect.right > gDisplayWindow->portRect.right )
      gCurrentXIncrement = - kXincrement;
   else if ( theRect.left < gDisplayWindow->portRect.left )
      gCurrentXIncrement = + kXincrement;
}
```

DetermineAnimationDirection() is called from AnimateOneFrame(). That means that before each movement of the balloon, its direction is determined. The global variable gCurrentXIncrement holds the current number of pixels in which the balloon should move at each pass through the animation loop. This variable is initialized to a value of kXincrement, or 1. When the balloon reaches the right edge of the window, its time for the balloon to travel from right to left. The variable -gCurrentXIncrement then gets set to -kXincrement, or –1. When the balloon then reaches the left edge, gCurrentXIncrement gets set back to 1. At any point in between, gCurrentXIncrement keeps whatever value it currently has.

The constant kXincrement establishes the number of pixels that the balloon moves at each pass through the animation loop. A value of 1 moves the balloon at a moderate pace. To speed things up, try changing the value of kXincrement to 2.

NOTE The balloon picture used in the GWorld program is set up for a kXincrement value of 1—the picture has a one pixel wide white border. If you change kXincrement to 2, change the picture border to two white pixels—otherwise one pixel of the balloon will get cut off as the balloon travels across the screen. You can easily add this border by cutting PICT 129 from the project's resource file and pasting it into a paint program. Then select the balloon, allowing for two extra pixels on each side. Copy the picture and paste it back into the resource project. Make sure that the new balloon picture has an ID of 129 before closing the resource file.

Before using CopyBits(), the example program makes calls to the Toolbox routines RGBForeColor() and RGBBackColor() to set the foreground color to black and the background color to white. Apple suggests doing this to avoid unwanted coloring of images. An application-defined routine named SetForeAndBackColors() accomplishes this by declaring two RGBColor variables and by then setting one to white and one to black.

A PixMap is accessed using a PixMapHandle. Because objects referenced by handles can move in memory, your application should call the Toolbox routine LockPixels() before calling CopyBits(). This function will ensure that a pixel map won't move in memory. After CopyBits(), call Unlock-Pixels(). LockPixels() and UnlockPixels() should be called for both the source and destination pixel maps. For simplicity, the example program doesn't nest each call to CopyBits() with lock and unlock calls. Instead, it just locks each pixel map at the start of the program and unlocks them as the program ends.

When your program is finished with an offscreen graphics world, call the Toolbox function `DisposeGWorld()`. Pass this routine a `GWorldPtr` to the graphics world that is to be disposed of.

Now, the much-awaited listing for the program that produces smooth, flicker-free color animation follows:

```
//_____

#include <QDOffscreen.h>

//_____

void      InitializeToolbox( void );
void      OpenDisplayWindow( void );
Boolean   AreGWorldsAvailable( void );
void      SetForeAndBackColors( void );
void      CreateGWorldsAndPixMaps( void );
void      PrepareForAnimation( void );
void      AnimateOneFrame( void );
void      DetermineAnimationDirection( void );

//_____

#define    rBackPicture        128
#define    rForePicture        129
#define    rDisplayWindow      128
#define    kXincrement           1

//_____

WindowPtr      gDisplayWindow;
short          gCurrentXIncrement = kXincrement;
GWorldPtr      gForeGWorldPtr;
GWorldPtr      gBackGWorldPtr;
GWorldPtr      gMergeGWorldPtr;
PixMapHandle   gForePixMap;
PixMapHandle   gBackPixMap;
PixMapHandle   gMergePixMap;
Rect           gWindowPixMapRect;
Rect           gGWorldPixMapRect;

//_____
```

```
void   main( void )
{
   Boolean    graphicsWorldsPresent;
   oolean    pixelsLocked;

   InitializeToolbox();

   HideCursor();

   graphicsWorldsPresent = AreGWorldsAvailable();
   if ( graphicsWorldsPresent == false )
      ExitToShell();

   SetForeAndBackColors();

   OpenDisplayWindow();

   CreateGWorldsAndPixMaps();

   pixelsLocked = LockPixels( gForePixMap );
   if ( pixelsLocked == false )
      ExitToShell();

   pixelsLocked = LockPixels( gBackPixMap );
   if ( pixelsLocked == false )
      ExitToShell();

   pixelsLocked = LockPixels( gMergePixMap );
   if ( pixelsLocked == false )
      ExitToShell();

   PrepareForAnimation();

   while ( !Button() )
      AnimateOneFrame();

   UnlockPixels( gForePixMap );
   UnlockPixels( gBackPixMap );
   UnlockPixels( gMergePixMap );

   DisposeGWorld( gForeGWorldPtr );
   DisposeGWorld( gBackGWorldPtr );
   DisposeGWorld( gMergeGWorldPtr );
}

//_____

Boolean  AreGWorldsAvailable( void )
```

```
{
   OSErr    theError;
   long     theResult;
   Boolean  worldAvail;

   theError = Gestalt( gestaltQuickdrawFeatures, &theResult );
   if ( theError != noErr )
      ExitToShell();

   worldAvail = theResult & ( 1 << gestaltHasDeepGWorlds );
   if ( worldAvail > 0 )
      return ( true );
   else
      return ( false );
}

//_____

void SetForeAndBackColors( void )
{
   RGBColor  theBlackColor;
   RGBColor  theWhiteColor;

   theBlackColor.red   = 0x0000;
   theBlackColor.green = 0x0000;
   theBlackColor.blue  = 0x0000;

   theWhiteColor.red   = 0xFFFF;
   theWhiteColor.green = 0xFFFF;
   theWhiteColor.blue  = 0xFFFF;

   RGBForeColor( &theBlackColor );
   RGBBackColor( &theWhiteColor );
}

//_____

void  OpenDisplayWindow( void )
{
   PicHandle  theBackPicture;
   Rect       theRect;

   theBackPicture = GetPicture( rBackPicture );
   if ( theBackPicture == nil )
      ExitToShell();

   theRect = (**theBackPicture).picFrame;
   OffsetRect( &theRect, - theRect.left, - theRect.top );
```

```
        gDisplayWindow = GetNewCWindow( rDisplayWindow, nil,
                                        (WindowPtr)-1L );
        ShowWindow( gDisplayWindow );
        SetPort( gDisplayWindow );

        DrawPicture( theBackPicture, &theRect );
    }

    //_____

    void  CreateGWorldsAndPixMaps( void )
    {
        PicHandle   theForePicture;
        QDErr       theError;

        theForePicture = GetPicture( rForePicture );
        if ( theForePicture == nil )
            ExitToShell();

        gGWorldPixMapRect = (**theForePicture).picFrame;
        OffsetRect( &gGWorldPixMapRect, - gGWorldPixMapRect.left,
                    - gGWorldPixMapRect.top );

        theError = NewGWorld( &gForeGWorldPtr, 0, &gGWorldPixMapRect,
                              nil, nil, noNewDevice );
        theError = NewGWorld( &gBackGWorldPtr, 0, &gGWorldPixMapRect,
                              nil, nil, noNewDevice );
        theError = NewGWorld( &gMergeGWorldPtr, 0, &gGWorldPixMapRect,
                              nil, nil, noNewDevice );

        gForePixMap = GetGWorldPixMap( gForeGWorldPtr );
        gBackPixMap = GetGWorldPixMap( gBackGWorldPtr );
        gMergePixMap = GetGWorldPixMap( gMergeGWorldPtr );

        SetGWorld( gForeGWorldPtr, nil );

        DrawPicture( theForePicture, &gGWorldPixMapRect );
    }

    //_____

    void  PrepareForAnimation( void )
    {
        gWindowPixMapRect = gGWorldPixMapRect;
        OffsetRect( &gWindowPixMapRect, 0, 25 );

        CopyBits( &(gDisplayWindow->portBits), (BitMap *)(*gBackPixMap),
                  &gWindowPixMapRect, &gGWorldPixMapRect, srcCopy, nil );
```

```
   CopyBits( (BitMap *)(*gBackPixMap), (BitMap *)(*gMergePixMap),
            &gGWorldPixMapRect, &gGWorldPixMapRect, srcCopy, nil );
}

//_____

void  AnimateOneFrame( void )
{
   Rect  theTempRect;

   DetermineAnimationDirection();

   theTempRect = gGWorldPixMapRect;
   OffsetRect( &theTempRect, gCurrentXIncrement, 0 );

   CopyBits( (BitMap *)(*gForePixMap), (BitMap *)(*gMergePixMap),
            &gGWorldPixMapRect, &theTempRect, transparent, nil );

   CopyBits( (BitMap *)(*gMergePixMap), &(gDisplayWindow->portBits),
            &gGWorldPixMapRect, &gWindowPixMapRect, srcCopy, nil );

   OffsetRect( &gWindowPixMapRect, gCurrentXIncrement, 0 );

   CopyBits( &(gDisplayWindow->portBits), (BitMap *)(*gMergePixMap),
            &gWindowPixMapRect, &gGWorldPixMapRect, srcCopy, nil );

   theTempRect = gGWorldPixMapRect;
   OffsetRect( &theTempRect, -gCurrentXIncrement, 0 );

   CopyBits( (BitMap *)(*gBackPixMap), (BitMap *)(*gMergePixMap),
            &gGWorldPixMapRect, &theTempRect, srcCopy, nil );

   CopyBits( (BitMap *)(*gMergePixMap), (BitMap *)(*gBackPixMap),
            &gGWorldPixMapRect, &gGWorldPixMapRect, srcCopy, nil );
}

//_____

void  DetermineAnimationDirection( void )
{
   Rect  theRect;

   theRect = gWindowPixMapRect;

   OffsetRect( &theRect, gCurrentXIncrement, 0 );

   if ( theRect.right > gDisplayWindow->portRect.right )
      gCurrentXIncrement = - kXincrement;
   else if ( theRect.left < gDisplayWindow->portRect.left )
```

```
        gCurrentXIncrement = + kXincrement;
}

//_____

void  InitializeToolbox( void )
{
    InitGraf( &qd.thePort );
    InitFonts();
    InitWindows();
    InitMenus();
    TEInit();
    InitDialogs( OL );
    FlushEvents( everyEvent, 0 );
    InitCursor();
}
```

Summary

To produce flicker-free black-and-white animation, you need to use off-screen `BitMaps` and the `CopyBits()` function. Your program will begin by creating three `BitMaps` offscreen—in memory, rather than in a window. Your program can then apply a foreground object to a background picture out of the sight of the user. After merging the object with the background, the combined result can be drawn to the screen. By repeatedly performing these steps offscreen, the flicker that would normally be noticeable to the user now takes place in memory.

Color animation is performed in much the same way as monochrome animation is. Both types of animation rely on the `CopyBits()` function and offscreen drawing areas. Color animation uses offscreen pixel maps rather than the offscreen `BitMaps` used in black-and-white animation. Because keeping track of color images is more complicated than keeping track of monochrome images, Apple provides the programmer with the offscreen graphics world—or GWorld. A GWorld is a color environment created specifically to support the offscreen preparation of complex color images.

CHAPTER 6

QuickDraw GX

For over a decade, QuickDraw has been the drawing environment of the Macintosh—and it still is. But now there is another QuickDraw—QuickDraw GX. This new version doesn't replace the original QuickDraw—it supplements it. Programs can still use only the original QuickDraw, or they can use both the old and the new together in a single application. In this chapter, you'll see how that's possible.

QuickDraw GX is a system extension that adds the power of the new QuickDraw to a Macintosh computer. It is also the set of function calls that allow the programmer to exploit this powerful new object-based graphics environment. In this chapter you'll see how to make your application ready for QuickDraw GX. You'll learn how to check for the presence of the QuickDraw GX extension, then to initialize it, and ready a window for QuickDraw GX drawing.

QuickDraw GX relies on objects. Every shape or string of text that is drawn is a shape—with its own set of properties, such as color and fill pattern. In this chapter, you'll learn about some of the many different QuickDraw shape objects. You'll read up on how to create them, modify their properties, and draw them to a window.

About QuickDraw GX

QuickDraw GX is a system extension that adds new drawing, typography, and printing capabilities to the Macintosh. QuickDraw GX is also an extensive set of functions ready to be integrated into Mac programs by Mac developers.

Object and Shapes

QuickDraw GX relies heavily on objects. Each shape that is drawn using QuickDraw GX functions is its own object, with its own set of properties. A shape has a type, such as a line, rectangle, or picture. The shape's *properties* further define what a particular shape will look like. Frame width, color, and fill pattern are all shape properties.

NOTE

C language programmers—don't let this mention of objects alarm you. While the QuickDraw GX API (application programming interface) is a natural in object-oriented C++ programs, it works just as well in C projects—as will be demonstrated by the example programs found in this chapter.

A QuickDraw GX shape, or object, is defined by a private data structure. This means that the inner workings of a shape's structure are unknown to an application. Such a "black box" approach relieves the programmer from trying to decipher the complexities of QuickDraw GX shape objects. Instead, the programmer only has to become familiar with the set of QuickDraw GX functions that exist to make object access possible. Just as a Mac programmer comes to know the fundamental and important Toolbox functions, so too will the Mac QuickDraw GX programmer gain insight into the QuickDraw GX functions that make shape creation, modifying, and drawing possible.

 **N O T E** There are seven Inside Macintosh volumes devoted to QuickDraw GX programming. This chapter will of course only touch on the topics presented in the more than 3500 pages that comprise those books. Consider this chapter an introduction to the vast world of QuickDraw GX programming.

Graphics programming is memory-intensive. Keeping track of the many properties of a shape—or of hundreds or thousands of shapes—requires a well thought-out memory management scheme. The Apple designers of QuickDraw GX have provided just such a memory model. First, an application that makes use of QuickDraw GX gains an extra partition of memory—one devoted just to QuickDraw GX. Second, a programmer who works with QuickDraw GX does not have to be nearly as knowledgeable or concerned with pointers and handles as the programmer who works with other areas of Macintosh programming. That's because QuickDraw GX doesn't return pointers or handles to objects. Instead, QuickDraw GX uses a single object-reference value to identify and work with an object. It is this reference value that your program will use when calling QuickDraw GX functions.

QuickDraw vs. QuickDraw GX

QuickDraw uses a *state-based architecture*. That is, the current state of the drawing environment determines how an image will be drawn. Consider the following QuickDraw call:

```
Line( 100, 0 );
```

By looking at the above call, you know that the line that is drawn will be 100 pixels in length. Unknown, however, are the other properties of the line—for example, its thickness. The thickness of the line is determined by the last call made to `PenSize()`. A call to `PenSize()` effects the thickness of every line that gets drawn subsequent to the call.

QuickDraw GX uses an *object-based architecture*. That is, a graphics shape, such as a line, is represented by an object. An object holds all of the information necessary to draw a shape. In QuickDraw GX, the thickness of a line is unaffected by a call to `PenSize()`. Instead, the thickness of the line is held as information that is a part of the line object.

The object-based architecture used by QuickDraw GX has the important advantage of freeing images from a dependency on the current state of the drawing environment. This means that all of the properties of a graphics shape are self-contained. This scheme becomes significant when it is time to update a graphics shape—the shape essentially can redraw itself.

Chapter Example: PoorMansQDGX

This chapter's first example program, PoorMansQDGX, doesn't use QuickDraw GX. Instead, it exists to give you an appreciation for the power of QuickDraw GX, and for some insight into the reduction in programming effort that this graphics extension provides.

If you like the idea of an object-based architecture—a system that frees you from keeping track of the current graphics environment—you don't have to use QuickDraw GX. Instead, you can write your own classes and member functions to define shapes that hold their own graphics information. For instance, a line shape could be defined by its starting point, its end point, and its thickness. The following `LineObject` class defines such a class.

```
class  LineObject
{
   private:
      short  thickness;
      short  xBegin;
      short  yBegin;
      short  xEnd;
      short  yEnd;

   public:
      void  SetLineSize( short );
      void  SetLineCoordinates( short, short, short, short );
      void  DrawLine( void );
};
```

To create a line object, declare a pointer to a `LineObject`, then use the C++ `new` operator:

```
LineObject  *theLine;

theLine = new LineObject;
```

To give the line a thickness, invoke the object's `SetLineSize()` member function. Here the line is being set to a thickness of 5:

```
theLine->SetLineSize( 5 );
```

The `SetLineSize()` member function is simple enough—it just sets the `thickness` data member to the value passed to it:

```
void  LineObject :: SetLineSize( short width )
{
    this->thickness = width;
}
```

To set the line object's window coordinates, invoke the `SetLine-Coordinates()` member function:

```
theLine->SetLineCoordinates( 20, 50, 120, 50 );
```

The `SetLineCoordinates()` function uses the four passed-in values to set the beginning point and ending point of the line:

```
void  LineObject :: SetLineCoordinates( short x1, short y1,
                                        short x2, short y2 )
{
    this->xBegin = x1;
    this->yBegin = y1;
    this->xEnd   = x2;
    this->yEnd   = y2;
}
```

Finally, to draw the line, call the `DrawLine()` member function:

```
theLine->DrawLine();
```

`DrawLine()` uses three Toolbox functions to set the graphics pen size and then draw the line. The result of this example is shown in Figure 6.1.

```
void  LineObject :: DrawLine( void )
{
    PenSize( this->thickness, this->thickness );
    MoveTo( this->xBegin, this->yBegin );
    LineTo( this->xEnd, this->yEnd );
}
```

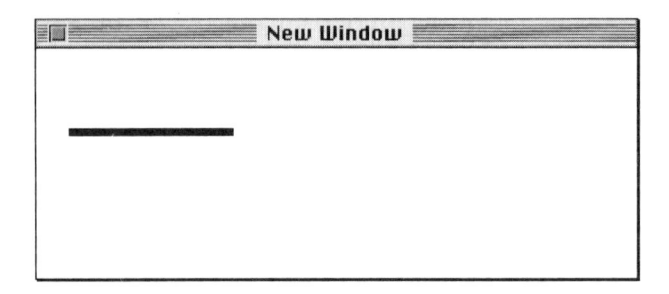

FIGURE 6.1 The result of running the PoorMansQDGX program.

Now, take a look at how QuickDraw GX works with a line object. Don't worry about the details of the following code snippets—those details will appear later in this chapter. First, declare a shape variable:

```
gxShape  theLineShape;
```

Though the variable name implies that the shape object is to be a line, the gxShape data type can be used for any kind of shape. A call to the QuickDraw GX function GXNewShape() establishes the shape type:

```
theLineShape = GXNewShape( gxLineType );
```

To set the thickness property of the new line object, call another QuickDraw GX function. The ff() function that is used as a parameter allows you to pass a short value in place of the Fixed data type that QuickDraw GX works with:

```
GXSetShapePen( theLineShape, ff(5) );
```

To set the coordinates for the line, declare a variable that was designed for just such a purpose. When declaring the gxLine variable you can set the starting point (20, 50) and the ending point (120, 50) for the line:

```
gxLine  theLineGeometry = { {ff(20), ff(50)}, {ff(120), ff(50)} };
```

Now apply the values in the gxLine variable to the shape object:

```
GXSetLine( theLineShape, &theLineGeometry );
```

Finally, draw the line shape:

```
GXDrawShape( theLineShape );
```

For ease of reading, the following snippet groups together the QuickDraw GX code shown separately above:

```
gxShape   theLineShape;
gxLine    theLineGeometry = { {ff(20), ff(50)}, {ff(120), ff(50)} };

theLineShape = GXNewShape( gxLineType );

GXSetShapePen( theLineShape, ff(5) );

GXSetLine( theLineShape, &theLineGeometry );

GXDrawShape( theLineShape );
```

You can see from the above snippet that creating a QuickDraw GX shape isn't difficult. Setting a shape's properties isn't difficult either—you rely on QuickDraw GX functions to do the work. Notice also that while you can easily set the properties of a line object, nowhere in the above code is it clear what the internal structure of a line looks like. As mentioned, QuickDraw GX data structures are private. You don't need to know the internal details of how QuickDraw GX defines a line object, and you don't have to directly access any of the line object's fields—the QuickDraw GX functions do that for you.

The following is the listing for the PoorMansQDGX program. As you look over the source code, consider that the LineObject class can be used to create a line with only a couple of properties: thickness and location. If the LineObject was to match the QuickDraw GX version of a line object, it would have to include code for many other properties.

```
//_____

class  LineObject
{
   private:
      short  thickness;
      short  xBegin;
      short  yBegin;
      short  xEnd;
```

```
       short   yEnd;

   public:
       void   SetLineSize( short );
       void   SetLineCoordinates( short, short, short, short );
       void   DrawLine( void );
};

//_____

void   LineObject :: SetLineSize( short width )
{
   this->thickness = width;
}

void   LineObject :: SetLineCoordinates( short x1, short y1,
                                         short x2, short y2 )
{
   this->xBegin = x1;
   this->yBegin = y1;
   this->xEnd   = x2;
   this->yEnd   = y2;
}

void   LineObject :: DrawLine( void )
{
   PenSize( this->thickness, this->thickness );
   MoveTo( this->xBegin, this->yBegin );
   LineTo( this->xEnd, this->yEnd );
}


//_____

void   main( void )
{
   WindowPtr   theWindow;
   LineObject  *theLine;

   InitGraf( &qd.thePort );
   InitFonts();
   InitWindows();

   theWindow = GetNewWindow( 128, nil, (WindowPtr)-1L );
   SetPort( theWindow );

   theLine = new LineObject;
```

```
theLine->SetLineSize( 5 );
theLine->SetLineCoordinates( 20, 50, 120, 50 );
theLine->DrawLine();

while ( !Button() )
    ;
}
```

Readying a Program for QuickDraw GX

QuickDraw GX may one day be built into the system of every Macintosh—just as QuickDraw is. When that happens, all Mac users will be able to enjoy the advantages of programs that use the sophisticated drawing features of QuickDraw GX. But for now, programs that make use of QuickDraw GX functionality can make no assumptions about the user's machine. Instead, a QuickDraw GX program should check for the presence of the QuickDraw GX extension at application startup. Further, if QuickDraw GX is present, this same application should make sure to perform the proper initializations.

Checking for QuickDraw GX

Before using any of the multitude of QuickDraw GX features, your program should verify that the user of your application indeed has the QuickDraw GX extension installed and enabled on his or her Macintosh. As usual, when checking for the presence of a system feature on the host machine your program should call the Toolbox function `Gestalt()`.

NOTE

Other examples of calls to `Gestalt()` appear in the check for sound recording capabilities (Chapter 3), and in the check for the presence of the QuickTime extension (Chapter 7).

To make a QuickDraw GX information request to the Toolbox, call `Gestalt()` two times—with a different selector code at each call. The QuickDraw GX extension consists of two parts: a graphics part and a printing part. That the extension consists of two parts is invisible to both you and user, and one part will never be present without the other. Knowing that, you'd be correct in assuming that checking for either part should be enough to determine if the extension is available. Why make both checks? The answer has to do with version numbers.

Each call to Gestalt() returns two pieces of information: the presence of the part (in the OSErr return value) and the part version number (in the response parameter). While the examples in this book don't examine the part versions, your code might. In the future, your program may rely on some special feature of QuickDraw GX graphics or QuickDraw GX printing—a feature only available in a particular version of one part or the other. In that case, you'll be able easily to add a check of the part version number.

In the first of two calls to Gestalt(), pass the Apple-defined selector code gestaltGraphicsVersion. In return, Gestalt() determines if the graphics part of the QuickDraw GX extension is installed and enabled. If it is, Gestalt() returns an OSErr value of noErr. If the graphics part isn't found, Gestalt() will return a value other than noErr. That means your code should examine the returned OSErr value to determine if your program can continue.

```
OSErr   theError;
long    theResult;

theError = Gestalt( gestaltGraphicsVersion, &theResult );
if ( theError != noErr )
   ExitToShell();
```

In the second call to Gestalt(), pass the Apple-defined selector code gestaltGXPrintingMgrVersion. Gestalt() will then return an OSErr value of noErr if the printing part of QuickDraw GX is available:

```
theError = Gestalt( gestaltGXPrintingMgrVersion, &theResult );
if ( theError != noErr )
   ExitToShell();
```

N O T E In the unlikely event that you do need to check a version number, examine the value returned in theResult. The fourth digit holds the version. Thus version 1.0 would be returned as 0x00010000. Because the last four digits aren't guaranteed to each be zero, do not assume that they will be. In other words, version 1 could be returned as 0x00018000. You'll want to set up your test using >= rather than ==:

```
if ( theResult == 0x00010000 )    // don't use == in this test!
```

Your application may be one that uses normal QuickDraw commands for much of its drawing, and QuickDraw GX commands only occasionally. In that situation, your program might not want to terminate if QuickDraw GX isn't on the user's machine. Instead, it could set a global flag and then examine this flag before calling any QuickDraw GX routines:

```
Boolean   gQuickDrawGXPresent;

if ( gQuickDrawGXPresent == true )
    // enable menu item that uses QuickDraw GX routines
else
    // disable menu item that uses QuickDraw GX routines
```

The global flag can be set near the start of your program's execution by calling an application-defined routine that performs the two calls to Gestalt():

```
Boolean   gQuickDrawGXPresent;

gQuickDrawGXPresent = IsQuickDrawGXAvailable();
```

Your application-defined function should look like the IsQuickDrawGX-Available() function shown below.

```
Boolean   IsQuickDrawGXAvailable( void )
{
   OSErr   theError;
   long    theResult;
```

```
theError = Gestalt( gestaltGraphicsVersion, &theResult );
if ( theError != noErr )
   return ( false );

theError = Gestalt( gestaltGXPrintingMgrVersion, &theResult );
if ( theError != noErr )
   return ( false );

return ( true );
}
```

Initializing QuickDraw GX

Once your application has verified that the QuickDraw GX extension is present, it will need to perform a few steps necessary to initialize of QuickDraw GX. The first of these steps is the allocation of a graphics client heap.

When a Macintosh application is launched, it gets loaded into a section of memory reserved for the application's own private use. This area, called the *application partition*, is composed of the application stack, the application heap, and a free area of memory between the stack and heap. It is from this free pool that both the stack and the heap obtain extra memory when either needs to grow in size.

The memory model that includes the application partition applies both to applications that use QuickDraw GX and to those that don't. Additionally, an application that uses QuickDraw GX reserves another area in memory. This section of memory, called the *graphics client heap*, is then used exclusively by QuickDraw GX to hold your application's QuickDraw GX objects.

Your application will request that QuickDraw GX allocate a graphics client heap from temporary memory as part of the QuickDraw GX initialization process. QuickDraw GX will then find and reserve a suitably sized area and claim it as the graphics client heap for your program. Figure 6.2 shows the memory layout for an application that uses QuickDraw GX.

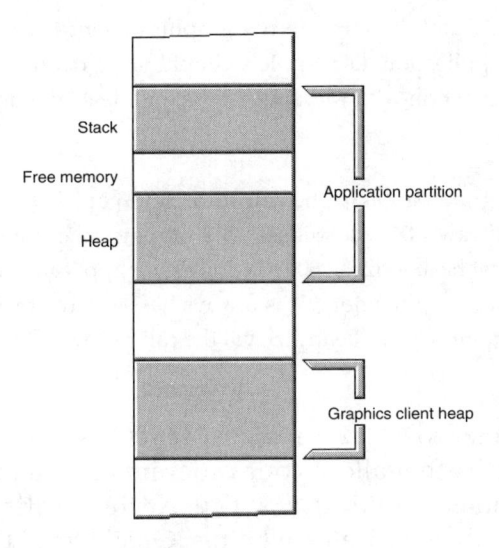

FIGURE 6.2 Memory model of a Macintosh application that uses QuickDraw GX.

QuickDraw GX defines a graphics client object, of type gxGraphicsClient, to keep track of the information in a graphics client heap. When initializing QuickDraw GX, your program should call the GXNewGraphicsClient() to create such an object:

```
#define      kGXClientHeapSizeBytes     150 * 1024

gxGraphicsClient  gGXClient;

gGXClient = GXNewGraphicsClient( nil, kGXClientHeapSizeBytes, OL );
```

The first parameter to GXNewGraphicsClient() is a pointer to a particular area in memory in which the graphics client heap should be placed. Your program should pass a nil pointer here to let QuickDraw GX have control of where the graphics client heap will be allocated.

The second parameter to GXNewGraphicsClient() is the size of the graphics client heap, in bytes. The above snippet uses the application-defined constant kGXClientHeapSizeBytes to request a 150 KB heap—a block of memory large enough for a small or moderate-size program.

To accurately determine the graphics client heap size-requirements for your application, use Apple's GraphicsBug debugger. GraphicsBug works in conjunction with MacsBug or the high-level debugger of your choice.

N O T E

A program can skip the call to `GXNewGraphicsClient()`. If it does so, QuickDraw GX will still set up a graphics client heap—but it will always give that heap a size of 600 KB. Since your application could very well use less or more heap memory, it is always best to have the application determine the graphics client heap size via the call to `GXNewGraphicsClient()`.

N O T E

The last parameter to `GXNewGraphicsClient()` is a single `long` value that holds a set of flags that allow your program to provide additional client heap specifications to QuickDraw GX. At this writing, only one flag is defined—a flag that indicates whether QuickDraw GX has permission to increase the graphics client heap size as needed (pass `0L`) or whether the heap must be left at the size specified in the second parameter to `GXNewGraphicsClient()` (pass `1L`, or the Apple-defined constant `gxStaticHeapClient`).

A call to `GXNewGraphicsClient()` creates a graphics client object to keep track of the graphics client heap, but it doesn't allocate the memory for the heap. A call to `GXEnterGraphics()` uses the information supplied in the preceding call to `GXNewGraphicsClient()` to allocate a graphics client heap and perform any necessary initializations.

```
GXEnterGraphics();
```

A program that skips the call to `GXNewGraphicsClient()` can also skip the call to `GXEnterGraphics()` as well. QuickDraw GX will then set up a default 600 KB graphics client heap. As mentioned in the preceding note, though, having the application specify the heap size is the preferred method.

N O T E

One of the advantages to calling `GXNewGraphicsClient()` and `GXEnter-Graphics()` is that you get to select the size of the graphics client heap. Another advantage is that you get to determine if enough memory was available for the allocation of the heap. After calling `GXEnterGraphics()`, call `GXGetGraphicsError()` to see if the call to `GXEnterGraphics()` succeeded. You can compare the returned error value to the following Apple-defined error out_of_memory:

```
gxGraphicsError  theGXgraphicsError;
theGXgraphicsError = GXGetGraphicsError( nil );
if ( theGXgraphicsError == out_of_memory )
   ExitToShell();
```

QuickDraw GX graphics routines don't return errors. Instead, they return a nil pointer as the function result. To check for an error, follow the QuickDraw GX call with a call to GXGetGraphicsError(). Although you can use the GXGetGraphicsError() function to determine if an error occurred after any QuickDraw GX call, it generally makes sense to do so only after GX calls that allocate blocks of memory.

NOTE The QuickDraw GX error-handling scheme is similar to the one used to handle resource errors. After calling a Resource Manager routine (such as FSpCreateResFile(), AddResource(), or GetResource()), you can call ResError() to determine if an error occurred. Here's an example:

```
theRefNum = FSpOpenResFile( theFSSpec, fsRdWrPerm );
theError = ResError();
if ( theError != noErr )
   // handle the error here
```

The following snippet shows how the preceding GX calls can be used to create a graphics client heap, allocate a block of memory for that heap, and then verify that the allocation was successful.

```
#define     kGXClientHeapSizeBytes     150 * 1024

gxGraphicsClient  gGXClient;

gxGraphicsError   theGXgraphicsError;
OSErr             theGXprintError;

gGXClient = GXNewGraphicsClient( nil, kGXClientHeapSizeBytes, 0L );

GXEnterGraphics();
theGXgraphicsError = GXGetGraphicsError( nil );
if ( theGXgraphicsError == out_of_memory )
   ExitToShell();
```

As mentioned earlier, QuickDraw GX consists of two parts: a graphics part and a printing part. After setting up your application's graphics client heap, the graphics initialization is complete. Now you should initialize the printing part of QuickDraw GX. To do that, make a call to GXInitPrinting():

```
OSErr   theGXprintError;

theGXprintError = GXInitPrinting();
```

Some QuickDraw GX printing routines don't return errors. Instead, a printing routine call can be followed with a call to GXGetJobError(). Other printing routines, however, do return an error—an OSErr. As you've just seen, GXInitPrinting() is such a routine. If GXInitPrinting() returns noErr, the initialization was successful. Any other value means that the initialization failed. The following snippet shows the check you should make after calling GXInitPrinting():

```
OSErr   theGXprintError;

theGXprintError = GXInitPrinting();
if ( theGXprintError != noErr )
   ExitToShell();
```

You can wrap all of the QuickDraw GX initialization calls into one function such as the application-defined InitializeQuickDrawGX() routine shown below.

```
#define     kGXClientHeapSizeBytes     150 * 1024

gxGraphicsClient  gGXClient;

void  InitializeQuickDrawGX( void )
{
   gxGraphicsError   theGXgraphicsError;
   OSErr             theGXprintError;

   gGXClient = GXNewGraphicsClient( nil, kGXClientHeapSizeBytes, 0L );

   GXEnterGraphics();
   theGXgraphicsError = GXGetGraphicsError( nil );
   if ( theGXgraphicsError == out_of_memory )
      ExitToShell();
```

```
      theGXprintError = GXInitPrinting();
      if ( theGXprintError != noErr )
         ExitToShell();
}
```

At the start of your program, perform the usual Toolbox initializations. Then make a call to the application-defined function IsQuickDrawGX-Available() to check for the availability of QuickDraw GX. If present, go ahead and initialize QuickDraw GX. If not present, exit or, if your program allows it, carry on but avoid calls to QuickDraw GX functions. The following snippet is similar to code used in each of this chapter's example programs.

```
InitializeToolbox();

gQuickDrawGXPresent = IsQuickDrawGXAvailable();
if ( gQuickDrawGXPresent == true )
   InitializeQuickDrawGX();
else
   // exit, or carry on without using GX routines
```

Terminating a QuickDraw GX Application

When the user chooses to terminate your application, respond by "cleaning up" QuickDraw GX. Unsurprisingly, the steps involved in exiting QuickDraw GX are related to the steps involved in initializing it.

If your application initializes printing using GXInitPrinting()—as shown in this chapter—it must exit the printing part of QuickDraw GX by calling GXExitPrinting(). Like GXInitPrinting(), GXExitPrinting() returns an OSErr value. Since your application is exiting at the time GXExitPrinting() is being called, it needn't check for an error.

```
OSErr  theGXprintError;

theGXprintError = GXExitPrinting();
```

To allocate the memory for a graphics client heap, your application called (either explicitly or implicitly) GXEnterGraphics(). To deallocate this block of memory, call GXExitGraphics(), as follows:

```
GXExitGraphics();
```

Finally, dispose of the graphics client object that was used to keep track of the graphics client heap. A call to GXDisposeGraphicsClient() handles this task. The one parameter to this function is the gxGraphicsClient type variable returned by GXNewGraphicsClient() at QuickDraw GX initialization:

```
GXDisposeGraphicsClient( gGXClient );
```

When combined into a single "clean up and exit" routine, your Quick-Draw GX exit calls should look like the ones shown in the application-defined function CleanUpQuickDrawGXandQuit():

```
OSErr   theGXprintError;

theGXprintError = GXExitPrinting();

GXExitGraphics();

GXDisposeGraphicsClient( gGXClient );
```

NOTE Notice that the calls to exit QuickDraw GX are in an order *opposite* those that initialize QuickDraw GX. This order is important—make sure that printing is deallocated before the graphics client object, and make sure that GXDisposeGraphicsClient() is the last QuickDraw GX function called.

Initializing QuickDraw GX:

```
GXNewGraphicsClient()        // create graphics client object
GXEnterGraphics()            // allocate graphics client heap
GXInitPrinting()             // initialize printing
```

Exiting QuickDraw GX:

```
GXExitPrinting()             // exit printing
GXExitGraphics()             // deallocate graphics client heap
GXDisposeGraphicsClient()    // dispose of graphics client object
```

Chapter Example: QDGXIntro

The QDGXIntro example demonstrates how to properly initialize QuickDraw GX at the start of a program and how to correctly exit

QuickDraw GX at the end of a program. In between, QDGXIntro opens a window that displays a message that tells whether or not QuickDraw GX is in the user's Extensions folder and enabled. Figure 6.3 shows that window.

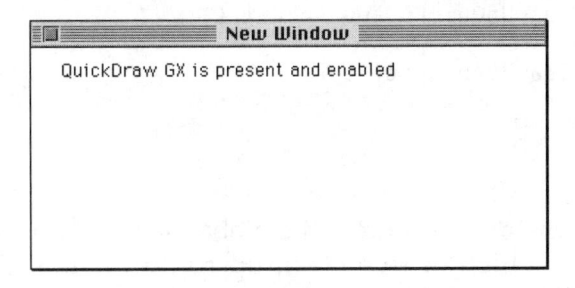

New Window

QuickDraw GX is present and enabled

FIGURE 6.3 The result of running the QDGXIntro program.

N O T E

To see the message that says "QuickDraw GX not present or not enabled", either move the QuickDraw GX extension out of the Extensions folder and reboot or uncheck it using the Extensions Manager control panel and reboot. Then run QDGXIntro again.

QDGXIntro uses the application-defined `IsQuickDrawGXAvailable()` function to determine if QuickDraw GX is present. If it is, the application-defined function `InitializeQuickDrawGX()` routine is called to create the graphics client heap and initialize printing. If QuickDraw GX isn't available, this initialization routine is skipped. After that, a simple function that opens a window and writes a message to it is called. A `while` loop that responds only to a click of the mouse button is used as a simple event loop. The program's `main()` function follows:

```
void  main( void )
{
    InitializeToolbox();

    gQuickDrawGXPresent = IsQuickDrawGXAvailable();
    if ( gQuickDrawGXPresent == true )
        InitializeQuickDrawGX();

    OpenDisplayWindow();
```

```
while ( gDone == false )
{
   if ( Button() )
   {
      if ( gQuickDrawGXPresent == true )
         CleanUpQuickDrawGXandQuit();
      else
         CleanUpAndQuit();
   }
}
}
```

At the click of the mouse button, the global flag `gQuickDrawGXPresent` is checked to see which of two clean-up routines should be called. If QuickDraw GX is present, a routine that performs both QuickDraw GX clean up and standard memory disposal tasks is called, as shown below:

```
void  CleanUpQuickDrawGXandQuit( void )
{
   OSErr  theGXprintError;

   if ( gDisplayWindow != nil )
      DisposeWindow( gDisplayWindow );

   GXExitGraphics();

   GXDisposeGraphicsClient( gGXClient );

   gDone = true;
}
```

If QuickDraw GX isn't present, a routine that handles only traditional memory management is called:

```
void  CleanUpAndQuit( void )
{
   if ( gDisplayWindow != nil )
      DisposeWindow( gDisplayWindow );

   gDone = true;
}
```

You'll want to spend a few extra minutes examining the QDGXIntro source code listing. That's because almost all of the code in this example will be reused in the remaining four example programs in this chapter. Because the next four examples will add to the code used here, only the new code will be shown in the remaining listings.

```
//_____

Boolean   IsQuickDrawGXAvailable( void );
void      InitializeToolbox( void );
void      InitializeQuickDrawGX( void );
void      OpenDisplayWindow( void );
void      CleanUpAndQuit( void );
void      CleanUpQuickDrawGXandQuit( void );

//_____

#define   kGXClientHeapSizeBytes    150 * 1024

//_____

gxGraphicsClient  gGXClient;
Boolean           gQuickDrawGXPresent;
WindowPtr         gDisplayWindow = nil;
Boolean           gDone = false;

//_____

void  main( void )
{
    InitializeToolbox();

    gQuickDrawGXPresent = IsQuickDrawGXAvailable();
    if ( gQuickDrawGXPresent == true )
        InitializeQuickDrawGX();

    OpenDisplayWindow();

    while ( gDone == false )
    {
        if ( Button() )
        {
            if ( gQuickDrawGXPresent == true )
                CleanUpQuickDrawGXandQuit();
            else
                CleanUpAndQuit();
        }
    }
}
```

```
}

//_____

4Boolean  IsQuickDrawGXAvailable( void )
{
   OSErr   theError;
   long    theResult;

   theError = Gestalt( gestaltGraphicsVersion, &theResult );
   if ( theError != noErr )
     return ( false );

   theError = Gestalt( gestaltGXPrintingMgrVersion, &theResult );
   if ( theError != noErr )
     return ( false );

   return ( true );
}

//_____

void  InitializeQuickDrawGX( void )
{
   gxGraphicsError  theGXgraphicsError;
   OSErr            theGXprintError;

   gGXClient = GXNewGraphicsClient( nil, kGXClientHeapSizeBytes, 0L );

   GXEnterGraphics();
   theGXgraphicsError = GXGetGraphicsError( nil );
   if ( theGXgraphicsError == out_of_memory )
      ExitToShell();

   theGXprintError = GXInitPrinting();
   if ( theGXprintError != noErr )
      ExitToShell();
}

//_____

void  OpenDisplayWindow( void )
{
   gDisplayWindow = GetNewCWindow( 128, nil, (WindowPtr)-1L );
   ShowWindow( gDisplayWindow );
   SetPort( gDisplayWindow );
   MoveTo( 20, 20 );
```

```
   if ( gQuickDrawGXPresent == true )
      DrawString( "\pQuickDraw GX is present and enabled" );
   else
      DrawString( "\pQuickDraw GX not present or not enabled" );
}

//_____

void  CleanUpQuickDrawGXandQuit( void )
{
   OSErr  theGXprintError;

   if ( gDisplayWindow != nil )
      DisposeWindow( gDisplayWindow );

   theGXprintError = GXExitPrinting();

   GXExitGraphics();

   GXDisposeGraphicsClient( gGXClient );

   gDone = true;
}

//_____

void  CleanUpAndQuit( void )
{
   if ( gDisplayWindow != nil )
      DisposeWindow( gDisplayWindow );

   gDone = true;
}

//_____

void  InitializeToolbox( void )
{
   InitGraf( &qd.thePort );
   InitFonts();
   InitWindows();
   InitMenus();
   TEInit();
   InitDialogs( 0L );
   FlushEvents( everyEvent, 0 );
   InitCursor();
}
```

Windows and QuickDraw GX

In the standard QuickDraw drawing environment, drawing takes place in a graphics port. After opening a window using `GetNewCWindow()` (or `GetNewWindow()`, `NewWindow()`, or `NewCWindow()`), your program calls `SetPort()` to ensure that subsequent QuickDraw drawing commands target the new window:

```
WindowPtr  gDisplayWindow;

gDisplayWindow = GetNewCWindow( 128, nil, (WindowPtr)-1L );
SetPort( gDisplayWindow );
```

In the QuickDraw GX environment, drawing takes place in a standard window—but in a *view* port rather than a *graphics* port. When using QuickDraw GX, your program will still execute the above code. Now, however, there'll be an additional function call—a call to `GXNewWindowViewPort()`:

```
WindowPtr   gDisplayWindow;
gxViewPort  gWindowViewPort;

gDisplayWindow = GetNewCWindow( 128, nil, (WindowPtr)-1L );
SetPort( gDisplayWindow );

gWindowViewPort = GXNewWindowViewPort( gDisplayWindow );
```

The `GXNewWindowViewPort()` function creates a new view port object and attaches, or associates, it with a window. Now the same window has a graphics port and a view port, and can thus accept both standard QuickDraw commands and new QuickDraw GX commands. Figure 6.4 illustrates. In this figure `SetRect()` and `FillRect()` calls have been made to draw a rectangle in the window. QuickDraw GX typography calls have been made to draw text to the window as well. While these two objects can be thought of as existing in two planes, the outcome is that they appear together in the window.

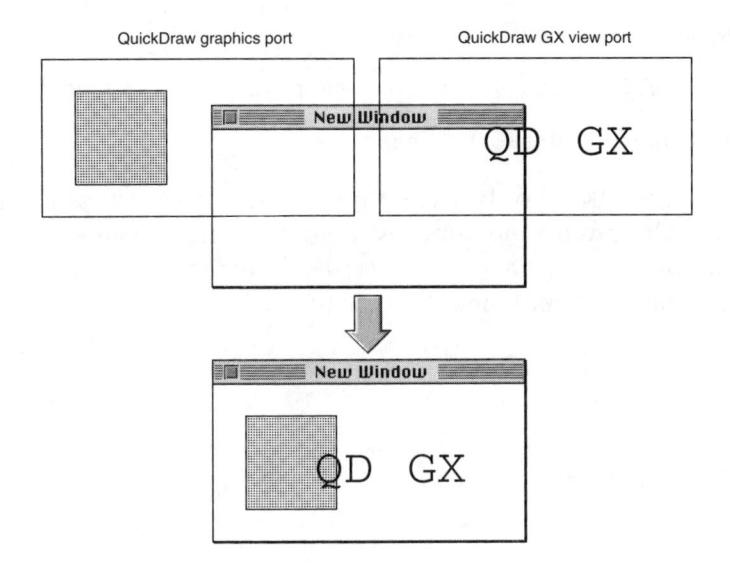

FIGURE 6.4 A single window can support both a
QuickDraw graphics port and a QuickDraw GX view port.

After a window has been given a view port, QuickDraw GX shapes can be drawn to that window. A shape can be created using the GXNewShape() function, paired with a view port using GXSetShapeViewPort(), and then drawn to that view port using GXDrawShape(). Shapes, and these QuickDraw GX functions, are covered later in this chapter. For now, the following snippet provides an overview of the process of drawing a shape to a window.

```
WindowPtr    gDisplayWindow;
gxViewPort   gWindowViewPort;

gDisplayWindow = GetNewCWindow( 128, nil, (WindowPtr)-1L );
SetPort( gDisplayWindow );

gWindowViewPort = GXNewWindowViewPort( gDisplayWindow );
```

```
// GXNewShape() - create a shape

// GXSetShapeViewPorts() - pair a shape with a view port

// GXDrawShape() - draw the shape
```

When a window that holds a view port closes, the view port should be disposed of along with the window. Before calling `DisposeWindow()`, call `GXDisposeViewPort()`. Pass the `gxViewPort` object that was created by the earlier call to `GXNewWindowViewPort()`.

```
WindowPtr    gDisplayWindow;
gxViewPort   gWindowViewPort;

GXDisposeViewPort( gWindowViewPort );
DisposeWindow( gDisplayWindow );
```

Chapter Example: QDGXWindow

QDGXWindow, like QDGXIntro, opens a window and writes a message to it. A click of the mouse closes the window and ends the program. Figure 6.5 shows the QDGXWindow.

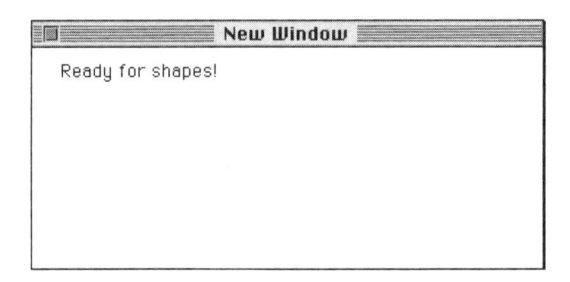

FIGURE 6.5 The result of running the QDGXWindow program.

QDGXWindow doesn't draw any QuickDraw GX shapes. Instead, the program serves as an example of how to ready a window for QuickDraw GX, and how to properly dispose of the window.

The QDGXWindow program adds one global variable to those used in the QDGXIntro example—a `gxViewPort` variable named `gWindowViewPort`:

```
gxGraphicsClient    gGXClient;
Boolean             gQuickDrawGXPresent;
WindowPtr           gDisplayWindow = nil;
gxViewPort          gWindowViewPort;
Boolean             gDone = false;
```

The main() function of QDGXWindow differs from that of QDGXIntro
in that QuickDraw GX is now required. If it isn't present, the program
will call ExitToShell() to terminate. Because QuickDraw GX must be
present, the event loop now doesn't check to see if QuickDraw GX clean
up should be performed upon quitting. Instead, a mouse click always
results in a call to CleanUpQuickDrawGXandQuit(). Each of the remaining
programs in this chapter work the same way.

```
void  main( void )
{
    InitializeToolbox();

    gQuickDrawGXPresent = IsQuickDrawGXAvailable();
    if ( gQuickDrawGXPresent == true )
        InitializeQuickDrawGX();
    else
        ExitToShell();

    OpenDisplayWindow();

    while ( gDone == false )
    {
        if ( Button() )
            CleanUpQuickDrawGXandQuit();
    }
}
```

OpenDisplayWindow() now includes a call to GXNewWindowViewPort() to
create a new view port object and to attach that object to the program's
window. The function also includes a few commented lines to hint at
the code that will appear in the next example program.

```
void  OpenDisplayWindow( void )
{
    gDisplayWindow = GetNewCWindow( 128, nil, (WindowPtr)-1L );
    ShowWindow( gDisplayWindow );
    SetPort( gDisplayWindow );
```

```
   MoveTo( 20, 20 );
   DrawString( "\pReady for shapes!" );

   gWindowViewPort = GXNewWindowViewPort( gDisplayWindow );

// GXNewShape() - create a shape

// GXSetShapeViewPorts() - pair a shape with a view port

// GXDrawShape() - draw the shape

}
```

The `CleanUpQuickDrawGXandQuit()` function now includes a call to `GXDisposeViewPort()`—as shown below.

```
void  CleanUpQuickDrawGXandQuit( void )
{
   OSErr  theGXprintError;

   if ( gDisplayWindow != nil )
   {
      GXDisposeViewPort( gWindowViewPort );
      DisposeWindow( gDisplayWindow );
   }

   theGXprintError = GXExitPrinting();

   GXExitGraphics();

   GXDisposeGraphicsClient( gGXClient );

   gDone = true;
}
```

Graphic Shape Objects

There are several types of objects that QuickDraw GX works with. Of these object types, it is the shape object with which you'll become the most familiar with. A shape object can be used to create, display, and manipulate lines, rectangles, polygons, bit maps, pictures, text, and more.

Creating and Drawing a Shape Object

The GXNewShape() function is used to create a new shape object. GXNewShape() accepts the type of shape to create as the single parameter and returns a gxShape—a new shape object. The shape type can be any of the following Apple-defined constants:

```
gxEmptyType
gxPointType
gxLineType
gxCurveType
gxRectangleType
gxPolygonType
gxPathType
gxBitmapType
gxTextType
gxGlyphType
gxLayoutType
gxFullType
gxPictureType
```

Before calling GXNewShape(), declare a gxShape variable to hold the returned shape. Then pass GXNewShape() one of the shape types listed above.

```
gxShape   theLineShape;

theLineShape = GXNewShape( gxLineType );
```

When you create a new shape, QuickDraw GX assigns default values to each of the shape's properties—the characteristics that define a shape. You can use QuickDraw GX functions to change any or all of a shape's properties. In all cases, you'll want to change the *shape geometry* property— the property that defines the space the shape occupies. QuickDraw GX uses a struct to define a shape's geometry. For a line, the struct is named gxLine and looks like this:

```
struct  gxLine
{
   struct  gxPoint  first;
   struct  gxPoint  last;
};
```

As a second example, QuickDraw GX uses a `gxRectangle` struct that looks like the following:

```
struct   gxRectangle
{
   Fixed   left;
   Fixed   top;
   Fixed   right;
   Fixed   bottom;
};
```

The line's geometry structure uses two fields of type `gxPoint` to define a line. Each `gxPoint` field consists of two `Fixed` values. The rectangle's geometry structure uses four `Fixed` values as well. The `Fixed` data type is easy for QuickDraw GX to work with, but not so easy for humans to use. For this reason, QuickDraw GX defines the `ff()` macro that is used to convert an integral number such as a `short` to a number in `Fixed` format. Whenever a QuickDraw GX routine requires that a parameter be of type `Fixed`, you can use a `short`—provided you use the `ff()` macro.

NOTE

The `Fixed` data type is defined to be a `long`. But the Macintosh doesn't interpret the `Fixed` in the same way that it does a `long`. A number in `Fixed` format holds a whole, or integer part, and a fractional part. QuickDraw GX makes extensive use of the `Fixed` format because manipulating `Fixed` numbers is quicker than manipulating floating-point, or float numbers.

To set up a new geometry for a new shape, declare a shape geometry variable that matches the shape's type. For a line object, declare a `gxLine` variable. For a rectangle object, declare a `gxRectangle` variable. When you declare the variable, initialize its fields. Recall that for a line, the gxLine structure requires the line's first and last points. For a line that is to start at (50, 100) and end at (300, 60), declare a shape geometry variable as shown below. Figure 6.6 shows the line that would be defined by the following geometry.

```
gxLine  theLineGeometry = { {ff(50), ff(100)}, {ff(300), ff(60)} };
```

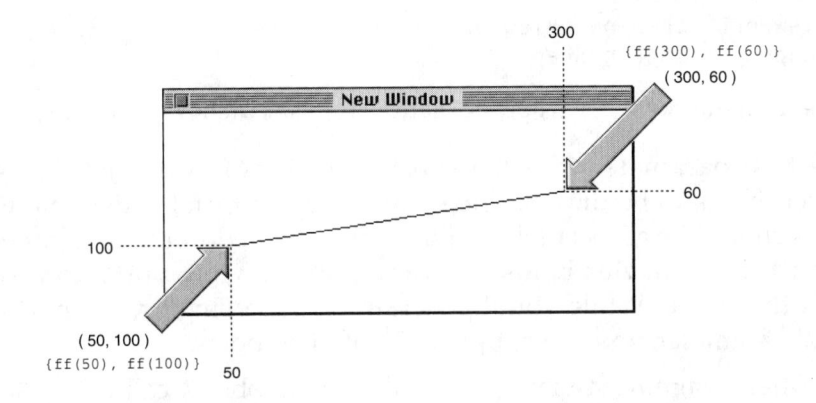

FIGURE 6.6 The geometry of a line specifies the line's end points

Each shape has its own geometry-setting function: a line's geometry is set by GXSetLine(), a rectangle's geometry is set by GXSetRectangle(), and so forth. For the line shape, after declaring and initializing the geometry variable, you'll call GXSetLine() to match the geometry to the shape object. The first parameter to GXSetLine() is the shape whose geometry is being set. The second parameter is a pointer to the geometry.

```
GXSetLine( theLineShape, &theLineGeometry );
```

The following snippet shows the complete code needed to create a line shape object and to set the shape geometry property of that line:

```
gxShape   theLineShape;
gxLine    theLineGeometry = { {ff(50), ff(100)}, {ff(300), ff(60)} };

theLineShape = GXNewShape( gxLineType );
GXSetLine( theLineShape, &theLineGeometry );
```

To draw a shape, call the GXDrawShape() function. Before doing so, though, you'll need to tell QuickDraw GX where the shape should be drawn. Just as QuickDraw needs to know which graphics port to draw an image to, QuickDraw GX needs to know which view port to draw a shape to. The GXSetShapeViewPorts() function is used for this task. A call to GXSetShapeViewPorts() follows:

```
gxViewPort   theWindowViewPort;
gxShape      theLineShape;

GXSetShapeViewPorts( theLineShape, 1, theWindowViewPort );
```

The first parameter to GXSetShapeViewPorts() is the gxShape shape object that is to be drawn. The second parameter tells how many view ports should be associated with the object named in the first parameter. The third parameter holds the view port, or view ports, to associate with the shape. While you'll generally name a single view port as the third parameter, you can supply a list of view ports.

After assigning a view port to the shape object, call GXDrawShape() to draw the shape to the view port:

```
gxShape   theLineShape;

GXDrawShape( theLineShape );
```

The following snippet demonstrates how to create a line shape object, set its geometry, and then draw that shape to a view port.

```
gxViewPort   theWindowViewPort;
gxShape      theLineShape;
gxLine       theLineGeometry = { {ff(50), ff(100)}, {ff(300), ff(60)} };

theLineShape = GXNewShape( gxLineType );
GXSetLine( theLineShape, &theLineGeometry );

GXSetShapeViewPorts( theLineShape, 1, &theWindowViewPort );

GXDrawShape( theLineShape );
```

Chapter Example: QDGXShape

The QDGXShape program draws the same line the was described on the previous pages—Figure 6.7 shows the window you'll see when you run the p rogram.

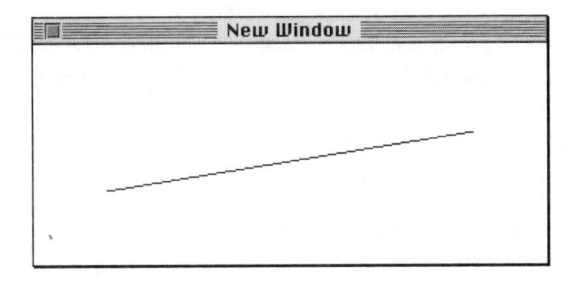

FIGURE 6.7 The result of running the QDGXShape program.

QDGXShape adds one more global variable to the ones used in the preceding program. The `gLineShape` variable will hold the line shape object.

```
gxGraphicsClient    gGXClient;
Boolean             gQuickDrawGXPresent;
WindowPtr           gDisplayWindow = nil;
gxViewPort          gWindowViewPort;
Boolean             gDone = false;
gxShape             gLineShape;
```

The application-defined `CreateGXLineShape()` function is used to create the new line shape object and to set the geometry of that object.

```
void  CreateGXLineShape( void )
{
   gxLine  theLineGeometry = { {ff(50), ff(100)}, {ff(300), ff(60)} };

   gLineShape = GXNewShape( gxLineType );
   GXSetLine( gLineShape, &theLineGeometry );
}
```

CreateGXLineShape() is called from OpenDisplayWindow(). When CreateGX-LineShape() returns, the global line shape object gets drawn to a view port:

```
void  OpenDisplayWindow( void )
{
   gDisplayWindow = GetNewCWindow( 128, nil, (WindowPtr)-1L );
   ShowWindow( gDisplayWindow );
   SetPort( gDisplayWindow );

   gWindowViewPort = GXNewWindowViewPort( gDisplayWindow );

   CreateGXLineShape();

   GXSetShapeViewPorts( gLineShape, 1, &gWindowViewPort );

   GXDrawShape( gLineShape );
}
```

Shape Object Properties

All shape objects have nine properties. The *shape type*, *shape geometry*, and *shape fill* are the three properties that define the shape itself. For example, a rectangle shape object would, of course, be a shape type of rectangle. QuickDraw GX uses the shape constant gxRectangleType to denote a shape that is a rectangle. A rectangle object's shape geometry is the coordinates of the rectangle. QuickDraw GX uses a gxRectangle struct to hold these four values. A rectangle's fill could be any of a number of fill types. For instance, QuickDraw GX would use the fill constant gxSolidFill as the shape fill for a rectangle drawn as a solid. Figure 6.8 shows these three important shape properties.

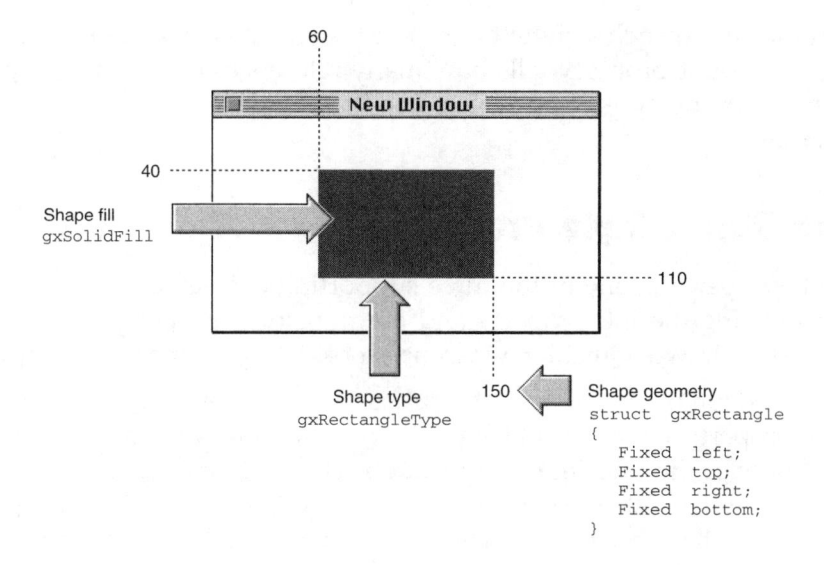

FIGURE 6.8 The three shape properties that define a shape.

Each shape object has a *style property, ink property,* and *transform property.* These three properties are used to modify the look of a shape. Each of these three properties is actually an object—a *supporting object.* Supporting objects don't need to be explicitly created by your program. When your application creates a new shape, three new supporting objects are also created. Your program doesn't have to keep track of a shape's supporting objects—the shape will know how to reference them as needed.

A shape's style property is used to vary such characteristics as the shape's pen width and pattern. The ink property of a shape is used to set the shape's color and its transfer mode—the way in which the shape covers the background it is set against. The transform property of a shape is used to change the mapping of a shape—that is, to scale, skew, or rotate the shape.

The remaining three shape properties are the object-related properties: the *shape attributes, owner count,* and *tag list.* The shape-attributes property holds information such as whether or not the shape is locked in memory. The owner- count property tells how many references exist to the shape. The tag list property is used if you need to attach application-specific information to an object.

Shape Object Style Properties

The style property is one of the three supporting objects for a shape (the other two being the ink property and the transform property). When a shape is to be drawn, QuickDraw GX first looks at the shape's style object.

Like a shape object, a style object has a set of properties of its own. Of these properties, you'll find the pen width the most familiar. To change the thickness of the lines that frame an object, call `GXSetShapePen()`. The first parameter to `GXSetShapePen()` is the shape object that the pen affects, while the second parameter is the new width, or thickness, of the pen. Because the second parameter should be in `Fixed` notation, use the `ff()` macro when passing the new width. The following snippet changes the pen width of the `theLineShape`:

```
gxShape  theLineShape;

GXSetShapePen( theLineShape, ff(15) );
```

After the above snippet executes, any calls to `GXDrawShape( theLineShape )` will result in a line with a thickness of 15 pixels being drawn.

> The details of the supporting objects can be found in the more than 650 pages of the *QuickDraw GX Objects* volume of *Inside Macintosh*—one of the seven *QuickDraw GX Inside Macintosh* books.

N O T E

Shape Object Ink Properties

The ink property is another of the three supporting objects for a shape. The ink object lets you add color and transfer mode information to a shape. To set the color property of an ink object, begin by declaring a `gxColor` variable:

```
gxColor  theRedColor;
```

As shown below, the gxColor structure consists of three members.

```
struct gxColor
{
   gxColorSpace      space;
   gxColorProfile    profile;
   union
   {
      ...
      ...
   }                 element;
};
```

The first gxColor member is the space field. This member specifies the color space—or color system—used to define the color for a shape. For Macintosh programmers, the most common example of a color space is the RGB space. RGB (for red, green, blue) is used by Color QuickDraw. Other color space examples are CMYK and the indexed color space. The gxColorSpace data type defines the different color spaces—a few of which are shown here:

```
enum  gxColorSpaces { ..., gxRGBSpace, ..., gxGraySpace, ... };
```

To set the color space of a gxColor variable, use one of the gxColorSpace constants. As mentioned, RGB is the most commonly used space:

```
gxColor  theRedColor;
```

```
theRedColor.space = gxRGBSpace;
```

The second gxColor member is the profile field. This field holds information used in color-matching when switching devices (monitors). If you set this field to nil, QuickDraw GX will use its default color profile:

```
theRedColor.profile = nil;
```

The last gxColor member is the element field. The element field holds one specific color. In the gxColor structure, the element field is defined as a union. Drawing on your C background you'll recall that a structure field that is a union is one that can have different data types, but only one type at any given time. The following is the complete definition of the element field of gxColor.

```
union
{
    struct  gxCMYKColor        cmyk;
    struct  gxRGBColor         rgb;
    struct  gxRGBAColor        rgba;
    struct  gxHSVColor         hsv;
    struct  gxHLSColor         hls;
    struct  gxXYZColor         xyz;
    struct  gxYXYColor         yxy;
    struct  gxLUVColor         luv;
    struct  gxLABColor         lab;
    struct  gxYIQColor         yiq;
    gxColorValue               gray;
    struct  gxGrayAColor       graya;
    unsigned  short            pixel16;
    unsigned  long             pixel32;
    struct  gxIndexedColor     indexed;
    gxColorValue               component[4];
} element;
```

If your shape object is using the RGB space for its color space, then it should use the rgb union member for the element field of the gxColor variable. In the above definition, you can see that the rgb field is of the type gxRGBColor:

```
struct  gxRGBColor
{
    gxColorValue  red;
    gxColorValue  green;
    gxColorValue  blue;
};
```

The gxColorValue type holds a value in the range of 0x0000 to 0xFFFF. A value of 0x0000 represents the least intense level of a color, while 0xFFFF represents the most intense level. To create a bright red color using the RGB space, use the following code:

```
theRedColor.element.rgb.red   = 0xFFFF;
theRedColor.element.rgb.green = 0x0000;
theRedColor.element.rgb.blue  = 0x0000;
```

NOTE If you aren't familiar with RGB colors, experiment with the Color Picker. This utility, pictured in Figure 6.9, can be found in the Color control panel of System 7.1. You can click on a color on the color wheel and the corresponding red, green, and blue values will be shown at the bottom left of the Color Picker. In Figure 6.9, the color red has been selected. If you know how to convert decimal to hexadecimal, you'll know that 65535 in decimal is 0xFFFF in hexadecimal. If you don't want to make the conversion, you can use the decimal values in your code. Append an L to each value to force the compiler to recognize the numbers as 4-byte longs:

```
theRedColor.element.rgb.red   = 65535L;
theRedColor.element.rgb.green = 0L;
theRedColor.element.rgb.blue  = 0L;
```

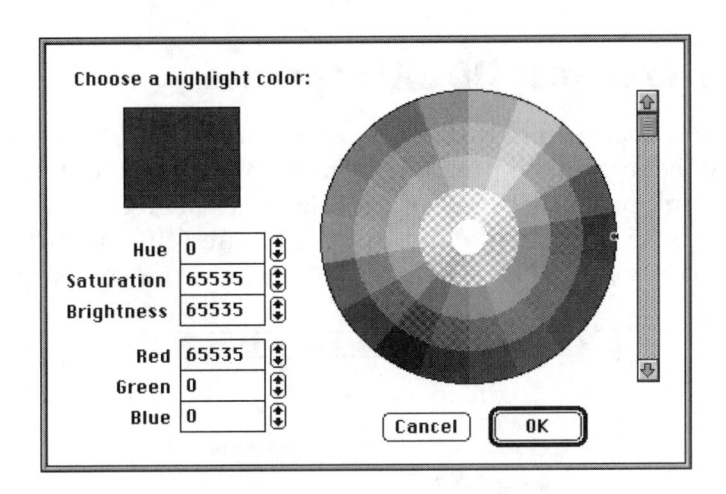

FIGURE 6.9 Apple's Color Picker can be used to find the RGB values of a color.

Once a color has been set up, assign it to a shape using the GXSetShape-Color() function:

```
gxColor   theRedColor;
gxShape   theLineShape;

GXSetShapeColor( theLineShape, &theRedColor);
```

The following snippet shows how to assign a gxColor variable a color of red using the RGB color space, and then how to associate that color with a shape.

```
gxColor  theRedColor;
gxShape  theLineShape;

theRedColor.space = gxRGBSpace;
theRedColor.profile = nil;
theRedColor.element.rgb.red   = 0xFFFF;
theRedColor.element.rgb.green = 0x0000;
theRedColor.element.rgb.blue  = 0x0000;

GXSetShapeColor( theLineShape, &theRedColor);
```

Chapter Example: QDGXProperties

The QDGXProperties program uses the gxShape variable theLineShape introduced in the previous program, QDGXShape. Here, the style property object and ink property object of the shape are altered to create a line shape that is 15 pixels wide and purple. Figure 6.10 shows the line—though, of course, you'll have to trust that the line is indeed purple.

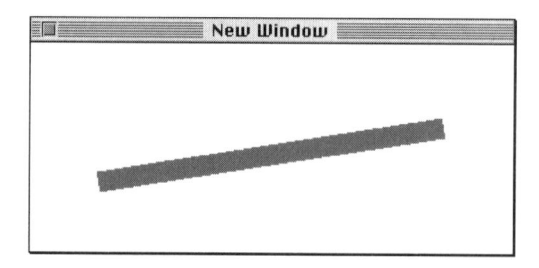

FIGURE 6.10 The result of running the QDGXProperties program.

All of the code that differs from the QDGXShape program is found in the application-defined CreateGXLineShape() function. In this function, a gxColor variable is declared, then set to the RGB color space. The color purple is achieved by mixing a moderate amount of red (in hexadecimal, 0x8000 is one half of 0xFFFF) with a moderate amount of blue. No green is used.

```
void  CreateGXLineShape( void )
{
   gxLine  theLineGeometry = { {ff(50), ff(100)}, {ff(300),
   ff(60)} };
   gxColor thePurpleColor;

   gLineShape = GXNewShape( gxLineType );
   GXSetLine( gLineShape, &theLineGeometry );

   thePurpleColor.space = gxRGBSpace;
   thePurpleColor.profile = nil;
   thePurpleColor.element.rgb.red   = 0x8000;
   thePurpleColor.element.rgb.green = 0x0000;
   thePurpleColor.element.rgb.blue  = 0x8000;

   GXSetShapePen( gLineShape, ff(15) );
   GXSetShapeColor( gLineShape, &thePurpleColor );
}
```

Shape Object Transform Properties

The style property and the ink property are two of the three supporting objects used with a shape. The third and final supporting object is the transform property object. As its name indicates, a transform object holds information that transforms a shape in some way. Scaling, rotating, skewing, and adding perspective are a few of the uses of the transform object.

Mapping is a general term used to describe some transforms. The mapping property of a transform object holds a matrix. QuickDraw GX multiplies the values in this matrix with the coordinates of a shape to transform the shape into a new one.

Chapter Example: QDGXMapping

The QDGXMapping program introduces a new shape—the rectangle shape. It also demonstrates how to use a transform property—scaling. Figure 6.11 shows a window with the program's original rectangle to the right, and a scaled version to the left.

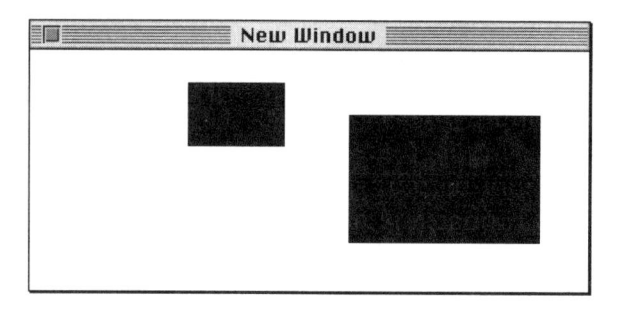

FIGURE 6.11 The result of running the QDGXMapping program.

All shapes—regardless of type—begin as a `gxShape` variable. In QDGX-Shape you saw that was the case for a line object. Here, you'll see that it holds true for a rectangle shape:

```
gxShape  gRectShape;
```

The particular shape type of a `gxShape` is determined when `GXNewShape()` is called. QDGXMapping uses a short application-defined routine to create a rectangle object and define that object's geometry.

```
void  CreateGXRectangleShape( void )
{
   gxRectangle  theRectGeometry = { ff(200), ff(40), ff(320), ff(120) };

   gRectShape = GXNewShape( gxRectangleType );
   GXSetRectangle( gRectShape, &theRectGeometry );
}
```

`CreateGXRectangleShape()` is called from `OpenDisplayWindow()`. Once the rectangle shape is created, `OpenDisplayWindow()` calls `GXDrawShape()` to draw it to a window. Figure 6.12 shows the coordinates of this rectangle.

```
gWindowViewPort = GXNewWindowViewPort( gDisplayWindow );

CreateGXRectangleShape();

GXSetShapeViewPorts( gRectShape, 1, &gWindowViewPort );

GXDrawShape( gRectShape );
```

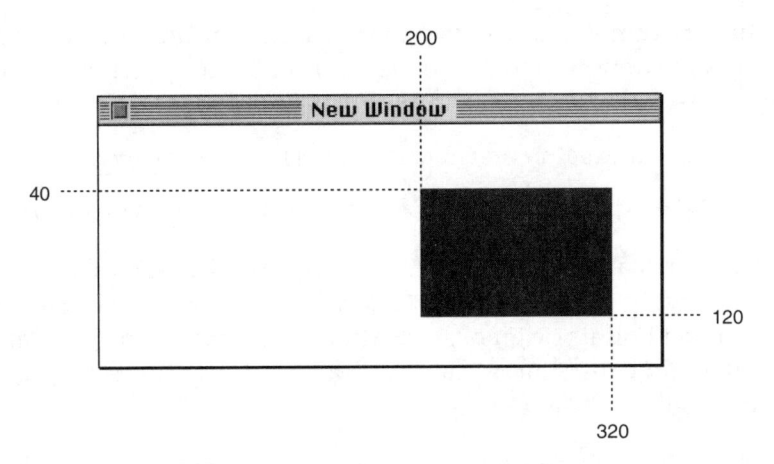

FIGURE 6.12 The geometry of a rectangle
the first time it is drawn using GXDrawShape().

After drawing the rectangle, OpenDisplayWindow() calls the application-defined function ScaleGXRectangleShape() to scale the rectangle to one-half its original size. This is accomplished using the QuickDraw GX function GXScaleShape(). Here's the prototype for that function:

```
void  GXScaleShape( gxShape  target,
                    Fixed    hScale,
                    Fixed    vScale,
                    Fixed    xOffset,
                    Fixed    yOffset )
```

Pass GXScaleShape() an object and this QuickDraw GX function will transform the shape by applying a mapping matrix to it. The second and third parameters determine the scaling factor for the shape. For instance, a value of one half for hScale would tell GXScaleShape() to reduce the horizontal geometry of a shape to one-half its current value. Because GXScaleShape() accepts Fixed values, you can't directly pass a value of one half. Instead, use the QuickDraw GX FixedDivide() function to create a Fixed format value equal to one half:

```
Fixed  theHorizScale;

theHorizScale = FixedDivide( ff(1), ff(2) );
```

The first parameter to `FixedDivide()` is the numerator, the second parameter is the denominator. Use the `ff()` macro to pass these values as `Fixed` numbers. Several more examples that use `FixedDivide()` follows:

```
theHorizScale = FixedDivide( ff(1), ff(4) );     // 1/4th original

theHorizScale = FixedDivide( ff(3), ff(1) );     // triple original
```

Finally, the fourth and fifth parameters to `GXScaleShape()` are x and y offsets. The following function uses `GXScaleShape()` to scale the `gRectShape` rectangle to one-half its original size. After `OpenDisplayWindow()` calls this function, it again calls `GXDrawShape()` to again draw the rectangle shape object. The result is shown in Figure 6.13.

```
void  ScaleGXRectangleShape( void )
{
   Fixed  theHorizScale;
   Fixed  theVertScale;
   Fixed  theXOffset = ff(0);
   Fixed  theYOffset = ff(0);

   theHorizScale = FixedDivide( ff(1), ff(2) );
   theVertScale  = FixedDivide( ff(1), ff(2) );

   GXScaleShape( gRectShape, theHorizScale, theVertScale,
                 theXOffset, theYOffset );
}
```

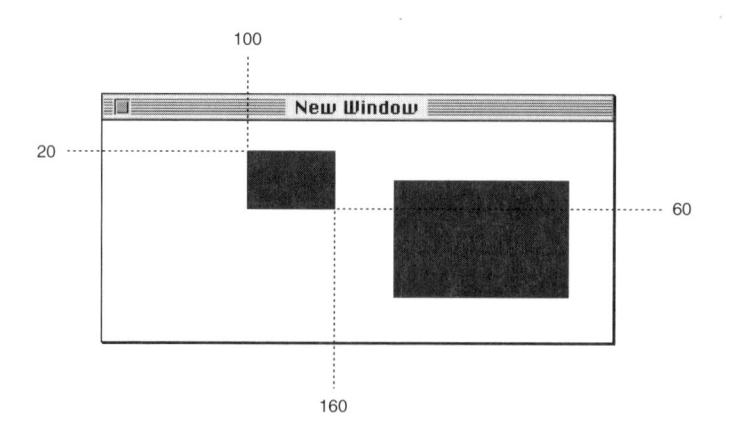

FIGURE 6.13 The geometry of a rectangle the second time
it is drawn using `GXDrawShape()`.

In Figure 6.13, notice that along with being reduced in size by a factor of two, the location of the shape has changed from its original position. That's because `GXScaleShape()` changes the geometry of the shape. The rectangle's original coordinates were set as follows:

```
gxRectangle  theRectGeometry  = { ff(200), ff(40), ff(320), ff(120) };
```

If a rectangle shape had its geometry set using the new scaled values, the initialization would look like the following:

```
gxRectangle  theScaleGeometry = { ff(100), ff(20), ff(160), ff(60) };
```

Summary

QuickDraw GX is a system software extension that adds new, powerful graphics functionality to the Macintosh. The new QuickDraw GX supplements rather than replaces the older QuickDraw.

In QuickDraw GX, shapes are objects. A shape can be as simple as a line and as complex as a bit-mapped image. In both cases, the shape is represented by an object. A new shape object is created using the QuickDraw GX function `GXNewShape()`. The shape can be drawn using the QuickDraw GX function `GXDrawShape()`. Before doing so, call `GXSetShapeViewPort()` to match the shape with a QuickDraw GX view port.

A shape has properties that define the shape itself and allow the shape to be modified. The shape type, geometry, and fill provide a description of the type of a shape. The style, ink, and transform properties hold information that modifies the look of a shape.

CHAPTER 7

QuickTime Movies

Apple's QuickTime system extension allows programmers to easily add movie-playing capabilities to any Macintosh applications. By adding little more than a page's worth of source code to a project, you can bring an ordinary, unassuming application to life. And with a little extra effort, you can further turn that same application into a multimedia showpiece. The dynamic content that movies add to your program make the incorporation of QuickTime a surefire way to hook users on your application.

In this chapter, you'll learn all about the Movie Toolbox—the set of movie-related Toolbox routines that enable you to add movie-playing and movie-editing features to any of your programs. You will also get an introduction to the basic Movie Toolbox routines that are used to open movie files, play movies, and add a movie controller to a movie. In Chapter 9, you'll read about additional routines that are all you need to add movie-editing and movie-saving features to a program.

A *movie controller* is the thin, three-dimensional control panel that appears at the bottom of a window that displays a QuickTime movie. As you peruse this chapter, you will learn the details of creating a movie controller, attaching it to a movie window, and implementing the buttons that appear on that controller.

The Movie Toolbox

QuickTime isn't an application that a Mac user runs—it's a system software extension. An *extension* is code that extends the power of the Macintosh. In order to access this code, Apple supplies an application programming interface (API), to it. Just as Macintosh Toolbox is the API that allow programmers to access Apple's graphical user interface code, so is the Movie Toolbox the API that allows programmers to access QuickTime code. When you know how to use the Macintosh Toolbox, you'll be able to have your application open and then automatically play a movie (as shown in Figure 7.1), display a movie in an area of a dialog box (as shown in Figure 7.2), or attach a movie controller to a movie to give the user the ability to control movie playing (as shown in Figure 7.3). In this chapter, you'll see explanations and source code examples that work with movies in each of these ways.

FIGURE 7.1 A QuickTime movie displayed in a window without a movie controller.

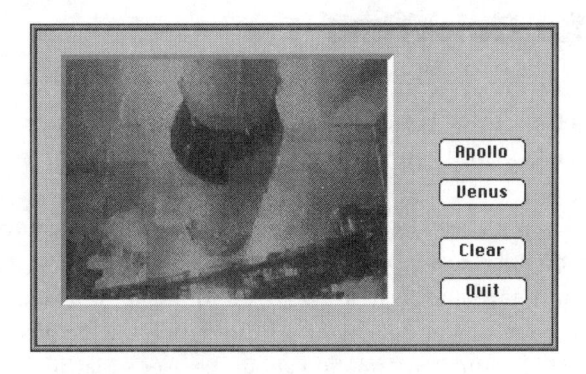

FIGURE 7.2 A QuickTime movie displayed in an area of a dialog box.

FIGURE 7.3 QuickTime movies displayed in windows that have movie controllers.

The original Macintosh Toolbox routines allow a programmer to add hundreds of interface features—a functional menu bar, multiple windows, a File Selection dialog box—to any application. The Movie Toolbox is nothing more than another set of routines available to aid in the programming of the Mac. While the Movie Toolbox doesn't contain several thousand routines as the Macintosh Toolbox does, it does contain enough functions to allow a programmer to incorporate any movie-related feature into any program.

Checking for QuickTime

Before playing a movie, your program should verify that the user of your application has the QuickTime extension installed on his or her Macintosh. To handle this task, you'll rely on the Toolbox function Gestalt().

N O T E   If you haven't used Gestalt() in the past, you should have! This powerful function exists to supply your program with a wealth of information about the hardware and system software found on a user's machine. When passed one of the dozens of Apple-defined selector codes as the first parameter, Gestalt() returns information about the user's Mac in the second parameter—the response parameter. To learn more about the available selector codes for Gestalt(), scroll through the **Gestalt.h** universal header file.

To request QuickTime information, pass Gestalt() the Apple-defined selector code gestaltQuickTime. In return, Gestalt() will determine if the QuickTime extension is installed in the user's Extensions folder. If it is, Gestalt() returns an OSErr value of noErr. If QuickTime isn't found, Gestalt() will return a value other than noErr. That means your code should examine the returned OSErr value to determine if your program can continue.

```
#include <Gestalt.h>

OSErr   theError;
long    theResult;

theError = Gestalt( gestaltQuickTime, &theResult );

if ( theError != noErr )
   ExitToShell();
```

While a general check for the availability of QuickTime will usually suffice, there may be times when your program needs to know if some minimum version of QuickTime is present. If, for instance, your program makes use of a new Movie Toolbox function that only became available with the release of QuickTime 2.0.1, you'll want to verify that the user has that version or a more recent one. If that's the case, examine the value of the response parameter—Gestalt() will have placed the QuickTime version number in that variable.

Gestalt() embeds the QuickTime version number in the upper two bytes of the four-byte response parameter, and does so in a hexadecimal format. If the user has QuickTime 1.0, the upper bytes of theResult will be 0x0100. If the user has version 1.6.1, the upper bytes will be 0x0161. As an example of version testing, consider the following snippet. If your application makes use of some new movie-related feature not found in QuickTime before version 2.0.1, your program can check to see if the user at least has that version, as follows:

```
if ( theResult < 0x02010000 )
   ExitToShell();
```

NOTE

Always search for a minimum version value—not an exact value. For instance, *don't* check for QuickTime 1.6.1 like this:

```
if ( theResult == 0x01610000 )    // don't use == in this test!
```

Only the first four digits are version-related. The last four digits aren't guaranteed to each be zero. If the user does have version 1.6.1, theResult could be returned as 0x01618000. In that event, the above test would fail.

Initializing the Movie Toolbox

Once your program has verified that QuickTime is present, the Movie Toolbox needs to be initialized. A single function call takes care of this chore. The Movie Toolbox function EnterMovies() reserves an area of memory that the Movie Toolbox will use to hold information about your application. Like many of the Movie Toolbox routines you'll encounter, EnterMovies() returns an OSErr value to let your program know if the call was executed successfully.

```
#include <Movies.h>

OSErr  theError;

theError = EnterMovies();

if ( theError != noErr )
   ExitToShell();
```

The function prototypes for all of the Movie Toolbox routines can be found in the **Movies.h** universal header file—so include that header file in every project that makes use of QuickTime.

Before checking for QuickTime or initializing the Movie Toolbox, your program should perform the familiar Macintosh Toolbox initializations required of all Mac applications. If you use a standard initialization routine like the application-define `InitializeToolbox()` function found throughout this book, consider appending to that routine the QuickTime check and Movie Toolbox initialization. Since two Toolboxes are now being initialized (and in the future, perhaps more), you might want to rename your standard initialization routine to something more appropriate than `InitializeToolbox()`.

```
void  InitializeAllToolboxes( void )
{
   OSErr  theError;
   long   theResult;

   InitGraf( &qd.thePort );
   InitFonts();
   InitWindows();
   InitMenus();
   TEInit();
   InitDialogs( 0L );
   FlushEvents( everyEvent, 0 );
   InitCursor();

   theError = Gestalt( gestaltQuickTime, &theResult );
   if ( theError != noErr )
      ExitToShell();

   theError = EnterMovies();
   if ( theError != noErr )
      ExitToShell();
}
```

Loading a Movie

When a Macintosh program needs to display a picture that is in a picture file (a file of type 'PICT'), it first opens the file, then loads the picture data into memory. Once the data is in memory, the application can access it whenever it needs to—typically, to draw the picture to a window. The display of text from a text file (a file of type 'TEXT') follows a similar course of action. So it should come as no surprise that the playing of a QuickTime movie, which resides in a QuickTime movie file (a file of type 'MooV'), also involves the steps of opening a file and loading data into memory.

Opening a Movie File

A QuickTime movie is stored in a QuickTime movie file. Before an application can play a movie, the file in which the movie resides must be opened. The Movie Toolbox function OpenMovieFile() takes care of this job.

```
OSErr    theError;
FSSpec   theFSSpec;
short    theFileRefNum;

theError = OpenMovieFile( &theFSSpec, &theFileRefNum, fsRdPerm );
```

The first of the three parameters to OpenMovieFile() is the file system specification for the movie file to open. After the file has been opened, OpenMovieFile() fills the second parameter with a file reference number. Subsequent calls to some other Movie Toolbox routines will rely on this reference number. The final parameter to OpenMovieFile() is a permission level for the opened file. Programs that will play a movie—but won't allow changes to the movie—should use the Apple-defined fsRdPerm constant here. Programs that will allow movie editing should use the Apple-defined constant fsRdWrPerm.

If you've worked with Macintosh files in the past, you know about the FSSpec data type. To let a Toolbox routine know where to find a particular file, you provide the routine with three pieces of information about the file: a reference number to the volume (the drive) that the file is on, the file's parent directory (the folder the file is in), and the file's name (as displayed on the desktop). Conveniently, all of this information can be stored in a single data structure—the FSSpec.

If at the time you write a program, you know the location and name of a file that is to be opened, you can call the Toolbox routine FSMakeFSSpec()

to create an FSSpec for a file. If, instead, your application will let the user select a file using the standard Open dialog box, you'll rely on that dialog box to create an FSSpec for the file the user selects. For simplicity, FSMakeFSSpec() will be used in this chapter's first example program. Later in the chapter, the standard Open dialog box will be used.

The following snippet creates an FSSpec for a file named **Charlie-Chaplin**. The file is assumed to be in the same folder as the application that will be opening it.

```
OSErr    theError;
FSSpec   theFSSpec;

theError = FSMakeFSSpec( 0, 0, "\pCharlieChaplin", &theFSSpec );
```

The first FSMakeFSSpec() parameter is a volume reference number. A value of 0 tells FSMakeFSSpec() that the volume is the default, or startup, drive. The second parameter is the parent directory of the file. A value of 0 tells FSMakeFSSpec() that the parent directory is the same folder as the one that houses the application. Because the third parameter is the name of the file. Because FSMakeFSSpec() expects the file name to be in the form of a Pascal string, include the leading "\p" characters— as shown above. The final parameter is a pointer to an FSSpec variable. After FSMakeFSSpec() uses the first three parameters to create the file system specification, the function will return the newly created FSSpec in this last parameter.

If your program will keep a collection of movie files in a *subdirectory*—a folder within the application folder—you can still use FSMakeFSSpec() to create the FSSpec. To do so, include the name of the subdirectory in the file name. Including a folder name with the file name makes the file name a *partial pathname*—the name now includes information regarding the path to the file. This is done by prefacing the file name with the folder name. Include a colon before both the folder name and the file name. The following snippet again creates an FSSpec for the **CharlieChaplin** movie file. This time it's assumed that the file is kept in a subdirectory named Movie Files *f*.

```
OSErr    theError;
FSSpec   theFSSpec;
Str255   theFileName = "\p:Movie Files f:CharlieChaplin";
```

```
theError = FSMakeFSSpec( 0, 0, theFileName, &theFSSpec );
```

Figure 7.4 shows the pathnames for a few different folder scenarios that each use the **CHARLIECHAPLIN** movie file. In each case it is assumed that both the volume reference number and the parent directory are set to 0 in the call to FSMakeFSSpec().

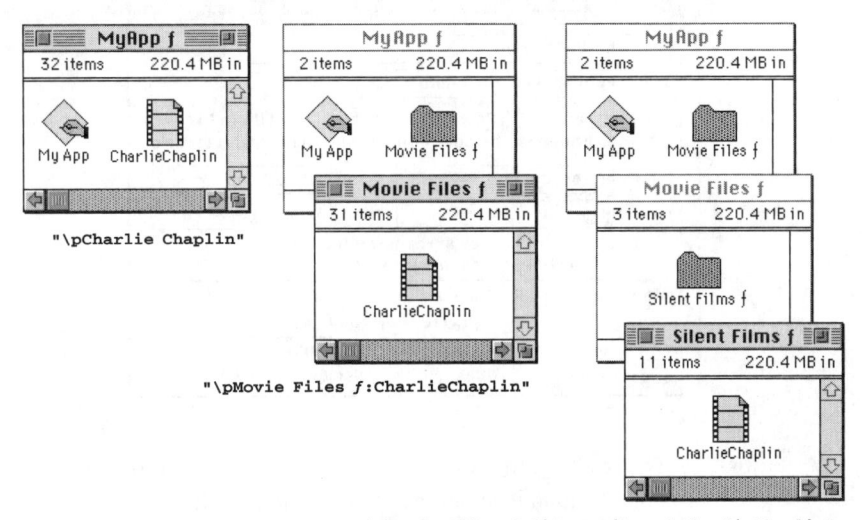

FIGURE 7.4 Movie names for a movie file located
in three different folder arrangements.

Loading a Movie from a File

A Macintosh QuickTime movie file (a file of type 'MooV') consists of a moov resource in the movie file's resource fork and movie data in the movie file's data fork. The moov resource holds information about the format of a movie—information such as the duration of the movie and how many tracks the movie has. The moov resource doesn't, however, contain the data that makes up the movie itself. That information is held in the movie file's data fork. Figure 7.5 shows the resource fork of a movie file. It also shows a **ResEdit Get Info** window that gives information about the movie file. By examining this window, you can see that the vast majority of a movie file's byte size is in the file's data fork.

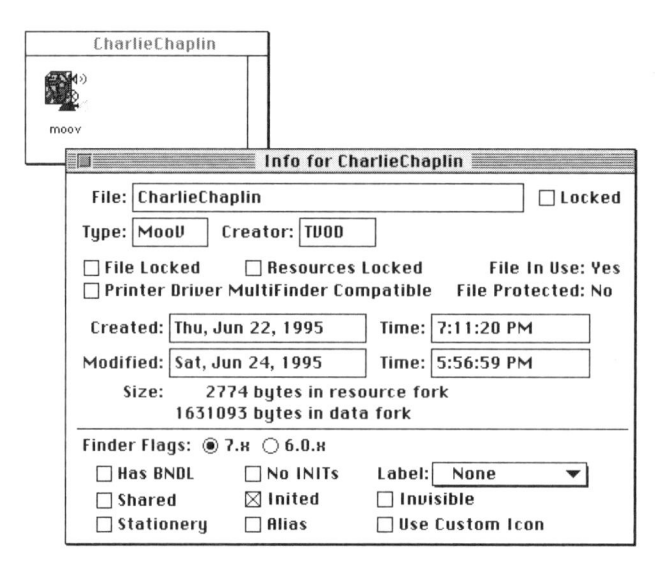

FIGURE 7.5 The resource fork of a movie file holds a moov resource, while the data fork holds the movie data itself.

A movie's data can even be held in a file, or files, other than the QuickTime movie file that holds the movie's moov resource. If that is the case, then the data fork holds references to the location of the movie's data.

N O T E

After opening a movie file with a call to OpenMovieFile(), the movie needs to be loaded into memory. A call to the Movie Toolbox routine NewMovieFromFile() accomplishes this. The NewMovieFromFile() function doesn't load all of the movie data into memory—the data for a large movie can easily exceed the amount of free RAM a user has. Instead, some data will be loaded, along with references to the location of other data. To a programmer, the most important aspect of NewMovieFromFile() is that this routine handles the data loading without any help—that

is, you'll never have to be concerned with the format of either the
moov resource or the data in the data fork. Here's how a call to
NewMovieFromFile() looks:

```
OSErr    theError;
short    theFileRefNum;
Movie    theMovie;
short    theMovieResID = 0;
Str255   theMovieResName;
Boolean  wasAltered;

theError = NewMovieFromFile( &theMovie, theFileRefNum,
                             &theMovieResID, theMovieResName,
                             newMovieActive, &wasAltered );
```

After the call to NewMovieFromFile() is complete, the first parameter will
hold an identifier to the loaded movie. This identifier, of the data type
Movie, will be useful in subsequent Movie Toolbox function calls. While
the data in memory may not consist of all of the data that makes up a
movie, the loading of the data and references is still referred to as "creating
a movie." Likewise, a variable of the type Movie—used to identify the data
and data references—is referred to as "a movie."

To load a movie into memory, NewMovieFromFile() needs two pieces
of information: the file that the movie is in and the ID of the moov
resource in that file. The file that holds the movie can be identified by the
file reference number returned by the call to the Toolbox routine that
precedes the call to NewMovieFromFile()—the routine OpenMovieFile().
This reference number is the second parameter to NewMovieFromFile().
Because it is possible to keep more than one moov resource in a single
movie file, a moov resource ID is also needed. If you specify a resource
ID of 0, NewMovieFromFile() will load the first moov resource in the specified
file. If there is only one moov resource, a value of 0 will of course tell
NewMovieFromFile() to load that resource.

Besides supplying an identifier to the movie, NewMovieFromFile()
returns three other pieces of information. However, in most instances,
your program will ignore this returned information. To begin, the third
parameter will be the ID of the moov resource that was used. If a value of 0
was used at the start of call, that value will be overwritten by the

resource ID at the completion of the call. The second piece of information provided by `NewMovieFromFile()` can be found in the fourth parameter. Here, you'll find the name of the `moov` resource. Notice that this is the name of the `moov` resource, not the name of the QuickTime movie file. The final returned information can be found in the last parameter. This `Boolean` value will tell you whether `NewMovieFromFile()` had to make any changes to the data references that were a part of the data in the data fork.

The only routine not yet described is the fifth one—`newMovieActive` in the above example. This parameter holds a flag that provides supplemental information to `NewMovieFromFile()`. Here, you'll want to pass the Apple-defined constant `newMovieActive` to activate the new movie—a movie needs to be active in order for it to be played.

The Toolbox call to create an `FSSpec` for a movie file and the Movie Toolbox function calls used to open a movie file and load the file's movie can be called one after another. The following snippet illustrates this.

```
OSErr    theError;
FSSpec   theFSSpec;
short    theFileRefNum;
Movie    theMovie;
short    theMovieResID = 0;
Str255   theMovieResName;
Boolean  wasAltered;

theError = FSMakeFSSpec( 0, 0, "\pCharlieChaplin", &theFSSpec );
theError = OpenMovieFile( &theFSSpec, &theFileRefNum, fsRdPerm );
theError = NewMovieFromFile( &theMovie, theFileRefNum,
                             &theMovieResID, theMovieResName,
                             newMovieActive, &wasAltered );
```

All three of the above function calls return an `OSErr` value. For brevity, no error-checking is shown. In actuality, you'd want to check the value of `theError` after each function call and either exit upon an error—as shown below—or, more likely, post an alert displaying an error message—as described in Appendix E.

```
theError = FSMakeFSSpec( 0, 0, "\pCharlieChaplin", &theFSSpec );
if ( theError != noErr )
   ExitToShell();
```

Closing a Movie File

If your application doesn't allow the user to edit the frames that make up a movie, the opened movie file can be closed immediately after the file's movie has been loaded. After a call to `NewMovieFromFile()`, your program has the movie's data—or references to all of the movie data—in memory. That means that the application knows where to find the movie's data. It also means the movie file no longer needs to be open. A call to the Movie Toolbox function `CloseMovieFile()` will handle the closing of the file.

```
short  theFileRefNum;

CloseMovieFile( theFileRefNum );
```

As its only parameter, `CloseMovieFile()` requires the reference number to the open file. This is the same reference number returned by `OpenMovieFile()` and used in the call to `NewMovieFromFile()`.

As you'll see later in this chapter, if a program allows movie editing, and the editing changes are to be saved, the program should keep the movie file open so that the changes can be written to the file.

Displaying a Movie

After loading a movie, a window in which to display the movie needs to be opened. There is no special "movie type" of window for this purpose—just call either of the Toolbox functions `GetNewCWindow()` or `NewCWindow()` to open a color window. While a QuickTime movie—even a color movie—can be displayed in a window opened with a call to `GetNewWindow()` or `NewWindow()`, QuickTime is more efficient at displaying a movie if a color window is used.

```
#define   rMovieWindow     128

WindowPtr  theWindow;

theWindow = GetNewCWindow( rMovieWindow, nil, (WindowPtr)-1L );
```

Setting the Movie Graphics World— SetMovieGWorld()

At this point, a movie is loaded and a window is open—but there's no link between the window and the movie that is to appear in it. As the movie plays, you'll of course want to make sure it's playing in the window it is meant to appear in. To pair the window to a movie, call SetMovieGWorld(). This Movie Toolbox function sets the pixel-display coordinate system of theMovie to the same system used by theWindow.

```
Movie      theMovie;
WindowPtr  theWindow;

SetMovieGWorld( theMovie, (CGrafPtr)theWindow, nil );
```

The first parameter to SetMovieGWorld() is the movie returned by NewMovieFromFile(). The second parameter can be a pointer to either a graphics port, a color graphics port, or a graphics world—the SetMovieGWorld() function can work with any of these types. In the above snippet, the WindowPtr variable is typecast to a color graphics port. The third parameter to SetMovieGWorld() is a handle to the movie's graphics device structure. Using nil for this parameter tells SetMovieGWorld() that the current device should be used.

No, you can't just go casting a variable of one data type to *any* data type and expect things to work out all right. The above cast is valid because a CGrafPtr and a WindowPtr both point to the same data structure—a GrafPort. If you recall that a WindowPtr points to a WindowRecord, you might question that statement. Keep in mind that the first field of a WindowRecord is a GrafPort—so that a WindowPtr can be thought of as pointing to either a WindowRecord or a GrafPort.

Resizing the Display Window

If you use a call to GetNewCWindow() to load the information for the window that will display a movie, you of course need to define a WIND resource. When you do, set the window to any size you wish—but make sure to uncheck the **Initially visible** checkbox if using ResEdit, or the

Visible checkbox if using Resorcerer. The window's initial size is unimportant because your application will resize the window to match the size of the movie that is to be displayed in the window. The window's initial invisibility is important so that this resizing takes place out of sight of the user.

Your program will rely on one Toolbox routine and two Movie Toolbox routines to resize a window to the size of a movie. First, a call to the Movie Toolbox function GetMovieBox() should be made to determine the size of a frame of the movie that is to be displayed. Pass GetMovieBox() the Movie variable that was returned by NewMovieFromFile() and a pointer to a rectangle. GetMovieBox() will measure the size of a frame from the movie and place those dimensions in the Rect variable:

```
Movie   theMovie;
Rect    theMovieBox;

GetMovieBox( theMovie, &theMovieBox );
```

At this point, the temptation may arise to set the window size to the dimensions held in the Rect variable theMovieBox. Before doing that, a couple of more steps are necessary. First, the Toolbox routine OffsetRect() should be called. While GetMovieBox() will provide the dimensions of a movie, it does so indirectly. For instance, the four fields of the Rect variable could have values similar to these:

```
theMovieBox.left      40
theMovieBox.right     240
theMovieBox.top       100
theMovieBox.bottom    235
```

As shown in Figure 7.6, the above values yield a movie that is 200 pixels in width and 135 pixels in height. To get the variable theMovieBox to reflect these dimensions, however, the rectangle should be offset by the left and top values:

```
Rect   theMovieBox;

OffsetRect( &theMovieBox, -theMovieBox.left, -theMovieBox.top );
```

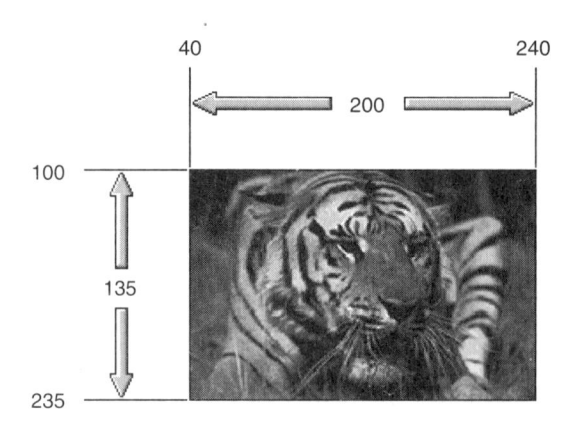

FIGURE 7.6 A movie's moviebox holds the movie's pixel dimensions,
but these values may not have an origin point of (0, 0).

After the offset, the four fields of theMovieBox variable used in the preceding example will have the following values:

```
theMovieBox.left       0
theMovieBox.right    200
theMovieBox.top        0
theMovieBox.bottom   135
```

Next, call the Movie Toolbox routine SetMovieBox() to make these new, offset values the boundaries for the rectangle that defines the size of the movie. The following is a snippet that adjusts a movie's boundaries.

```
Movie   theMovie;
Rect    theMovieBox;

GetMovieBox( theMovie, &theMovieBox );
OffsetRect( &theMovieBox, -theMovieBox.left, -theMovieBox.top );
SetMovieBox( theMovie, &theMovieBox );
```

After the above calls, the movie rectangle, or movie box, has been adjusted—but these changes don't apply to the window that is to display the movie. To do that, call the Toolbox function SizeWindow(). Pass SizeWindow() the window to resize, along with the right and bottom coordinates of the movie's rectangle. In the above example, that would be theWindow, 200, and 135. The last parameter to SizeWindow() is a Boolean value that indicates whether or not an update event should be generated.

```
WindowPtr   theWindow;
Rect        theMovieBox;

SizeWindow( theWindow, theMovieBox.right, theMovieBox.bottom, true );
```

At this point, the window is properly sized to match the dimensions of the movie that will be displayed in it. And, because the window was invisible, the user didn't see the window resizing take place. Now it's time to display the window in preparation for the display of the movie.

```
WindowPtr   theWindow;

ShowWindow( theWindow );
```

Playing a QuickTime Movie

A movie can be played directly by your application—without any user intervention—or it can display a movie controller that gives the user full control of movie playing. In this section, you'll see how to play a movie using the first method. Later in this chapter, you'll read about playing movies using a movie controller.

Preparing a Movie for Playing

When you create a new movie, or edit an existing one, you save the movie to file. When a movie is saved, the current frame is also saved. Consider the following scenario. You paste a frame into the middle of a movie using a program such as Apple's Movie Player. Then you save the edited movie and close it. The next time that movie is opened, it will be opened to the frame at which the movie was saved. To open a movie and guarantee that the movie will be rewound to the first frame, call the Movie Toolbox function GoToBeginningOfMovie(). The only parameter this function needs is the name of the movie to rewind.

```
Movie   theMovie;

GoToBeginningOfMovie( theMovie );
```

After rewinding the movie, call the Movie Toolbox routine `Start-Movie()`. Contrary to its name, this function doesn't actually start the movie playing. Instead, it readies the movie for playing by making the movie active and setting the movie's playback rate. Pass `StartMovie()` the movie that is to be played.

```
Movie  theMovie;

StartMovie( theMovie );
```

Playing a Movie

To play a movie your program should call the Movie Toolbox routine `MoviesTask()`. This function doesn't play a movie from start to finish, however. Instead, it processes only a small part of the movie, updating the display of the movie by drawing a frame. That means that `MoviesTask()` needs to be called repeatedly until the movie has completed playing. You can use another Movie Toolbox routine to determine when a movie has finished. When passed a Movie variable, `IsMovieDone()` returns a `Boolean` value that tells whether or not that movie has finished playing.

```
Movie  theMovie;

do
{
   MoviesTask(theMovie, 0);
}
while ( IsMovieDone( theMovie ) == false );
```

The first parameter to `MoviesTask()` is the movie to *service*. A single call to `MoviesTask()` is capable of servicing more than one movie. If more than one movie is open on the screen, rather than pass a movie your application should pass a value of `nil` as the first parameter. That tells the Movie Toolbox to service every active movie on the screen.

The second parameter to `MoviesTask()` is the number of milliseconds that your application is willing to give the Movie Toolbox for its task of servicing movies. If one active movie is open, the Movie Toolbox will spend no more than this time servicing that movie. If more than one active movie is open, then the Movie Toolbox will service as many of those movies as it can, in the time specified by this second parameter.

To make sure that all active movies get serviced, pass a value of 0 as this second parameter—that tells the Movie Toolbox to service each active movie once.

Cleaning Up

When your application has finished with a movie, release the memory occupied by both the movie and the window the movie is displayed in. A call to the Movie Toolbox routine `DisposeMovie()` frees the movie memory, while a call to the Toolbox function `DisposeMovie()` deallocates the window memory.

```
DisposeMovie( theMovie );
DisposeWindow( theWindow );
```

Chapter Example: QuickPlay

This chapter's first example program demonstrates the basics of QuickTime movie playing. When you run the QuickPlay program, a window will open and a short clip from a silent movie will play in the window. The movie has a sound track, so you'll hear a musical score play as the movie runs. When the movie ends, the program will end too. Figure 7.7 shows the QuickPlay window and a frame from the movie.

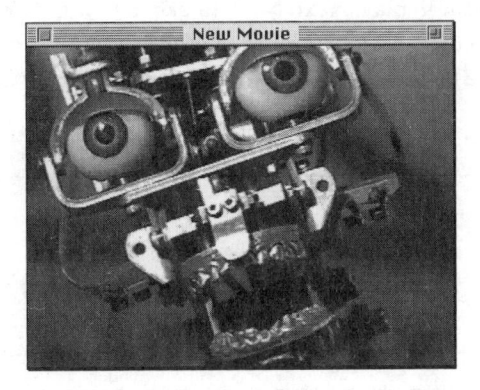

FIGURE 7.7 The Robot movie, as viewed in the QuickPlay example program.

The type of window that the movie plays in is established in a WIND resource—the only resource used by the QuickPlay project. Figure 7.8 shows this resource. Notice in the figure that the resource size of the window—100 pixels by 100 pixels—has no correlation to the size of the window as displayed in the program. Also note that the **Initially visible** checkbox is *not* checked. The source code listing for QuickPlay needs no walk-through—all of the code has been discussed at length in this chapter.

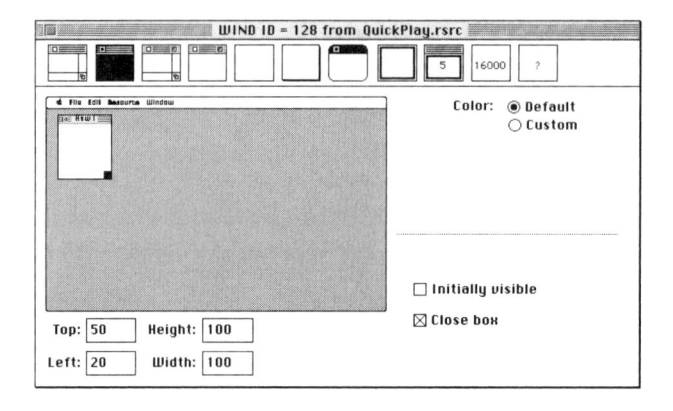

FIGURE 7.8 The WIND resource for the window that will display the Robot movie.

NOTE

If you'd like QuickPlay to play a different QuickTime movie, change the kMovieName constant from "\pRobot" to the name of the movie you want the program to play. Next, *build* (make) a new QuickPlay application from the QuickPlay project. Finally, before running the QuickPlay program, make sure that the movie is in the same folder as the QuickPlay application.

```
//_____

#include <Movies.h>

//_____

void  InitializeAllToolboxes( void );

//_____

#define      rMovieWindow                    128
#define      kMovieName        "\pRobot"
```

```
//_____

void  main( void )
{
    OSErr       theError;
    FSSpec      theFSSpec;
    short       theFileRefNum;
    Movie       theMovie;
    short       theMovieResID = 0;
    Str255      theMovieResName;
    Boolean     wasAltered;
    WindowPtr   theWindow;
    Rect        theMovieBox;

    InitializeAllToolboxes();

    theError = FSMakeFSSpec( 0, 0, kMovieName, &theFSSpec );
    theError = OpenMovieFile( &theFSSpec, &theFileRefNum, fsRdPerm
    );
    theError = NewMovieFromFile( &theMovie, theFileRefNum,
                                 &theMovieResID, theMovieResName,
                                 newMovieActive, &wasAltered );

    CloseMovieFile( theFileRefNum );

    theWindow = GetNewCWindow( rMovieWindow, nil, (WindowPtr)-1L );
    SetMovieGWorld( theMovie, (CGrafPtr)theWindow, nil );

    GetMovieBox( theMovie, &theMovieBox );
    OffsetRect( &theMovieBox, -theMovieBox.left, -theMovieBox.top );
    SetMovieBox( theMovie, &theMovieBox );

    SizeWindow( theWindow, theMovieBox.right, theMovieBox.bottom,
                true );
    ShowWindow( theWindow );

    GoToBeginningOfMovie( theMovie );

    StartMovie( theMovie );

    do
    {
        MoviesTask(theMovie, 0);
    }
    while ( IsMovieDone( theMovie ) == false );
    DisposeMovie( theMovie );
    DisposeWindow( theWindow );
```

```
}
//_____

void  InitializeAllToolboxes( void )
{
   OSErr  theError;
   long   theResult;
   InitGraf( &qd.thePort );
   InitFonts();
   InitWindows();
   InitMenus();
   TEInit();
   InitDialogs( OL );
   FlushEvents( everyEvent, 0 );
   InitCursor();
   theError = Gestalt( gestaltQuickTime, &theResult );
   if ( theError != noErr )
      ExitToShell();

   theError = EnterMovies();
   if ( theError != noErr )
      ExitToShell();
}
```

Chapter Example: MovieDialog

The QuickPlay program played a movie in a fixed window and didn't use a movie controller. While the main purpose for creating a program of such simplicity was to keep the source code listing of the first QuickTime example brief and to the point, there are instances where an application might display and play a movie without a movie controller. Examples include a game that opens and plays a movie in response to some user action, or a program that advertises a line of products and plays one of several movies depending on which selection a user makes from a menu.

The MovieDialog Program

Before moving on to the topic of movie controllers, this section examines a program that makes use of movies that are played without controllers.

MovieDialog provides a practical example of how a multimedia program might use movies without implementing movie controllers. It also demonstrates how to play a movie within an area of a dialog box rather than sizing a window to match the dimensions of a movie. When run, the MovieDialog program opens a dialog box like the one pictured in Figure 7.9.

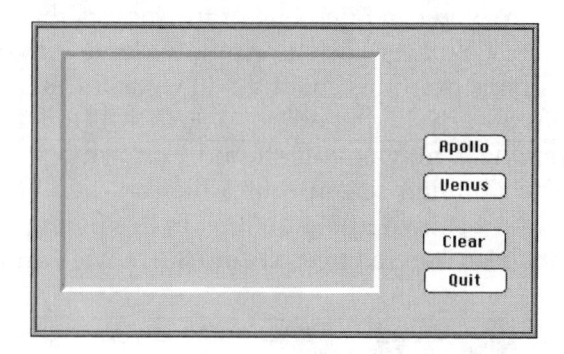

FIGURE 7.9 The dialog box that is opened by the MovieDialog program.

Clicking on the **Apollo** button plays a movie of the launching of one of the Apollo rockets—as shown in Figure 7.10. Clicking on the **Venus** button plays a movie of the Venus space probe. When a movie has finished playing, its last frame remains in the movie-playing area of the dialog box. To clear this area and return it to its original light gray state, click the **Clear** button.

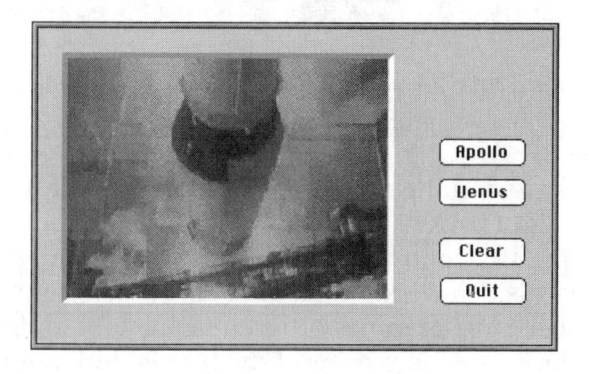

FIGURE 7.10 The MovieDialog dialog box, with a movie playing in it.

The MovieDialog Resources

You'll create three resources for the MovieDialog project: a `DLOG`, a `DITL`, and a `PICT`. Of most interest will be the picture resource—it provides the three-dimensional look for the movie-playing area of the MovieDialog dialog box. To create the picture, you can open one of the movies that will be used by MovieDialog. A movie player such as Apple's Movie Player or any one of the example programs from this chapter will work for this task (you'll find compiled versions of each chapter example on the CD that accompanies this book). After opening a movie, you should perform a screen capture, or screen dump. The resulting screen dump file can then be opened with a graphics program—as shown in Figure 7.11. In this figure, you can also see that the movie has been selected from within the movie window.

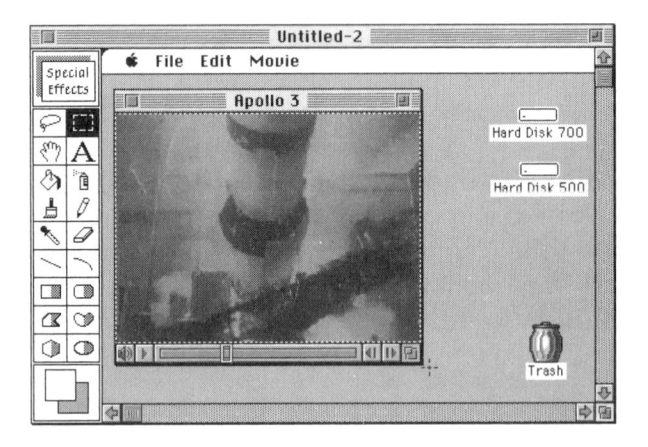

FIGURE 7.11 A screen dump of a movie is opened in a
graphics program, and the movie is selected.

Now cut the movie and then clear, or erase, the rest of the window. Fill this area with a light background color. This shaded background is only necessary to provide a contrast for the white frame that will soon border the movie on two sides. Next, paste the cut movie frame back into the window. Then use your graphics program's line tool to draw two white lines and two dark-gray lines around the movie. In Figure 7.12, the pen has been set to a width of four pixels before drawing the line. Then the corners were touched up with a narrow pen-setting.

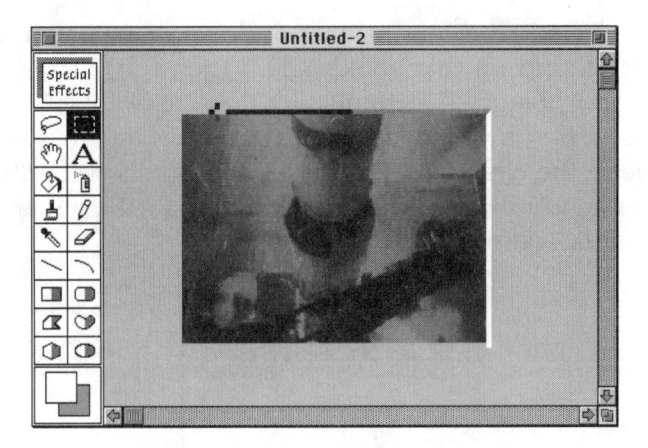

FIGURE 7.12 A frame with a three-dimensional look is drawn around the movie.

Next, the movie again cut the movie frame from the window. Fill the remaining white area with a light-gray color that will match the dialog box background when the dialog box is laid out. The last step with the graphics program is to select the picture and cut it from the window— as is being done in Figure 7.13.

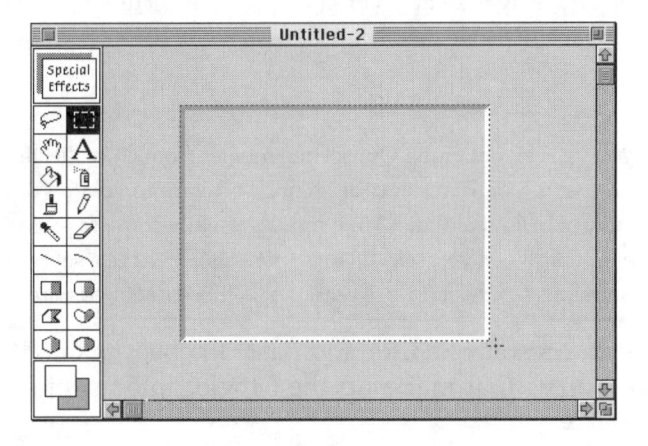

FIGURE 7.13 The frame is selected and copied to the clipboard.

You'll need to know the exact size of the picture when placing it in the DITL resource. Your graphics program may provide this information when a picture is selected from one of its windows. If not, you can use the PictSize utility found on this book's CD. When run, PictSize opens the window shown in Figure 7.14 to display the size of the current contents of the clipboard. If you've copied the picture from the graphics program, it will still be in the clipboard. Simply double-click on the **PictSize** icon to launch this handy utility. When you do that, PictSize will respond by displaying the clipboard contents—in pixels.

FIGURE 7.14 The PictSize utility provides the pixel dimensions
of any picture that is currently in the Clipboard.

 If you're using System 7.5 or later, paste the picture in the Scrapbook. The Scrapbook will give the picture's size.

NOTE

 If you've been obtaining QuickTime movies from CD collections, or if you've been using a digitizer and digitizing software to create your own movies, you've noticed that QuickTime movies usually come in just a few sizes. That means that when you select a topic, you should have a set of movies of equal dimensions—perfect for use with the method described here.

NOTE

Next, launch your resource editor and paste the picture into it. Figure 7.15 shows the resources that make up the MovieDialog project—including the PICT resource.

 Earlier it was stated that you'll create three resources for the MovieDialog project—yet Figure 7.15 shows four resources. The dctb resource is a dialog color-table resource that is automatically created by the resource editor when you add color to a dialog box.

NOTE

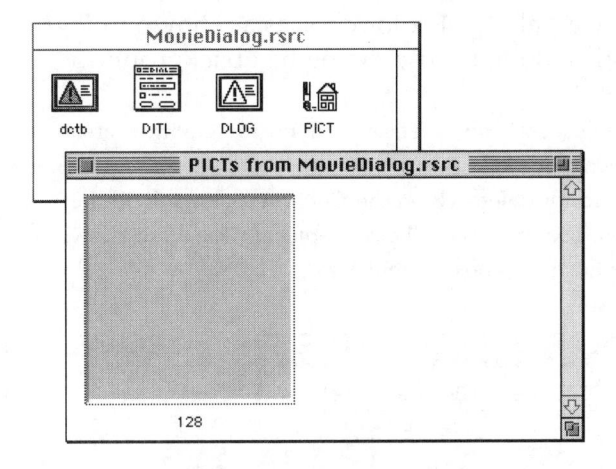

FIGURE 7.15 The picture frame that was copied from the
graphics program is pasted into the project's Resource file.

When you create the DITL that holds the dialog box items, you'll add this
picture as a Picture item. If you've noted the picture's dimensions, you'll be
able to set the picture's size properly in the DITL—as shown in Figure 7.16.

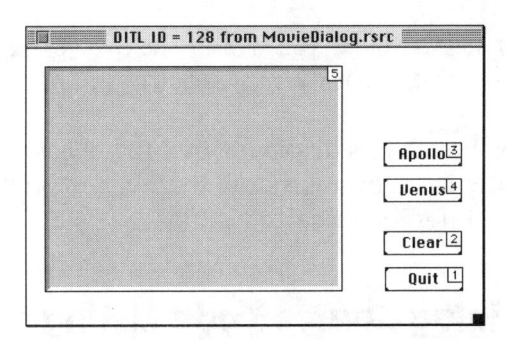

FIGURE 7.16 A Picture item is added to a DITL resource,
and the ID of the item is set to that of the PICT resource.

The dialog box displayed in MovieDialog has a light-gray background.
If you wish, you can use your resource editor to give the entire dialog
box a matching background. In ResEdit, create a DLOG resource, then
click on the **Custom** button in DLOG editor. Next, click on the **Content**

box to display a palette of color choices as shown in Figure 7.17. Select a color from this palette for the dialog box background.

NOTE If you use Resorcerer as your resource editor, create a new dialog box. Select **Set Dialog Info** from the Dialog menu. In the Settings window that opens, double-click on the **Content** dialog box in the **Window Colors** section. That brings up the color-picker wheel that allows you to select a color for the dialog box content area.

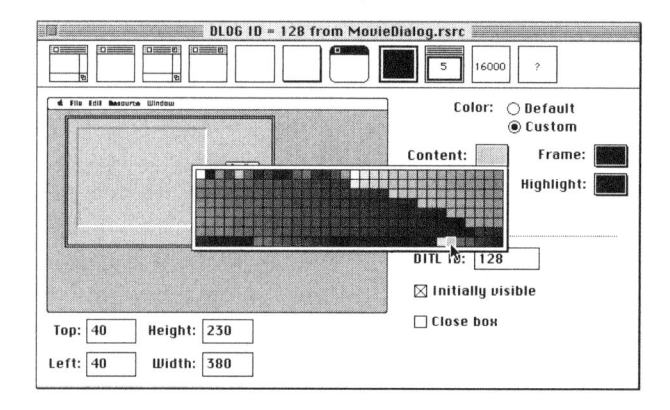

FIGURE 7.17 ResEdit allows you to easily add color, or gray shading, to the content area of a DLOG resource.

Because the dialog box that is displayed by MovieDialog won't need to be resized—as was the case for a window that was to be the exact size of a movie—you can set it to be initially visible.

The MovieDialog Source Code Listing

There isn't anything unique about the dialog box displayed by MovieDialog— the code that handles this dialog box is similar to code you've written for any other program that displays a modal dialog box. The listing for OpenDisplayDialog()—the routine that handles the dialog box—is provided just ahead. Here's an outline of what the function does:

```
declare variables
```

```
open the dialog box

begin loop

    call ModalDialog() to get number of a clicked-on item

    case Apollo button item:
       play Apollo movie

    case Venus button item:
       play Venus movie

    case Clear button item:
       clear movie display area

    case Quit button item:
       quit program

end loop

dispose of the dialog box
```

An application-defined routine named LoadAndRunMovie() handles a click on either the **Apollo** or **Venus** button—the two movie-playing buttons. That routine will be described in just a few pages. When a movie finishes playing in MovieDialog, its last frame remains displayed in the dialog box. If the user wishes to clear the movie-area, the **Clear** button can be used.

```
#define      kMovieFramePicture      128    // resource ID of PICT
#define      kFrameButton              5    // item number of picture

DialogPtr  theDialog;
short      theType;
Handle     theHandle;
Rect       theRect;
PicHandle  thePicture;

GetDialogItem( theDialog, kFrameButton,
                  &theType, &theHandle, &theRect );
thePicture = GetPicture( kMovieFramePicture );
DrawPicture( thePicture, &theRect );
```

The playing of a movie is handled by the program's LoadAndRunMovie() routine. Most of the code that makes up this function is similar to code seen in this chapter's QuickPlay example. One thing that differs is the determination of the rectangle in which a movie will play.

In QuickPlay, the movie rectangle is offset so that the upper left corner of the movie is at point (0, 0). That places the movie in the upper left corner of the window it will play in. The movie is the exact size of the window, as planned. In MovieDialog, the movie won't be the same size as the dialog box, and won't appear in the dialog box's upper left corner. The code that determines the placement of the movie in the dialog box is shown below.

```
#define        kFramePixelSize      4      // pixel width of frame
#define        kFrameButton         5      // item number of picture

Movie        theMovie;
Rect         theMovieBox;
DialogPtr    theDialog;
short        theType;
Handle       theHandle;
Rect         theRect;

GetMovieBox( theMovie, &theMovieBox );
OffsetRect( &theMovieBox, -theMovieBox.left, -theMovieBox.top );
GetDialogItem( theDialog, kFrameButton,
               &theType, &theHandle, &theRect );
OffsetRect( &theMovieBox, theRect.left + kFramePixelSize,
            theRect.top + kFramePixelSize );
```

In the above snippet, the movie box is obtained with a call to GetMovieBox(), and then offset so that its upper left corner appears at point (0, 0)—just as was done in QuickPlay. If the movie was displayed at this point, it would appear in the dialog box as shown in the top part of Figure 7.18.

Next, a call to GetDialogItem() is made to get the rectangle of the PICT item. This is close to the area in which the movie should be displayed—as shown in the middle part of Figure 7.18. This rectangle, however, doesn't take into account the frame of the picture.

Finally, the upper left corner of the movie box rectangle is offset from point (0, 0). The offset amount equals the top and left boundaries of the PICT rectangle, with the pixel size of the frame added. That results in the movie being placed directly in the movie area of the picture—as shown in the bottom part of Figure 7.18.

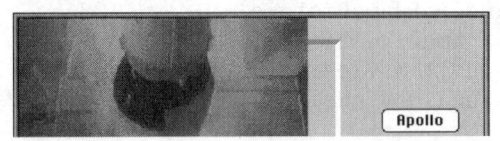

If the rectangle used in the first call to `OffsetRect()` was used, the movie would appear in the upper-left corner of the dialog box

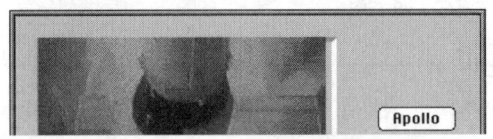

If the rectangle returned by `GetDialogItem()` was used, the movie wouldn't appear centered in the movie-area picture

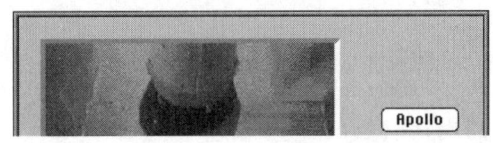

The second call to `OffsetRect()` accounts for the size of the frame that is a part of the movie-area picture

FIGURE 7.18 A movie is centered in the picture item of the dialog box.

The following is the source code listing for the MovieDialog program that you'll find on this book's CD.

```
//_____

#include <Movies.h>

//_____

void    InitializeAllToolboxes( void );
void    OpenDisplayDialog( void );
void    LoadAndRunMovie( DialogPtr, Str255 );

//_____

#define         rMovieWindow            128
#define         rMovieDialog            128
#define         kQuitButton               1
#define         kClearButton              2
#define         kApolloButton             3
#define         kVenusButton              4
#define         kFrameButton              5
```

```
#define        kMovieFramePicture       128
#define        kFramePixelSize            4
#define        kApolloMovieName      "\p:Movie ƒ:Apollo 3"
#define        kVenusMovieName       "\p:Movie ƒ:Venus Probe"

//_____

Boolean  gAllDone  = false;

//_____

void  main( void )
{
   InitializeAllToolboxes();
   OpenDisplayDialog();
}

//_____

void  OpenDisplayDialog( void )
{
   DialogPtr   theDialog;
   short       theItem;
   Boolean     allDone = false;
   short       theType;
   Handle      theHandle;
   Rect        theRect;
   PicHandle   thePicture;

   theDialog = GetNewDialog( rMovieDialog, nil, (WindowPtr)-1L );
   ShowWindow( theDialog );
   SetPort( theDialog );

   while ( allDone == false )
   {
      ModalDialog( nil, &theItem );

      switch ( theItem )
      {
         case kApolloButton:
            LoadAndRunMovie( theDialog, kApolloMovieName );
            break;
         case kVenusButton:
            LoadAndRunMovie( theDialog, kVenusMovieName );
            break;

         case kClearButton:
```

```
            GetDialogItem( theDialog, kFrameButton,
                        &theType, &theHandle, &theRect );
            thePicture = GetPicture( kMovieFramePicture );
            DrawPicture( thePicture, &theRect );
            break;

        case kQuitButton:
            allDone = true;
            break;
    }
}
    DisposeDialog( theDialog );
}

//_____

void  LoadAndRunMovie( DialogPtr theDialog, Str255 theMovieName )
{
    OSErr    theError;
    FSSpec   theFSSpec;
    short    theFileRefNum;
    Movie    theMovie;
    short    theMovieResID = 0;
    Str255   theMovieResName;
    Boolean  wasAltered;
    Rect     theMovieBox;
    short    theType;
    Handle   theHandle;
    Rect     theRect;

    theError = FSMakeFSSpec( 0, 0L, theMovieName, &theFSSpec );
    theError = OpenMovieFile( &theFSSpec, &theFileRefNum, fsRdPerm );
    theError = NewMovieFromFile( &theMovie, theFileRefNum,
                        &theMovieResID, theMovieResName,
                        newMovieActive, &wasAltered );

     CloseMovieFile( theFileRefNum );

    SetMovieGWorld( theMovie, (CGrafPtr)theDialog, nil);

    GetMovieBox( theMovie, &theMovieBox );

    OffsetRect( &theMovieBox, -theMovieBox.left, -theMovieBox.top );
    GetDialogItem( theDialog, kFrameButton,
                &theType, &theHandle, &theRect );
    OffsetRect( &theMovieBox, theRect.left + kFramePixelSize,
                theRect.top + kFramePixelSize );
```

```
SetMovieBox( theMovie, &theMovieBox );

GoToBeginningOfMovie( theMovie );

StartMovie( theMovie );

do
{
   MoviesTask(theMovie, 0);
}
while ( IsMovieDone( theMovie ) == false );
DisposeMovie( theMovie );
}
```

Improving the MovieDialog Program

MovieDialog uses a little shading to provide a three-dimensional effect for the area of the dialog box that displays movies. For a more polished look, this 3-D effect could be carried over to the buttons as well. Figure 7.19 shows how this dialog box might look if custom controls (CDEFs) were used to create shaded, three-dimensional buttons.

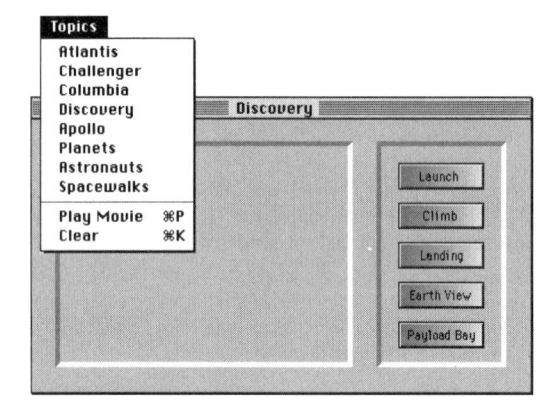

FIGURE 7.19 The simple MovieDialog program could be modified into a full-featured application.

Figure 7.19 also shows that a more sophisticated version of MovieDialog could include a menu that lets the user select a general topic. Selecting a topic would cause a change in the titles of the buttons in the dialog box. The figure shows the buttons after the Discovery menu item is selected.

One means of achieving this "button switch" would involve having a different `DITL` resource for every topic. Selecting a topic from the menu would cause the dialog box to display a different `DITL`.

If you need the details of implementing custom controls, and information on creating a dialog box that uses multiple dialog item lists, refer to *More Mac Programming Techniques* by M&T Books.

N O T E

```
void  PlayMovie( Movie theMovie )
{
   GoToBeginningOfMovie( theMovie );

   StartMovie( theMovie );

   do
   {
      MoviesTask(theMovie, 0);
   }
   while ( IsMovieDone( theMovie ) == false );
}
```

To see an example of a shareware program that plays a movie within a picture—as MovieDialog does—run the TheaterMaker program that is included on this book's CD.

N O T E

Chapter Example: SelectMovie

The QuickPlay and MovieDialog programs demonstrate how to open and play a movie when the movie file's name and location are known at the time of compilation. Using `FSMakeFSSpec()` to create an `FSSpec` for a movie file—as both these programs did—works fine for programs that play movies from a predetermined group of movie files. Other programs, however, will let the user select the movie to play. To do that your program should use the Movie Toolbox routine `StandardGetFilePreview()`. The result of calling this function is shown in Figure 7.20. In that figure you can see that `StandardGetFilePreview()` displays a standard Open dialog box. Beneath the dialog box list is a **Show Preview** checkbox that, when checked, expands the dialog box to display a small view of the first frame of the movie (a *thumbnail*) that is highlighted in the dialog box list.

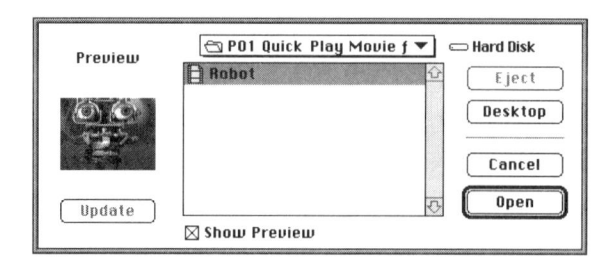

FIGURE 7.20 The standard Open dialog box with a preview, or thumbnail, of a movie.

To allow the user to select a file to open, call StandardGetFilePreview() in place of FSMakeFSSpec():

```
SFTypeList          typeList = { MovieFileType, 0, 0, 0 };
StandardFileReply   theReply;

StandardGetFilePreview( nil, 1, typeList, &theReply );
```

The first three StandardGetFilePreview() parameters describe the type or types of files that are to be shown in the dialog box list. The first parameter holds a pointer to an optional filter function that aids in filtering out files that should not be displayed. In general, StandardGetFile-Preview() handles file filtering without the need for this function—so a value of nil can be passed here. The second parameter specifies the number of file types to list. If your application will only open movies, give this parameter a value of 1. The third parameter is a list that indicates which file types to display. For example, if StandardGetFilePreview() is to display text files, the file list should contain the 'TEXT' type. If both text files and picture files are to be displayed, the list should contain an entry of 'TEXT' and an entry of 'PICT' (and the second parameter should be set to a value of 2). To display movie files, the list should have an entry of 'MooV'—the file type for QuickTime movie files. Apple defines the constant MovieFileType to have a value of 'MooV', so you can use this constant to make it clear just which type of file 'MooV' refers to. To create a file type list, declare a variable of type SFTypeList. To fill the list with up to four file types, enclose the types in braces. If less than four types are being assigned to the list, use zeros—as is being done here:

```
SFTypeList  typeList = { MovieFileType, 0, 0, 0 };
```

The above declaration is identical to this declaration:

```
SFTypeList  typeList = { 'MooV', 0, 0, 0 };
```

The last parameter to StandardGetFilePreview() is a pointer to a *standard file reply structure*. After the call to StandardGetFilePreview() has completed, the StandardFileReply data structure will have all of its several members filled. To determine if the user selected a file (as opposed to clicking on the **Cancel** button), examine the sfGood member. If it has a value of true, the user double-clicked on a file name or clicked once on a file name and then clicked on the **Open** button. If sfGood *is* true, your code should proceed with the opening of the movie file and with the loading of the movie. When doing so, use the sfFile member of the StandardFileReply—it holds an FSSpec for the file the user selected. Note that the File Manager takes care of creating this FSSpec—your code doesn't need to call FSMakeFSSpec().

The following snippet shows how a call to StandardGetFilePreview() can be used to open a movie file. If the user presses the standard Open file dialog box **Cancel** button, the code exits the program. Figure 7.21 shows the changes that were made to the code of this chapter's QuickPlay example to turn that program into the SelectMovie program. In that figure, the lines that have been commented out are from the QuickPlay program.

```
SFTypeList          typeList = { MovieFileType, 0, 0, 0 };
StandardFileReply   theReply;

StandardGetFilePreview( nil, 1, typeList, &theReply );

if ( theReply.sfGood == true )
{
   theError = OpenMovieFile( &theReply.sfFile, &theFileRefNum,
   fsRdPerm );
   theError = NewMovieFromFile( &theMovie, theFileRefNum,
                                &theMovieResID, theMovieResName,
                                newMovieActive, &wasAltered );
   CloseMovieFile( theFileRefNum );
}
else
```

```
{
   ExitToShell();
}
```

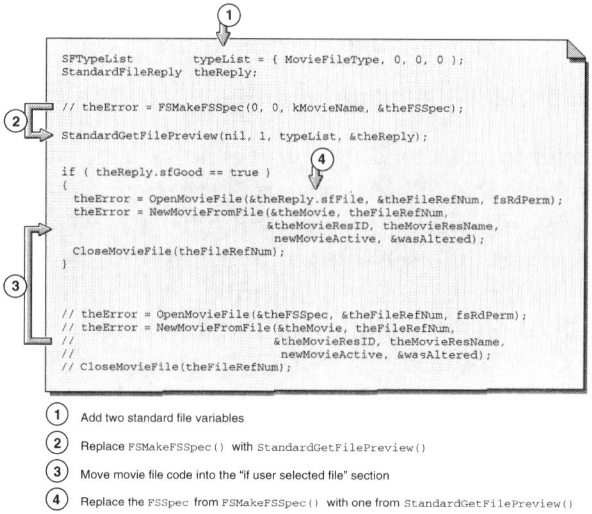

```
SFTypeList         typeList = { MovieFileType, 0, 0, 0 };
StandardFileReply  theReply;

// theError = FSMakeFSSpec(0, 0, kMovieName, &theFSSpec);

StandardGetFilePreview(nil, 1, typeList, &theReply);

if ( theReply.sfGood == true )
{
  theError = OpenMovieFile(&theReply.sfFile, &theFileRefNum, fsRdPerm);
  theError = NewMovieFromFile(&theMovie, theFileRefNum,
                              &theMovieResID, theMovieResName,
                              newMovieActive, &wasAltered);
  CloseMovieFile(theFileRefNum);
}

// theError = OpenMovieFile(&theFSSpec, &theFileRefNum, fsRdPerm);
// theError = NewMovieFromFile(&theMovie, theFileRefNum,
//                             &theMovieResID, theMovieResName,
//                             newMovieActive, &wasAltered);
// CloseMovieFile(theFileRefNum);
```

① Add two standard file variables

② Replace `FSMakeFSSpec()` with `StandardGetFilePreview()`

③ Move movie file code into the "if user selected file" section

④ Replace the `FSSpec` from `FSMakeFSSpec()` with one from `StandardGetFilePreview()`

FIGURE 7.21 Minimal changes to the QuickPlay source code
turn it into the SelectMovie source code.

Movie Controllers

Opening and playing a QuickTime movie can be a task initiated and handled by the application—as you've seen in this chapter. Many programs, however, need to provide the user with the power to control the playing of a movie. To make this happen, your program should make use of movie controllers.

About Movie Controllers

If you want your application to display a movie that can be controlled by the user, it should make use of a movie controller. By using Apple's standard movie controller, you'll be providing users of your program with an easily recognized—and easy to use—movie-playing tool. Figure 7.22 shows a movie controller and its parts.

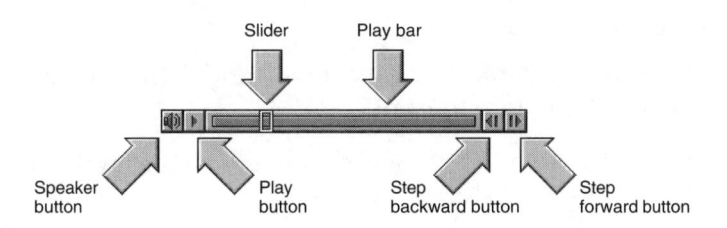

FIGURE 7.22 The parts of a movie controller.

A movie controller can be attached to any open movie. Once attached, the controller acts as a part of the window the movie is displayed in. When the movie is moved on screen, the controller moves with it. The Movie Toolbox provides numerous routines that allow you easily to take advantage of the movie-playing and movie-editing powers of the movie controller.

Attaching a Movie Controller to a Movie

If a movie *won't* be using a movie controller, the act of opening and readying the movie for playing can be summed up in the following ten steps:

1. Open a movie file.
2. Load the movie.
3. Close the movie file.
4. Open a window.
5. Set the movie's graphics world to that of the window.
6. Get the movie box.
7. **Offset the movie box rectangle.**
8. **Set the movie box to the new rectangle.**
9. Size the window.
10. Show the window.

If movie *will* be using a movie controller, the above script—with very little modification—can be used. Steps 7 and 8 are shown in bold because those two steps are the only ones that need to be replaced in order to attach a controller to a movie.

In the QuickPlay example, you saw steps 7 and 8 implemented through the use of the following two lines of code:

```
OffsetRect( &theMovieBox, -theMovieBox.left, -theMovieBox.top );
SetMovieBox( theMovie, &theMovieBox );
```

When adding a movie controller, the above two lines will be replaced by the following:

```
theController = NewMovieController( theMovie, &theMovieBox,
                                    mcTopLeftMovie);

MCGetControllerBoundsRect( theController, &theBoundsRect );
```

The first Movie Toolbox routine to call is `NewMovieController()`. This routine creates a movie controller and attaches it to the movie named in the first parameter.

The second parameter holds the size of the movie box. As before, this rectangle is obtained from a call to the Movie Toolbox function `GetMovieBox()`. The movie box is necessary so that `NewMovieController()` can properly size the new controller so that the controller will have the same width as the movie.

The last parameter to `NewMovieController()` is an Apple-defined constant that tells the Movie Toolbox where the movie will be placed within a window. This information allows the Movie Toolbox to determine where the top of the controller should go. A value of `mcTopLeftMovie` indicates that the movie will fit snugly into the top left corner of the window. The use of this constant in this function call replaces the need to call `OffsetRect()` and `SetMovieBox()`—steps 7 and 8 in the list of steps necessary to ready a movie for playing.

The "mc" in the constant `mcTopLeftMovie` stands for "movie controller." The same applies to Movie Toolbox routines that begin with "MC"—such as the `MCGetControllerBoundsRect()` function used above and described just ahead.

N O T E

When `NewMovieController()` finishes executing, a `MovieController` variable will be returned. This `MovieController` can be used throughout the program to access the controller. The following snippet shows a call to `NewMovieController()`.

```
MovieController   theController;
Movie             theMovie;
Rect              theMovieBox;

theController = NewMovieController( theMovie, &theMovieBox,
                                    mcTopLeftMovie);
```

Figure 7.23 illustrates the controller's placement in the movie's window. The `mcTopLeftMovie` constant tells the Movie Toolbox that the movie will go in the window's upper left corner, and that the new controller should be placed directly beneath the movie—regardless of the size of the window. Remember, the initial size of the window that will hold the movie is arbitrary and gives no indication of the final size of the window.

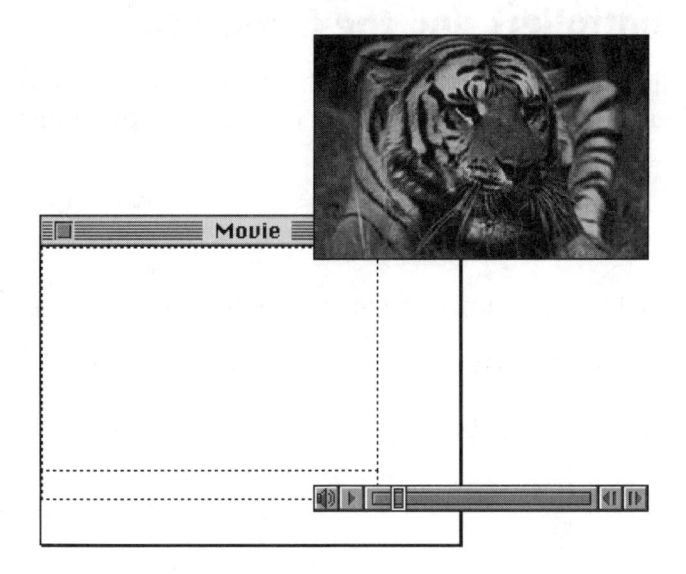

FIGURE 7.23 The `mcTopLeftMovie` constant dictates that the movie will appear in the window's upper left corner and the controller will appear directly beneath the movie.

After the call to `NewMovieController()`, call the Movie Toolbox routine `MCGetControllerBoundsRect()`.

```
MovieController  theController;
Rect             theBoundsRect;

MCGetControllerBoundsRect( theController, &theBoundsRect );
```

When passed a `MovieController` variable, the `MCGetControllerBoundsRect()` function returns the rectangle that bounds both the movie and controller. In the QuickPlay program, the window was sized to match the boundaries of the movie box. Now, with a controller attached, the window must be set to a size large enough to hold both the movie box and the controller area beneath the movie box. The rectangle variable `theBoundsRect` represents the size that the window should be resized to:

```
SizeWindow( theWindow, theBoundsRect.right, theBoundsRect.bottom,
            true );
```

Movie Controllers and the Event Loop

For simplicity, many of the short example programs in this book don't have an event loop. To add an event loop to one of these programs, you could first declare a couple of new variables:

```
Boolean       allDone = false;
EventRecord   theEvent;
```

Next, include the following code near the end of `main()`:

```
while ( allDone == false )
{
   WaitNextEvent( everyEvent, &theEvent, 15L, nil );

   switch ( theEvent.what )
   {
      case keyDown:
         allDone = true;
         break;
   }
}
```

While the this event loop looks for only a press of a key, it satisfies the requirements of a basic event loop: it makes a call to `WaitNextEvent()`, examines the `what` field of the returned event, and then responds to the type of event that occurred.

The structure of the above event loop is perfect for handling most event types, such as a click of the mouse button. Occasionally, though, a program will need to respond to a single event type in different ways. A movie with a movie controller is one such situation. When the user clicks the mouse button, the way in which the `mouseDown` event is handled depends on whether the cursor was over a movie controller or over some other part of the Mac interface. Before entering the loop's `switch` statement, your event loop should determine if an event is controller-related. If it is, the event should be handled—if the controller's **Play** button was clicked, the movie should play; if the **Step forward** button was clicked, the movie should advance a single frame, and so forth. After that, the event can be considered handled and the `switch` statement can be skipped during this pass through the event loop. The following version of the event loop adds a few comments to show how, in general terms, a movie controller event should be handled.

```
Boolean           allDone = false;
EventRecord       theEvent;
MovieController   theController;

while ( allDone == false )
{
   WaitNextEvent( everyEvent, &theEvent, 15L, nil );
// if the event is controller-related, handle it here
// if the event was controller-related, event was handled:
// skip the following code this pass through the while loop
   {
      switch ( theEvent.what )
      {
         case keyDown:
            allDone = true;
            break;
      }
   }
}
```

To determine if an event is controller-related, call the Movie Toolbox routine `MCIsPlayerEvent()`. When passed a movie controller and an event, this function determines if the event involves the movie controller. If it did, a value of 1 is returned. If it didn't, a value of 0 is returned. Here's a call to `MCIsPlayerEvent()`:

```
MovieController    theController;
EventRecord        theEvent;
Boolean            isControllerEvent;

isControllerEvent = MCIsPlayerEvent( theController, &theEvent );
```

The controller will be the `MovieController` returned by a previous call to `NewMovieController()`. The event will be the `EventRecord` returned by a call to `WaitNextEvent()`.

> The return type for `MCIsPlayerEvent()` is actually `ComponentResult`, which is defined to be a `long`. Since the returned values of 1 and 0 match the definitions for `true` and `false`, you can use the returned value as a `Boolean`.

NOTE

The `MCIsPlayerEvent()` function is one of the most important and powerful Movie Toolbox routines. Not only does it provide feedback as to whether an event was controller related—it also handles that event, if it was. If the user clicks on the **Speaker**, **Play**, **Step backward**, or **Step forward** button, or clicks and drags the slider, `MCIsPlayerEvent()` will perform the appropriate action. Your code will not need to call any other routines to handle these user actions. The calls that are necessary to play a movie that doesn't have a controller (`StartMovie()`, `MoviesTask()`, and `IsMovieDone()`) are no longer necessary for a movie that uses a controller.

The following snippet provides a look at a simple event loop that is capable of handling movie controller events. Notice that the `switch` statement will only be executed if `MCIsPlayerEvent()` returns a value of `false`—that is, only if `MCIsPlayerEvent()` finds that the event isn't controller-related and returns a value of 0.

```
Boolean            allDone = false;
EventRecord        theEvent;
```

```
MovieController   theController;
Boolean           isControllerEvent;

while ( allDone == false )
{
   WaitNextEvent( everyEvent, &theEvent, 15L, nil );

   isControllerEvent = MCIsPlayerEvent( theController, &theEvent );

   if ( isControllerEvent == false )
   {
      switch ( theEvent.what )
      {
         case keyDown:
            allDone = true;
            break;
      }
   }
}
```

NOTE   If you've ever included a modeless dialog box in a program, you've done something similar to the above. Before entering the `main()` switch statement, your program called `DialogEvent()` and `DialogSelect()` to determine if an event occurred in a modeless dialog box. If it did, additional code (an application-defined routine, most likely) handled the event and the `switch` statement was skipped.

Chapter Example: QuickController

The QuickController source code has much in common with the QuickPlay code. The change are, of course, controller-related—as described in the preceding text. When you run QuickController, you'll again see the Robot movie. This time, however, it will have a movie controller attached to it—as shown in Figure 7.24. You can use the controller to change the sound volume, play the movie, or step through it. When finished, press any key to quit.

FIGURE 7.24 The Robot movie, as viewed in the
QuickController example program.

As always, you can use any movie in place of the supplied one by changing the value of the kMovieName constant to that of the new movie file, rebuilding the program, and then placing the movie in the folder with the QuickController application

N O T E

When QuickController starts, the program opens a movie and attaches a controller to the movie. Before the user gets a chance to interact with the program, the movie controller has a value (it points to the data that makes up the controller). In your programs, this won't be the case. Typically, a user will select a menu item to open a movie. Before that, the MovieController variable won't point to any valid data. Because the MovieController is used in the main event loop, this could cause problems—at each pass through the event loop your code will be passing MCIsPlayerEvent() a controller variable that doesn't point to valid data:

```
isControllerEvent = MCIsPlayerEvent( theController, &theEvent );
```

To remedy this problem, assign the controller variable a value of nil when it is declared and when a movie is closed. In other words, if no movie is on the screen, then no controller is, either—and the variable `theController` should reflect that fact. The following snippet introduces the Movie Toolbox function `DisposeMovieController()` and shows how to properly assign values to `theController`.

```
MovieController  theController = nil;

// theController gets a value when NewMovieController() is called

// when it's time to close the movie, use the following code:

DisposeMovieController( theController );
theController = nil;
DisposeMovie( theMovie );
DisposeWindow( theWindow );
```

Next, test the value of `theController` before calling `MCIsPlayerEvent()`. If the `MovieController` variable has a value of `nil`, no movie is open and any event that occurs cannot be controller-related. If the `MovieController` variable has a value other than `nil`, then the variable points to valid controller data and `MCIsPlayerEvent()` should be called to see if any event is controller-related.

```
if ( theController == nil )
   isControllerEvent = false;
else
   isControllerEvent = MCIsPlayerEvent( theController, &theEvent );
```

The following is the source code listing for QuickController. You'll find that most of the code is identical to the code used in the preceding text.

```
//_____

#include <Movies.h>

//_____

void  InitializeAllToolboxes( void );
//_____

#define      rMovieWindow                    128
#define      kMovieName         "\pRobot"

//_____
```

```
void  main( void )
{
   OSErr           theError;
   FSSpec          theFSSpec;
   short           theFileRefNum;
   Movie           theMovie;
   short           theMovieResID = 0
   Str255          theMovieResName;
   Boolean         wasAltered;
   WindowPtr       theWindow;
   Rect            theMovieBox;
   Rect            theBoundsRect;
   MovieController theController = nil;
   EventRecord     theEvent;
   Boolean         isControllerEvent;
   Boolean         allDone = false;

   InitializeAllToolboxes();

   theError = FSMakeFSSpec( 0, 0, kMovieName, &theFSSpec );
   theError = OpenMovieFile( &theFSSpec, &theFileRefNum, fsRdPerm );
   theError = NewMovieFromFile( &theMovie, theFileRefNum,
                            &theMovieResID, theMovieResName,
                            newMovieActive, &wasAltered );

   CloseMovieFile( theFileRefNum );
   theWindow = GetNewCWindow( rMovieWindow, nil, (WindowPtr)-1L );
   SetMovieGWorld( theMovie, (CGrafPtr)theWindow, nil );
   GetMovieBox( theMovie, &theMovieBox );
   theController = NewMovieController( theMovie, &theMovieBox,
                                    mcTopLeftMovie);

   MCGetControllerBoundsRect( theController, &theBoundsRect );

   SizeWindow( theWindow, theBoundsRect.right,
             theBoundsRect.bottom, true );
   ShowWindow( theWindow );

   while ( allDone == false )
   {
      WaitNextEvent( everyEvent, &theEvent, 15L, nil );
      if ( theController == nil )
         isControllerEvent = false;
      else
         isControllerEvent = MCIsPlayerEvent( theController,
                                          &theEvent );
```

```
    if ( isControllerEvent == false )
    {
        switch ( theEvent.what )
        {
            case keyDown:
                allDone = true;
                break;
        }
    }
}

DisposeMovieController( theController );
theController = nil;
DisposeMovie( theMovie );
DisposeWindow( theWindow );
}
```

Movie Controllers and Movie Looping

When a new movie controller is created, MCIsPlayerEvent() handles mouse clicks that occur on that movie controller in a predictable manner. A click on the **Play** button plays the movie one time, for instance. In general, these default actions will be appropriate for your applications. Occasionally, though, you'll want to change how MCIsPlayerEvent() handles certain events. The Movie Toolbox routine MCDoAction() gives your program the ability to do just that.

The MCDoAction() function acts on one specific controller—the controller that is passed in the routine's first parameter. The second parameter— the *action parameter*—specifies what action should be affected. Apple defines several constants that specify different actions. The third parameter is a pointer to additional information. The nature of this additional information varies with the action being passed to MCDoAction().

Movie looping is one of the most common reasons for using MCDoAction(). Passing the Apple-defined constant mcActionSetLooping as the second parameter and a pointer to the value true as the third parameter tells MCDoAction() to turn looping on for the controller named in the first parameter. Here's an example:

```
MovieController  theController;

MCDoAction( theController, mcActionSetLooping, (Ptr)true );
```

Calling `MCDoAction()` won't immediately start the movie looping. Instead, it sets the controller's **Play** button to looping mode. From that point on, a mouse click on the controller's **Play** button will cause the movie in the controller's window to play repeatedly until the user again clicks the **Play** button.

To return a movie controller's **Play** button to its original state, again call `MCDoAction()` with an action parameter of `mcActionSetLooping`. This time, pass a pointer to a value of `false`:

```
MCDoAction( theController, mcActionSetLooping, (Ptr)false );
```

QuickTime allows a movie controller to loop through a movie in palindrome mode. Palindrome looping means that the movie will first play forward, then backward. This back-and-forth playing pattern will repeat until the user again clicks on the controller's **Play** button. The following is a snippet that sets a controller to palindrome mode:

```
MCDoAction( theController, mcActionSetLoopIsPalindrome, (Ptr)true );
```

Turning palindrome looping off is as simple as turning normal looping off:

```
MCDoAction( theController, mcActionSetLoopIsPalindrome,
    (Ptr)false );
```

Chapter Example: MovieLooping

The MovieLooping example demonstrates just how easy it is to add looping to a movie. The source code for MovieLooping is identical to that of the QuickController program except for the addition of a single line of code. If you compare the source code listings for the two programs, you'll find that the MovieLooping code has the following line after the controller is created, whereas the QuickController listing doesn't:

```
MCDoAction( theController, mcActionSetLooping, (Ptr)true );
```

 The call to `MCDoAction()` doesn't have to appear immediately after a new controller is created. As long as a valid `MovieController` is passed in as the first parameter, `MCDoAction()` can be used at any point in a program. For instance, if your program includes a **Looping** menu item in a Movies menu, you can call `MCDoAction()` in response to this item being selected.

N O T E

Chapter Summary

The Movie Toolbox is the set of Toolbox routines that enable you to add movie-related features to a Mac program. Before making use of this Toolbox, you should call Gestalt() to verify that the user of your program has QuickTime installed on his or her computer. If QuickTime is present, make sure to initialize the Movie Toolbox by making a call to the EnterMovies() routine.

A QuickTime movie resides in a QuickTime movie file. Before a movie can be played, the file in which the movie is must be opened and the movie must be loaded into memory. After that, your program needs to open a standard color window in which the movie will be displayed. After the window is resized to match the dimensions of the movie that will appear in it, the movie can be displayed and then played. To play the movie, call the MoviesTask() function repeatedly until the movie has finished.

If your program is to give control of movie playing to the user, attach a movie controller to an open movie. After that, call MCIsPlayerEvent() from the program's main event loop. This powerful Movie Toolbox routine will handle a mouse click on any of the buttons that make up a movie controller.

CHAPTER 8

QuickTime Musical Instruments

If you have System 7.5 or later on your Macintosh, your programs can make use of QuickTime and QuickTime Musical Instruments. Chapter 7 supplied you with all the information you need to add movie-playing capabilities to your programs. It is now time to add music-playing capabilities as well.

In this chapter, you'll see how the QuickTime Musical Instruments extension—and the Toolbox functions designed to work with this system software—makes it easy to add music and sound effects to any of your programs. And unlike storing digitized sounds in your application's resource fork, you'll find that using the QuickTime Musical Instruments to play sounds adds very little extra size to your application.

Here, you'll see that—with just a few Toolbox calls—you can play sounds from any of 128 predefined instruments—the standardized MIDI (Musical Instrument Digital Interface) instruments that other programs have used for years. These MIDI instruments don't just allow you to play crystal-clear music from such instruments as a grand piano, acoustic guitar, or tenor saxophone—many of these "instruments" allow you to add great special effects and synthesized noises such as seashore noise, the whir of a helicopter, and telephone rings to your programs.

About QuickTime Music

The QuickTime Music Architecture, or QMA, is the QuickTime Musical Instruments system software extension used in conjunction with the QuickTime extension and the host of new music-related routines that you can add to any of your programs.

QMA consists of three software components, each corresponding to a level of access to the devices that are used to create sound. The three components, or layers, are described here.

> *Tune Player* The top layer that provides timing for *sequences*—the instruments and notes of a musical composition.
>
> *Note Allocator* The next level down from the Tune Player. This layer is responsible for playing individual notes on specific synthesizer devices.
>
> *Music Component* The lowest layer. The Music Component provides routines that allow access to the settings of synthesizer devices.

If your application is to set up a complex musical score, it will make use of the Tune Player. If your program only needs to play a note or notes from one of the many available instruments, the Note Allocator can be used. The Music Component layer is normally used only by the other layers—a program should seldom or never need to make use of it directly. This chapter deals with the Note Allocator. By using this one QMA component, you can quickly and easily add a wide variety of sounds to any program.

The Note Allocator

The Note Allocator is the midlevel QuickTime Music Architecture component that is used to play individual musical notes. This component makes it possible for your application to play a wide variety of instruments and music with just a few Toolbox calls.

Opening a Note Allocator Component

A program that makes use of the QuickTime Music Architecture must open an *instance* of a Note Allocator component before even a single note can be played. To do this, call the Toolbox function `OpenDefaultComponent()`. This routine isn't QMA-specific—it is used to open any type of component. You'll find its definition in the **Components.h** universal header file.

```
NoteAllocator   gNoteAllocatorComp;

gNoteAllocatorComp = OpenDefaultComponent( kNoteAllocatorType, 0 );
```

The first parameter to `OpenDefaultComponent()` is the component type. Supply the Apple-defined constant `kNoteAllocatorType` (which is defined to be 'nota', for Note Allocator) to tell `OpenDefaultComponent()` to open a Note Allocator component. The second parameter is a component subtype—pass 0 here.

`OpenDefaultComponent()` returns a Note Allocator component. Save a reference to this component in a variable of type `NoteAllocator`. The above snippet stores the component in the global variable `gNoteAllocatorComp`.

ToneDescription: Describing an Instrument

After opening an instance of a Note Allocator component, a note channel needs to be opened. When your program requests a note channel, it will supply specific information about the music that will be played from that channel. Some of this information will be about the instrument type that will be used to produce the sound that emanates from the channel. Apple defines the `ToneDescription` data structure to hold this instrument information:

```
struct  ToneDescription
{
   OSType   synthesizerType;
   Str31    synthesizerName;
```

```
    Str31     instrumentName;
    long      instrumentNumber;
    long      gmNumber;
};
```

The first field of the `ToneDescription` structure is a number that specifies the type of synthesizer that should be used. A synthesizer is a software or hardware device used to create sound. Each synthesizer has its own Music Component—a low-level component that serves as the software interface to the synthesizer. The QuickTime Music Architecture includes a built-in synthesizer.

The second field of `ToneDescription` is the name of the synthesizer specified in the first field. If the built-in synthesizer is used, this field will be filled in with the string "Macintosh Built In."

The `instrumentName` field of the structure holds the name of the instrument that will be used to generate a sound. This field will hold one of the strings listed in Appendix A.

The fourth field holds a number that represents the instrument to be used. This field will have a value in the range of 1 to 128. These numbers correspond to the instruments listed in Appendix A. The value of this field will usually match the value in the `gmNumber` field.

The `gmNumber` field holds one of the 128 General MIDI Instrument numbers shown in Appendix A. Your program can open an Instrument Picker dialog box (discussed later) that allows the user to select an instrument by name. If that happens, the `gmNumber` field will be filled in with the matching instrument number from Appendix A. If instead your program specifies an instrument to play, your program will supply a gmNumber value in the range of 1 to 128. If your program supplies a number outside of this range, the QMA will select a valid number, place that value in the `instrumentNumber` field, and use that instrument.

To fill in a `ToneDescription`, first declare a `ToneDescription` variable:

```
ToneDescription  gToneDesc;
```

Next, fill in the five fields. You can supply zeros in the first three fields and a General MIDI Instrument number in the fourth and fifth fields. The following snippet creates a `ToneDescription` for the Xylophone instrument:

```
ToneDescription  gToneDesc;

gToneDesc.synthesizerType = 0;
gToneDesc.synthesizerName[0] = 0;
gToneDesc.instrumentName[0] = 0;
gToneDesc.instrumentNumber = 14;
gToneDesc.gmNumber = 14;
```

In preparation for the opening of a note channel and the playing of a note, you can write a short application-defined routine like the Initialize-Instrument() function shown here. It opens a Note Allocator component, then sets the fields of a ToneDescription.

```
NoteAllocator       gNoteAllocatorComp;
ToneDescription  gToneDesc;

void InitializeInstrument( void )
{
    gNoteAllocatorComp = OpenDefaultComponent( 'nota', 0 );

    gToneDesc.synthesizerType = 0;
    gToneDesc.synthesizerName[0] = 0;
    gToneDesc.instrumentName[0] = 0;
    gToneDesc.instrumentNumber = 15;
    gToneDesc.gmNumber = 15;
}
```

Describing a Note Channel

The ToneDescription defines the instrument that will be used to play a note. There are a couple of other attributes that are needed before a note channel can be opened. The NoteRequest data structure defines the information needed to define a note channel:

```
struct  NoteRequest
{
    long                polyphony;
    Fixed               typicalPolyphony;
    ToneDescription  tone;
};
```

The first field of the `NoteRequest` structure is the channel's polyphony. In music, `polyphony` has to do with the combining of melodies—as in a harmony. The polyphony field holds the maximum number of notes, or voices, that can be played at one time by the channel.

The `typicalPolyphony` field of the `NoteRequest` structure is used by the Note Allocator to help it return a note channel that best satisfies the information in the rest of the `NoteRequest` structure. Pass a value of `0x00010000` for this `Fixed` field type.

The final `NoteRequest` field is a `ToneDescription` like the one described earlier. The `ToneDescription` tells the Note Allocator what type of instrument will be used in the note channel.

The following snippet fills in a `NoteRequest` for use in opening a new note channel. The `tone` field is filled in with the `ToneDescription` global variable discussed earlier—`gToneDesc`.

```
NoteRequest  theNoteRequest;

theNoteRequest.polyphony = 4;
theNoteRequest.typicalPolyphony = 0x00010000;
theNoteRequest.tone = gToneDesc;
```

Opening a Note Channel

Finally, it's time to open a new note channel. A call to `NANewNoteChannel()` does that:

```
NoteAllocator     gNoteAllocatorComp;
NoteChannel       theNoteChannel;
NoteRequest       theNoteRequest;
ComponentResult   theError;

theError = NANewNoteChannel( gNoteAllocatorComp, &theNoteRequest,
                             &theNoteChannel );
```

The first parameter to `NANewNoteChannel()` is an instance of a Note Allocator component. This is the NoteAllocator returned by the call to the Toolbox function `OpenDefaultComponent()`.

The second parameter to `NANewNoteChannel()` is a variable of type `NoteRequest`. The third field of this `NoteRequest` structure should hold the filled-in `ToneDescription` that specifies the type of General MIDI Instrument that is to be used with the channel.

After opening a new note channel, `NANewNoteChannel()` returns in the third parameter a `NoteChannel` with the qualities described in the `NoteRequest` structure.

If you haven't already realized it, the leading "NA" in a function name tells you the function is Note Allocator–related.

N O T E

After opening a new note channel, notes and music can be played—as you'll see just ahead.

When through with a note channel, your application can dispose of it using the `NADisposeNoteChannel()` function. Pass this routine both the instance of the Note Allocator component and the `NoteChannel` that were the first and third parameters in the call to `NANewNoteChannel()`.

```
NoteAllocator      gNoteAllocatorComp;
NoteChannel        theNoteChannel;
ComponentResult    theError;

theError = NADisposeNoteChannel( gNoteAllocatorComp, theNoteChannel );
```

Playing a Note

With a note channel open, it's time to play some music. A call to `NAPlayNote()` does that. The following snippet plays a middle C note from whatever instrument, and at whatever polyphony, was specified in the `NoteRequest` structure passed to `NANewNoteChannel()`:

```
NoteAllocator    gNoteAllocatorComp;
NoteChannel      theNoteChannel;
short            thePitch;
long             theLong;
```

```
thePitch = 60;

NAPlayNote( gNoteAllocatorComp, theNoteChannel, thePitch, 127 );
```

The first parameter to `NAPlayNote()` is the instance of the Note Allocator component returned by `OpenDefaultComponent()` and used in the call to `NANewNoteChannel()`. The second parameter to `NAPlayNote()` is the note channel from which to play the music.

Skipping the third parameter for a moment, the value in the fourth parameter specifies the *velocity* of the note. The velocity refers to how hard a key on a keyboard would be struck to produce this note on a piano. Simplistically, the velocity is the note's volume. A value of 0 produces silence, while a value of 127 produces maximum volume.

Back to the third `NAPlayNote()` parameter. This value is the *pitch*, or frequency, of the note. The value of 60 produces a middle C note. This parameter should have a value in the range of 0 to 127. Each of these 128 pitch values corresponds to a MIDI key number. If you're familiar with music, you know that pitch is related to a particular key. Figure 8.1 shows how the possible pitch values of 0 through 127 correspond to the C keys of each of the eleven octaves of a piano.

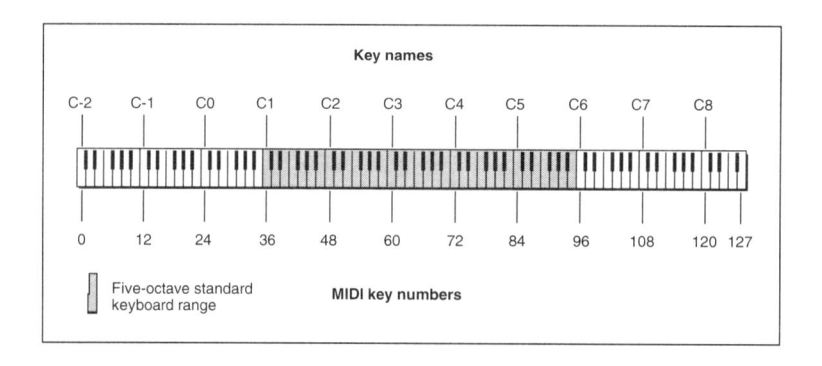

FIGURE 8.1 Piano keys each have a key name and a MIDI key, or note, value.

NOTE Don't confuse the MIDI note values of 0 to 127 that correspond to piano keys with the General MIDI Instrument numbers (listed in Appendix A), which have a range of 1 to 128. Any one of the 128 MIDI instruments can play any of the 128 MIDI notes.

Each pitch value corresponds to a MIDI note value. Each MIDI note value corresponds to a note in the scale of a particular octave. Figure 8.1 shows the MIDI note values related to the keys of a piano and to the C notes in the scales of the octaves. Table 8.1 shows the MIDI note values related to each note in all of the octaves. For example, specifying a pitch of 37 will produce a C# note in the scale of the fourth octave. The highlighted pitch values 36 through 96 are the pitch values that fall into the range of the standard five-octave keyboard.

Table 8.1 A MIDI note value corresponds to a scale value in a particular octave.

	A	A#	B	C	C#	D	D#	E	F	F#	G	G#
Octave 1				0	1	2	3	4	5	6	7	8
Octave 2	9	10	11	12	13	14	15	16	17	18	19	20
Octave 3	21	22	23	24	25	26	27	28	29	30	31	32
Octave 4	33	34	35	36	37	38	39	40	41	42	43	44
Octave 5	45	46	47	48	49	50	51	52	53	54	55	56
Octave 6	57	58	59	60	61	62	63	64	65	66	67	68
Octave 7	69	70	71	72	73	74	75	76	77	78	79	80
Octave 8	81	82	83	84	85	86	87	88	89	90	91	92
Octave 9	93	94	95	96	97	98	99	100	101	102	103	104
Octave 10	105	106	107	108	109	110	111	112	113	114	115	116
Octave 11	117	118	119	120	121	122	123	124	125	126	127	

When `NAPlayNote()` is called, a note specified by the pitch is played on the instrument specified by the setup of the note channel. As long as the velocity value is nonzero, this note will play indefinitely—`NAPlayNote()` includes no provision for setting the duration of the note. To stop the note, again call `NAPlayNote()`. This time, use a velocity of 0. If you make the second call to `NAPlayNote()` immediately after the first call, the note will stop immediately. To set a duration, add a delay between the two calls to `NAPlayNote()`. You can use the Toolbox function `Delay()` to accomplish this task—as shown in this snippet:

```
NoteAllocator    gNoteAllocatorComp;
NoteChannel      theNoteChannel;
short            thePitch;
long             theLong;

thePitch = 60;

NAPlayNote( gNoteAllocatorComp, theNoteChannel, thePitch, 127 );
Delay( 10, &theLong );
NAPlayNote( gNoteAllocatorComp, theNoteChannel, thePitch, 0 );
```

The first parameter to `Delay()` specifies the length of the delay in ticks—sixtieths of a second. The above snippet causes the note to play for ten sixtieths, or one sixth, of a second. Similarly, a first parameter of 60 would play the note for one second while a first parameter of 180 would play the note for three seconds. The second parameter to `Delay()` is a pointer to a `long` variable. `Delay()` returns the number of ticks that have taken place from the time of the computer's startup to the call to `Delay()`—a value that you won't be concerned with.

Chapter Example: PlayNote

This chapter's first example uses QuickTime Musical Architecture functions to play the sound of a helicopter for 5 seconds. The setting of the `ToneDescription` field `gmNumber` to a value of 126 in the application-defined `InitializeInstrument()` function specifies that the Helicopter General MIDI Instrument should be used. To change the sound, refer to Appendix A. Select any of the 128 MIDI instrument numbers, set `gmNumber` to that value, and recompile and run the program.

You can slow the helicopter sound down or speed it up by changing the value of the pitch in the `PlayMusicFromNoteChannel()` function. Choose a value in the range of 0 to 127. Lower values slow the helicopter blade down; higher values speed it up.

You can change the length which the sound plays by changing the value of the first parameter in the `Delay()` function called from `PlayMusicFromNoteChannel()`.

// _____

```
#include <QuickTimeComponents.h>
```

```
//_____

void  InitializeToolbox( void );
void  InitializeInstrument( void );
void  PlayMusicFromNoteChannel( void );

//_____

NoteAllocator      gNoteAllocatorComp;
ToneDescription  gToneDesc;

//_____

void  main( void )
{
   InitializeToolbox();

   InitializeInstrument();

   PlayMusicFromNoteChannel();
}

//_____

void InitializeInstrument( void )
{
   gNoteAllocatorComp = OpenDefaultComponent( kNoteAllocatorType, 0 );

   gToneDesc.synthesizerType = 0;
   gToneDesc.synthesizerName[0] = 0;
   gToneDesc.instrumentName[0] = 0;
   gToneDesc.instrumentNumber = 126;
   gToneDesc.gmNumber = 126;
}

//_____

void  PlayMusicFromNoteChannel( void )
{
   NoteRequest       theNoteRequest;
   NoteChannel       theNoteChannel;
   short             thePitch;
   ComponentResult theError;
   long              theLong;

   theNoteRequest.polyphony = 4;
   theNoteRequest.typicalPolyphony = 0x00010000;
   theNoteRequest.tone = gToneDesc;
```

```
    theError = NANewNoteChannel( gNoteAllocatorComp, &theNoteRequest,
                            &theNoteChannel );
    thePitch = 60;

    NAPlayNote( gNoteAllocatorComp, theNoteChannel, thePitch, 127 );
    Delay( 300, &theLong );
    NAPlayNote( gNoteAllocatorComp, theNoteChannel, thePitch, 0 );

    theError = NADisposeNoteChannel( gNoteAllocatorComp,
                            theNoteChannel );
}

//_____

void  InitializeToolbox( void )
{
    InitGraf( &qd.thePort );
    InitFonts();
    InitWindows();
    InitMenus();
    TEInit();
    InitDialogs( 0L );
    FlushEvents( everyEvent, 0 );
    InitCursor();
}
```

Chapter Example: PlayScale

The PlayScale program is very similar to the PlayNote example you just
experimented with. One of the differences is in the instrument used to
play the sound. In PlayScale, the gmNumber is set to 1, which selects the
Acoustic Grand Piano instrument (again, refer to Appendix A).

```
void InitializeInstrument( void )
{
    gNoteAllocatorComp = OpenDefaultComponent( kNoteAllocatorType, 0 );

    gToneDesc.synthesizerType = 0;
    gToneDesc.synthesizerName[0] = 0;
    gToneDesc.instrumentName[0] = 0;
    gToneDesc.instrumentNumber = 1;
```

```
    gToneDesc.gmNumber = 1;
}
```

More important than the change to the `InitializeInstrument()` function is the change to `PlayMusicFromNoteChannel()`. In PlayScale, the calls to `NAPlayNote()` and `Delay()` have been placed in the body of a `for` loop. At each pass through the loop, the pitch is incremented by a value of 1. The effect is that of running your finger from left to right across the shaded piano keys in Figure 8.1.

```
for ( thePitch = 36; thePitch <= 96; thePitch++ )
{
   NAPlayNote( gNoteAllocatorComp, theNoteChannel, thePitch, 127 );
   Delay( 10, &theLong );
   NAPlayNote( gNoteAllocatorComp, theNoteChannel, thePitch, 0 );
}
```

The remainder of the PlayScale code is identical to that of the PlayNote program. You can refer to this book's CD for the complete source code listing.

Selecting an Instrument

The QuickTime Music Architecture provides a powerful and easy to implement means of both experimenting with MIDI instruments and of allowing users of your programs to select the MIDI instrument to use. Figure 8.2 shows the Instrument Picker dialog box that your program can open with a single Note Allocator function call.

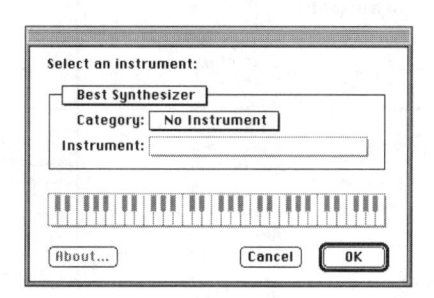

FIGURE 8.2 The Pick Instrument dialog box.

Clicking on the synthesizer pop-up menu in the Instrument Picker dialog box displays a list of synthesizers to choose from. As shown in Figure 8.3, Apple supplies one synthesizer with the QuickTime Musical Instruments extension—third-party synthesizers may be available. You can leave this menu at the Best Synthesizer item to let the QMA select the best choice.

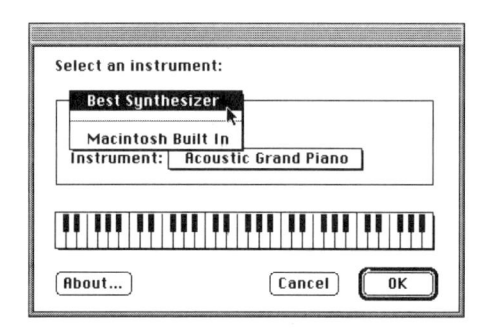

FIGURE 8.3 The synthesizer pop-up menu in the Pick Instrument dialog box.

As shown in Figure 8.4, the Category pop-up menu allows you to select a category of instruments. Selecting a category determines the contents of the next pop-up menu, the Instrument menu.

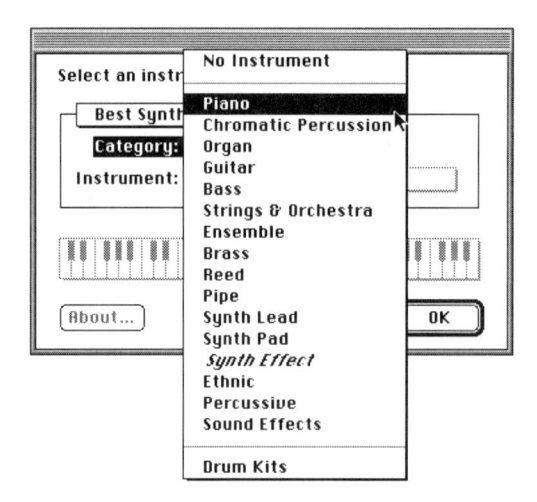

FIGURE 8.4 The Category pop-up menu in the Pick Instrument dialog box.

After selecting an instrument category, select a particular instrument from that category by using the Instrument pop-up menu—shown in Figure 8.5.

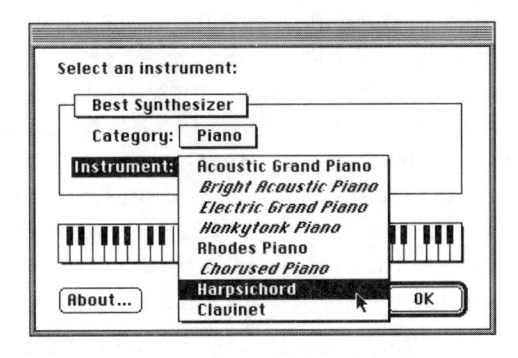

FIGURE 8.5 The Instrument pop-up menu in the Pick Instrument dialog box.

Once you've selected an instrument, click on any key of the Instrument Picker keyboard. If you click on a key and hold the mouse button down, the note will play until you release the mouse button. You can also hold the mouse button down and move the cursor across the keys to play any number of notes in a single mouse-click.

Adding the Instrument Picker Dialog Box to a Program

The Instrument Picker dialog box is great for experimenting with *all* of the one hundred-plus MIDI instruments. When added to one of your own programs, it serves to quickly and easily show off the capabilities of the QuickTime Musical Instruments extension.

A single Toolbox call displays the Instrument Picker dialog box and handles all of its functionality. The following snippet makes use of the powerful `NAPickInstrument()` function.

```
NoteAllocator      gNoteAllocatorComp;
ToneDescription    gToneDesc;
ComponentResult    theResult;
Str31              thePrompt = "\pPick an instrument:";
```

```
theResult = NAPickInstrument( gNoteAllocatorComp, nil, thePrompt,
                              &gToneDesc, 0, 0, 0, 0 );
```

The first parameter to `NAPickInstrument()` is the Note Allocator component that was returned in the call to `OpenDefaultComponent()`. The second parameter holds an optional filter function—the above snippet simply sets this parameter to `nil`. The third parameter holds a string that will be displayed in the dialog box—refer to Figure 8.5 to see the placement of this string. The fourth parameter to `NAPickInstrument()` is a pointer to a `ToneDescription` variable. Unlike the `ToneDescription` variables used in preceding example programs, the one used here does not need to be initialized. Instead, the `NAPickInstrument()` function will fill the fields of this variable based on the user's instrument selection.

The last four parameters to `NAPickInstrument()` can each be set to `0`. The fifth parameter can be used to hold a flag that limits the user's instrument choices. Passing the Apple-defined constant `kPickDontMix` will dim the last menu item in the Category pop-up menu—the **Drum Kits** item. Refer to Figure 8.4 to see this item. Passing the Apple-defined constant `kPickSameSynth` will dim all synthesizer items in the synthesizer menu except for the **Best Synthesizer** item.

The sixth parameter is used to hold a reference constant—the above snippet sets this value to `0`. The seventh and eighth parameters are reserved by Apple and *must* be set to `0`.

Chapter Example: PickInstrument

The PickInstrument example program displays the Pick Instrument dialog box. You can experiment with this dialog box to your heart's content—it won't be dismissed until you click either the **Cancel** or **OK** button.

After initializing the Macintosh Toolbox, PickInstrument calls the application-defined `InitializeInstrument()` function to set the instrument number to 0. A value of `0` in the `gmNumber` field of the `ToneDescription` structure means that the Category pop-up menu will display a **No Instrument** item, the Instrument pop-up menu will be disabled, and the dialog box keyboard will be disabled as well. That should be an indication to the user that a selection from the Category menu is in order. Once a selection other than **No Instrument** is made, the rest of the dialog box will become enabled.

```
void InitializeInstrument( void )
{
    gNoteAllocatorComp = OpenDefaultComponent( kNoteAllocatorType, 0 );

    gToneDesc.synthesizerType = 0;
    gToneDesc.synthesizerName[0] = 0;
    gToneDesc.instrumentName[0] = 0;
    gToneDesc.instrumentNumber = 0;
    gToneDesc.gmNumber = 0;
}
```

To demonstrate that `NAPickInstrument()` fills in the `ToneDescription` structure that is passed as the fourth parameter, turn your compiler's debugging option on. If you break at the end of the `InitializeInstrument()` function you'll see that the `gToneDesc` fields have been filled as expected—Figure 8.6 shows this using the Metrowerks debugger.

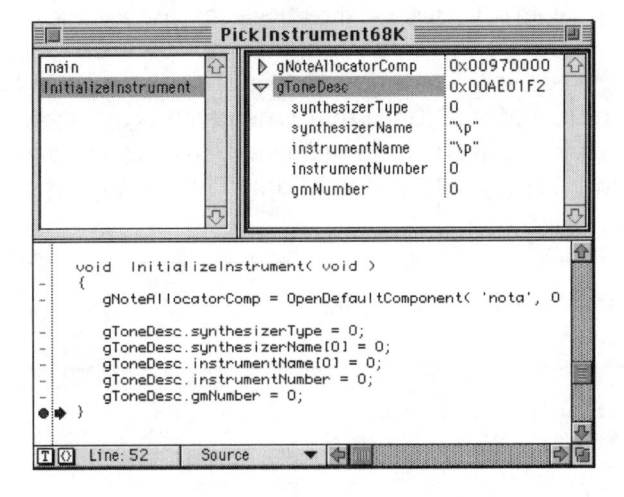

FIGURE 8.6 The fields of the `ToneDescription` structure are initialized to 0.

Next, set a breakpoint after the call to `NAPickInstrument()`—as shown in Figure 8.7. When this breakpoint is reached you'll find that the fields of the `gToneDesc ToneDescription` structure have been filled—including both the MIDI name and number of the instrument selected by the user.

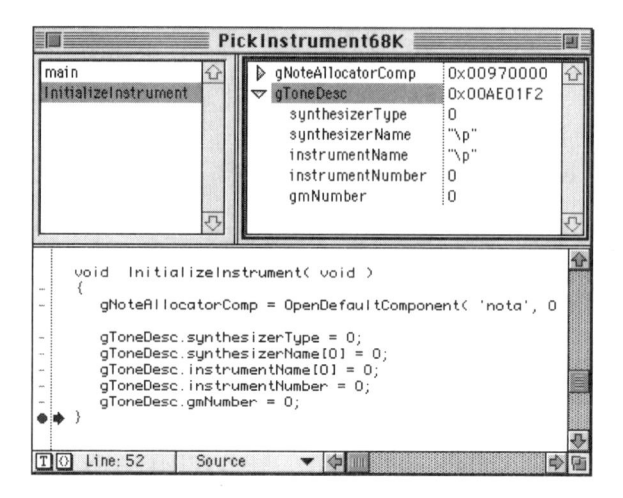

FIGURE 8.7 The `NAPickInstrument()` function will change
the values of the fields of the `ToneDescription` structure.

The following very short listing is the entire source code listing for the PickInstrument program. Notice that when `NAPickInstrument()` is called, no new note channel needs to be allocated. `NAPickInstrument()` handles the creation and disposal of the note channel it uses to play music.

```
//_____

#include <QuickTimeComponents.h>

//_____

void   InitializeToolbox( void );
void   InitializeInstrument( void );

//_____

NoteAllocator       gNoteAllocatorComp;
ToneDescription     gToneDesc;
```

```
//_____

void  main( void )
{
    ComponentResult  theResult;
    Str31            thePrompt = "\pSelect an instrument:";

    InitializeToolbox();

    InitializeInstrument();

    theResult = NAPickInstrument( gNoteAllocatorComp, nil, thePrompt,
                                  &gToneDesc, 0, 0, 0, 0 );
    if ( theResult != noErr )
        ExitToShell();
}

//_____

void InitializeInstrument( void )
{
    gNoteAllocatorComp = OpenDefaultComponent( kNoteAllocatorType, 0 );

    gToneDesc.synthesizerType = 0;
    gToneDesc.synthesizerName[0] = 0;
    gToneDesc.instrumentName[0] = 0;
    gToneDesc.instrumentNumber = 0;
    gToneDesc.gmNumber = 0;
}

//_____

void  InitializeToolbox( void )
{
    InitGraf( &qd.thePort );
    InitFonts();
    InitWindows();
    InitMenus();
    TEInit();
    InitDialogs( OL );
    FlushEvents( everyEvent, 0 );
    InitCursor();
}
```

Chapter Example: PickAndPlay

The last example program in this chapter adds to the PickInstrument program you just looked over. When you run PickAndPlay, you'll again see the Pick Instrument dialog box. If you select an instrument and then click the **OK** button, the dialog box will be dismissed and a series of notes from the selected instrument will be played. The `PlayMusicFromNoteChannel()` routine used in this chapter's PlayScale example takes care of this task. You'll find that this version of `PlayMusicFromNote-Channel()` is identical to the previous version—it's a direct copy and paste from PlayScale.

PlayScale demonstrates that while the Pick Instrument dialog box may sidetrack the user for quite a while, this dialog box is more than a simple diversion. It allows your application to let the user choose the instrument to be used. This dialog box also allows your program to save the user's instrument selection for later use. By having a global variable for the `ToneDescription` parameter that is passed to `NAPickInstrument()`, your program can recall the user's instrument selection at any time.

If the user clicks the **Cancel** button rather than the **OK** button, PickAndPlay assumes that the user doesn't want the selection saved. If the user doesn't make an instrument selection, the program again assumes that no music is to be played. In both cases, PickAndPlay exits—your program will handle a **Cancel** hit or a nonselection in a more graceful manner.

```
theResult = NAPickInstrument( gNoteAllocatorComp, nil, thePrompt,
                              &gToneDesc, 0, 0, 0, 0 );

if ( ( gToneDesc.instrumentNumber == 0 ) || ( theResult != noErr ) )
   ExitToShell();
else
   PlayMusicFromNoteChannel();
```

N O T E The above snippet will exit the program if the user clicks the Pick Instrument dialog box **Cancel** button—the variable `theResult` will have a value of `userCanceledErr`. If your program needs to know if this button was clicked, make a comparison using the following Apple-defined constant:

```
if ( theResult == userCanceledErr )
   // handle user canceled instrument choice
```

Now that you're familiar with the fields of the `ToneDescription` structure and how they can be initialized, the application-defined `Initialize-Instrument()` function has been redesigned. It now calls the Toolbox function `NAStuffToneDescription()`.

Rather than filling in the fields of `gToneDesc` one at a time—as was done in previous examples—a single call to `NAStuffToneDescription()` is now used. When passed a Note Allocator component and a `gmNumber` value in its first two parameters, this function fills in the fields of the `ToneDescription` variable passed as the third parameter. `InitializeInstrument()` now accepts a single parameter—the General MIDI Instrument number of the instrument to initialize the `ToneDescription` structure to. Here's the new `InitializeInstrument()` function, along with a call to it.

```
#define        kMIDInoInstrument        0

long  theInstrument = kMIDInoInstrument;

InitializeInstrument( theInstrument );

void InitializeInstrument( long theInstrument )
{
   ComponentResult  theResult;

   gNoteAllocatorComp = OpenDefaultComponent( kNoteAllocatorType, 0 );

   theResult = NAStuffToneDescription( gNoteAllocatorComp,
                                 theInstrument, &gToneDesc );
}
```

The MIDI instrument that is passed to `InitializeInstrument()` in the form of a `gmNumber` value will be the instrument that appears in the Instrument pop-up menu of the Pick Instrument dialog box when the dialog box opens. Try changing the value passed to `InitializeInstrument()` to verify that it has this effect.

```
//_____

#include <QuickTimeComponents.h>

//_____

void  InitializeToolbox( void );
void  InitializeInstrument( long );
```

```c
void  PlayMusicFromNoteChannel( void );

//_____

#define        kMIDInoInstrument        0

//_____

NoteAllocator      gNoteAllocatorComp;
ToneDescription   gToneDesc;

//_____

void  main( void )
{
   ComponentResult   theResult;
   Str31             thePrompt = "\pSelect an instrument:";
   long              theInstrument = kMIDInoInstrument;

   InitializeToolbox();

   InitializeInstrument( theInstrument );

   theResult = NAPickInstrument( gNoteAllocatorComp, nil, thePrompt,
                                 &gToneDesc, 0, 0, 0, 0 );

   if ( ( gToneDesc.instrumentNumber == 0 ) || ( theResult != noErr ) )
      ExitToShell();
   else
      PlayMusicFromNoteChannel();
}

//_____

void InitializeInstrument( long theInstrument )
{
   ComponentResult   theResult;

   gNoteAllocatorComp = OpenDefaultComponent( kNoteAllocatorType, 0 );

   theResult = NAStuffToneDescription( gNoteAllocatorComp,
                                       theInstrument, &gToneDesc );
}

//_____

void  PlayMusicFromNoteChannel( void )
{
   NoteRequest      theNoteRequest;
```

```
    NoteChannel      theNoteChannel;
    short            thePitch;
    ComponentResult  theError;
    long             theLong;

    theNoteRequest.polyphony = 4;
    theNoteRequest.typicalPolyphony = 0x00010000;
    theNoteRequest.tone = gToneDesc;

    theError = NANewNoteChannel( gNoteAllocatorComp, &theNoteRequest,
                               &theNoteChannel );

    for ( thePitch = 36; thePitch <= 96; thePitch++ )
    {
       NAPlayNote( gNoteAllocatorComp, theNoteChannel, thePitch, 127 );
       Delay( 10, &theLong );
       NAPlayNote( gNoteAllocatorComp, theNoteChannel, thePitch, 0 );
    }

    theError = NADisposeNoteChannel( gNoteAllocatorComp,
                                   theNoteChannel );
}

//_____

void  InitializeToolbox( void )
{
    InitGraf( &qd.thePort );
    InitFonts();
    InitWindows();
    InitMenus();
    TEInit();
    InitDialogs( OL );
    FlushEvents( everyEvent, 0 );
    InitCursor();
}
```

Summary

System 7.5 includes an extension called *QuickTime Musical Instruments*. This system software—and the new Movie Toolbox functions that work with this system software—make it simple to add quality music and sound effects to any Mac program.

To play a musical note, your program first needs to open a Note Allocator component. A call to `OpenDefaultComponent()` takes care of this. Next, your program should create and fill in a `ToneDescription` structure that describes the type of instrument that will be used to play the music. After that, a `NoteRequest` structure needs to be filled in. One of the three fields of this structure is the `ToneDescription` that was created earlier. Finally, a new note channel needs to be allocated using the `NANewNoteChannel()` function. After that, your application is ready to use the `NAPlayNote()` function to play one or more notes.

To display the standard Pick Instrument dialog box, your program should call `NAPickInstrument()`. This powerful routine opens the dialog box and handles all user action in it—including opening a new note channel for the user-selected instrument.

CHAPTER 9

Application: QuickTime Movie Editor

Each example program in the previous nine chapters was a short, simple application written with one purpose: to provide a working demonstration of the topic that appeared just before the program. The code listings for those programs are meant to serve as sources from which you can select code snippets to paste and modify in the source file of your own, larger graphics and sound application. While having the individual pieces of a puzzle can be helpful, it is also nice to have a complete puzzle to serve as a model. Enter the FilmEdit program.

In this chapter, you'll see the development of a QuickTime movie editor named *FilmEdit*. You'll see how the QuickTime topics presented in Chapter 7 can be applied to a program that uses menus and supports multiple movie windows. FilmEdit is a full-blown Mac application that can serve as a sort of framework for your own program. Much of the code is written to be reusable "as is," or with only slight modification. And, of course, much of the code is written to demonstrate techniques presented in this book.

As you read about FilmEdit, you'll see the general technique of creating a program that supports any number of open windows—even different types of windows. You'll also see the more specific technique of implementing all of the Edit menu items so that they work on Quick-Time movies. You'll also learn how to save a movie that has been edited—either to the same file from which the movie came or to a new file.

Movie Editing

Your application might allow users to play movies, but not make changes to them. Before you place that limitation on the user, consider that the Movie Toolbox makes the addition of movie-editing capabilities to an application a very simple task.

Movie Editing and the Movie Controller

When a movie has a movie controller attached to it, the user can use the **Step forward** and **Step backward** buttons to move to any frame in that movie. If a program implements **Copy** and **Cut** commands, they can be used on whichever frame is currently being displayed. If the **Shift** key is held down while the slider is moved (or either of the **Step** buttons are clicked), a selection of a number of frames can be made. When that's done, the Play bar highlights the selection (see Figure 9.1) and **Copy** and **Cut** commands apply to all the frames within the selection.

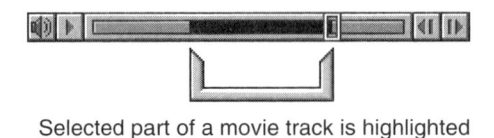

Selected part of a movie track is highlighted

FIGURE 9.1 A movie controller and its parts.

You may recall that when a movie file is opened, you provide some level of read or write permission for the movie in that file. In past examples, the level has been set to read-only—fsRdPerm. To allow editing of a movie to take place, instead open the movie's file with a permission level of read and write—fsRdWrPerm. The following snippet makes the necessary change to the call to OpenMovieFile().

```
OSErr   theError;
FSSpec  theFSSpec;
short   theFileRefNum;

theError = OpenMovieFile( &theFSSpec, &theFileRefNum, fsRdWrPerm );
```

You'll need to use only a handful of Movie Toolbox routines to be able to create an Edit menu that works as well for movie frames as it does for text and graphics. The first of these functions is MCEnableEditing(). When a controller is created, it initially doesn't support editing. Calling MCEnable-Editing() gives the controller the permission it needs to allow editing.

```
MovieController  theController;

MCEnableEditing( theController, true );
```

The first parameter to MCEnableEditing() is the controller attached to the movie to edit. The second parameter is a Boolean value that tells the Movie Toolbox whether to enable editing (true) or disable editing (false) for this movie controller.

Enabling editing for a movie controller (and thus for a movie) is a one-time task. Once the movie file has been opened with a write permission level and the movie's controller has had editing enabled, editing functions performed on the movie will work properly.

Movie Toolbox Movie Editing Routines

The Movie Toolbox holds editing routines that take care of the work involved in editing a movie. Each routine requires a controller as a parameter. By specifying a controller, you also specify the movie that is to receive the editing.

To cut the current frame or current selection of a movie, call the Movie Toolbox function MCCut().

```
MovieController  theController;
Movie            theTempMovie;

theTempMovie = MCCut( theController );
```

The movie controller is the only parameter `MCCut()` needs. After removing the current selection, `MCCut()` returns it to your program as a `Movie`. You'll need this movie as a parameter to another Movie Toolbox routine, `PutMovieOnScrap()`. The Movie Toolbox doesn't take the liberty of automatically placing the cut movie to the clipboard, or scrap. Doing so would overwrite the existing contents of the scrap—something every application may not want to do. To place the cut movie on the scrap, follow a call to `MCCut()` with a call to `PutMovieOnScrap()`:

```
MovieController   theController;
Movie             theTempMovie;

theTempMovie = MCCut( theController );
PutMovieOnScrap( theTempMovie, movieScrapOnlyPutMovie );
```

`PutMovieOnScrap()` gives you the option of placing the cut movie on the scrap and overwriting whatever is already there, or adding the cut movie to whatever is currently on the scrap. To overwrite the current contents of the scrap, pass the Apple-defined constant `movieScrapOnly-PutMovie` as the second parameter to `PutMovieOnScrap()`. To add the cut movie to whatever is already on the scrap, use the Apple-defined constant `movieScrapDontZeroScrap`.

Because movies can be quite large, your application is through with one, dispose of it. As you've seen, that's what the example applications have done by calling the Movie Toolbox routine `DisposeMovie()`. In the above snippet, you saw that a `Movie` variable named `theTempMovie` held the cut movie. Make sure to free the memory occupied by this temporary movie by disposing of it:

```
theTempMovie = MCCut( theController );
PutMovieOnScrap( theTempMovie, movieScrapOnlyPutMovie );
DisposeMovie( theTempMovie )
```

To copy the current selection of a movie, make a call to the Movie Toolbox routine `MCCopy()`. Then, as was done for cutting a part of a movie, call `PutMovieOnScrap()` to store the copied movie to the scrap. Then, again as was done for cutting a movie, dispose of the temporary movie by making a call to `DisposeMovie()`.

```
MovieController   theController;
Movie             theTempMovie;
```

```
theTempMovie = MCCopy( theController );
PutMovieOnScrap( theTempMovie, movieScrapOnlyPutMovie );
DisposeMovie( theTempMovie )
```

After cutting or copying a part of a movie, the user should be able either to paste this movie from the scrap to a different spot in the same movie or a different existing movie, or to form a new movie altogether. To paste, call the Movie Toolbox routine `MCPaste()`.

```
MovieController  theController;

MCPaste( theController, nil );
```

`MCPaste()` will paste to the current frame of the active window of a program. And, this function can be written such that it will paste any movie there—not just the movie on the scrap. The second parameter to `MCPaste()` is the movie to paste. If you pass a value of `nil`, as shown above, `MCPaste()` will use the contents of the scrap in the paste. If you specify a particular `Movie` variable as the second parameter, `MCPaste()` will instead use that movie in the paste, and ignore the contents of the scrap.

NOTE

Passing a value of `nil` as the second parameter in `MCPaste()` will allow your program to paste the contents of the clipboard to the selected movie—whether the clipboard contains a movie, a picture, or text.

Most programs that include a functioning Edit menu have a **Clear** menu item in that menu. This item cuts the current selection, but doesn't save it to the scrap. Not saving it allows the user to remove selected frames while still preserving whatever is already on the Clipboard. You can clear the current selection by calling the Movie Toolbox routine `MCClear()`. `MCClear()` cuts the current selection but doesn't return the cut movie to your application—thereby saving the you the effort of disposing of the movie.

```
MovieController  theController;

MCClear( theController );
```

Adding an **Undo** menu item to your application's Edit menu is easy with the Movie Toolbox. Just call `MCUndo()` to undo the most recently performed editing operation:

```
MovieController   theController;

MCUndo( theController );
```

Compared to the implementation of the other editing operations, adding a **Select All** menu item to an Edit menu requires a little extra effort. Before selecting an entire movie, your program needs to be made aware of the movie's length. Timing information for a movie can be saved in a data structure of type `TimeRecord`:

```
struct   TimeRecord
{
   CompTimeValue   value;
   TimeScale       scale;
   TimeBase        base;
};
```

Movie time is measured on a scale. Applications have the freedom of setting the scale to a unit of measurement of their choice. A unit value of 1 means that a time coordinate system of seconds is used. A unit value of 60 means that a time coordinate system of sixtieths of a second is used. Thus a movie with a running time of 2 seconds would be of length 2 in the seconds scale and length 120 in the sixtieths of a second scale. The second field of `TimeRecord` holds the scale for a movie. You can find out what time scale a movie is in by calling the Movie Toolbox routine `GetMovieTimeScale()`. The returned value can be placed in the `scale` field of a `TimeRecord`:

```
TimeRecord   theTimeRecord;
Movie        theMovie;

theTimeRecord.scale = GetMovieTimeScale( theMovie );
```

The first member of the `TimeRecord` is used to hold a specific point in time of a movie. For instance, if a movie was 2 seconds in length, and its time scale was in sixtieths of a second, then the duration of the movie would be 120 and the midpoint of the movie would be at a time value of 60. In order to hold very large time values, the `TimeRecord` uses two 32-bit integers to hold a single time. The `value` field itself is thus composed of two fields. The `hi` field holds the high-order 32 bits of the value and the `lo` field holds the low-order 32 bits. To set the current value of a movie to its start, you'd set both the `hi` and `lo` fields of the `value` to 0:

```
TimeRecord   theTimeRecord;

theTimeRecord.value.hi = 0;
theTimeRecord.value.lo = 0;
```

To set a `TimeRecord` value field to the end of a movie, call the Movie Toolbox routine `GetMovieDuration()`. This function returns a `long` value that can be stored in the lower 32 bits of the value field:

```
Movie        theMovie;
TimeRecord   theTimeRecord;

theTimeRecord.value.lo = GetMovieDuration( theMovie );
```

NOTE

The maximum value of a 32-bit `long` is over 4 billion, so that even the value representing the duration of a very long movie should fit in the low-order 32 bits of the `value` field.

The third and final field of a `TimeRecord` holds a movie's time base. The `base` field holds a single value that encapsulates a movie's play direction and speed—its rate. Because editing takes place on a movie that isn't playing, the base value can be set to 0:

```
TimeRecord   theTimeRecord;

theTimeRecord.base = 0;
```

After filling a `TimeRecord` scale with a movie's scale, and then setting the value and base to 0, call `MCDoAction()` to tell the movie's controller that this location is to be used as the start of the edit selection. Recall that `MCDoAction()` accepts a variety of second parameter constants that act on the controller passed as the first parameter. The third parameter holds a pointer to data that varies with the type of action that is to be performed. You'll pass a pointer to the `TimeRecord`, as follows:

```
MovieController   theController;
TimeRecord        theTimeRecord;
```

```
Movie              theMovie;

theTimeRecord.value.hi = 0;
theTimeRecord.value.lo = 0;
theTimeRecord.base = 0;

theTimeRecord.scale = GetMovieTimeScale( theMovie );
MCDoAction( theController, mcActionSetSelectionBegin, &theTimeRecord)
```

The start of the selection is made by passing MCDoAction() the Apple-defined action constant mcActionSetSelectionBegin. The end of the selection is made by again calling MCDoAction()—this time with an action constant of mcActionSetSelectionEnd. Before doing this, call GetMovieDuration() to change the value field of the TimeRecord from the beginning of the movie (value = 0) to of the end of the movie:

```
MovieController  theController;
TimeRecord       theTimeRecord;
Movie            theMovie;

theTimeRecord.value.lo = GetMovieDuration( theMovie );
MCDoAction( theController, mcActionSetSelectionDuration,
            &theTimeRecord );
```

The following snippet shows the complete code for setting a movie's edit selection to the entire movie. When the code completes, the entire Play bar of the movie's controller will be highlighted.

```
MovieController  theController;
TimeRecord       theTimeRecord;
Movie            theMovie;

theTimeRecord.value.hi = 0;
theTimeRecord.value.lo = 0;
theTimeRecord.base = 0;

theTimeRecord.scale = GetMovieTimeScale( theMovie );
MCDoAction( theController, mcActionSetSelectionBegin,
            &theTimeRecord );
theTimeRecord.value.lo = GetMovieDuration( theMovie );
MCDoAction( theController, mcActionSetSelectionDuration,
            &theTimeRecord );
```

Saving an Edited Movie

If your application allows movie editing, it should also provide the means for the user to save any changes that were made to a movie. Providing **Save** and **Save As** menu items in the File menu of your application will allow the user to do just that.

Saving a Movie with a "Save" Menu Item

In Chapter 7, you saw how a QuickTime movie-playing program used the Movie Toolbox routine `OpenMovieFile()` to load a movie from a movie file. There, the `fsRdPerm` permission level was used. For applications that allow movie editing, you'll need to open a movie file with the `fsRdWrPerm` permission constant. In Chapter 7, you also saw that after a movie was loaded into memory, the file from which the movie came was closed. If your program is going to save changes made to a movie, you'll want instead to keep the movie file open—the changes will need to be written to the file. The following snippet uses the standard Open dialog box to get an `FSSpec` for a movie, `OpenMovieFile()` to open the movie file, and `NewMovieFromFile()` to load into memory the file's movie. Notice that the call to `OpenMovieFile()` uses the `fsRdWrPerm` constant, and that the snippet *doesn't* make a call to `CloseMovieFile()`. The snippet also checks both returned `OSErr` values to ensure that no errors have occurred.

```
OSErr              theError;
SFTypeList         typeList = { MovieFileType, 0, 0, 0 };
StandardFileReply  theReply;
Movie              theMovie;
short              theFileRefNum;
short              theMovieResID;
Str255             theMovieResName;

Boolean            wasAltered;

StandardGetFilePreview( nil, 1, typeList, &theReply );
if ( theReply.sfGood == false )
   return;

theError = OpenMovieFile( &theReply.sfFile, &theFileRefNum,
   fsRdWrPerm );
```

```
if ( theError != noErr )
   ExitToShell();

theError = NewMovieFromFile( &theMovie, theFileRefNum,
                             &theMovieResID, theMovieResName,
                             newMovieActive, &wasAltered );
if ( theError != noErr )
   ExitToShell();
```

If a user of your program makes editing changes to a movie and then selects **Save** from the File menu, your program will only need to call one Movie Toolbox routine—`UpdateMovieResource()`:

```
Movie  theMovie;
short  theFileRefNum;
short  theMovieResID;

UpdateMovieResource( theMovie, theFileRefNum, theMovieResID, nil );
```

Pass `UpdateMovieResource()` the movie to save to disk in the first parameter. Pass the reference number of the file that the movie is to be saved to as the second parameter. The third parameter is the movie resource ID of the movie's `moov` resource. Looking at the above two snippets you can see that these second and third parameters—`theFileRefNum` and `theMovieResID`—come from the calls to `OpenMovieFile()` and `NewMovieFromFile()`. The fourth parameter to `UpdateMovieResource()` is a pointer to a new name for the movie's `moov` resource. If you're content with the current name, pass a value of `nil` here. Notice that this is the name of the `moov` resource, not the name of the QuickTime movie file.

Saving a Movie with a "Save As" Menu Item

If the user has made changes to a movie and wants to save the edited version as a new movie, you should provide a **Save As** menu item in your application. Before describing the Movie Toolbox routine that helps you do this, a quick look at QuickTime movie file formats is in order.

QuickTime movies are capable of having data spread out among more than one file. In such a case, the `moov` resource of the QuickTime movie file holds the information about which file or files contain the movie's data. While this resolution of *data dependencies* goes unnoticed by the user (who can simply double-click on the one movie file to run it), it necessitates that all of the data files be present on the user's machine. That can cause a problem for the user if he or she copies the movie file to a disk for use on a different machine. When the user attempts to run the movie on that machine, the movie won't run because the supporting data files aren't present. Instead, the user will see an alert like the one shown in Figure 9.2.

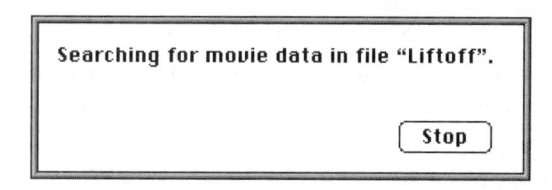

FIGURE 9.2 Data from a single movie can be spread across more than one movie file.

Why spread a single movie across multiple files? If several versions of a single movie are being made, than this method will save disk space. One large version will hold the entire movie. Smaller version could contain only selected frames from the larger movie. Each smaller version would then consist of only references to the frames from the large movie—not the frames themselves. Consider a large movie named Liftoff. If the Liftoff movie is edited so that it contains only half the number of frames as the original version, it can be saved to a file that is considerably smaller than half the size of the original. If, on the other hand, the copy is saved as a self-contained—or flattened—movie, it will be much larger. Figure 9.3 shows how Apple's MoviePlayer program provides the user with the option of saving a file in either format.

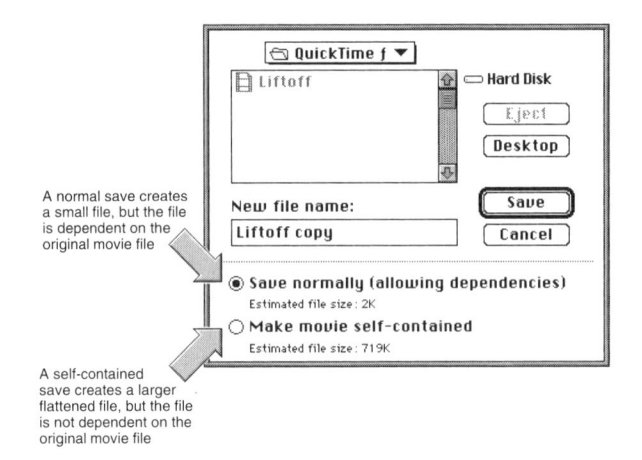

A normal save creates a small file, but the file is dependent on the original movie file

A self-contained save creates a larger flattened file, but the file is not dependent on the original movie file

FIGURE 9.3 Programs can be written to allow movies to be saved with dependencies or flattened.

If you want your application to allow users to save movies, you should let them save movies in a flattened format. That way, the user can copy his or her movies to a disk without thought of whether or not the entire movie has been copied.

In response to a request to save a movie to a new file, your program should display the standard Save dialog box. A call to the Toolbox routine `StandardPutFile()` takes care of this:

```
StandardFileReply   theReply;

StandardPutFile( "\pSave as:", "\pUntitled", &theReply );
```

The first parameter to `StandardPutFile()` is the prompt that the user will see in the Save dialog box. The second parameter is the default file name that will be placed in the dialog box when it opens. The user, of course, is free to change this default name to a file name of his or her choice. The last parameter is a `StandardFileReply` variable that will be filled in by the Toolbox after the user clicks on the **Save** button in the Save dialog box.

After checking the `sfGood` field of the `StandardFileReply` to verify that the user did in fact click on the **Save** button, call the Movie Toolbox routine `FlattenMovie()` to create a new flattened movie file that holds the movie's `moov` resource and all of the movie's data. Here's a typical call to `FlattenMovie()`:

```
Movie   theMovie;

FlattenMovie( theMovie, flattenAddMovieToDataFork,
              &theReply.sfFile, 'TVOD', smSystemScript,
              createMovieFileDeleteCurFile, nil, nil );
```

The first parameter to `FlattenMovie()` is the movie to save. The second parameter is a flag that tells the Movie Toolbox where to put the movie's data. Use the Apple-defined constant `flattenAddMovieToDataFork` to add the data to the data fork and the `moov` resource to the resource fork.

The third parameter to `FlattenMovie()` is a pointer to the file system specification for the movie file that will be created. This `FSSpec` was returned by the call to `StandardPutFile()`.

The fourth parameter is the creator that will be associated with the file. If you want a double-click on your movie file to launch your application, supply your application's creator type here. In the above snippet the creator `'TVOD'` is the creator of Apple's MoviePlayer movie-playing application.

For an application file, the creator is a four-character string that identifies the program to the Finder. For a data file, the creator string generally matches the creator string of the application that created the data file. For

N O T E   instance, Apple's MoviePlayer program has a creator of `'TVOD'`. Movies created by MoviePlayer have this same creator. That lets the Finder know the relationship between applications and files.

The fifth parameter to `FlattenMovie()` specifies the script for the movie. Scripts define the way the Finder displays a file's name. You can use the Apple-defined constant `smSystemScript`.

After the script specification comes a flag that tells whether or not to delete an existing file. If the file to be saved is given the same name as a file that already exists, delete the existing file and replace it with a new one by using the Apple-defined constant `createMovieFileDeleteCurFile`.

The next-to-last parameter to `FlattenMovie()` is a pointer to a `short` that holds the resource ID for the new `moov` resource. Passing a value of `nil` for this parameter tells the Toolbox to assign a unique resource ID to the new `moov` resource. In the above snippet, a new, empty file is being created—so this parameter is unimportant. Finally, the eighth parameter is a pointer to a string that holds the name of the new `moov` resource. Passing a value of `nil` means that no name will be given to the resource. As in the call to `UpdateMovieResource()`, this string is the name of the `moov` resource, not the name of the QuickTime movie file.

Working with Multiple Movies

A program that displays and plays a movie with little or no user-intervention—such as the MovieDialog example in Chapter 7—may not require more than a single movie to be on the screen at one time. Programs that give the user more control of movie playing, such as a movie editor—will. For such programs you'll need to implement a multiple window-handling strategy. That way, when the user has two or more movie windows open, selecting **Cut** will cut a frame from the correct movie, selecting **Close** will close the correct movie window, and pressing the **Play** button on more than one movie controller will cause each movie to play at the same time.

In this section, you'll see a technique that provides for the proper handling of any number of open movie windows—the maximum number of open movies is limited only by the amount of free memory on the user's Macintosh. This multiple-window technique is one you can apply to any Macintosh program that opens more than one window at a time—it's not just for applications that use QuickTime.

Window Records and Extra Window Data

The Macintosh data type `WindowRecord` is a data structure that holds information about a window—information such as the size of the window and what the window frame looks like. The Macintosh data type `WindowPtr` serves as a pointer to the first field of a `WindowRecord`. This first field is the `GrafPort` member of the `WindowRecord`. The `GrafPort` itself is a data structure. It consists of several fields that describe the drawing environment of a window. These `GrafPort` fields are of the most interest to a programmer—information such as the font to be used in the display of text and the dimensions of lines to be drawn can be found in the `GrafPort` fields.

Usually, a programmer doesn't need to access any information from a `WindowRecord` other than that found in the fields of its `GrafPort`. That's why—by definition—a `WindowPtr` variable is allowed access only to the `GrafPort`, and not to the remainder of the `WindowRecord`. Occasionally, though, a programmer may need access to another field of a `WindowRecord`. The Macintosh data type `WindowPeek` exists for that purpose. Like the `WindowPtr`, the `WindowPeek` points to the start of a `WindowRecord`—to the `GrafPort` field. Unlike the `WindowPtr`, the `WindowPeek` is defined so that a variable of the `WindowPeek` type is free to access any field of a `WindowRecord`. Figure 9.4 summarizes this.

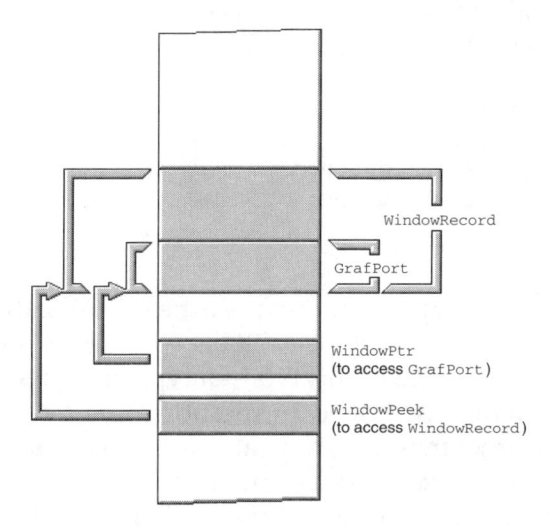

FIGURE **9.4** A `WindowPtr` is used to access only the `GrafPort` field of a `WindowRecord`, while a `WindowPeek` is used to access any field of a `WindowRecord`.

NOTE

An object such as a structure is placed in memory starting at a lower address and progressing towards a higher address. Because Macintosh memory is pictured with lower-numbered addresses at the bottom of memory, an object in memory appears to be "upside down." That is, the first field of a structure is at the bottom of the structure.

Every window that your program opens has its own `WindowRecord` in memory—it's created by a call to the Toolbox function `GetNewWindow()` or `GetNewCWindow()`. This same function call also returns a `WindowPtr` to your program—a pointer to the `GrafPort` of this `WindowRecord`. Because each window has a `WindowRecord` and a `WindowPtr`, these two data types provide a good basis for tying additional data to each window.

Consider an application that is to make use of two types of windows—one type that shows a QuickTime movie and another that displays a picture. You might want to have this window-type information accompany every window open on the screen. To keep track of this new data, your program should define a data structure that consists of a `WindowRecord` and this new data, as follows:

```
typedef  struct
{
   WindowRecord   theWindRecord;
   short          theWindType;

}  BigWindRecord, *BigWindRecordPeek;
```

The above `struct` definition creates a new application-defined data type—a type named `BigWindRecord`. It also defines a data type that serves as a pointer to a structure of this type—a type named `BigWindRecordPeek`. Because a structure is placed in memory one field after another, a `BigWindRecord` structure would appear in memory as shown in Figure 9.5. The first of the two `BigWindRecord` members is `theWindRecord`—an entire `WindowRecord` (which includes a `GrafPort` as its first field). Above that would be the next member of the `BigWindRecord`—the short `theWindType`. As shown, a variable of type `BigWindRecordPeek` would have access to the entire `BigWindRecord` structure.

NOTE

An application-defined window structure will usually contain more information than just a `WindowRecord` and a window-type field. Later, you'll see that this chapter's FilmEdit program defines a window structure that consists of six fields.

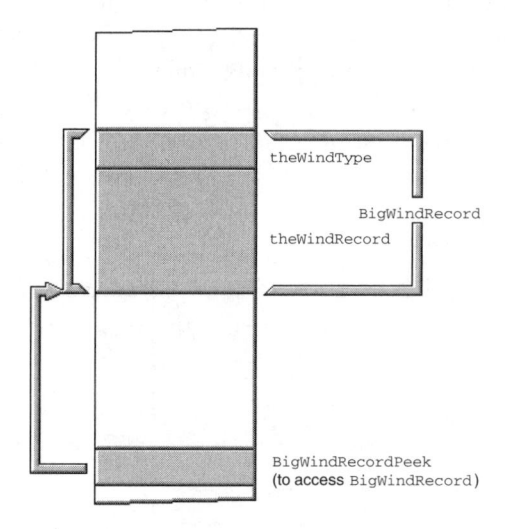

FIGURE 9.5 The fields of the application-defined `BigWindRecord` struct are accessed through a `BigWindRecordPeek`.

NOTE

The two fields of the `BigWindRecord` shown in Figure 9.5 aren't shown to scale. A `WindowRecord` itself consists of many fields, and would occupy considerably more memory than the 2-byte `theWindType` field. You can assume that the remainder of the memory figures in this chapter are not drawn to scale.

The first part of the multiple window-handling scheme is now established: define a data structure that has a `WindowRecord` as a first member and any other window data as additional members. When defining this data structure, also define a data type that points to a structure of this type.

Accessing the Application-Defined Window Structure

If you've followed closely, you may have noticed one important fact. A WindowPtr, a WindowPeek, and a BigWindRecordPeek all point to the same thing—the start of a WindowRecord. The difference among the three types is not what they point to, but how far into memory each is allowed to access. The WindowPtr can access only a GrafPort, the WindowPeek can access the entire WindowRecord, and a BigWindRecordPeek can access the WindowRecord and the data that lies beyond it—the other field of the BigWindRecord structure. Figure 9.6 illustrates.

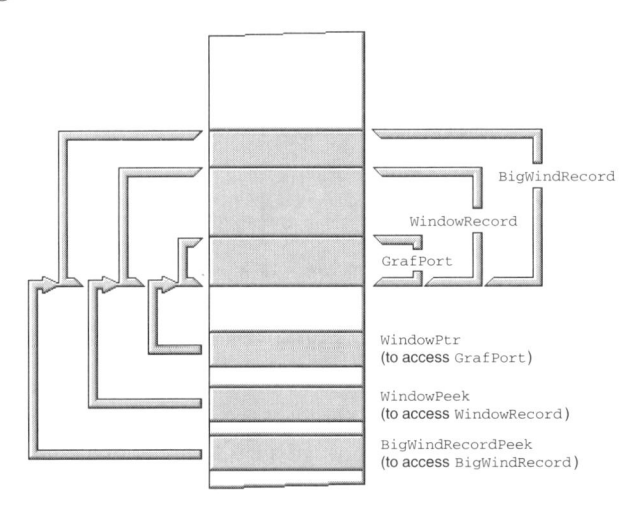

FIGURE 9.6 The different pointer types can access different structures.

The BigWindRecord data type is application-defined—the Toolbox doesn't know anything about this type. That means that when you open a new window you can't immediately get a BigWindRecordPeek pointer to it. Instead, you'll first get a WindowPtr to a window, then typecast that pointer to a BigWindRecordPeek. This will be possible because a WindowPtr and a BigWindRecordPeek point to the same data structure—a WindowRecord. The BigWindRecordPeek just happens to be able to access information beyond the WindowRecord.

Begin by calling GetNewCWindow() to open a window and receive a WindowPtr to the window. In the past, you've probably let the Window

Manager reserve memory for a `WindowRecord` by passing a value of `nil` as the second parameter to `GetNewCWindow()`. Here, you'll tell the Window Manager how much memory to reserve by first setting up a pointer to an area of memory the size of a `BigWindRecord` data structure. When you open the window, use this pointer as the second parameter. The way to do that follows:

```
WindowPtr   theWindow;
Ptr         theWindowStorage;

theWindowStorage = NewPtr( sizeof( BigWindRecord ) );
theWindow = GetNewCWindow( 128, theWindowStorage, (WindowPtr)-1L );
```

After the above snippet executes, a program will have a `WindowPtr` that points to a color window. More accurately, `theWindow` will point to a `WindowRecord`. Note that even though enough memory was reserved for a `BigWindRecord`, the variable `theWindow` can only access the `WindowRecord`—that's the limitation of a `WindowPtr`. To access fields of data beyond the `WindowRecord`, declare a `BigWindRecordPeek` variable and then typecast the `WindowPtr` variable to a `BigWindRecordPeek`:

```
BigWindRecordPeek   theBigPeek;

theBigPeek = (BigWindRecordPeek)theWindow;
```

Now, the variable `theBigPeek` can be dereferenced to access the second member of the `BigWindRecord` data structure. In the following snippet, a value of 2 is being assigned to `theWindType` field. Figure 9.7 shows how memory would look after this assignment takes place.

```
BigWindRecordPeek   theBigPeek;

theBigPeek = (BigWindRecordPeek)theWindow;
theBigPeek->theWindType = 2;
```

NOTE

If you prefer dereferencing with the dot operator, the above code could be written as follows:

```
BigWindRecordPeek   theBigPeek;

theBigPeek = (BigWindRecordPeek)theWindow;
(*theBigPeek).theWindType = 2;
```

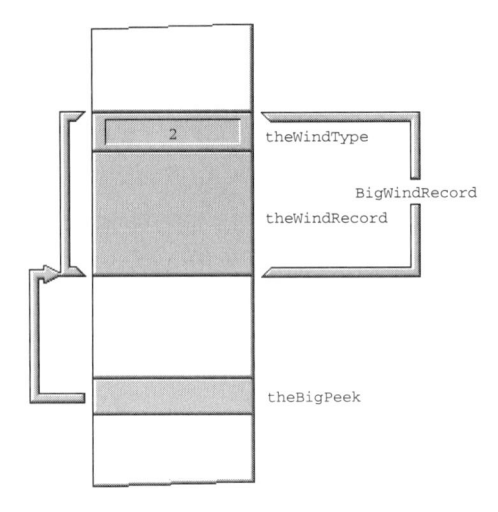

FIGURE 9.7 Dereferencing theBigPeek allows access to the WindType field.

Figure 9.7 shows the result of setting the value of a BigWindRecord data structure member. This value can be retrieved by again typecasting. If your program wants to know the type of a window, it should get a WindowPtr to that window, typecast that pointer to a BigWindRecordPeek, and then examine the theWindType field of the BigWindRecord. Usually your program will want information about the active window. The Toolbox routine FrontWindow() can be used to get a WindowPtr to that window—as shown below:

```
WindowPtr            theWindow;
BigWindRecordPeek    theBigPeek;
short                theCurrentWindowType;

theWindow = FrontWindow();
theBigPeek = (BigWindRecordPeek)theWindow;
theCurrentWindowType = theBigPeek->theWindType;
```

Assuming memory is as pictured in Figure 9.7, after the above snippet executes theCurrentWindowType will have a value of 2. The variable theCurrentWindowType can then be used to determine how the window should be handled:

```
switch ( theCurrentWindowType )
{
    case 1:
        // handle type 1 window
        break;

    case 2:
        // handle type 2 window
        break;
}
```

For clarity, your code can define a constant for each window type your program uses. For instance, if a program has a type of window that plays a QuickTime movie and another that displays a picture, the above snippet might become:

```
#define      kMovieWindowType      1
#define      kPictureWindowType    2
switch ( theCurrentWindowType )
{
    case kMovieWindowType:
        // handle QuickTime movie window
        break;

    case kPictureWindowType:
        // handle picture window
        break;
}
```

An application will access data from the window structure frequently. For instance, every time a new window is opened, the window's theWindType field will need to be set to the window's type. And every time a window needs to be updated, the application will need to retrieve the value in this theWindType field in order to determine how the window should be updated. To eliminate redundant code, you'll want to define a routine that sets the value of the window-type field and another routine that gets the value from that field. The routine that sets the theWindType member follows:

```
void  SetWindowType( WindowPtr theWindow, short type )
{
```

```
   BigWindRecordPeek  theBigPeek;

   theBigPeek = (BigWindRecordPeek)theWindow;
   theBigPeek->theWindType = type;
}
```

After making a call to GetNewCWindow() to create a new window, the window's type can be set by making a call to SetWindowType():

```
#define       kMovieWindowType        1

WindowPtr  theWindow;

SetWindowType( theWindow, kMovieWindowType );
```

To get a window's type, a routine like GetWindowType() should be defined:

```
short  GetWindowType( WindowPtr theWindow )
{
   BigWindRecordPeek  theBigPeek;

   theBigPeek = (BigWindRecordPeek)theWindow;
   return ( theBigPeek->theWindType );
}
```

Every time some action takes place involving a window, your application will want to determine the window's type before handling the action. Consider a mouse click in a window's close box. If the window holds a QuickTime movie, you'll want to dispose of the movie, the movie controller, and the window. If the window is of a type that *doesn't* hold a movie, then there will be no movie and no controller to dispose of. The following is a snippet that uses the GetWindowType() function to test a window's type before closing the window.

```
if ( GetWindowType( theWindow ) == kMovieWindowType )
{
   DisposeMovieController( theController );
   DisposeMovie( theMovie );
   DisposeWindow( theWindow );
}
else
{
   DisposeWindow( theWindow );
}
```

As you'll see a little later, most application's that use an application-defined window structure define that structure to hold several pieces of information about a window—not just the window's type as has been done for this current example. Such application's should then define a "set" and "get" routine for each window data field that follows the WindowRecord in the window structure definition.

Example Program: FilmEdit

FilmEdit is a program that serves as a demonstration of this chapter's multiple window-handling technique. It also shows how all of the items in an Edit menu can be made to work on movie selections. FilmEdit allows the user to cut or copy frames from a movie and paste these frames back into a different location in that same movie. FilmEdit also allows the user to open a second window and paste the frames into that movie. After editing is finished, the user can save an altered movie using the File menu **Save** or **Save As** menu items.

In response to the user choosing Open from the File menu, FilmEdit displays the standard Open dialog box—as shown in Figure 9.8. After opening a movie, the user is free to again select Open to open another QuickTime movie. As shown in Figure 9.9, movies don't have to be the same size. If you run the FilmEdit program and experiment with it, you'll see that editing operations can be performed on different-size movies. That is, you can copy a frame or frames from a large movie and paste them into a smaller movie, or vice versa.

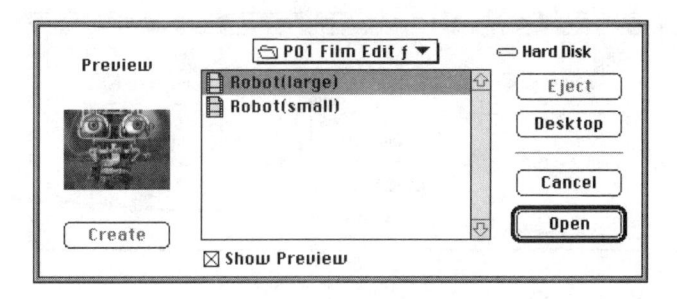

FIGURE 9.8 The **Open** menu item brings up the standard Open dialog box.

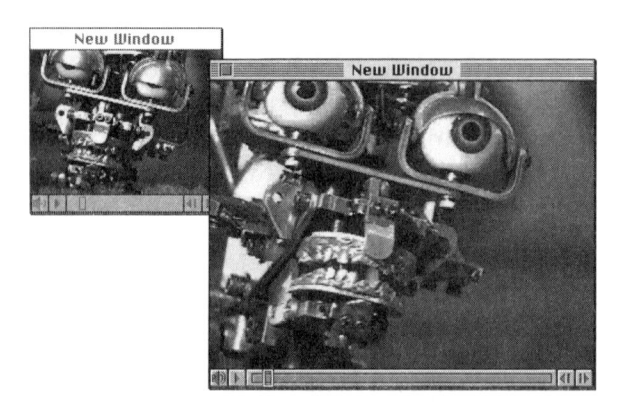

FIGURE 9.9 FilmEdit allows multiple windows to be open.

The FilmEdit Resources

The FilmEdit project requires three resource types. To display a movie, a WIND is required. As you saw in Chapter 7, the size of the window defined by the WIND is unimportant. For the menus, three MENU resources are needed—they're shown in Figure 9.10. To define the order in which these menus will appear in the menu bar, a single MBAR resource is needed. Figure 9.11 shows the MBAR.

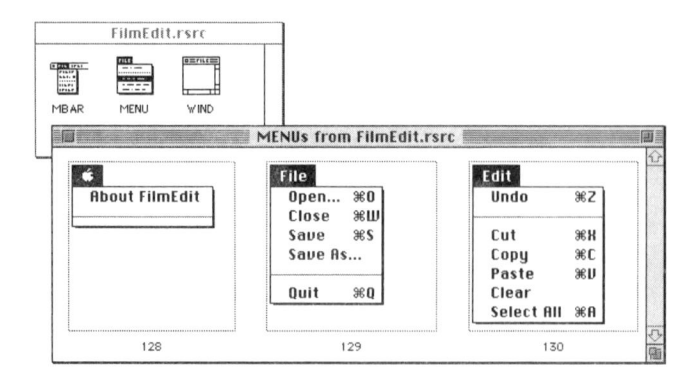

FIGURE 9.10 The MENU resources for the FilmEdit project.

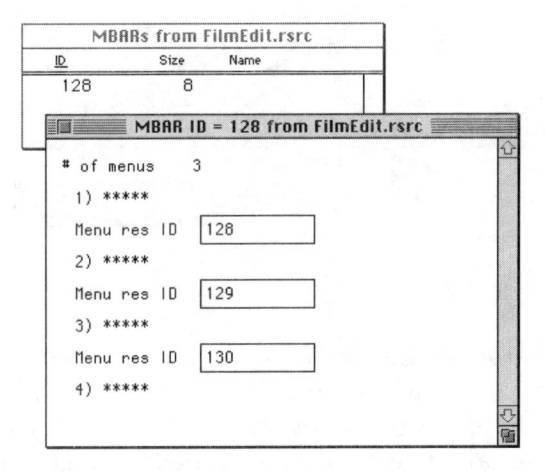

FIGURE **9.11** The MBAR resource for the FilmEdit project.

Program Initialization

Most Macintosh applications share a great deal of similar code—the code that implements the graphical interface and handles events. FilmEdit is no different. Much of the FilmEdit code can be reused—with very little modification—in other applications. This "generic" source code has been grouped into three source files in the FilmEdit project: **Globals.c**, **Initialize.c**, and **Generic.c.** Later in this chapter, there'll be more mention of the FilmEdit project's file organization.

The starting point of FilmEdit is, of course, main(). This routine initializes the Toolbox and Movie Toolbox, sets up the program's menu bar, and then enters the program's event loop. The following is the complete listing of main(). Figure 9.12 shows the function- calling chain for main().

```
void  main( void )
{
    InitializeAllToolboxes();

    SetUpMenuBar();

    EventLoop();
}
```

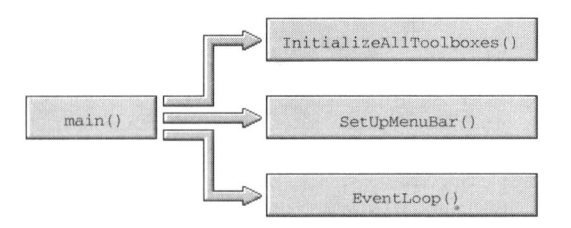

FIGURE 9.12 Application-defined routines called by main().

InitializeAllToolboxes() is similar to the version developed in Chapter 7. It does, however, have a couple of additions that can be used in any Mac program. After initializing the Toolbox, the Toolbox function MoreMasters() is called twice to allocate extra master pointers. These calls aren't strictly necessary—the system would call MoreMasters() on its own if the need ever arose for more master pointers. But by explicitly calling MoreMasters() early in the life of a program, InitializeAllToolboxes() ensures that these nonrelocatable blocks of pointers will appear low in the heap—and that reduces the likelihood of fragmentation. The second addition to InitializeAllToolboxes() is a call to the Toolbox function MaxApplZone(). This call expands the application heap to the application heap limit, thereby reducing the potential for heap fragmentation later on in the program.

```
void  InitializeAllToolboxes( void )
{
   OSErr  theError;
   long   theResult;

   InitGraf( &qd.thePort );
   InitFonts();
   InitWindows();
   InitMenus();
   TEInit();
   InitDialogs( 0L );
   FlushEvents( everyEvent, 0 );
```

```
InitCursor();
MoreMasters();
MoreMasters();
MaxApplZone();

theError = Gestalt( gestaltQuickTime, &theResult );
if ( theError != noErr )
   ExitToShell();
theError = EnterMovies();
if ( theError != noErr )
   ExitToShell();
}
```

After initializations take place, the FilmEdit menu bar is set up. The
SetUpMenuBar() function, shown below, uses the application-defined
constants rMenuBar and mApple. These constants, defined in the **Defines.h**
header file, are used to hold the IDs of the project's MBAR resource and the
Apple menu's MENU resource. SetUpMenuBar() doesn't do anything
fancy—it just makes several Toolbox calls to load the menu bar, add the
Apple menu items, and then draw the menu bar.

```
#define      rMenuBar      128
#define      mApple        128

void  SetUpMenuBar( void )
{
   Handle       theMenuBar;
   MenuHandle   theAppleMenu;

   theMenuBar = GetNewMBar( rMenuBar );
   SetMenuBar( theMenuBar );
   DisposeHandle( theMenuBar );

   theAppleMenu = GetMHandle( mApple );
   AddResMenu( theAppleMenu, 'DRVR' );

   DrawMenuBar();
}
```

The Main Event Loop and Menus

The last routine called from main() is EventLoop(). This event loop is similar to the one developed in Chapter 7—with a couple of notable exceptions. Here's the event loop—changes to it are discussed after the listing. Figure 9.13 provides an overview of the function calls EventLoop() makes.

```
void  EventLoop( void )
{
   EventRecord  theEvent;
   Boolean      isControllerEvent;

   while ( gDone == false )
   {
      WaitNextEvent( everyEvent, &theEvent, 0, nil );

      AdjustAllMenus();

      isControllerEvent = UpdateAllOpenMovies( theEvent );

      if ( isControllerEvent == false )
      {
         switch ( theEvent.what )
         {
            case activateEvt:
               HandleActivateEvent( theEvent );
               break;

            case updateEvt:
               HandleUpdateEvent( theEvent );
               break;

            case keyDown:
               HandleKeyDownEvent( theEvent );
               break;

            case mouseDown:
               HandleMouseDownEvent( theEvent );
               break;
         }
      }
   }
}
```

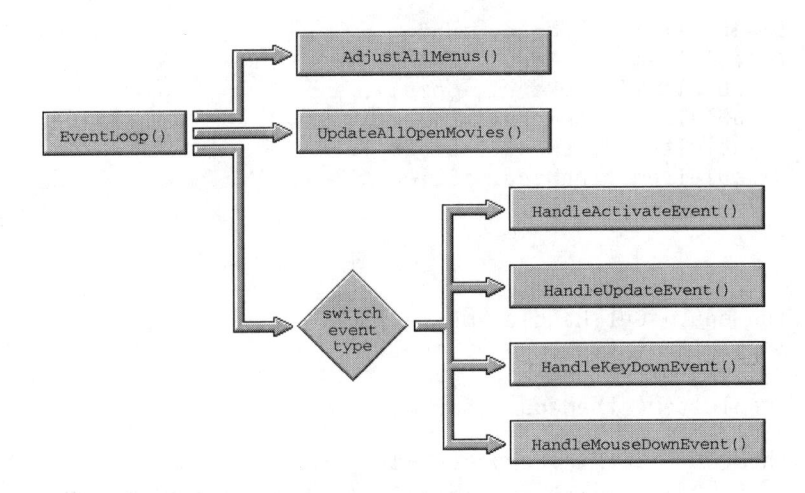

FIGURE 9.13 Application-defined routines called by EventLoop().

The event loop used in Chapter 7 was used in the very simple Quick-Controller example. Because that program didn't support menus, the event loop had no provision for updating, or adjusting, menu items. The FilmEdit event loop does. At every pass through the event loop, the application-defined routine AdjustAllMenus() is called. The numerous "m" and "i" constants, such as mFile and iClose, are all application-defined constants found in the project's Defines.h file.

```
void  AdjustAllMenus( void )
{
    WindowPtr         theWindow;
    MovieController   theController;
    MenuHandle        theMenu;

    theWindow = FrontWindow();

    if ( theWindow == nil )
    {
        theMenu = GetMHandle( mFile );
        DisableItem( theMenu, iClose );
        DisableItem( theMenu, iSave );
        DisableItem( theMenu, iSaveAs );

        theMenu = GetMHandle( mEdit );
```

```
            DisableItem( theMenu, iUndo );
            DisableItem( theMenu, iCut );
            DisableItem( theMenu, iCopy );
            DisableItem( theMenu, iPaste );
            DisableItem( theMenu, iClear );
            DisableItem( theMenu, iSelectAll );
        }
        else
        {

            theMenu = GetMHandle( mFile );
            EnableItem( theMenu, iClose );
            EnableItem( theMenu, iSave );
            EnableItem( theMenu, iSaveAs );

            theMenu = GetMenuHandle( mEdit );
            if ( GetWindowType( theWindow ) == kMovieWindowType )
            {
                theController = GetWindowController( theWindow );
                MCSetUpEditMenu( theController, 0, theMenu );
                EnableItem( theMenu, iSelectAll );
            }
            else
            {
                EnableItem( theMenu, iUndo );
                EnableItem( theMenu, iCut );
                EnableItem( theMenu, iCopy );
                EnableItem( theMenu, iPaste );
                EnableItem( theMenu, iClear );
                EnableItem( theMenu, iSelectAll );
            }
        }
    }
}
```

AdjustAllMenus() checks to see if there is an open window on the screen. If there isn't, the routine dims the menu items that are not applicable to a windowless screen. If a window is open, the appropriate menu items are enabled. If a window is open, AdjustAllMenus() makes one other check—to see if the front window is a QuickTime movie window. If it is, AdjustAllMenus() relies on the Movie Toolbox function MCSetUpEditMenu() to adjust the Edit menu.

NOTE Why check for the type of window, when FilmEdit only supports one type—the kMovieWindowType? Perhaps, in a future release, FilmEdit will make use of other application-defined window types. If that happens, changes to the source code will be minimal.

This handy function will enable the **Cut**, **Copy**, **Paste**, and **Clear** items. If there is something to undo, the **Undo** item will also be enabled. Further, MCSetUpEditMenu() will append additional text to the **Undo** menu item to add clarity to the item. For instance, if the last editing action performed with a movie's controller was a **Cut**, then the **Undo** item will be enabled and its text will change to **Undo Cut**. If the last action was a **Paste**, the item will again be enabled, but this time its text will change to **Undo Paste**. Figure 9.14 illustrates how the File and Edit menus look after they are adjusted.

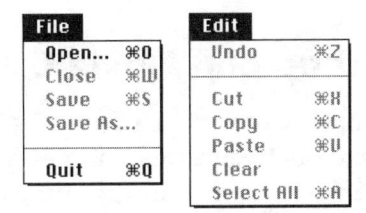

FilmEdit menus when no windows are open

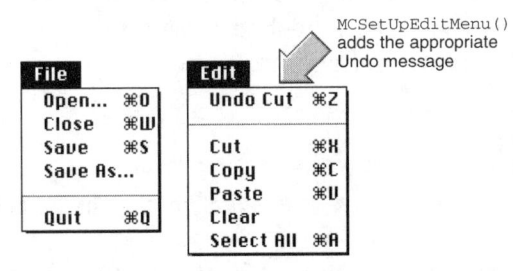

FilmEdit menus when a QuickTime movie window is open

FIGURE 9.14 The AdjustAllMenus() function enables and disables File and Edit menu items.

NOTE As you can see from AdjustAllMenus(), the basic FilmEdit source code isn't completely generic. What if you were adapting the FilmEdit source code for a project that didn't play movies? You could leave AdjustAllMenus() as it is. If a program doesn't use movie windows, GetWindowType() will never return a window type of kMovieWindowType—and the MCSetUpEditMenu() function will thus never get called. In general, you can leave any movie-specific code in the listings provided that:

1. The code executes only if a check of a window reveals that the window is a movie window.
2. You #include the **Movies.h** universal header file so that the linker recognizes Movie Toolbox calls.

Another approach would be to simply cut out or comment out the if section and leave just the six EnableItem() calls that are now found under the else.

The Main Event Loop and Movie Controllers

Menu adjustment is one trick that the Chapter 7 event loop didn't perform. The other difference between this chapter's event loop and that found in Chapter 7 examples is in the updating of QuickTime movie windows. The Chapter 7 examples allowed only one movie to be open at a time. To determine if MCIsPlayerEvent() should be called to update a movie, those examples checked to see if the MovieController variable theController had a value other than nil:

```
if ( theController == nil )
   isControllerEvent = false;
else
   isControllerEvent = MCIsPlayerEvent( theController, &theEvent );
```

In FilmEdit, MCIsPlayerEvent() can't just be called a single time. That's because MCIsPlayerEvent() updates only a single controller—the one passed to it in the first parameter. Because FilmEdit allows multiple movies to be open, there is the potential for MCIsPlayerEvent() to be called more than one time at each pass through the event loop. EventLoop() calls an application-defined routine named UpdateAllOpenMovies() to do the work of determining how many movie windows are open, and then calling `MCIsPlayerEvent()` for each. When `UpdateAllOpenMovies()` completes, it will return a `Boolean` value that indicates whether the event was handled.

```
isControllerEvent = UpdateAllOpenMovies( theEvent );
```

The details of `UpdateAllOpenMovies()` are discussed a little later in this chapter.

Again, what about adapting this code to a project that doesn't use QuickTime? Just remove or comment out the `isControllerEvent` variable and the call to `UpdateAllOpenMovies()`. Then remove the `if ( isControllerEvent == false )` test so that the `switch` statement always gets executed.

The Main Event Loop and Event Handling

FilmEdit watches for activate, update, key-down, and mouse-down events. An activate event is handled by `HandleActivateEvent()` routine—without help from any other application-defined routines. If the window turns out to be a movie window, the window's controller is retrieved from the window structure and passed to `MCActivate()`. This Movie Toolbox routine activates or deactivates a movie controller. Passing a value of `true` as the last parameter to `MCActivate()` indicates that the event was an activate event. A value of `false` tells the routine that the event was a deactivate event. You should perform an AND operation on the `modifiers` field of the event record and the Apple-defined constant `activeFlag` to get this information.

```
void  HandleActivateEvent( EventRecord theEvent )
{
    WindowPtr        theWindow;
    Boolean          isActivateEvent;
    MovieController  theController;

    theWindow = (WindowPtr)theEvent.message;
    SetPort( theWindow );
    isActivateEvent = ( theEvent.modifiers & activeFlag ) != 0;

    if ( GetWindowType( theWindow ) == kMovieWindowType )
    {
```

```
      theController = GetWindowController( theWindow );
      MCActivate( theController, theWindow, isActivateEvent );
   }
}
```

Like an activate event, an update event is simple to handle. The routine's source code listing follows:

```
void  HandleUpdateEvent( EventRecord theEvent )
{
   WindowPtr  theWindow;

   theWindow = (WindowPtr)theEvent.message;
   BeginUpdate( theWindow );
      EraseRect( &(theWindow->portRect) );
//    update "nonQuickTime" window here
   EndUpdate( theWindow );
}
```

Recall that movie windows are updated by calls to MCIsPlayerEvent()— not by the event loop switch statement. For this reason, when an update event occurs in a QuickTime movie window, HandleUpdateEvent() *won't* be called. Since FilmEdit doesn't use any window types except the movie type, HandleUpdateEvent() will *never* get called. Nonetheless, the routine is included for the sake of expansion. If FilmEdit is ever upgraded to make use of a second type of window, then the code is in place for the handling of an update to that window. Assuming that a window type that displayed pictures was added to FilmEdit, HandleUpdateEvent() might be changed as follows:

```
void  HandleUpdateEvent( EventRecord theEvent )
{
   WindowPtr  theWindow;

   theWindow = (WindowPtr)theEvent.message;
   BeginUpdate( theWindow );
      EraseRect( &(theWindow->portRect) );
      if ( GetWindowType( theWindow ) == kPictureWindowType )
         UpdatePictureTypeWindow( theWindow );
   EndUpdate( theWindow );
}
```

Activate events and update events are completely handled by `HandleActivateEvent()` and `HandleUpdateEvent()`, respectively. A mouse down event, on the other hand, may require the involvement of other application-defined routines besides the `HandleMouseDownEvent()` function. For instance, if the mouse click occurs in the menu bar, application-defined routines will be called to determine which menu and which menu item were involved.

A key-down event is examined in `HandleKeyDownEvent()` routine to see if the **Command** key is involved. If it is, the key press is treated as a menu selection—the same application-defined routine that handles a mouse-down event in the menu bar is invoked. Figure 9.15 provides an overview of the application-defined routines that get called by key-down and mouse-down events.

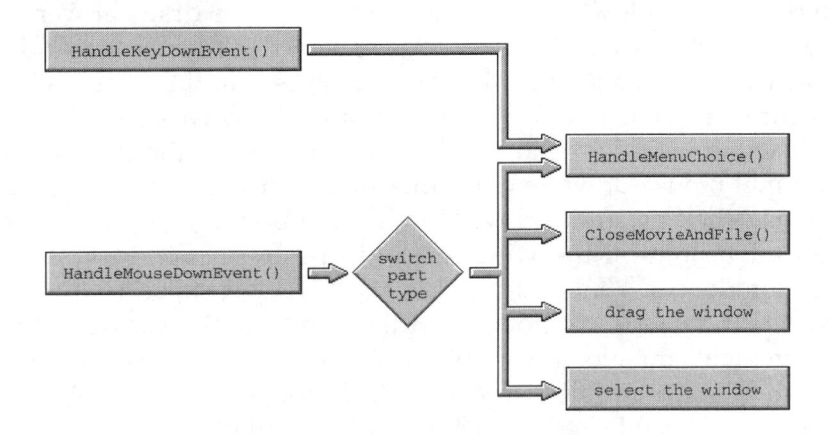

FIGURE 9.15 Application-defined routines called by `HandleKeyDownEvent()` and `HandleMouseDownEvent()`.

The following is the listing for the `HandleKeyDownEvent()` function. This routine determines which character is represented by the pressed key. Then it determines if the **Command** key was pressed during the keystroke. If it was, the application-defined `HandleMenuChoice()` routine is called to treat the keystroke as a menu selection.

```
void  HandleKeyDownEvent( EventRecord theEvent )
{
```

```
short   theChar;
long    theMenuAndItem;

theChar = theEvent.message & charCodeMask;

if ( ( theEvent.modifiers & cmdKey ) != 0 )
{
   if ( theEvent.what != autoKey )
   {
      theMenuAndItem = MenuKey( theChar );
      HandleMenuChoice( theMenuAndItem );
   }
}
}
```

The HandleMouseDownEvent() takes care of mouse clicks that occur in the menu bar, in a window's close box, or in a window's drag bar. Very little of the HandleMouseDownEvent() code is specific to movie windows. Remember, MCIsPlayerEvent() handles events—including mouse clicks—that occur in a movie's controller. If a mouse click occurs elsewhere over a movie window—such as in the window's drag bar—the click is treated as a normal mouse down event rather than a movie controller event. If the mouse click occurs in a window's close box, a check needs to be made to determine if the window holds a movie. If it does, then the application-defined routine CloseMovieAndFile() is called to dispose of the movie, the movie controller, and the window. CloseMovieAndFile() also decrements the global variable gWindowCount. This variable is one of only two global variables used by FilmEdit—the other is gDone. The gWindowCount variable keeps track of the total number of windows that are open at any given time.

```
void  HandleMouseDownEvent( EventRecord theEvent )
{
   WindowPtr  theWindow;
   short      thePart;
   long       theMenuAndItem;

   thePart = FindWindow( theEvent.where, &theWindow );

   switch ( thePart )
   {
      case inMenuBar:
         theMenuAndItem = MenuSelect( theEvent.where );
```

```
            HandleMenuChoice( theMenuAndItem );
            break;

        case inGoAway:
            if ( TrackGoAway( theWindow, theEvent.where ) )
            {
                if ( GetWindowType( theWindow ) != kMovieWindowType )
                {
                    DisposeWindow( theWindow );
                    —gWindowCount;
                }
                else
                    CloseMovieAndFile( theWindow );
            }
            break;

        case inDrag:
            DragWindow( theWindow, theEvent.where,
                        &qd.screenBits.bounds );
            break;

        case inContent:
            SelectWindow( theWindow );
            break;
    }
}
```

If a mouse click occurs in the menu bar, or if a key is pressed in conjunction with the **Command** key, HandleMenuChoice() gets called. This routine, shown below and in Figure 9.16, serves as nothing more than a branching station. A separate application-defined routine exists for the handling of each menu. As you can see from the listing, HandleMenuChoice() can be used for any project that uses the three standard menus.

```
void  HandleMenuChoice( long theMenuAndItem )
{
    short   theMenu;
    short   theMenuItem;

    if ( theMenuAndItem != 0 )
    {
        theMenu = HiWord( theMenuAndItem );
        theMenuItem = LoWord( theMenuAndItem );

        switch ( theMenu )
```

```
      {
         case mApple:
            HandleAppleChoice( theMenuItem );
            break;

         case mFile:
            HandleFileChoice( theMenuItem );
            break;

         case mEdit:
            HandleEditChoice( theMenuItem );
            break;
      }
      HiliteMenu(0);
   }
}
```

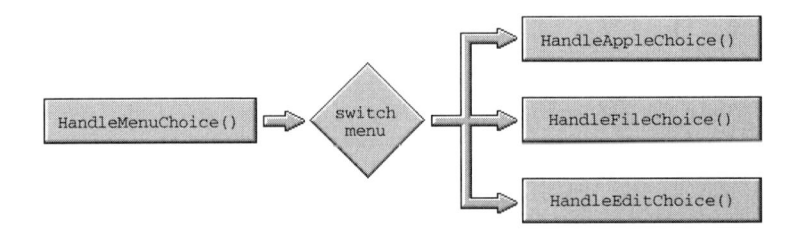

FIGURE 9.16 Application-defined routines called by `HandleMenuChoice()`.

Like `HandleMenuChoice()`, each of the three routines that handle a menu selection is nothing more than a branch point. And, again, like `Handle-MenuChoice()`, these three routines can be used as-is in many other projects. The listing for the routine that handles a click in the Apple menu follows. Its calling chain is shown in Figure 9.17.

```
void  HandleAppleChoice( short theMenuItem )
{
   switch ( theMenuItem )
   {
      case iAbout:
         HandleAppleMenuAboutItem();
         break;
```

```
         default:
            HandleAppleMenuDefaultItem( theMenuItem );
            break;
      }
}
```

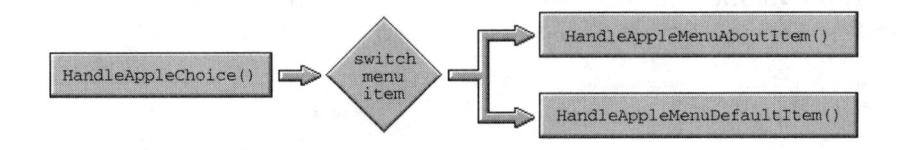

FIGURE 9.17 Application-defined routines called by `HandleAppleChoice()`.

The File and Edit menus are handled in a manner similar to the Apple menu: the menu item is determined, then a routine written to handle just that item is invoked.

```
void  HandleFileChoice( short theMenuItem )
{
   switch ( theMenuItem )
   {
      case iOpen:
         HandleFileMenuOpenItem();
         break;

      case iClose:
         HandleFileMenuCloseItem();
         break;

      case iSave:
         HandleFileMenuSaveItem();
         break;

      case iSaveAs:
         HandleFileMenuSaveAsItem();
         break;

      case iQuit:
         HandleFileMenuQuitItem();
         break;
```

```
    }
}
```

Giving each specific menu item its own routine makes it easy to keep application-specific code separate from the more general event-handling code. FilmEdit has a separate source code file named **FileMenu.c** that holds the five File menu routines shown above and in Figure 9.18. The same applies for Apple menu routines, which can be found in the **AppleMenu.c** file, and Edit menu routines, which are located in **EditMenu.c**.

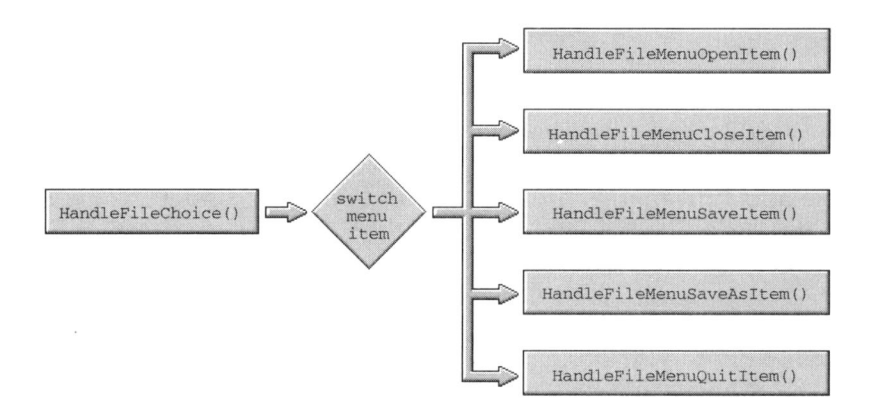

FIGURE 9.18 Application-defined routines called by `HandleFileChoice()`.

As mentioned, each Edit menu item selection is handled by its own routine—as shown in the `HandleEditChoice()` listing and in Figure 9.19.

```
void  HandleEditChoice( short theMenuItem )
{
   switch ( theMenuItem )
   {
      case iUndo:
         HandleEditMenuUndoItem();
         break;

      case iCut:
         HandleEditMenuCutItem();
         break;

      case iCopy:
```

```
         HandleEditMenuCopyItem();
         break;

    case iPaste:
       HandleEditMenuPasteItem();
       break;

    case iClear:
       HandleEditMenuClearItem();
       break;

    case iSelectAll:
       HandleEditMenuSelectAllItem();
       break;
   }
}
```

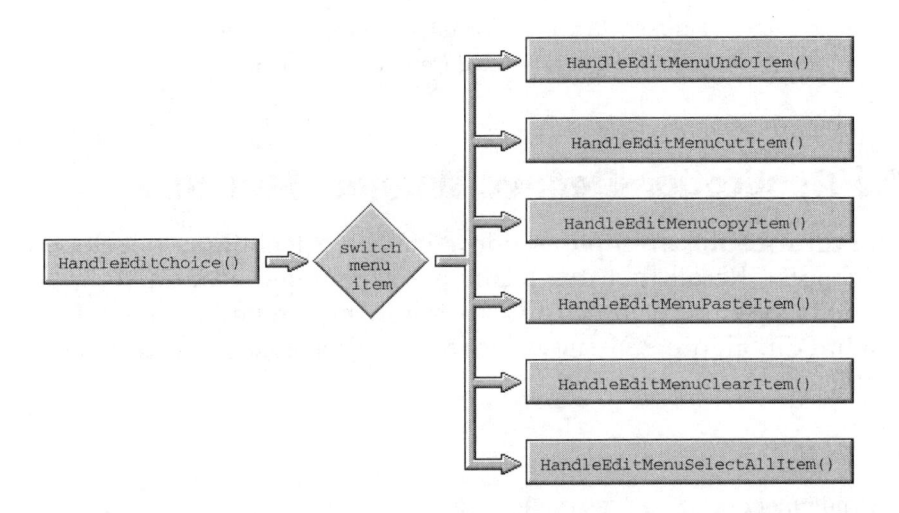

FIGURE 9.19 Application-defined routines called by HandleEditChoice().

A single menu selection, such as **Cut** from the Edit menu, sets off a chain of application-defined function calls—as shown in Figure 9.20. If the FilmEdit code were to be adapted for use in another program that uses the **Cut** menu item, only the body of the HandleEditMenuCutItem() function would need to be modified.

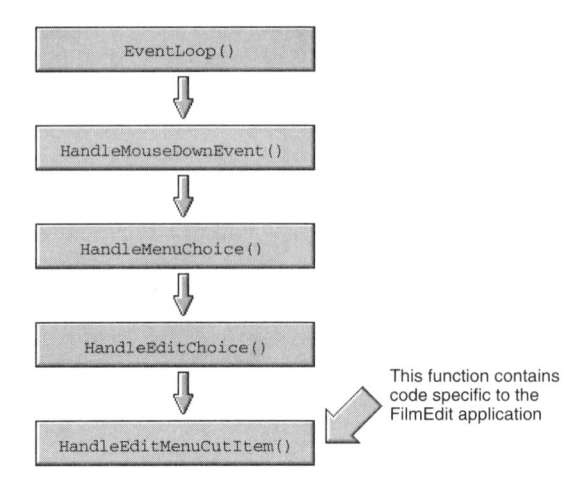

FIGURE 9.20 Application-defined routines called
when **Cut** is selected from the Edit menu.

The Application-Defined Window Structure

FilmEdit uses the multiple window-handling technique developed in
this chapter. Recall that this technique is centered around an application-defined window structure. The following structure is the one used
by FilmEdit. Figure 9.21 shows how a `BigWindRecord` structure looks in
memory.

```
typedef struct
{
   WindowRecord     theWindRecord;
   short            theWindType;
   short            theFileReference;
   short            theMovieResourceID;
   Movie            theMovie;
   MovieController  theController;

} BigWindRecord, *BigWindRecordPeek;
```

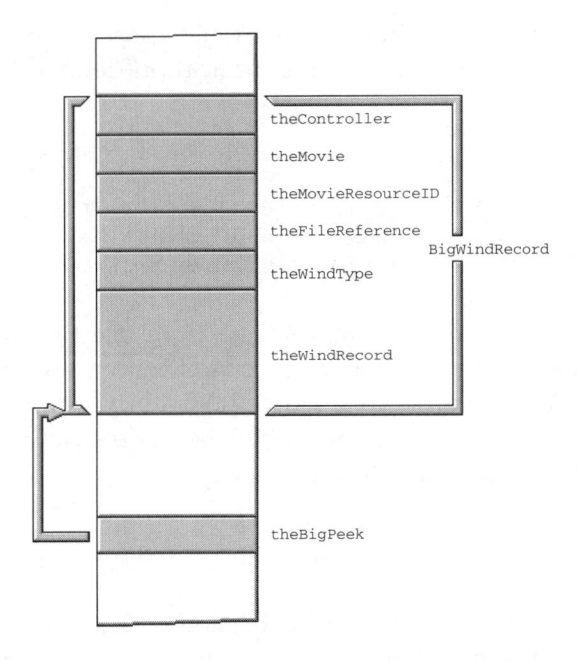

FIGURE 9.21 The FilmEdit version of a `BigWindRecord`.

The FilmEdit version of the `BigWindRecord` structure begins with a `WindowRecord` and a field that holds the window's type—the two fields you saw in this chapter's introduction to this structure. Next comes two fields that will come in handy when saving a movie. Recall that when a movie is to be saved, a call is made to `UpdateMovieResource()`:

```
UpdateMovieResource( theMovie, theFileRefNum, theMovieResID, nil );
```

`UpdateMovieResource()` depends on the file's reference number and the movie's resource ID in order to write a movie to a file. When a movie is opened and loaded into memory, these two values can be written to the movie window's structure using application-defined "set" routines:

```
SetWindowFileReference( theWindow, theFileRefNum );
SetWindowMovieResourceID( theWindow, theMovieResID );
```

Later, when it is time to save the movie, these values can be retrieved from the window's structure using application-defined "get" routines:

```
short  theFileRefNum;
short  theMovieResID;

theFileRefNum = GetWindowFileReference( theWindow );
theMovieResID = GetWindowMovieResourceID( theWindow );
UpdateMovieResource( theMovie, theFileRefNum, theMovieResID, nil );
```

The last two fields in the `BigWindRecord` are used to keep track of the movie and the movie controller associated with a window. Like the file reference number and movie resource ID fields, the movie and controller field values can be set right after a QuickTime movie window is opened and a controller is attached to the movie:

```
SetWindowMovie( theWindow, theMovie );
SetWindowController( theWindow, theController );
```

Once a movie and a controller are associated with a window, either or both can be retrieved from the window structure when needed. For instance, if a QuickTime movie window is being closed, its movie and controller should be disposed of. In the following snippet, the Toolbox routine `FrontWindow()` is used to determine which window is to be closed. Once the window is known, its movie and controller can be found.

```
WindowPtr         theWindow
MovieController   theController;
Movie             theMovie

theWindow = FrontWindow()

theController = GetWindowController( theWindow )
DisposeMovieController( theController );

theMovie = GetWindowMovie( theWindow );
DisposeMovie( theMovie );
```

```
DisposeWindow( theWindow );
```

Figure 9.22 shows what memory might look like after a new QuickTime movie window has been opened. Notice that the `theMovie` and `theController` fields hold addresses. This is because variables of type `Movie` and `MovieController` are identifiers, or pointers, to movie and controller data in memory.

NOTE For programs that use different types of windows, the `BigWindRecord` should be modified to include fields that pertain to each window type. For example, a program that has a QuickTime window and a picture window might have two additional fields in the `BigWindRecord`. As shown below, the new version of the structure can now keep track of a handle to a picture and a title for the picture. A QuickTime movie window (as determined by the `theWindType` field) would simply ignore these last two fields. A picture window (again, as determined by `theWindType`) would ignore the `theMovieResourceID`, `theMovie`, and `theController` fields. If the program allowed picture windows to be saved to disk, then a picture window could use `theFileReference` field to keep track of an open 'PICT' file—just as a QuickTime movie uses this field to keep track of an open 'MooV' file.

```
typedef struct
{
    WindowRecord        theWindRecord;
    short               theWindType;
    short               theFileReference;
    short               theMovieResourceID;
    Movie               theMovie;
    MovieController      theController;
    PicHandle           thePicture;
    Str255              thePictName;

}  BigWindRecord, *BigWindRecordPeek;
```

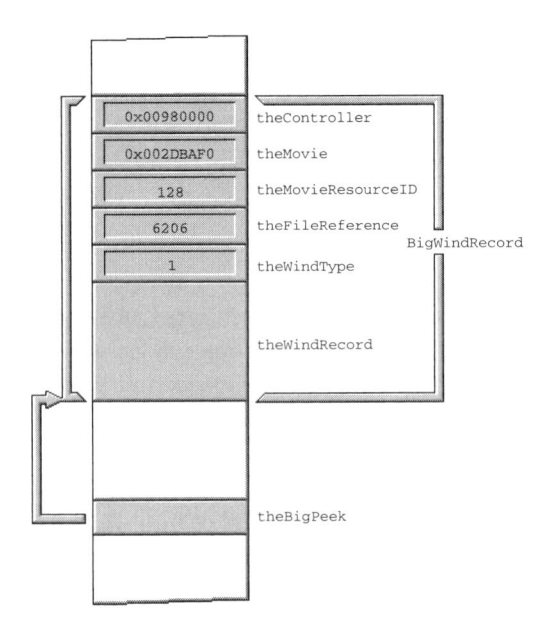

FIGURE 9.22 A BigWindRecord after a QuickTime movie window is opened.

Earlier in this chapter it was suggested that your application should define a "set" and "get" routine for each data item being stored in a window structure. You've already seen SetWindowType() and GetWindowType() for the first item—theWindType. FilmEdit defines similar routines for the other four private data items—the data items that belong to one window and that can be accessed only through a WindowPtr typecast to a BigWindRecordPeek. The routines follow for setting a window's movie controller and for retrieving that same information.

```
void  SetWindowController( WindowPtr theWindow,
                           MovieController theController )
{
   BigWindRecordPeek   theBigPeek;

   theBigPeek = (BigWindRecordPeek)theWindow;
   theBigPeek->theController = theController;
}

MovieController  GetWindowController( WindowPtr theWindow )
```

```
{
   BigWindRecordPeek  theBigPeek;

   theBigPeek = (BigWindRecordPeek)theWindow;
   return ( theBigPeek->theController );
}
```

 You can get a movie window's movie at any time by calling the application-defined GetWindowMovie() function. Alternatively, if you know a window's controller, you can use the Movie Toolbox routine MCGetMovie() to get the window's movie:

N O T E

```
MovieController  theController;
Movie            theMovie;

theMovie = MCGetMovie( theController );
```

Updating Multiple Movies

In the FilmEdit event loop, you saw that an application-defined routine named UpdateAllOpenMovies() was responsible for taking care of the updating of QuickTime movies:

```
isControllerEvent = UpdateAllOpenMovies( theEvent );
```

UpdateAllOpenMovies() begins by setting the variable theWindow to the front window on the screen. Then the function cycles through a for loop, checking each open window to see if it is a QuickTime movie window. If a window is a movie window, UpdateAllOpenMovies() calls MCIsPlayer-Event(). If MCIsPlayerEvent() handles the event, the function is considered over and it returns a value of true (for event handled). If MCIsPlayerEvent() doesn't handle the event, then this current event didn't affect the controller. UpdateAllOpenMovies() then looks at the next window that is open on the screen. This looping takes place until the movie controller at which the event is directed is found. If no open window has a controller, or if the event doesn't pertain to any window with a controller, the event is not controller-related and UpdateAllOpenMovies() returns a value of false (for event not handled). The following is an outline of what takes place in the UpdateAllOpenMovies() function.

```
set window to front window
begin loop
   begin if window is QuickTime window
      get movie controller
      call MCIsPlayerEvent() for that controller
      if event handled
         return(true)
   end if
   determine next open window
end loop
return(false)
```

You can see in the above outline that UpdateAllOpenMovies() "bails out" of the loop once the event is handled by MCIsPlayerEvent(). If you consider the case of a movie that is playing, this makes sense—MCIsPlayerEvent() updates the playing movie and the event is considered handled. What about the case when two movies are playing at the same time? The code still exits after one movie is updated. UpdateAllOpenMovies() only handles one event—the event that is passed to it. The second movie will get updated at the next pass through the event loop, and thus at the next call to UpdateAllOpenMovies(). The UpdateAllOpenMovies() code follows:

```
Boolean  UpdateAllOpenMovies( EventRecord theEvent )
{
    int              i;
    WindowPtr        theWindow;
    WindowPeek       theWindPeek;
    MovieController  theController;
    Boolean          eventWasHandled;

    theWindow = FrontWindow();

    for (i = 0; i < gWindowCount; i++)
    {
        if ( GetWindowType( theWindow ) == kMovieWindowType )
        {
            theController = GetWindowController( theWindow );
            eventWasHandled = MCIsPlayerEvent( theController, &theEvent);
            if ( eventWasHandled == 1 )
                return ( true );
        }
        theWindPeek = ((WindowPeek)theWindow)->nextWindow;
        theWindow = (WindowPtr)theWindPeek;
```

```
    }
    return ( false );
}
```

In order to get a pointer to each open window, `UpdateAllOpenMovies()` relies on the `WindowRecord` field of a window structure. The Apple-defined `WindowRecord` contains several fields—one of which is the nextWindow field. This `WindowRecord` member holds a pointer to the next window. The first window pointer is obtained by making a call to `FrontWindow()`. After that, the next window is found by casting the window pointer to a `WindowPeek`. Recall that a `WindowPtr` can access only the `GrafPort` member of a `WindowRecord`. The `WindowPeek`, on the other hand, can access any member. Figure 9.23 illustrates this.

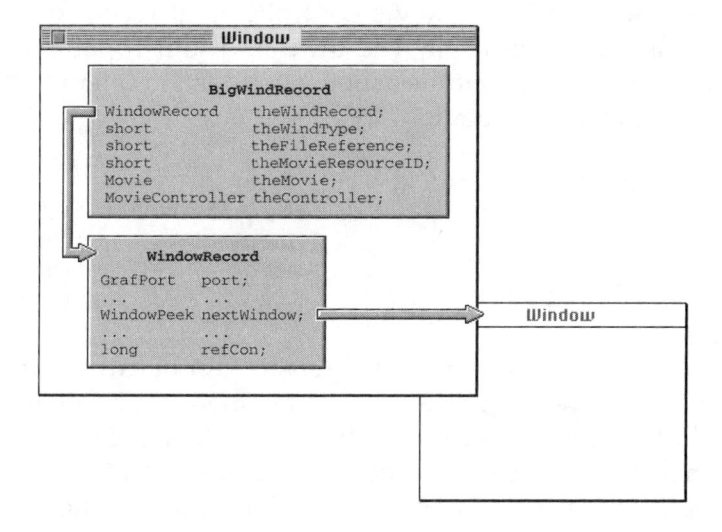

FIGURE 9.23 The nextWindow field of a window's WindowRecord can be used to find the next open window.

The Movie Controller Action Filter Function

A movie controller can make use of an optional action filter function. Whenever an action takes place that involves the controller, the controller will call the filter function. Your application will never directly call the filter function—it is always the controller itself that calls the routine.

 Routines called by the system rather than by an application should be a familiar concept to you. If you've worked with user items in dialog boxes, recall that the drawing procedure used to update a user item in a dialog box is called by the system. Chapter 2 of this book provides another example: the callback routine used during asynchronous sound play is called by the system, not an application.

An action filter is defined using the following format. First comes the pascal identifier, then a return type of `Boolean`. Next comes the action filter function name—any name of your choosing. Next come the four parameters. The first is the movie controller that received the action. The second is the action itself. The third and fourth parameters hold additional information about the action—your action filter function may or may not need this information.

```
pascal  Boolean  SizeChangeMCActionFilter(
                              MovieController theController,
                              short           theAction,
                              void            *theParams,
                              long            theRefCon )
```

Because an action filter can be written to handle different types of actions, the filter should use a `switch` statement. The following filter, used in FilmEdit, responds to one action—the changing of a controller's size. When a controller's size changes, so must the controller's window size. When looking for this action, use the Apple-defined `mcAction-ControllerSizeChanged`.

```
pascal  Boolean  SizeChangeMCActionFilter(
                              MovieController theController,
                              short           theAction,
                              void            *theParams,
                              long            theRefCon )
{
   Rect    theBoundsRect;
```

```
short   theWidth;
short   theHeight;

switch ( theAction )
{
    case mcActionControllerSizeChanged:
        MCGetControllerBoundsRect( theController, &theBoundsRect );
        theWidth  = theBoundsRect.right - theBoundsRect.left;
        theHeight = theBoundsRect.bottom - theBoundsRect.top;
        SizeWindow( (WindowPtr)theRefCon, theWidth, theHeight, true );
        break;
}
    return false;
}
```

mcActionControllerSizeChanged is by far the most common action used in a filter, but it isn't the only action that a controller can respond to. *Inside Macintosh: Sound* lists others.

When the action filter gets called with a controller size-change action, the filter will call `MCGetControllerBoundsRect()` to determine the new size of the window in which the movie and controller appear. This routine returns the rectangle in which the newly sized controller and movie will appear. The window's new width and height can then be found from this rectangle. Next, a call to `SizeWindow()` resizes the window.

One typical scenario that involves a resizing controller is during a paste operation. If the user copies a frame from a large movie and pastes that frame into a smaller movie, QuickTime will automatically enlarge the small movie to the size of the pasted frame. When the movie (and window) size change, so must the controller size. When the user performs the paste, the system will call the controller's action filter function to resize the window.

An action filter should return a value of `false` if further action processing is to be left to the controller. If the action filter has performed all necessary processing, return a value of `true`. In general, you'll want to return a value of `false` in case the controller has any additional tasks that it might routinely perform for a given action.

If a controller is to make use of an action filter, it needs to become aware of this application-defined routine. After creating a new controller with the `NewMovieController()` Movie Toolbox function, call `MCSetActionFilterWithRefCon()`:

```
MCSetActionFilterWithRefCon( theController,
    NewMCActionFilterWithRefConProc( SizeChangeMCActionFilter ),
                                 (long)theWindow );
```

The first parameter is the controller to which the action filter should be associated. The second parameter is a pointer to that filter function. Before the Power Macs, a parameter such as this would have been passed as a `ProcPtr`. Now, a universal procedure pointer (UPP) should be used. Fortunately, creating a UPP for a filter function is painless—when passed the name of a filter function, the Movie Toolbox routine `NewMCActionFilterWithRefConProc()` creates the necessary UPP.

 The universal procedure pointer, or UPP, is an important part of writing code that will compile using both a 68K and a PowerPC compiler.

N O T E

The third parameter to `MCSetActionFilterWithRefCon()` is of type `long` and serves as a link between the filter function and the movie window. This scheme works for two reasons. First, variable `theWindow` is a pointer, or 4-byte address—the same size as a `long`. Second, no two windows share the same `WindowPtr` value (two `WindowPtr`s may have the same value, but that only means they both point to the same window). Because a `WindowPtr` is a unique value, its value can be used to associate a window with an action routine.

If you look back at the definition of `SizeChangeMCActionFilter()`, you'll see that the last parameter to this routine is a long named `theRefCon`. This is the same `long` that was used in the call to `MCSetActionFilterWithRefCon()`. When the system calls the movie controller action filter function, it passes this value so that the filter knows which window is involved in the action. In the action filer, `theRefCon` is used in resizing the window—after first typecasting it back to a `WindowPtr`:

```
SizeWindow( (WindowPtr)theRefCon, theWidth, theHeight, true );
```

Handling Apple Menu Item Selections

FilmEdit uses just a few lines of code to handle menu item selections from the Apple menu. for simplicity, a click in the **About** item results in a single playing of the system alert sound—you can go the more traditional route of displaying an alert or dialog box with program information.

```
void  HandleAppleMenuAboutItem( void )
{
    SysBeep( 1 );
}
```

A selection from any of the other Apple menu items results in that item being launched. FilmEdit uses the same code that has always been used in the past to open desk accessories.

```
void  HandleAppleMenuDefaultItem( short theMenuItem )
{
    Str255      theAppleMenuItemName;
    short       theAppleMenuItemNumber;
    MenuHandle  theAppleMenu;
    theAppleMenu = GetMHandle( mApple );
    GetItem( theAppleMenu, theMenuItem, theAppleMenuItemName );
    theAppleMenuItemNumber = OpenDeskAcc( theAppleMenuItemName );
}
```

Handling the File Menu Open Item

An **Open** selection from the File menu results in a posting of the standard Open dialog box. After the user makes a file selection, the movie in that file is opened. Because FilmEdit allows a movie to be saved back to disk at any time, the movie's file is left open. Next, memory for a structure the size of a BigWindRecord is reserved, and then a window is opened and its data stored in that memory. Next, the action filter function is associated with the new movie by calling MCSetActionFilterWithRefCon(). After that, the window and controller-bounding rectangle is found and the window is resized to match that rectangle.

After the window is open, HandleFileMenuOpenItem() stores the movie type, the movie itself, the controller, the open 'MooV' file reference number, and the `moov` resource ID number in the window's `BigWindRecord` data structure. Finally, the open window count is incremented.

```
void  HandleFileMenuOpenItem( void )
{
    SFTypeList          typeList = { MovieFileType, 0, 0, 0 };
    StandardFileReply   theReply;
    OSErr               theError;
    short               theFileRefNum,
    Movie               theMovie;
    short               theMovieResID = 0;
    Str255              theMovieResName;
    Boolean             wasAltered;
    WindowPtr           theWindow;
    Ptr                 theWindowStorage;
    Rect                theMovieBox;
    Rect                theBoundsRect;
    MovieController     theController;

    StandardGetFilePreview( nil, 1, typeList, &theReply );

    if ( theReply.sfGood == false )
        return;

    theError = OpenMovieFile( &theReply.sfFile,
                              &theFileRefNum, fsRdWrPerm );
    if ( theError != noErr )
        ExitToShell();

    theError = NewMovieFromFile( &theMovie, theFileRefNum,
                                 &theMovieResID, theMovieResName,
                                 newMovieActive, &wasAltered );
    if ( theError != noErr )
        ExitToShell();

    theWindowStorage = NewPtr( sizeof ( BigWindRecord ) );
    theWindow = GetNewCWindow( rMovieWindow, theWindowStorage,
                               (WindowPtr)-1L );

    SetMovieGWorld( theMovie, (CGrafPtr)theWindow, nil );

    GetMovieBox( theMovie, &theMovieBox );

    theController = NewMovieController( theMovie, &theMovieBox,
                                        mcTopLeftMovie);
```

```
MCSetActionFilterWithRefCon( theController,
        NewMCActionFilterWithRefConProc( SizeChangeMCActionFilter ),
        (long)theWindow );

MCGetControllerBoundsRect( theController, &theBoundsRect );

SizeWindow( theWindow, theBoundsRect.right,
            theBoundsRect.bottom, true );
ShowWindow( theWindow );

MCEnableEditing( theController, true );

SetWindowType( theWindow, kMovieWindowType );
SetWindowMovie( theWindow, theMovie );
SetWindowController( theWindow, theController );
SetWindowFileReference( theWindow, theFileRefNum );
SetWindowMovieResourceID( theWindow, theMovieResID );

++gWindowCount;
}
```

Handling the File Menu Close Item

Selecting **Close** from the File menu results in a call to HandleFileMenu-
CloseItem(). This routine determines which window is frontmost, then
calls the application-defined function CloseMovieAndFile() to close that
window.

```
void  HandleFileMenuCloseItem( void )
{
    WindowPtr  theWindow;

    theWindow = FrontWindow();
    CloseMovieAndFile( theWindow );
}
```

CloseMovieAndFile() calls three application-defined "get" routines to
retrieve data about the frontmost window. First, the reference number of
the 'MooV' file that holds the movie is obtained. Recall that this movie file
remains open as long as its movie is in memory. With the movie window
about to close, it's time to close the file. The Movie Toolbox routine
CloseMovieFile() does that. Next, the movie's controller is retrieved and

disposed of, then the movie is retrieved and disposed of. Then the memory for the window itself is deallocated. The `DisposeMovieController()` and `DisposeMovie()` routines are Movie Toolbox functions described in Chapter 7. Finally, the global variable `gWindowCount` is decremented.

```
void  CloseMovieAndFile( WindowPtr theWindow )
{
   MovieController  theController;
   Movie            theMovie;
   short            theFileRefNum;

   theFileRefNum = GetWindowFileReference( theWindow );
   CloseMovieFile( theFileRefNum );

   theController = GetWindowController( theWindow );
   DisposeMovieController( theController );
   theMovie = GetWindowMovie( theWindow );

   DisposeMovie( theMovie );
   DisposeWindow( theWindow );

   -gWindowCount;
}
```

Handling the File Menu Save Item

The **Save** menu item is handled as described earlier in this chapter: A call to the Movie Toolbox function `UpdateMovieResource()` saves the movie named in the first parameter to the file and resource specified in the second and third parameters. The fourth parameter of `nil` tells the function that the `moov` resource should not be given a new name.

```
void  HandleFileMenuSaveItem( void )
{
   WindowPtr  theWindow;
   Movie      theMovie;
   short      theFileRefNum;
   short      theMovieResID;
```

```
theWindow = FrontWindow();

if ( GetWindowType( theWindow ) == kMovieWindowType )
{
    theMovie = GetWindowMovie( theWindow);
    theFileRefNum = GetWindowFileReference( theWindow );
    theMovieResID = GetWindowMovieResourceID( theWindow );
    UpdateMovieResource( theMovie, theFileRefNum, theMovieResID,
                         nil );
}
}
```

Handling the File Menu Save As Item

Like the **Save** menu item, the **Save As** item is handled as discussed earlier
in this chapter: A call to the Movie Toolbox function FlattenMovie() saves
a movie to a new file. The parameters to this call to FlattenMovie() are
identical to the ones used in this chapter's earlier discussion of
FlattenMovie().

After the movie is saved to a new file, HandleFileMenuSaveAsItem()
calls the Toolbox function SetWTitle() to change the movie window's title
to the name the user has selected for the movie.

```
void  HandleFileMenuSaveAsItem( void )
{
    StandardFileReply   theReply;
    WindowPtr           theWindow;
    Movie               theMovie;

    StandardPutFile( "\pSave as:", "\pUntitled", &theReply );

    if ( theReply.sfGood == false )
        return;

    theWindow = FrontWindow();

    theMovie = GetWindowMovie( theWindow );
```

```
FlattenMovie( theMovie, flattenAddMovieToDataFork,
              &theReply.sfFile, 'TVOD', 0,
              createMovieFileDeleteCurFile, nil, nil );

SetWTitle( theWindow, theReply.sfFile.name );
}
```

Handling the File Menu Quit Item

Many programs handle the Quit menu item by simply setting a global variable (such as the FilmEdit `Boolean` variable `gDone`) to `true` to end the main event loop and thus end the program. FilmEdit does that, but it also does a little cleanup work.

In this chapter's section on updating movie windows, you saw that the Toolbox function `FrontWindow()` could be used to get a pointer to the first, or front, window on the screen. Then the `nextWindow` field of the first window's `WindowRecord` could be used to obtain a pointer to the next open window. This same technique is used by `HandleFileMenuQuitItem()`. This routine uses a `for` loop to get a `WindowPtr` to each open window. For each window that is of type `kMovieWindowType`, the application-defined function `CloseMovieAndFile()` is called to close the movie's file and dispose of the memory occupied by the movie, controller, and window.

```
void  HandleFileMenuQuitItem( void )
{
   int         i;
   int         theNumWindows;
   WindowPtr   theWindow;
   WindowPeek  theWindPeek;
   WindowPtr   theNextWindow;

   theNumWindows = gWindowCount;
   theWindow = FrontWindow();

   for (i = 0; i < theNumWindows; i++)
   {
      theWindPeek = ((WindowPeek)theWindow)->nextWindow;
      theNextWindow = (WindowPtr)theWindPeek;
      if ( GetWindowType( theWindow ) == kMovieWindowType )
         CloseMovieAndFile( theWindow );
      theWindow = theNextWindow;
```

```
   }
   gDone = true;
}
```

NOTE True enough—all of the FilmEdit windows will be of type kMovieWindow-Type. But if you're thinking of adding some functionality to FilmEdit, this check should remind you that other windows will be closed in a different manner. In particular, there'll be no movie or controller memory to deallo-cate. If your version of FilmEdit will also support, say, a picture window, then you might add an else to the if statement—as shown below. The application-defined routine ClosePictureWindow() would handle any memory deallocation particular to this picture type of window (such as calling ReleaseResource() to release the memory occupied by a PICT resource).

```
if ( GetWindowType( theWindow ) == kMovieWindowType )
   CloseMovieAndFile( theWindow );
else
   ClosePictureWindow( theWindow );
```

Handling Edit Menu Item Selections

Each Edit menu item is handled by a short application-defined function. Each begins by calling FrontWindow() to acquire a pointer to the front-most window—the window in which the editing operation is to take place. After that, the window's movie controller is obtained through a call to the movie controller "get" function—GetWindowController(). Next, the appropriate Movie Toolbox function is called. The handling of the **Undo** menu item by the HandleEditMenuUndoItem() routine is typical of the Edit menu routines.

```
void  HandleEditMenuUndoItem( void )
{
   WindowPtr         theWindow;
   MovieController   theController;

   theWindow = FrontWindow();
   theController = GetWindowController( theWindow );

   MCUndo( theController );
```

```
}
```

The **Cut**, **Copy**, **Paste**, and **Clear** menu items are all handled as discussed earlier in this chapter.

```
void   HandleEditMenuCutItem( void )
{
   WindowPtr         theWindow;
   MovieController   theController;
   Movie             theTempMovie;
   theWindow = FrontWindow();
   theController = GetWindowController( theWindow );

   theTempMovie = MCCut( theController );
   PutMovieOnScrap( theTempMovie, movieScrapOnlyPutMovie );
   DisposeMovie( theTempMovie );
}

//_____

void   HandleEditMenuCopyItem( void )
{
   WindowPtr         theWindow;
   MovieController   theController;
   Movie             theTempMovie;

   theWindow = FrontWindow();
   theController = GetWindowController( theWindow );

   theTempMovie = MCCopy( theController );
   PutMovieOnScrap( theTempMovie, movieScrapOnlyPutMovie );
   DisposeMovie( theTempMovie );
}

//_____

void   HandleEditMenuPasteItem( void )
{
   WindowPtr         theWindow;
   MovieController   theController;

   theWindow = FrontWindow();
   theController = GetWindowController( theWindow );

   MCPaste( theController, nil );
}
```

```
//_____

void  HandleEditMenuClearItem( void )
{
    WindowPtr         theWindow;
    MovieController   theController;

    theWindow = FrontWindow();
    theController = GetWindowController( theWindow );
    MCClear( theController );
}
```

Handling of the **Select All** menu item relies on setting the values of the fields of a `TimeRecord`—as discussed earlier in this chapter.

```
void  HandleEditMenuSelectAllItem( void )
{
    WindowPtr         theWindow;
    MovieController   theController;
    TimeRecord        theTimeRecord;
    Movie             theMovie;

    theWindow = FrontWindow();
    theController = GetWindowController( theWindow );
    theMovie = GetWindowMovie( theWindow );

    theTimeRecord.value.hi = 0;
    theTimeRecord.value.lo = 0;
    theTimeRecord.base = 0;

    theTimeRecord.scale = GetMovieTimeScale( theMovie );
    MCDoAction( theController, mcActionSetSelectionBegin,
                &theTimeRecord);

    theTimeRecord.value.lo = GetMovieDuration( theMovie );
    MCDoAction( theController, mcActionSetSelectionDuration,
                &theTimeRecord );
}
```

The FilmEdit Project File Organization

Up to this point, the source-code for each of the example programs in this book has appeared in a single source-code file. While appropriate for a small example, a single-source code file isn't typical of real-world Mac projects. The FilmEdit example is large enough that its source code can be divided into several files. Figure 9.24 shows that the FilmEdit project consists of eight source-code files.

File	Code	Data	📄	✳
▽ **Generic Source**	**1K**	**4**	•	▾
Globals.c	0	4	•	▸
Initialize.c	190	0	•	▸
Generic.c	1326	0	•	▸
▽ **Application Source**	**2K**	**34**	•	▾
WindRecordAccess.c	450	0	•	▸
MovieUtilities.c	362	0	•	▸
AppleMenu.c	122	0	•	▸
FileMenu.c	804	34	•	▸
EditMenu.c	588	0	•	▸
▽ **Resources**	**0**	**0**		▾
FilmEdit.rsrc	n/a	n/a		▸
▽ **Libraries**	**30K**	**0**		▾
MacOS.lib	31554	0		▸
10 file(s)	**34K**	**38**		

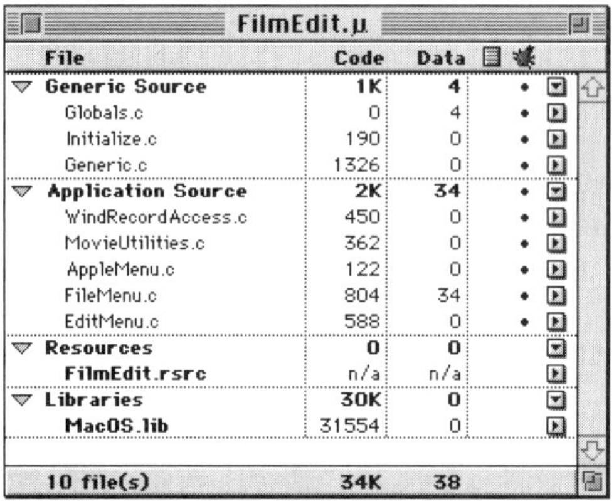

FIGURE 9.24 The Metrowerks version of the FilmEdit
project lists the eight source-code files.

Only for purposes of organization, the eight files have been placed into two groups. The first group holds the files that consist of the generic, or framework, code of FilmEdit. The global variables and routines found in the **Globals.c**, **Initialize.c**, and **Generic.c** files could be used in just about any other project.

The FilmEdit project uses three header files to make the #defines, data type, and global variables known to other files. If a function in any source file needs to be aware of any of this application-defined information, the source file should include the appropriate header file or files. For instance, routines in the **Generic.c** file include code that makes reference to many of the #defines, the BigWindRecord structure, and both of the global variables. For that reason, you'll find that **Generic.c** has the following lines near the top of the file:

```
#include "Defines.h"
#include "DataTypes.h"
#include "Globals.h"
```

Figure 9.25 shows the preceding #include directives in the **Generic.c** file. Notice also that because code in **Generic.c** makes use of Movie Toolbox functions, **Generic.c** also includes the **Movies.h** universal header file.

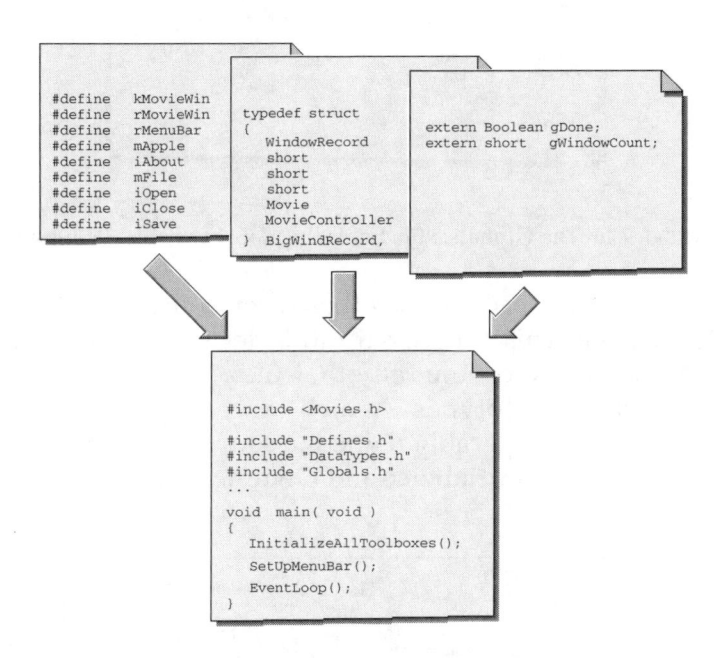

FIGURE 9.25 Any source-code file can be made aware of #defines, data types, and global variables.

In Figure 9.25, you'll notice that the global variables in **Globals.h** are defined using the extern keyword. The extern keyword is necessary here because your compiler will not allow the same variable to be declared more than one time. Without the use of the extern keyword, the compiler would view each appearance of a variable as a declaration. And because several source code files include the **Globals.h** file, there are several appearances of each variable. Variables do have to be declared once, however, and the **Globals.c** file takes care of this. Figure 9.26 shows that this file is where the global variables are declared and initialized. Because this file is a source file rather than a header file, it has been added to the project along with all of the other **.c** files. If you make additions to the FilmEdit project, make sure to add *each* new global variable to *both* the **Globals.c** and **Globals.h** files.

```
Boolean  gDone       = false;
short    gWindowCount = 0;
```

FIGURE 9.26 The **Globals.c** file holds the global variable definitions.

Aside from **Globals.c**, each of the other seven source-code files also has its own header file. This is necessary in order to make the functions in each file known to the code in all other files. Thus each **.h** header file holds the function prototypes—which serve as *public interfaces*—for each routine in the comparably named .c source file. Figure 9.27 shows the header files for the **Initialize.c** and **Generic.c** source files.

```
void   InitializeAllToolboxes( void );
void   SetUpMenuBar( void );
```

```
void  EventLoop( void );
void  AdjustAllMenus( void );

void  HandleMouseDownEvent( EventRecord );
void  HandleKeyDownEvent( EventRecord );
void  HandleActivateEvent( EventRecord );
void  HandleUpdateEvent( EventRecord );

void  HandleMenuChoice( long );
void  HandleAppleChoice( short );
void  HandleFileChoice( short );
void  HandleEditChoice( short );
```

FIGURE 9.27 The public interfaces for the **Initialize.c** and **Generic.c** source code files.

Initialize.c and **Generic.c** hold the reusable code for the FilmEdit project. The remaining five source files hold application-specific code. Figure 9.28 shows the header files for the menu-handling code found in the **AppleMenu.c**, **FileMenu.c**, and **EditMenu.c** source-code files. Note that there is one routine for each menu item—as discussed earlier.

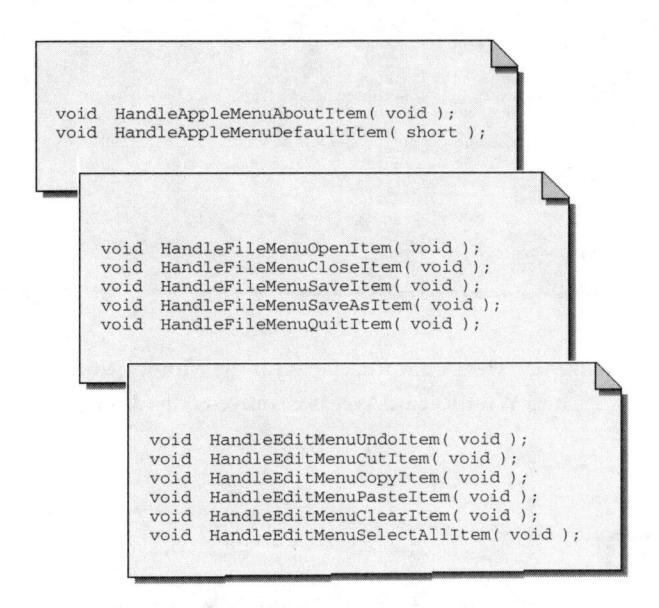

```
void  HandleAppleMenuAboutItem( void );
void  HandleAppleMenuDefaultItem( short );

void  HandleFileMenuOpenItem( void );
void  HandleFileMenuCloseItem( void );
void  HandleFileMenuSaveItem( void );
void  HandleFileMenuSaveAsItem( void );
void  HandleFileMenuQuitItem( void );

void  HandleEditMenuUndoItem( void );
void  HandleEditMenuCutItem( void );
void  HandleEditMenuCopyItem( void );
void  HandleEditMenuPasteItem( void );
void  HandleEditMenuClearItem( void );
void  HandleEditMenuSelectAllItem( void );
```

FIGURE 9.28 The public interfaces for the **AppleMenu.c**,
FileMenu.c, and **EditMenu.c** source code files.

The **MovieUtilities.c** file holds three routines that work with movie windows. Figure 9.29 shows the public interfaces for these three functions. The **WindRecordAccess.c** file holds the source code for the "get" and "set" routines that are used to access the fields of data in the BigWindRecord structure. Besides the WindowRecord field, the BigWindRecord consists of five other members. You can see from the **WindRecordAccess.h** header file that there is a "get" and "set" routine defined for each of these five members.

```
long    UpdateAllOpenMovies( EventRecord );
void    CloseMovieAndFile( WindowPtr );
pascal  Boolean SizeChangeMCActionFilter( MovieController,
                                   short, void *, long );
```

```
#include <Movies.h>

void    SetWindowType( WindowPtr, short );
void    SetWindowFileReference( WindowPtr, short );
void    SetWindowMovieResourceID( WindowPtr, short );
void    SetWindowMovie( WindowPtr, Movie );
void    SetWindowController( WindowPtr, MovieController );

short   GetWindowType( WindowPtr );
short   GetWindowFileReference( WindowPtr );
short   GetWindowMovieResourceID( WindowPtr );
Movie   GetWindowMovie( WindowPtr );
MovieController  GetWindowController( WindowPtr );
```

FIGURE 9.29 The public interfaces for the **MovieUtilities.c**
and **WindRecordAccess.c** source code files.

Summary

Your QuickTime application can easily support movie editing by using Movie Toolbox routines. The MCCut() and MCCopy() functions are used in response to **Cut** and **Copy** choices from the Edit menu. PutMovieOnScrap() adds the cut or copied section of a movie to the clipboard. MCPaste() is used when **Paste** is selected from the Edit menu. MCClear() is used when the **Clear** menu item is selected. This function cuts a selected part of a movie and doesn't save the cut selection. Any of these actions can be undone—when the user chooses **Undo** from the Edit menu, call MCUndo().

If your application allows the user to edit a movie, then it should also allow the user to save the changes made in an editing session. To overwrite the previous version of a movie, call the Movie Toolbox function UpdateMovieResource(). To save the new version to its own new file, call the Movie Toolbox function FlattenMovie().

Many example programs use a single window to demonstrate the topic at hand. Real world applications, however, allow multiple windows to be open at any time. To keep track of each window, your application should define a window structure. The first member of this structure should be a `WindowRecord`. The remaining members can be used to hold any application-specific window information. When an event occurs, call the Toolbox function `FrontWindow()` to receive a `WindowPtr` to the window to which the event applies. Then use that pointer to access the data for that window.

APPENDIX A

General MIDI Instrument Numbers

The QuickTime Musical Instruments system software extension is capable of playing sounds generated by any of the 128 predefined General MIDI Instruments. Each instrument has both a number and a name. Refer to Chapter 8 for information about using these instruments from within your applications.

1	Acoustic Grand Piano
2	Bright Acoustic Piano
3	Electric Grand Piano
4	Honky-tonk Piano

5	Rhodes Piano
6	Chorused Piano
7	Harpsichord
6	Chorused Piano
8	Clavinet
9	Celesta
10	Glockenspiel
11	Music Box
12	Vibraphone
13	Marimba
14	Xylophone
15	Tubular bells
16	Dulcimer
17	Draw Organ
18	Percussive Organ
19	Rock Organ
20	Church Organ
21	Reed Organ
22	Accordion
23	Harmonica
24	Tango Accordion
25	Acoustic Nylon Guitar
26	Acoustic Steel Guitar

27	Electric Jazz Guitar
28	Electric clean Guitar
29	Electric Guitar muted
30	Overdriven Guitar
31	Distortion Guitar
32	Guitar Harmonics
33	Wood Bass
34	Electric Bass Fingered
35	Electric Bass Picked
36	Fretless Bass
37	Slap Bass 1
38	Slap Bass 2
39	Synth Bass 1
40	Synth Bass 2
41	Violin
42	Viola
43	Cello
44	Contrabass
45	Tremolo Strings
46	Pizzicato Strings
47	Orchestral Harp
48	Timpani
49	Acoustic String Ensemble 1

50	Acoustic String Ensemble 2
51	Synth Strings 1
52	Synth Strings 2
53	Aah Choir
54	Ooh Choir
55	Synvox
56	Orchestra Hit
57	Trumpet
58	Trombone
59	Tuba
60	Muted Trumpet
61	French Horn
62	Brass Section
63	Synth Brass 1
64	Synth Brass 2
65	Soprano Sax
66	Alto Sax
67	Tenor Sax
68	Baritone Sax
69	Oboe
70	English Horn
71	Bassoon
72	Clarinet

73	Piccolo
74	Flute
75	Recorder
76	Pan Flute
77	Bottle blow
78	Shakuhachi
79	Whistle
80	Ocarina
81	Square Lead
82	Saw Lead
83	Calliope
84	Chiffer
85	Synth Lead 5
86	Synth Lead 6
87	Synth Lead 7
88	Synth Lead 8
89	Synth Pad 1
90	Synth Pad 2
91	Synth Pad 3
92	Synth Pad 4
93	Synth Pad 5
94	Synth Pad 6
95	Synth Pad 7

96	Synth Pad 8
97	Ice Rain
98	Soundtracks
99	Crystal
100	Atmosphere
101	Bright
102	Goblin
103	Echoes
104	Space
105	Sitar
106	Banjo
107	Shamisen
108	Koto
109	Kalimba
110	Bagpipe
111	Fiddle
112	Shanai
113	Tinkle bell
114	Agogo
115	Steel Drums
116	Woodblock
117	Taiko Drum
118	Melodic Tom

119	Synth Tom
120	Reverse Cymbal
121	Guitar Fret Noise
122	Breath Noise
123	Seashore
124	Bird Tweet
125	Telephone Ring
126	Helicopter
127	Applause
128	Gunshot

APPENDIX B

The A5 World

For the typical Macintosh programmer, the A5 world and the A5 register are topics that arise only occasionally. Because of this, many programmers ignore the details of how the Mac works with the central processing unit's A5 register. You'll gain a greater understanding of Macintosh code if you don't follow this trend and instead take a careful look at what goes on in this important register.

Discussion of the A5 register and the A5 world are important only to programs that will be running on 68K-based Macs. PowerPC-based computers don't have an A5 world. Because it's most likely that your application will be written such that it can run on both older 68K-based Macs and the newer PowerPC-based computers, the topic of the A5 world isn't entirely dated—and shouldn't be ignored.

Switching the Contents of A5

The CPU's A5 register holds a pointer that tells an application where to find its own global variables. When a Toolbox routine executes, the system may alter the contents of the A5 register. When the Toolbox routine has completed, the application needs to again have access to the A5 register—

with its original value back in it. Because of this, some scheme is necessary so that both an application and the system can share this single register.

Macintosh Memory, the A5 World, and the A5 Register

When an application is launched, the system locates a free area in RAM in which to hold part or all of the application. This section of RAM is called an application partition. Each currently executing program has its own partition. An application partition is composed of an A5 world, a stack, a heap, and an area of free memory between the stack and heap—as shown in Figure B.1.

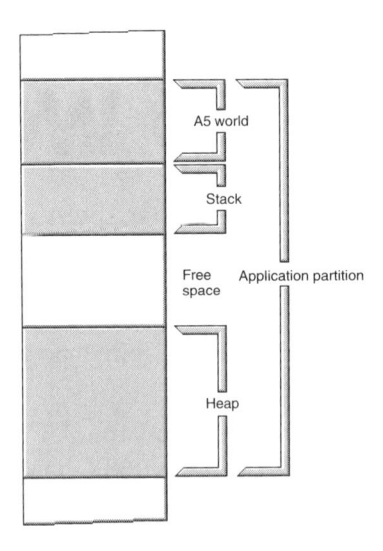

FIGURE **B.1** The memory layout of an application partition.

An application's stack holds local variables and function parameters. The application heap holds objects such as resource data, executable code, and data structures created by the program. The free space that lies between the stack and the heap serves as a pool of RAM available for use by both the stack and the heap. One of the purposes of the A5 world is to hold an application's global variables. The A5 world, and the CPU's A5 register, are the central topics of this appendix.

The memory model shown in Figure B.1 is a simplification of an application partition in that it doesn't show any details of the A5 world. The A5 world holds data that is fixed in size for the duration of a program's running. Global variables meet this criteria—the number and size of them is fixed when a program launches.

In Figure B.2 you can see that a section of the A5 world is devoted to an application's global variables. The figure also shows one address in the A5 world, and that same address in the A5 register in the central processing unit. The address that separates the A5 world's application global variable section from the A5 world data above it is referred to as the current A5, and is represented in code by the system global variable CurrentA5.

 The address shown in Figure B.2, 0x00464000, has no particular significance—it was randomly selected for this figure just to give you something concrete to refer to. The actual address of the boundary between the global

N O T E   variables and other A5 world data depends entirely on where in RAM the operating system places an application partition when a program is launched. Once a program is launched this address is stored in the *system* global variable named CurrentA5.

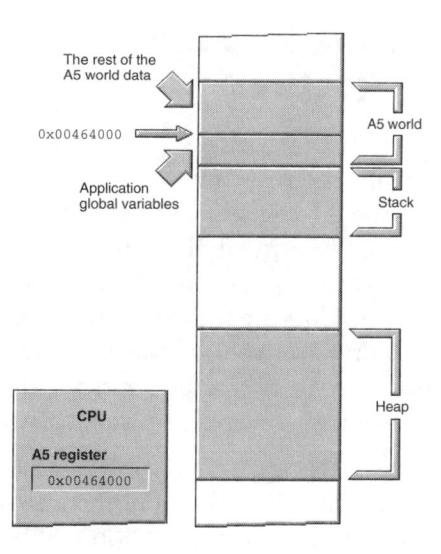

FIGURE **B.2** The A5 register holds the address of the section of the A5 world that holds an application's global variables.

NOTE Like Figure B.1, Figure B.2 is a simplification of Macintosh memory. The A5 world actually consists of a jump table, application parameters, QuickDraw global variables, and a pointer to those QuickDraw variables. For this discussion, though, only the application global variables section of the A5 world is of importance. For a more complete discussion of Macintosh memory, including the stack, the heap, and the A5 world, refer to the M&T book *Macintosh Programming Techniques* or the *Memory* volume of the *Inside Macintosh* series of books.

When a program accesses an application global variable, it has to first find the variable in the A5 world. It does so by using the current A5 address in the A5 register as a base address, then subtracting some offset value to move to the particular global variable.

NOTE The address in the A5 register is the address of the boundary between the A5 global variables and other A5 data—it's not the address of the start of the A5 globals. Because smaller addresses appear lower in figures, the global variables appear at addresses smaller than the boundary address in the A5 register.

Keeping Track of the Value in an Application's A5 Register

When a program launches, the address that separates the application's global variable space from the rest of the application's A5 world data—CurrentA5—is stored in the A5 register. If this address remained steadfast in this register for the duration of the program's execution, things would be very simple from a programmer's standpoint—one would never have to be concerned about the contents of this register. The A5 register, however, doesn't retain its value for the duration of the program. That, in fact, is the entire reason this appendix exists. Fortunately, the Macintosh operating system takes care of most of the work of keeping track of the A5 register for you.

There are some situations when the operating system needs to make use of the A5 register. Because your application needs the contents of this register, a conflict arises as to how this one register can be shared by both your application and the operating system. To resolve this dilemma, the operating system always takes the necessary step of preserving the current contents of the A5 register before altering the contents for its own use. When the operating system is finished with the A5 register, it places the saved address back in the register. Then it's safe for your application to again refer to the register's value to find its own global variables.

Figure B.3 shows what happens to the A5 register when a Toolbox routine is called by your program. Some Toolbox functions use the A5 register for their own purposes. When a routine does, it stores the original contents of the A5 register, changes the contents as it executes, and then finally restores the contents of the A5 register—as described above.

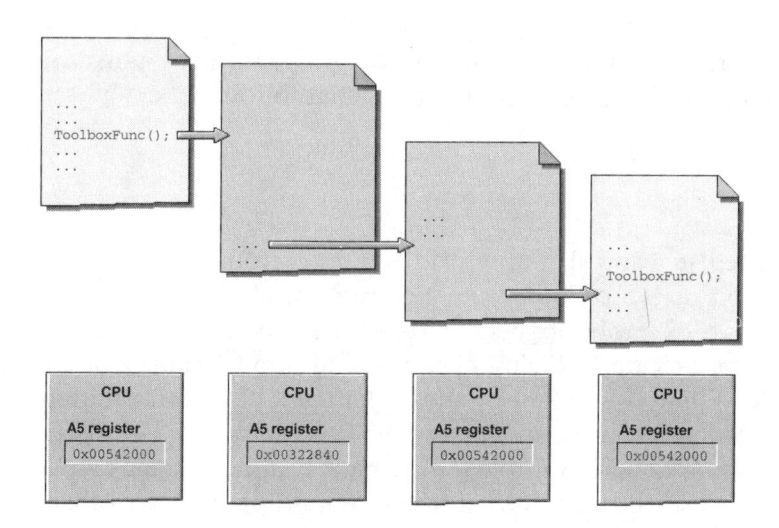

FIGURE B.3 Application code and Toolbox code cooperate
by saving and restoring the A5 register value.

In the leftmost code snippet of Figure B.3, an application is making a call to a hypothetical Toolbox routine named ToolboxFunc(). The importance of this example lies not in *which* Toolbox routine gets called, but rather that *a* Toolbox routine is called. The snippet that appears second from the left in the figure shows that when the Toolbox routine starts executing, it saves the value in the A5 register. This is the address of the application's global variables in the application's A5 world—CurrentA5. As the Toolbox routine executes, it makes use of the A5 register—note that in the CPU pictured under the second snippet from the left, the contents of A5 have now changed. In the third snippet from the left you can see that the Toolbox routine has completed and that the `ToolboxFunc()` code has now restored the saved, original contents of the A5 register. Finally, in the rightmost snippet you can see that, as the application code again executes, it once more can rely on the A5 register to supply it with the address of its own global variables.

Callback Routines and the A5 Register

The particulars of how an application accesses an application global variable are usually unimportant to the programmer—you simply make an assignment statement like the ones that follow:

```
short   gTotalScore = 0;

++gTotalScore;
```

The A5 register and the A5 world become important to you when your application uses a *callback routine* (sometimes referred to as a *completion routine*). An example of such a program appears in the AsynchSndPlay asynchronous sound playing example found in Chapter 2 of this book. A callback routine is invoked by the system—not by your program. Exactly when a callback routine will be executed is unknown. For instance, in the asynchronous sound example the callback routine executes when a sound is done playing. Because asynchronous sound play allows other actions to take place as a sound is playing, you have no way of predetermining exactly what code will be executing at the time a sound completes.

If your program invokes a callback routine when a Toolbox routine happens to be executing, the callback routine will not be able to access any of your program's global variables. That's because some Toolbox routines use the A5 register for their own purposes—as you saw back in Figure B.3. When such a Toolbox function is being executed, the value in the A5 register may not represent the address of the application's global variable section in the A5 world.

If a callback routine is to be able to access application global variables, it needs to know the original value of the A5 register. The approach to making this possible is to save the `CurrentA5` value *before* the callback routine is invoked. Then, once the callback routine is called, it should save the value in A5—just in case the operating system is in the middle of executing a Toolbox routine that is using A5. After saving A5, the callback routine should set the A5 register to the previously saved A5 value. At that point it is safe for the callback routine to access application global variables. When the callback routine is about to exit, it should restore the A5 register contents to the value that was in the register at the time the callback routine started. That will let the Toolbox routine continue to use A5.

Don't be alarmed if you feel that it's hard to follow all of the A5 switching—things are a little complicated. Thankfully, the above kind of code interruption isn't too common. The step-by-step list below, along with Figure B.4, should help make sense of how the A5 register is used by both an application and the system. As you read the following steps, follow along in Figure B.4.

1. Application is executing.
2. Application saves its `CurrentA5` value.
3. Toolbox routine begins executing.
4. Toolbox routine saves application A5, then uses and alters A5.
5. Callback routine begins executing *while* Toolbox routine is still executing.
6. Callback routine saves whatever value the Toolbox has placed in A5.
7. Callback routine sets A5 to the application A5 saved in Step 2.
8. Callback routine safely accesses application global variables.
9. Callback routine restores Toolbox A5 value saved in Step 6.
10. Toolbox routine continues, and completes, executing.
11. Toolbox routine restores application A5 value saved in Step 4.

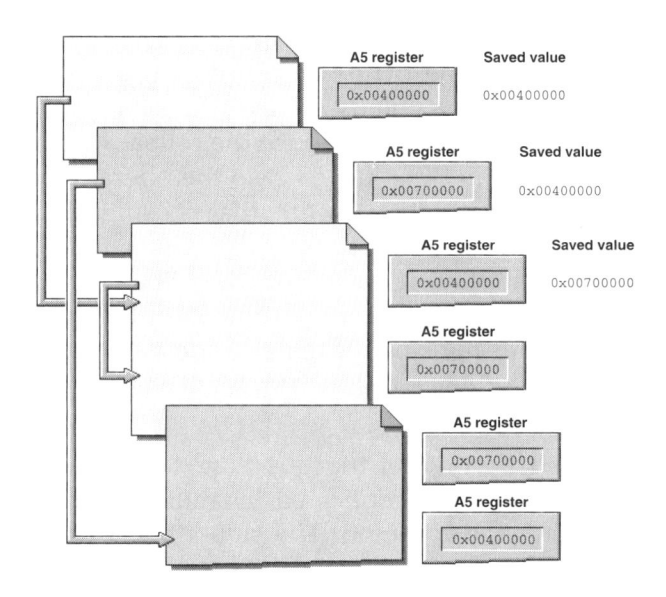

FIGURE **B.4** The Toolbox saves the A5 value when it starts executing,
as does the callback routine when it executes.

The top snippet of Figure B.4 is from an application's source code. Here the value in the A5 register (0x00400000) is saved for use later in the program. The arrow that starts at this first snippet ends at the point that this saved value is used. In the second snippet from the top of the figure you see that a Toolbox routine has been called and is executing. The first thing the Toolbox routine does is save the contents of the A5 register (0x00400000), then the routine uses the A5 register for its own purpose. In the course of running A5, the value in the register changes (to 0x00700000).

As the Toolbox code is executing, a callback routine is invoked (perhaps a sound has just finished playing and its callback routine was invoked). When this happens, the callback routine saves the contents of the A5 register—as shown in the third snippet from the top of Figure B.4. When the callback routine finishes, control will return to the Toolbox routine so that it too can finish. Here you see that the callback routine first preserves the value (0x00700000) left in the A5 register by the Toolbox function. The callback routine then sets A5 to the CurrentA5 value (0x00400000) saved back in the very top snippet. Now the callback routine has access to application global variables. When finished, the callback routine restores A5 to the value (0x00700000) it had when the callback took control—the value left in A5 by the Toolbox function.

When the callback routine completes, the interrupted Toolbox routine gets to finish. The callback routine properly restored the A5 register contents to the value (0x00700000) that the Toolbox routine was using when it got interrupted, so that the Toolbox routine immediately takes up where it left off. When its finished, it restores the A5 register contents to the value (0x00400000) that was in A5 when the Toolbox routine first started to execute back in the second snippet from the top of the figure.

The AsynchSndPlay Example Program

In Chapter 2 you saw that the AsynchSndPlay program uses a callback routine. By looking at some of the AsynchSndPlay source code, you'll be able to see an example of the theory discussed on the previous pages.

The AsynchSndPlay program saves the A5 register value by calling the Toolbox routine SetCurrentA5() from the application-defined routine InstallCallbackCommand(). SetCurrentA5() sets the A5 register to the value of the system global variable CurrentA5. This action isn't important here because, at this point, the A5 register already has this value. The real reason for calling SetCurrentA5() here is to take advantage of another task this function performs. Before setting the A5 register to CurrentA5, the function returns the current value in A5. The effect is the same as examining the system global variable CurrentA5 and placing that value in the param2 field of theCommand.

```
OSErr  InstallCallbackCommand( SndChannelPtr theChannel )
{
   OSErr        theError;
   SndCommand   theCommand;
   duty
   theCommand.cmd    = callBackCmd;
   theCommand.param1 = 0;
   theCommand.param2 = SetCurrentA5();

   theError = SndDoCommand( theChannel, &theCommand, true );

   return ( theError );
}
```

N O T E If you look at the AsynchSndPlay source code you'll see that the Install-CallbackCommand() routine includes an #ifndef powerc conditional directive. When the AsynchSndPlay source code is compiled with a PowerPC compiler, this directive eliminates the call to SetCurrentA5() and replaces it with a simple assignment statement that sets param2 to 0. This is done because PowerPC-based Macs don't have an A5 world, and don't need to go through the effort of preserving the value of the A5 register. For easier reading (and because this appendix deals only with 68K code), this directive has been eliminated from this example.

By saving the A5 value in a sound command parameter and then calling SndDoCommand(), the A5 value ends up in the queue of a sound channel. Figure B.5 shows how the call to SetCurrentA5() achieves the first step from Figure B.4.

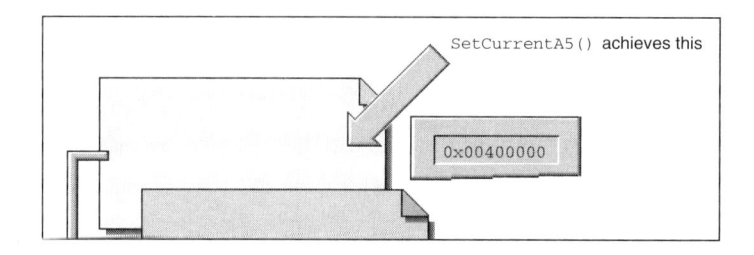

SetCurrentA5() achieves this

0x00400000

FIGURE B.5 A callback command saves the application's
A5 value in one of its three fields—param2.

When AsynchSndPlay finishes playing a sound, the program's callback routine is called. SoundChannelCallback() is shown below.

```
pascal void  SoundChannelCallback( SndChannelPtr theChannel,
                                   SndCommand theCommand )
{
   long  theA5;

   theA5 = SetA5( theCommand.param2 );

   gCallbackExecuted = true;
   gSoundPlaying = false;

   theA5 = SetA5( theA5 );
}
```

As in the `InstallCallbackCommand()` function, the AsynchSndPlay source code listing found in Chapter 2 uses the `#ifndef powerc` directive. If you look back at that chapter you'll see that the `SoundChannelCallback()` routine includes two `#ifndef powerc` conditional directives. When the AsynchSndPlay source code is compiled with a PowerPC compiler, these directives effectively eliminate the two lines of code that set the A5 register. Because PowerPC-based Macs don't have an A5 world, that's the desired effect. Again, for easier reading, these directives have been eliminated from this example.

For the sake of this example, assume that when the callback routine is called, the AsynchSndPlay program happens to be in the middle of executing a Toolbox routine. That means that A5 may have been altered. The callback routine too makes this assumption, and saves whatever value is in A5 before setting this register to the saved application A5 value. To do so, the Toolbox function `SetA5()` is called. The `SetA5()` function sets the A5 register to whatever value is passed to it. Before doing this, however, it returns the current value in A5, which is saved in the local variable `theA5`. Figure B.6 reminds you that it is a call to `SetA5()` that saves the A5 value being used by the Toolbox.

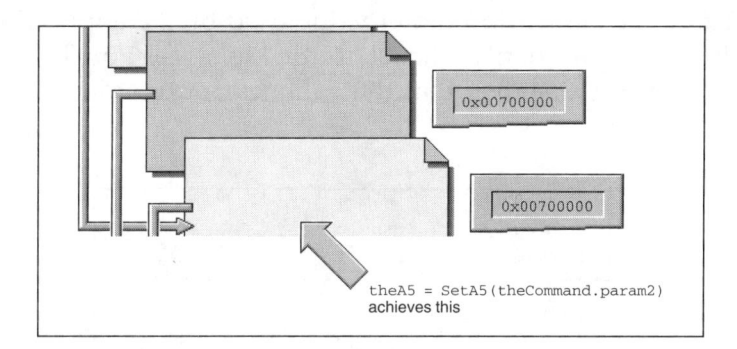

FIGURE **B.6** When a callback routine starts, it saves the A5 register value that was set by the interrupted Toolbox routine.

After saving the Toolbox-supplied value of A5, the callback routine sets A5 to the application A5 value that's been stored in the `param2` parameter of the `callBackCmd` sound command. Remember, until it sets up A5, the callback routine cannot access application global variables. That's why the application A5 value was initially saved in the sound channel queue. The callback routine has access to the passed-in sound command (which isn't a global variable). Figure B.7 shows this second purpose of calling the SetA5() Toolbox function (the first being to save the Toolbox-set A5 value).

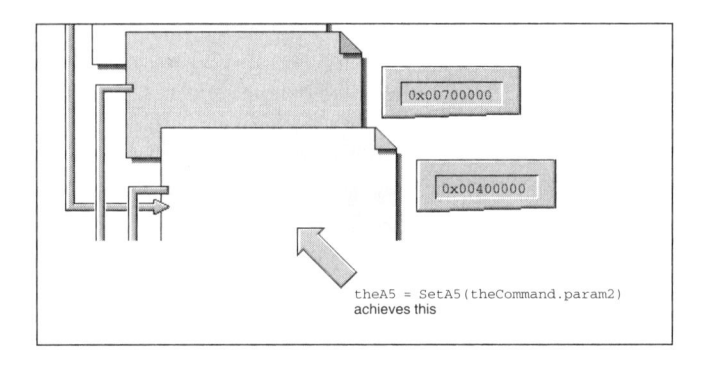

Figure B.7 After saving the A5 value set by the Toolbox,
a callback routine changes A5 to the application A5 value.

The call to SetA5() has now saved the A5 value used by the Toolbox, and set A5 to the A5 world pointer value used by the application. Now it's safe for the application's callback routine to access application global variables. Figure B.8 shows that the callback routine does in fact use two global variables.

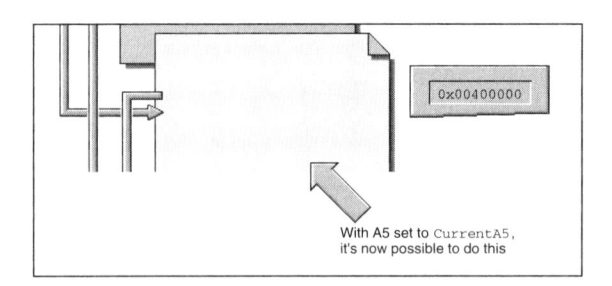

FIGURE B.8 Once the callback routine has set A5 to the original
application A5 value, the callback routine can access global variables.

When the callback routine has finished, it restores the A5 register to the value that was present when the callback function started—the value that was in A5 when the Toolbox function was executing. As shown in Figure B.9, another call to SetA5() does this. This time, the parameter to SetA5() is the local variable theA5. Recall that the last call to SetA5() returned the Toolbox-set A5 value to the variable theA5. Because the callback routine is ending, the value returned by SetA5() (which is saved in theA5) is ignored.

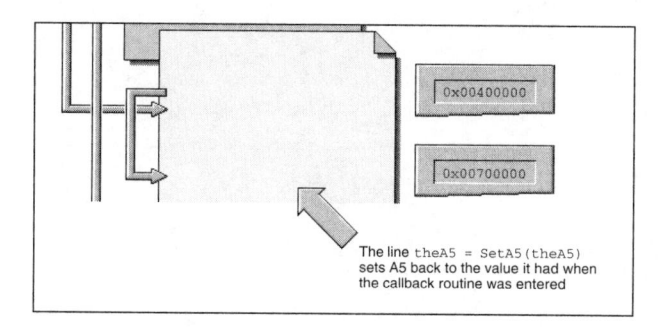

FIGURE B.9 Before exiting, a callback routine restores the A5 register to the state it was in when the callback routine started.

Figure B.10 recaps how the AsynchSndPlay callback routine fits the A5-switching pattern presented in the appendix.

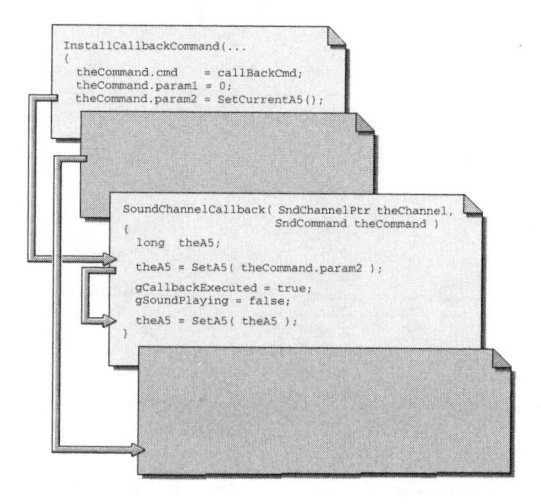

FIGURE B.10 The Chapter 2 AsynchSndPlay example program uses the A5-saving scheme described in this appendix.

INDEX

About the CD

The CD in the back of this book contains all the sample code discussed in both Metrowerks CodeWarrior and Symantec C++ projects. On the CD, you'll find a folder titled "M&T Graphics & Sound Examples." Inside this folder are the projects divided into folders for each compiler. The projects are further divided by chapter so you can find them easily.

Having a CD-ROM allows for a great deal more material for really the same price. As such, you're getting not only about 60M of programming examples and sample programs, but we've also included a folder titled "Goodies." Inside, you'll find some sample sounds, graphics, movies, and some shareware graphics toolkits. Don't let the shareware title bother you. These are tools you will probably find very useful. And, if you do, please pay the registration fees. Someone worked very hard to create these for you.